THE

50 GREATEST PLAYERS

IN

GREEN BAY PACKERS

HISTORY

THE
50 GREATEST PLAYERS
IN
GREEN BAY PACKERS
HISTORY

ROBERT W. COHEN

GUILFORD, CONNECTICUT

An imprint of The Rowman and Littlefield Publishing Group, Inc.
4501 Forbes Blvd., Ste. 200
Lanham, MD 20706
www.rowman.com

Distributed by NATIONAL BOOK NETWORK

British Library Cataloguing in Publication Information Available

Library of Congress Cataloging-in-Publication Data available

Names: Cohen, Robert W., author.
Title: The 50 greatest players in Green Bay Packers history / Robert W. Cohen.
Other titles: Fifty greatest players in Green Bay Packers history
Description: Guilford, Connecticut : Lyons Press, [2018] | "Distributed by
  NATIONAL BOOK NETWORK"—T.p. verso. | Includes bibliographical
references.
Identifiers: LCCN 2018009936 (print) | LCCN 2018012601 (ebook) | ISBN
  9781493031894 (e-book) | ISBN 9781493031887 (hardback : alk. paper)
Subjects: LCSH: Green Bay Packers (Football team)—History. | Football
  players—Rating of—United States.
Classification: LCC GV956.G7 (ebook) | LCC GV956.G7 C65 2018 (print) | DDC
  796.332/640977561—dc23
LC record available at https://lccn.loc.gov/2018009936

∞™ The paper used in this publication meets the minimum requirements of American National Standard for Information Sciences—Permanence of Paper for Printed Library Materials, ANSI/NISO Z39.48-1992.

Printed in the United States of America

CONTENTS

ACKNOWLEDGMENTS

I wish to thank Troy Kinunen of MEARSonlineauctions.com, Kate of RMYauctions.com, Richard Albersheim of Albersheims.com, Claremont shows.com, BidAmi.com, Collectauctions.com, Pristineauction.com, HeritageAuctions.com, LegendaryAuctions.com, Sportsmemorabilia.com, Mainlineautographs.com, George A. Kitrinos, Mike Morbeck, Leivur R. Djurhuus, Keith Allison, Chris Garrison, Kyle Engman, and Paul Cutler, each of whom generously contributed to the photographic content of this work.

INTRODUCTION

THE PACKER LEGACY

Founded on August 11, 1919, by former high school football rivals Earl "Curly" Lambeau and George Whitney Calhoun, the Green Bay Packers spent their first two seasons competing against other semi-pro teams located in the Midwest, before joining the American Professional Football Association (APFA), the forerunner of today's NFL, in 1921. Named after their sponsor, the Indian Packing Company, from whom Lambeau solicited funds for uniforms and equipment, the Packers found themselves plagued by financial difficulties until 1923, when a group of local businessmen known as the "Hungry Five" purchased the team and formed the Green Bay Football Corporation, which continues to run the franchise to this day, making the Packers the only community-owned major-league professional sports team based in the United States.

The Packers experienced a moderate amount of success from 1921 to 1924 while playing their home games at Bellevue Park and Hagemeister Park, compiling an overall record of 21-11-5 under player-coach Lambeau, who continued to function in that dual role until 1929, when he retired as an active player. However, they began to establish themselves as an NFL powerhouse shortly after they moved into City Stadium, which remained their primary home from 1925 to 1956. After posting an overall mark of 28-15-7 from 1925 to 1928, the Packers compiled the best record in the league in each of the next three seasons, finishing a combined 34-5-2 during that time, en route to winning the NFL title each year (the league did not institute a playoff system until 1933). Particularly dominant in 1929, the Packers finished the season with a record of 12-0-1, outscoring their opponents by a margin of 198–22, with their stifling defense shutting out the opposition eight times. After posting a mark of 10-3-1 the following year, the Packers won their third straight league championship in 1931 by compiling a record of 12-2, this time outscoring their opponents by a combined margin of 291–87. In addition to the outstanding coaching of Lambeau, the Packers benefited greatly from the brilliant two-way play of ends Johnny (Blood) McNally, LaVern "Lavvie" Dilweg, and Verne Lewellen, as well as the dominant line play of future Hall of Famers Cal Hubbard and Mike Michalske.

Following their championship run, the Packers remained competitive the next few seasons, posting as many as 10 victories in 1932, before winning the NFL title again in 1936, when, buoyed by the emergence of second-year wide receiver Don Hutson as the game's premier offensive weapon, they began their next period of excellence. After compiling a record of 10-1-1 during the regular season, the Packers defeated the Boston Redskins by a score of 21–6 in the NFL championship game, claiming in the process their fourth NFL title. Returning to the championship game again in 1938, the Packers suffered a 23–17 defeat at the hands of the New York Giants, before avenging that loss the following year by recording a lopsided 27–0 victory over New York. After failing to make it back to the NFL title game in any of the next four years, the Packers laid claim to their sixth league championship in 1944 by once again defeating the Giants, this time by a score of 14–7.

Although Curly Lambeau remained the face of the Packers in many ways until 1949, when he surrendered his coaching duties, Don Hutson established himself as easily the team's most dominant figure on the playing field. A brilliant receiver who has been credited with inventing pass patterns, Hutson led the NFL in receptions eight times, touchdown receptions nine times, and receiving yards seven times between 1935 and 1946, setting numerous NFL records along the way, many of which still stand. An exceptional two-way player, Hutson also starred at safety on defense, leading the league in interceptions and interception-return yards once each. Yet, the Packer squads for which he played featured several other excellent players as well whose contributions to those three NFL championship teams cannot be overstated. Arnie Herber and Cecil Isbell served as Green Bay's primary signal-callers throughout most of Hutson's career, combining with him at different times to form the league's deadliest passing combination. Clarke Hinkle excelled at both running back and linebacker, rivaling Chicago's legendary Bronko Nagurski as the most physically intimidating skilled position offensive player of the day. And Charley Brock and Charles "Buckets" Goldenberg starred on both sides of the ball, with the former gaining notoriety for his outstanding play at center and linebacker.

After winning the NFL title in 1944, the Packers spent the next three years toiling in mediocrity, compiling an overall record of 18-14-1 from 1945 to 1947, before suffering through just the second losing season in franchise history in 1948, when they finished an embarrassing 3-9. With the Packers posting a mark of just 2-10 the following year and the franchise in dire financial straits, Lambeau elected to resign his post prior to the start of the 1950 campaign, ending his 31-year association with the club with a regular-season coaching record of 209-104-21, an overall record of 231-108-21, and six league championships to his credit.

Following Lambeau's departure, the Packers entered into the darkest period in franchise history, failing to compile a winning record in any of the next nine seasons, during which time they posted an overall mark of just 34-74-2, as head-coaching duties passed from Gene Ronzani, to Lisle Blackbourn, and, finally, to Ray "Scooter" McLean. Meanwhile, the NFL threatened to move the Packers to Milwaukee full-time unless they constructed a new stadium to replace their antiquated home ballpark, which seated only 25,000 paying customers on uncomfortable wooden benches. The city of Green Bay responded by building a new 32,150-seat City Stadium for the team, making it the first facility built exclusively for an NFL team. After first opening its doors to the public in 1957, City Stadium became officially known as Lambeau Field in 1965, when the team chose to honor the legendary coach after he passed away earlier in the year. Since then, the ballpark has been renovated and expanded several times, so that it is now capable of seating 72,928 patrons.

After the Packers posted a franchise-worst 1-10-1 record in 1958, things finally began to turn around for them when they hired former New York Giants assistant Vince Lombardi to be their new head coach and general manager on February 2, 1959. Bringing with him to Green Bay a strong work ethic, a winning mentality, and extraordinary motivational skills, Lombardi soon instilled in his players a positive attitude and a sense of selflessness that helped the Packers emerge as the team of the 1960s. After improving their record to 7-5 in Lombardi's first year at the helm, the Packers advanced to the NFL title game in each of the next three seasons, losing to the Philadelphia Eagles by a score of 17–13 in 1960, before defeating the Giants by scores of 37–0 and 16–7 the next two years. Although they failed to represent the Western Conference in each of the next two title tilts, the Packers continued to perform well under Lombardi, compiling an overall record of 19-7-2 from 1963 to 1964, before winning the next three NFL titles and the first two Super Bowls. Oddly enough, the Packers' lopsided victories over Kansas City (35–10) and Oakland (33–14) in the first two meetings between the NFL and AFL champions proved to be somewhat anticlimactic, because they first had to get past the Dallas Cowboys in a pair of classic NFL title games, one of which, later referred to as the "Ice Bowl" for its frigid temperatures and unbearable playing conditions, remains to this day arguably the most famous football game ever played. Still, even though Lombardi served as the driving force behind the Packers' extraordinary run, he proved to be quite fortunate in that he coached a team with a considerable amount of talent. Defensive linemen Willie Davis and Henry Jordan, linebackers Ray Nitschke and Dave Robinson, and defensive backs Willie Wood and Herb Adderley all eventually gained induction into the Pro Football Hall of Fame. Meanwhile, quarterback Bart Starr did an expert job of running the offense behind an offensive line that included standouts Jim Ringo, Forrest Gregg, Jerry Kramer, and Fuzzy Thurston. Those aforementioned linemen also opened up huge holes in the running game for future Hall of Famers Jim Taylor and Paul Hornung.

Unfortunately, Lombardi chose to relinquish his coaching duties following the conclusion of the 1967 campaign, having led the Packers to five NFL championships in his final seven seasons. He then spent one year serving as the team's general manager, before leaving the organization in 1969 to become head coach and minority owner of the Washington Redskins. However, he ended up spending just one season in Washington, leading the Redskins to their first winning record in 14 years, before dying unexpectedly from cancer on September 3, 1970. In recognition of Lombardi's extraordinary accomplishments with the Packers, the NFL renamed the Super Bowl trophy the Vince Lombardi Trophy. Meanwhile, the city of Green Bay renamed Highland Avenue in his honor in 1968, placing Lambeau Field at 1265 Lombardi Avenue.

Longtime Green Bay assistant Phil Bengtson assumed head coaching duties following Lombardi's departure, but, inheriting an aging team and lacking his predecessor's leadership skills, he ended up directing the team to an overall record of just 20-21-1 over the course of the next three seasons before being relieved of his duties. Dan Devine succeeded Bengtson but fared little better, leading the Packers to just one winning season between 1971 and 1974, although they managed to finish first in the newly formed NFC Central Division in 1972 by posting a mark of 10-4. However, they exited the postseason tournament quickly, being eliminated in the opening round by the eventual NFC champion Washington Redskins.

A lengthy period of mediocrity followed, as head coaching duties passed from Bart Starr (1975–1983), to Forrest Gregg (1984–1987), and, finally, to Lindy Infante (1988–1991), with the Packers compiling a winning record just three times over the course of those 17 seasons. Yet, even as the team continued to struggle, several players distinguished themselves in Green Bay, with wide receivers James Lofton and Sterling Sharpe, and linebackers Fred Carr and John Anderson all gaining widespread acclaim.

With the Packers' on-field performance throughout the period being hampered by poor personnel decisions that included ill-advised trades and draft picks that exhibited a lack of sound judgment, the organization experienced a shakeup in the front office in 1991 that left new GM Ron Wolf in full control of the team's football operations. Displaying a considerable amount of foresight, Wolf hired former San Francisco 49ers offensive coordinator Mike Holmgren to be the Packers' new head coach prior to the start of the 1992 campaign—a move that proved to be just the first of many that helped restore the team to prominence.

Shortly after hiring Holmgren, Wolf acquired quarterback Brett Favre from the Atlanta Falcons for a first-round draft pick, obtaining in the process the man who served as the cornerstone of the team for the next 16 years. Starting 253 consecutive games behind center for the Packers from 1992 to 2007, Favre set numerous league and franchise records along the way, including most pass attempts and pass completions by an NFL quarterback, and most passing yards and touchdown passes by a Green Bay signal-caller. Favre's superb play, which earned him nine Pro Bowl selections, six All-Pro nominations, and three NFL MVP awards, ended up leading the Packers to seven division titles, four NFC championship game appearances, two Super Bowl appearances, and one league championship, which they claimed with a 35–21 victory over New England in Super Bowl XXXI. Yet, while Favre served as the central figure in the Packers' successful run that saw them compile a winning record 13 times between 1992 and 2007, he received a considerable amount of help from Hall of Fame defensive lineman Reggie White, Pro Bowl defensive backs LeRoy Butler, Darren Sharper, and Charles Woodson, star wide receivers Antonio Freeman and Donald Driver, and standout running back Ahman Green, the franchise's all-time leading rusher.

The Packers remained consistent winners throughout most of Favre's tenure with the team even though they underwent numerous changes in leadership, both on and off the field. Mike Holmgren handed in his resignation days after the Packers suffered a 30–27 defeat at the hands of the San Francisco 49ers in the 1998 playoffs, leaving the coaching duties to Ray Rhodes, who subsequently led Green Bay to an 8-8 record in his one year at the helm. After replacing Rhodes in 2000, Mike Sherman led the Packers to four playoff appearances and three division titles in his six seasons in charge, before passing the baton to Mike McCarthy, who has coached the Pack since 2006. Meanwhile, Ron Wolf left the organization prior to the start of the 2001 campaign, with Mike Sherman subsequently serving as both GM and head coach until 2005, when former Seattle Seahawks vice president of operations Ted Thompson assumed the role of the new executive vice president, general manager, and director of football operations.

The Packers continued to thrive after Thompson began rebuilding the team's roster following a dismal 4-12 performance in 2005 that led to Sherman's dismissal. And they transitioned almost seamlessly into a new era of Packers football after saying goodbye to Brett Favre following the conclusion of the 2007 campaign, experiencing just one losing season, before advancing to the playoffs eight straight times. More than anyone else, Aaron Rodgers has been responsible for the success the Packers have experienced since 2009. Assuming the starting quarterback duties in 2008 after spending his first three years in Green Bay serving as Favre's backup, Rodgers has performed brilliantly over the course of the last 10 seasons, establishing himself during that time as arguably the finest signal-caller in all of football. En route to earning six Pro Bowl selections, three All-Pro nominations, and two league MVP trophies, Rodgers has led the Packers to five division titles, three NFC championship game appearances, and one league championship, which they attained with a 31–25 victory over Pittsburgh in Super Bowl XLV.

Unfortunately, Rodgers suffered a serious injury during the early stages of the 2017 campaign that forced him to miss most of the year, leaving the Packers unable to advance to the postseason tournament for the first time in nine seasons. However, a healthy Rodgers is likely to make the Packers a leading contender in the NFC once again in 2018. Their next NFC championship will be their fourth. The Packers have also won 15 division titles, 11 Western Conference championships, four Super Bowls, and 13 NFL titles, the most in league history. And 24 members of the Pro Football Hall of Fame spent a significant amount of time playing for the Packers.

FACTORS USED TO DETERMINE RANKINGS

It should come as no surprise that selecting the 50 greatest players ever to perform for a team with the rich history of the Packers presented quite a challenge. Even after narrowing the field down to a mere 50 men, I still needed to devise a method of ranking the elite players that remained. Certainly, the names of Don Hutson, Ray Nitschke, Forrest Gregg, Bart Starr, Brett Favre, and Aaron Rodgers would appear at, or near, the top of almost everyone's list, although the order might vary somewhat from one person to the next. Several other outstanding performers have gained general recognition through the years as being among the greatest players ever to wear a Packers uniform. Herb Adderley, Jim Taylor, Willie Davis, James Lofton, Reggie White, and Clay Matthews head the list of other Packer icons. But, how does one compare players who lined up on opposite sides of the ball with any degree of certainty? And practically everyone who performed for the team prior to 1950 played on both offense and defense, compounding the issue. Furthermore, how does one differentiate between the pass-rushing and run-stopping skills of players such as Willie Davis and Reggie White and the ball-hawking and kickoff return abilities of a Herb Adderley? And, on the offensive end, how can a direct correlation be made between the contributions made by Hall of Fame lineman Forrest Gregg and skill position players such as Bart Starr and James Lofton? After initially deciding whom to include on my list, I then needed to determine what criteria I should use to formulate my final rankings.

The first thing I decided to examine was the level of dominance a player attained during his time in Green Bay. How often did he lead the NFL in a major statistical category? Did he ever capture league MVP honors? How many times did he earn a trip to the Pro Bowl or a spot on the All-Pro Team?

I also chose to assess each player's statistical accomplishments while wearing a Packers uniform, reviewing where he ranks among the team's all-time leaders in those categories most pertinent to his position. Of course, even the method of using statistics as a measuring stick has its inherent flaws. Although the level of success a team experiences rushing and passing the ball is affected greatly by the performance of its offensive line, there really is no way to quantifiably measure the level of play reached by each individual offensive lineman. Conversely, the play of the offensive line affects tremendously the statistics compiled by a team's quarterback and running backs. Furthermore, the NFL did not keep an official record of defensive numbers such as tackles and quarterback sacks until the 1980s. In addition, when examining the statistics compiled by offensive players, the era during which a quarterback, running back, or wide receiver competed must be factored into the equation.

To illustrate my last point, rules changes instituted by the league office have opened up the game considerably over the course of the last two decades. Quarterbacks are accorded far more protection than ever before, and officials have also been instructed to limit the amount of contact defensive backs are allowed to make with wide receivers. As a result, the game has experienced an offensive explosion, with quarterbacks and receivers posting numbers players from prior generations rarely even approached. One must place the numbers Aaron Rodgers has compiled during his career in their proper context when comparing him to other top Packer quarterbacks such as Bart Starr and Arnie Herber. The latter had the additional disadvantage of spending almost his entire career attempting to throw the oddly shaped ball that the NFL employed during the league's formative years. Not only did early receivers such as John (Blood) McNally and Verne Lewellen have to catch that roundish sphere, but they also competed during an era defined by its in-the-trenches style of play that stressed running over passing. As a result, Donald Driver's and Jordy Nelson's huge receiving totals must be viewed in moderation when compared to the figures compiled by players such as McNally and Lewellen, as well as later receivers such as Don Hutson, Boyd Dowler, and James Lofton.

Other important factors I considered were the overall contributions a player made to the success of the team, the degree to which he improved the fortunes of the club during his time in Green Bay, the manner in which he affected the team, both on and off the field, and the degree to which he added to the Packer legacy of winning. While the number of championships and division titles the Packers won during a particular player's years with the team certainly entered into the equation, I chose not to deny a top performer his rightful place on the list if his years in Green Bay happened to coincide with a lack of overall success by the club. As a result, the names of players such as Bobby Dillon and Sterling Sharpe will appear in these rankings.

One other thing I should mention is that I only considered a player's performance while playing for the Packers when formulating my rankings. That being the case, the names of outstanding players such as Billy Howton and Darren Sharper, both of whom had many of their best years while playing for other teams, may appear lower on this list than one might expect, while the names of other standout performers such as Emlen Tunnell and Ted Hendricks are nowhere to be found.

Having established the guidelines to be used throughout this book, we are ready to examine the careers of the 50 greatest players in Packers history, starting with number 1 and working our way down to number 50.

DON HUTSON

The greatness of Brett Favre is undeniable. The holder of practically every franchise passing record, Favre made an enormous impact on the Packers in his 16 years with the team, leading them to seven division titles, two conference championships, and one Super Bowl win. Establishing himself as one of the game's most decorated players during his time in Green Bay, Favre earned nine trips to the Pro Bowl, six All-Pro selections, and three NFL MVP trophies. Certainly, most Packer fans born after 1960 would consider him to be the most influential player to perform for the team during their lifetimes.

Nevertheless, Don Hutson, who had many of his finest seasons for the Packers more than half a century before Favre threw his first pass for the Green and Gold, left behind him a legacy even greater than that of the legendary signal-caller. Generally considered to be the first true wide receiver in NFL history, Hutson is viewed by most football historians as one of the handful of greatest receivers ever to play the game. Credited with inventing pass patterns, the speedy Hutson revolutionized the sport with his ability to navigate his way past opposing defenses, bringing the game out of the dark ages and into the modern era. Easily the most prolific offensive player of his day, Hutson led the NFL in pass receptions eight times, touchdown receptions nine times, receiving yards seven times, yards from scrimmage three times, touchdowns scored eight times, and points scored five times, with his brilliant play helping the Packers claim four Western Conference championships and three NFL titles between 1935 and 1945. The Packers' all-time leader in touchdowns scored (105) and touchdown receptions (99), Hutson earned four trips to the Pro Bowl, 11 consecutive All-Pro nominations, two league MVP awards, a spot on the NFL's 75th Anniversary Team, a place in the Pro Football Hall of Fame, and a number six ranking on the *Sporting News'* 1999 list of the 100 Greatest Players in NFL History. In the end, Hutson's extraordinary list of accomplishments made him the only possible choice for the top spot on this list.

Don Hutson revolutionized the game of football with his pass-catching skills.
Courtesy of RMYAuctions.com

Born in Pine Bluff, Arkansas, on January 31, 1913, Donald Montgomery Hutson first displayed his exceptional all-around athletic ability while attending Pine Bluff High School, earning All-State honors in both football and basketball, while also playing baseball for the town team. Later identifying basketball as his favorite sport, Hutson once revealed, "I'm like most athletes. I'd rather see football, but I'd rather play basketball."

After enrolling at the University of Alabama, Hutson spent three seasons starring on the gridiron for the Crimson Tide, with Arkansas native and coaching legend Paul "Bear" Bryant, who served as a teammate of Hutson for two years, recalling, "He [Hutson] was something to see, even then. We'd hitchhike to Pine Bluff just to watch him play. I saw him catch five touchdown passes in one game in high school." Earning First-Team All-America honors as a senior in 1934, Hutson drew praise from Georgia Tech head coach Bill Alexander, who stated, "All Don Hutson can do is beat you with clever hands and the most baffling change of pace I've ever seen." Meanwhile, Hutson's College Football Hall of Fame profile reads: "Fluid in motion, wondrously elusive with the fake, inventive in his patterns, and magnificently at ease when catching the ball . . . Hutson and fellow Hall of Famer Millard 'Dixie' Howell became football's most celebrated passing combination."

Yet, despite his exceptional play at the collegiate level, Hutson did not initially intend to turn pro due to the NFL's lack of popularity in the South. His plans changed, though, when Packers head coach Curly Lambeau offered him a contract for the then-princely sum of $300 a game. Reflecting back on Lambeau's offer, Hutson noted, "That was far and above what they had ever paid a player. Each week, they'd give me a check for $150 from one bank and $150 from another so nobody would know how much I was getting paid."

Laying claim to the starting split end job immediately upon his arrival in Green Bay, Hutson had a solid rookie season in 1935, earning Second-Team All-Pro honors for the first of three straight times by ranking among the league leaders with 18 receptions and 420 receiving yards, while topping the circuit with six touchdown catches. Improving upon his performance the following year, Hutson helped the Packers win the NFL title by setting new league marks with 34 receptions, 536 receiving yards, and eight touchdown receptions. Continuing his outstanding play in each of the next two seasons, Hutson totaled 73 receptions, 1,100 receiving yards, and 16 TD catches from 1937 to 1938, leading the league in the last category both times, while earning the first of his eight consecutive First-Team All-Pro selections in the second of those campaigns.

Combining with Green Bay quarterback Arnie Herber his first few years in the league to form the NFL's deadliest passing combination, Hutson established himself as the most dangerous offensive weapon in the game. Capable of running the 100-yard dash in 9.7 seconds, the 6'1", 183-pound Hutson had the ability to run by most defenders. But, while Hutson relied heavily on his speed to break down opposing defenses, he also possessed a wide variety of moves and fakes that made him almost impossible to cover one-on-one, with Philadelphia Eagles head coach Greasy Neale commenting, "Hutson is the only man I ever saw who could feint in three different directions at the same time."

Coach Luke Johnsos of the Chicago Bears suggested that defending against Hutson proved to be extremely difficult because "half the time, he didn't know himself where he was going."

In describing his team's best player, Curly Lambeau said, "Hutson would glide downfield, leaning forward, as if to steady himself close to the ground. Then, as suddenly as you gulp or blink an eye, he'd feint one way and go the other, reach up like a dancer, gracefully squeeze the ball and leave the scene of the accident, the accident being the defensive backs who tangled their feet up and fell trying to cover him."

Former teammate Bernie Scherer also acknowledged the greatness of Hutson when he stated, "He was the Jerry Rice of my era. He'd jump up with two guys and get the ball, and, once he got the ball, it was his ball. When he hit the ground, he wasn't tethered down. Boy! He was gone. He was just so tricky. He wasn't big, he was just fast and agile, and he ran with a peculiar lope. He was hard to cover."

Hutson also drew praise from Cecil Isbell, who spent parts of five seasons running the Green Bay offense. In discussing his former teammate, Isbell noted, "He had triple speed. The man could do the most amazing things. He had finesse. He could freeze a defensive back better than anybody I've seen."

An intelligent player as well who worked extremely hard at his craft, Hutson once claimed, "For every pass I caught in a game, I caught a thousand passes in practice." Continuing to excel after Isbell became the Packers' primary signal-caller, Hutson totaled 79 catches, 1,510 receiving yards, and 13 touchdown receptions from 1939 to 1940, before beginning an extraordinary four-year run during which he led the NFL in every major receiving category. Here are the numbers he compiled over the course of those four seasons:

YEAR	RECS	REC YDS	TD RECS	TDS	POINTS
1941	58	738	10	12	95*
1942	74	1,211	17	17	138
1943	47	776	11	11	117
1944	58	866	9	9	85

* Please note that any numbers printed in bold throughout this book indicate that the player led the NFL in that statistical category that year.

In addition to leading the league in receptions, receiving yards, and TD catches all four years, Hutson topped the circuit in touchdowns and points scored each season, with his brilliant play earning him recognition in both 1941 and 1942 as the winner of the Joe F. Carr Trophy, presented at that time to the league's most outstanding player (the Associated Press MVP award did not come into existence until 1957). Hutson also led the NFL in yards from scrimmage in three of those four seasons and annually placed near the top of the league rankings in all-purpose yards, finishing second on two separate occasions. Hutson's total of 1,211 receiving yards in 1942, which bettered by nearly 400 yards the league-mark he established three years earlier, remained a single-season franchise record until Billy Howton surpassed it 10 years later. Meanwhile, his 17 touchdown catches that same season remained an NFL record until 1984, when Mark Clayton hauled in 18 TD passes for the Miami Dolphins. An outstanding defender as well, Hutson recorded a total of 30 interceptions from his safety position over the course of his career, leading the league in picks once (six in 1940) and interception-return yards once (197 in 1943). Serving as the Packers' primary placekicker for much of his career, Hutson also led the league in field goals made once and extra points made three times.

Although it should be noted that Hutson, whose three daughters made him exempt from military service during World War II, compiled some of those numbers against inferior talent, he dominated anyone against whom he ever competed, prompting Paul Hornung to squash the notion that he exploited watered-down defenses by proclaiming, "I'm a believer. Am I a believer! You know what Hutson would do in this league today? The same things he did when he played."

Hutson once again posted outstanding numbers for the Packers in 1945, leading the league with 47 receptions, while finishing second in the circuit with 834 receiving yards, nine TD catches, 10 touchdowns, and 97 points scored. However, after announcing his retirement during each of the three previous offseasons, only to later change his mind, Hutson retired for good following the conclusion of the 1945 campaign, ending his career with 18 NFL single-game, single-season, and career records, including 488 pass receptions, 7,991 receiving yards, 8,275 yards from scrimmage, 99 touchdown receptions, 105 touchdowns, and 823 points scored. At the time of his retirement, Hutson's 488 receptions more than doubled the total amassed by any other player in league history. Meanwhile, his 99 touchdown catches stood as an NFL record for 44 years, until Seattle's Steve Largent finally surpassed it in 1989.

More than 70 years after he played his last game for the Packers, Hutson continues to hold franchise records for most touchdowns and most touchdown receptions.
Courtesy of MearsOnlineAuctions.com

Following his playing days, Hutson remained with the Packers as an assistant on Curly Lambeau's coaching staff until 1948, when he left the game to begin a career in business. Hutson, who earned a degree in business at Alabama and earlier operated the Packer Playdium Bowling Alley during his playing career, opened the Hutson Motor Car Co. dealership and purchased Chevrolet and Cadillac agencies in Racine, Wisconsin, in 1951. After retiring from the dealership business, Hutson settled in Rancho Mirage, California, where he lived until his death on June 26, 1997, at the age of 84.

Upon learning of Hutson's passing, Packers general manager Ron Wolf said, "He most certainly was the greatest player in the history of this franchise."

Longtime Dallas Cowboys executive and current football analyst Gil Brandt is another who greatly admired Hutson. Brandt, who grew up in Wisconsin during the height of Hutson's career, said that he saw him play "as a very little boy" and added that he has seen and evaluated nearly every great player since. In speaking of Hutson, Brandt offered, "He was without question one of the greatest players of all-time. His pass-catching, his technique of catching was totally different for his time—he caught the ball in his hands. He didn't trap the ball."

Brandt went on to say, "Nobody knows how great Hutson was based on passes caught. As an example, we [the Cowboys] had a fellow by the name of Drew Pearson. He had around 450 catches in his career and led the league in receptions twice with around 55 catches. Fifty-five catches doesn't mean scratch today. People think 'well, he must not have been very good.' But we very seldom threw the ball in those days. We ran it so much more than we threw it."

Brandt then added, "That was even more true in Hutson's time. You look today, and you see completion rates are 62-to-66 percent. In those days, if teams completed 30 percent of their passes, that was good. For him to catch the number of passes he caught was a true exception."

Perhaps Hutson's greatest admirer, though, is sportswriter and football historian Peter King, who said during a 2010 interview:

> I just think that, when you compare him to the guys in the first 25 years of NFL history, which is all you can do, he's head-and-shoulders above, in speed, in production, in toughness, in versatility . . . I think Don Hutson is the most dominant single player at his position of any in NFL history. . . . If you look at guys who dominate their sports over a long period of time—a guy like Wilt Chamberlain in basketball, maybe Wayne Gretzky in hockey—I think the only one who comes close to what Hutson did with the touchdown catch is Babe Ruth with home runs. . . . When he retired, he had three times as many touchdown receptions as any receiver in the first 25 years of pro football . . . I truly believe that Don Hutson would have been a prolific receiver in 1997, as well as

1937. Don Hutson is the best receiver of all-time, and I call him the best player of all-time.

CAREER HIGHLIGHTS

Best Season

Although Hutson had several sensational seasons for the Packers, he proved to be most dominant in 1941 and 1942, earning NFL MVP honors both years. After leading the league with 58 receptions, 738 receiving yards, 10 touchdown receptions, 12 touchdowns, and 95 points scored in the first of those campaigns, Hutson reached his zenith in 1942, when, in addition to establishing new NFL marks by making 74 receptions, amassing 1,211 receiving yards, recording 17 touchdown receptions, and scoring 138 points, he finished second in the league with 1,286 all-purpose yards and seven interceptions. Upon naming Hutson the winner of the Joe F. Carr Trophy as the league's most valuable player, the selection committee declared, "Also considered were his nuisance value as a disrupter of enemy defenses and his ability to transform the Packers into a confident, powerful aggregation in clutch situations."

Memorable Moments/Greatest Performances

Hutson didn't wait long to establish himself as an offensive force in the NFL, giving the Packers a 7–0 victory over the Chicago Bears on September 22, 1935, by collaborating with Arnie Herber on an 83-yard touchdown pass on the first play from scrimmage in just his second game as a pro.

Hutson scored the first non-offensive touchdown of his career during a 13–9 win over the Detroit Lions on October 20, 1935, when he returned a blocked punt 41 yards for a TD.

Hutson followed that up by scoring a pair of fourth-quarter touchdowns that turned a 14–3 deficit to the Chicago Bears into a 17–14 Packers win on October 27, 1935, with one of his TDs coming on a 69-yard connection with quarterback Arnie Herber. Hutson finished the game with five receptions for 103 yards.

Hutson led the Packers to a 26–17 victory over the Detroit Lions on November 29, 1936, by making a 58-yard touchdown reception and returning a blocked punt 40 yards for another score.

Hutson performed well for the Packers in the 1936 NFL championship game, helping them record a 21–6 victory over the Boston Redskins by scoring the game's first touchdown on a 48-yard hookup with Arnie Herber and making five catches for a total of 76 yards.

Hutson caught three touchdown passes in one game six times during his career, accomplishing the feat for the first time during a 35–10 win over the Cleveland Rams on October 17, 1937, when he made a 5-yard TD catch and scored twice from 35 yards out.

Hutson had a big day against Chicago on November 7, 1937, making five catches for 140 yards and scoring a 78-yard touchdown during a 24–14 win over the Bears.

Hutson starred during Green Bay's 26–17 win over the Rams in the 1938 regular-season opener, scoring all three Packer touchdowns on pass plays that covered 7, 53, and 18 yards.

Hutson again scored three touchdowns against Cleveland on October 30, 1938, leading the Packers to a 28–7 win over the Rams by hooking up with Cecil Isbell from 53 yards out, before hauling in a pair of TD passes from Bob Monnett that covered 31 and 50 yards. Hutson finished the game with six catches for 148 yards.

Hutson recorded one of the longest scoring plays in Packers history on October 8, 1939, when he caught a 92-yard TD pass from Arnie Herber during a 27–20 win over the Chicago Cardinals.

Although Hutson made only two receptions during a 26–7 victory over the Detroit Lions on October 22, 1939, he made them both count, collaborating with Arnie Herber and Cecil Isbell on scoring plays that covered 60 and 51 yards, respectively.

Hutson helped the Packers defeat the Washington Redskins by a score of 22–17 in the 1941 regular-season finale by hooking up with Cecil Isbell on three second-half touchdowns, the longest of which went for 40 yards. He finished the game with nine catches for 135 yards.

Hutson amassed more than 200 receiving yards for the first time during a 45–28 victory over the Cleveland Rams on October 18, 1942, making 13 receptions for 209 yards and two touchdowns.

Hutson again topped 200 yards during a 55–24 pasting of the Chicago Cardinals on November 1, 1942, making five catches for 207 yards and three touchdowns, with his scoring plays covering 40, 73, and 65 yards.

Hutson again made three touchdown receptions during a 30–12 win over the Cleveland Rams on November 8, 1942.

Hutson set a franchise record that still stands by making 14 receptions during a 21–21 tie with the Giants on November 22, 1942, finishing the day with 134 receiving yards and two touchdowns.

Hutson had a tremendous all-around game on October 31, 1943, leading the Packers to a 35–21 win over the Giants by making eight catches for 103 yards and two TDs, kicking five extra points, and completing the only pass of his career—a 38-yard scoring strike to Harry Jacunski.

Hutson starred on both sides of the ball during a 35–14 win over the Chicago Cardinals on November 14, 1943, making a pair of touchdown receptions and returning an interception 84 yards for another score.

Hutson followed that up by making eight catches, scoring two touchdowns, and amassing a career-high 237 receiving yards during a lopsided 31–7 victory over the Brooklyn Dodgers on November 21, 1943, with his scoring plays covering 51 and 79 yards. Hutson also kicked a 23-yard field goal during the contest.

Hutson again went over the 200-yard mark on October 8, 1944, when he helped lead the Packers to a 34–7 trouncing of a combined Chicago Cardinals/Pittsburgh Steelers squad by making 11 receptions for 207 yards and two touchdowns, which included a 55-yard connection with Irv Comp for the game's first score.

Hutson turned in one of his most memorable performances during a 57–21 manhandling of the Detroit Lions on October 7, 1945, when he set an NFL record by making four touchdown receptions in the second quarter. In addition to scoring on plays that covered 56, 46, 17, and 6 yards, Hutson kicked five extra points during the period, giving him a total of 29 points, which remains the league record for most points scored by any player in a single quarter.

Hutson scored three touchdowns for the final time in his career during a 33–14 win over the Chicago Cardinals on October 28, 1945, hooking up with Irv Comp on TD passes that covered 19 and 39 yards, and rushing 12 yards for another score.

NOTABLE ACHIEVEMENTS

- Surpassed 50 receptions three times, topping 70 catches once (74 in 1942).
- Surpassed 800 receiving yards four times, topping 1,000 yards once (1,211 in 1942).

- Surpassed 10 touchdown receptions three times, making 17 TD catches in 1942.
- Averaged more than 20 yards per reception twice.
- Recorded at least six interceptions three times.
- Recorded more than 100 interception-return yards once (197 in 1943).
- Led NFL in: pass receptions eight times; TD catches nine times; receiving yards seven times; yards from scrimmage three times; average yards per catch twice; TDs scored eight times; points scored five times; interceptions once; interception-return yards once; and field goals made once.
- Finished second in NFL in: pass receptions twice; touchdown receptions twice; receiving yards three times; yards from scrimmage twice; all-purpose yards three times; average yards per reception twice; touchdowns scored once; points scored three times; and interceptions once.
- Finished third in NFL in: receiving yards once; yards from scrimmage twice; all-purpose yards twice; average yards per catch twice; TDs scored once; points scored once; and interceptions once.
- Holds NFL records for: most seasons leading league in pass receptions (8); most consecutive seasons leading league in pass receptions (5); most seasons leading league in receiving yards (7); most consecutive seasons leading league in receiving yards (4); most seasons leading league in touchdown receptions (9); most consecutive seasons leading league in touchdown receptions (5); most seasons leading league in total touchdowns scored (8); most seasons leading league in points scored (5); most consecutive seasons leading league in points scored (5); most touchdowns scored in a quarter (4); and most points scored in a quarter (29).
- Holds Packers single-game records for most pass receptions (14 vs. New York Giants on 11/22/42) and most touchdown receptions (4 vs. Detroit Lions on 10/7/45).
- Holds Packers single-season record for most yards per reception (24.88 in 1939).
- Holds Packers career records for most touchdowns scored (105) and most TD catches (99).
- Ranks among Packers career leaders with: 488 pass receptions (5th); 7,991 receiving yards (5th); 8,275 yards from scrimmage (5th); 8,709 all-purpose yards (6th); 823 points scored (3rd); average of 16.38 yards per reception (5th); and 30 interceptions (9th).
- Ranks 11th in NFL history with 99 touchdown receptions.

- Retired as NFL's all-time leader in: pass receptions, touchdown receptions, receiving yards, touchdowns scored, and points scored.
- Four-time Western Conference champion (1936, 1938, 1939, and 1944).
- Three-time NFL champion (1936, 1939, and 1944).
- Four-time Pro Bowl selection (1939, 1940, 1941, and 1942).
- Eight-time First-Team All-Pro (1938, 1939, 1940, 1941, 1942, 1943, 1944, and 1945).
- Three-time Second-Team All-Pro (1935, 1936, and 1937).
- Two-time NFL MVP (1941 and 1942).
- NFL 1930s All-Decade Team.
- Pro Football Hall of Fame All-1930s Team.
- Pro Football Reference All-1930s First Team.
- #14 retired by Packers.
- Named to Packers 50th Anniversary Team in 1969.
- Named to NFL's 50th Anniversary Team in 1969.
- Named to NFL's 75th Anniversary All-Time Team in 1994.
- Named to NFL's 75th Anniversary All-Time Two-Way Team in 1994.
- Named Greatest Green Bay Packer of All-Time by the NFL Network in 2012.
- Number six on the *Sporting News*' 1999 list of 100 Greatest Players in NFL History.
- Number nine on NFL Films' 2010 list of 100 Greatest Players in NFL History.
- Elected to Pro Football Hall of Fame in 1963.

2

BRETT FAVRE

The first NFL quarterback to throw for 70,000 yards, pass for 500 touchdowns, complete 6,000 passes, and attempt 10,000 passes, Brett Favre currently ranks first all-time in pass attempts (10,169), pass completions (6,300), interceptions (336), games started (298), and consecutive games started (297). Compiling most of his record-setting numbers during his time in Green Bay, Favre spent 16 seasons directing the Packers offense, throwing for more than 3,000 yards in every one of those campaigns, while also completing more than 30 touchdown passes on eight separate occasions. En route to establishing himself as the franchise's all-time leader in practically every passing category, Favre led NFL signal-callers in pass completions twice, passing yards twice, touchdown passes four times, and pass completion percentage once, earning in the process nine trips to the Pro Bowl, six All-Pro nominations, five All-NFC selections, and three league MVP awards. Favre's brilliant play, which helped restore the Packers to prominence during the 1990s, also earned him a spot on the NFL 1990s All-Decade Team, a number 20 ranking on NFL Films' 2010 list of the 100 Greatest Players in NFL History, and a place in the Pro Football Hall of Fame.

Born in Gulfport, Mississippi, on October 10, 1969, Brett Lorenzo Favre attended Hancock North Central High School, where he played baseball and football, starring on the diamond as a pitcher, while also excelling on the gridiron at quarterback in a primarily option, run-oriented offense coached by his father. Yet, despite his outstanding play in high school, Favre drew little interest from college scouts, prompting him to enroll at the University of Southern Mississippi, from which he received his only scholarship offer.

After beginning his freshman year as the Golden Eagles' seventh-string quarterback, Favre gradually worked his way into the starter's role, displaying over the course of his college career a toughness that his teammates admired and a propensity for producing late-game heroics. Still, Favre nearly saw his playing days end abruptly prior to the start of his senior year,

Brett Favre helped restore the Packers to prominence during the 1990s.
Courtesy of MearsOnlineAuctions.com

when his involvement in a serious car accident almost cost him his life. Losing control of his car while going around a bend not far from his parents' home, Favre remained inside the automobile as it flipped over three times before finally coming to rest against a tree. After being freed from the vehicle by his brother, Favre was rushed to the hospital, where doctors removed 30 inches of his small intestine. Amazingly, Favre led Southern Mississippi to a comeback victory over Alabama just six weeks later, prompting Crimson Tide coach Gene Stallings to later proclaim, "You can call it a miracle, or a legend, or whatever you want to. I just know that, on that day, Brett Favre was larger than life."

Having set many school records by the time he graduated, Favre subsequently entered the 1991 NFL Draft, where the Atlanta Falcons selected him in the second round, with the 33rd overall pick. He then spent his rookie season sitting on the bench behind starting quarterback Chris Miller, before being pried away from the Falcons following the conclusion of the campaign by Packers general manager Ron Wolf, who sent the 19th overall pick of the 1992 NFL Draft to Atlanta in exchange for his services.

Joining a team in Green Bay that had posted a winning record in just four of the previous 22 seasons, including a mark of only 4-12 one year earlier, Favre made an immediate impact after he replaced Don Majkowski behind center four games into the 1992 campaign, leading the Packers to a record of 9-7 for the first of three straight times. Earning the first of his 11 Pro Bowl selections in 1992, Favre completed just over 64 percent of his passes, threw for 3,227 yards and 18 touchdowns, and posted a passer rating of 85.3. Although Favre earned Pro Bowl honors again the following year by placing sixth in the league with 3,303 yards passing, he compiled less impressive overall numbers, finishing the season with a pass-completion percentage of 60.9, a passer rating of just 72.2, 19 TD passes, and a league-leading 24 interceptions. He followed that up with a strong showing in 1994, ranking among the league leaders with 3,882 yards passing, 33 touchdown passes, and a passer rating of 90.7, while completing 62.4 percent of his passes and throwing only 14 interceptions. However, the best had yet to come, as Favre subsequently began an exceptional three-year run during which he established himself as arguably the finest quarterback in the game, compiling the following numbers over the course of those three seasons:

YEAR	YARDS PASSING	TD PASSES	INTS	COMP PCT	PASSER RATING
1995	**4,413**	38	13	63.0	99.5
1996	3,899	39	13	59.9	95.8
1997	3,867	35	16	59.3	92.6

In addition to leading the league in touchdown passes each year, Favre annually ranked among the leaders in passing yards, completion percentage, and passer rating, with his 4,413 yards through the air in 1995 leaving him just 45 yards short of Lynn Dickey's then–single-season franchise record of 4,458, which he set in 1983. More importantly, the Packers won three straight division championships, two NFC titles, and one NFL champion-ship, with Favre passing for 246 yards and two touchdowns during their 35–21 victory over New England in Super Bowl XXXI. Favre's superb play throughout the period earned him three consecutive league MVP awards, making him the first and only player to be so honored that many times in succession (he shared the award with Barry Sanders in 1997).

As Favre emerged as arguably the NFL's most recognizable figure, he developed into the Packers' unquestioned on-field leader and one of the team's most popular players, using his down-home, country-boy charm to ingratiate himself to his teammates. In discussing Favre's ability to make the other players around him feel comfortable, former Packers head coach Mike Sherman later revealed, "He was never one to say a lot in the locker room before or after the game. He was at his best, however, and felt most comfortable talking to the players while in the huddle on the field. He did his best talking in the huddle—and it wasn't always about the game! He kept them loose when they needed to be loose, and he challenged them when that was what they needed. He was at home—very comfortable—in the huddle."

Favre also became known for his ability to succeed in the face of adver-sity, his unbridled enthusiasm for the game, and his fearlessness, which eventually earned him the nickname "The Gunslinger." In addressing those attributes, Sherman stated:

> Brett Favre was unique in many ways. First and foremost, he made those around him better. Players played at a higher level with him on the field. Second, he was at his best when things around him were at their worst. Injured, adversity, back against the wall, death of his Dad . . . he always found a way not just to play . . . but to play well. Third, he was the true Gunslinger. He never let a bad play interfere with the next play. He was always ready for the next play . . . to win that play with complete confidence.

Sherman also praised Favre for his strong work ethic and dedication to his profession, saying, "Media people would ask me after a game if I was shocked or impressed by some 'once in a lifetime' throw they saw him make during the game. I'd usually have to tell them 'No, I've seen him make that throw in practice before.' I know he made things look easy—but he prac-ticed hard. He practiced like he played."

Unfortunately, the success Favre experienced during the relatively early stages of his career came at a price, because, while being treated for various injuries, he developed an addiction to the painkiller Vicodin. After suffering

Favre set NFL records for most yards passing and most touchdown passes during his time in Green Bay.
Courtesy of Heritage Auctions

a seizure during a hospital visit, Favre made his condition known to the public in May 1996 and subsequently entered a rehabilitation center, where he underwent 46 days of treatment to cure him of his addiction. Just a few months later, he led the Packers to their first Super Bowl win in nearly 30 years, after which he was named league MVP for the second consecutive time.

Favre continued to perform at an elite level the next several years, throwing for more than 3,300 yards each season from 1998 to 2004, while also completing at least 30 touchdown passes in four of those seven seasons. Particularly effective in 1998 and 2001, Favre threw 31 TD passes and led the league with 4,212 passing yards and a completion percentage of 63 in the first of those campaigns, before earning Pro Bowl and Second-Team All-Pro honors three years later by passing for 3,921 yards and 32 touchdowns, completing 61.6 percent of his passes, and posting a passer rating of 94.1.

However, after passing for 4,088 yards and tossing 30 touchdown passes in 2004, Favre spent the next three offseasons conducting himself very much like a diva, forcing the Green Bay front office to hold its breath while he decided whether or not he wished to continue playing. Waiting until the last possible moment to announce his decision each year, Favre invariably elected to return to the Packers, forcing Aaron Rodgers, who the team selected in the first round of the 2005 NFL Draft, to remain on the bench.

Finally, on March 4, 2008, Favre formally announced his retirement, stating during a tearful press conference, "I know I can still play, but I don't think I want to. And that's really what it comes down to." Four months later, though, Favre changed his mind and contacted the Packers about a possible return to the team. Speaking publicly for the first time about a potential comeback, Favre said during a July 14, 2008, interview on the Fox News Channel's *On the Record with Greta Van Susteren* that he was "guilty of retiring early," that he was "never fully committed" to retirement, and that he had been pressured by the Packers to make a decision before the NFL Draft and the start of the free agent signing period. He added that he had no intention of returning to the Packers as a backup, expressed his sympathy for Aaron Rodgers's predicament, and affirmed that he was fully committed to playing football in 2008.

Subsequently told during a lengthy meeting with Packers general manager Ted Thompson and head coach Mike McCarthy that the team had committed itself to Rodgers as its new quarterback, Favre agreed with both men that the time had come for the two sides to part ways. A few days later, on August 7, 2008, the Packers traded Favre to the New York Jets for a conditional fourth-round pick in the 2009 NFL Draft, ending in the process his 16-year association with the club. Over the course of those 16 seasons, Favre passed for 61,655 yards, threw 442 touchdown passes and 286 interceptions, completed 61.4 percent of his passes, and posted a passer rating of 85.8. Appearing in a franchise-record 255 games, Favre led the Packers to an overall record of 160-93 as a starter.

Favre ended up spending just one season in New York, leading the Jets to a record of 9-7 in 2008, before joining the Minnesota Vikings for two years. Experiencing a rebirth in Minnesota, Favre earned the last of his 11 Pro Bowl selections in 2009 by passing for 4,202 yards, throwing 33 touchdown passes and only seven interceptions, and establishing career-high marks in completion percentage (68.4) and passer rating (107.2). However, after passing for just 2,509 yards and throwing only 11 TD passes the following year, Favre elected to announce his retirement, ending his career as the NFL's all-time leader in seven different categories, including passing yards (71,838) and touchdown passes (508). He subsequently returned to Mississippi, where he became an assistant football coach at Oak Ridge High School in Hattiesburg. Asked by the St. Louis Rams to return to the NFL in 2013, Favre declined the offer, telling WSPZ radio in Washington, DC, that he suffered from memory loss he attributed in part to the multiple concussions he suffered during his playing career.

Upon learning that Favre had been elected to the Pro Football Hall of Fame on February 6, 2016, former Packers vice president and general manager Ron Wolf stated, "When I traded for Brett Favre, I thought he would be sensational. He became incomparable. They say that old Yankee Stadium was the house that Ruth built. Well, the Lambeau Field reconstruction is the house that Favre built."

PACKERS CAREER HIGHLIGHTS

Best Season

With so many great seasons from which to choose, this ended up being a difficult choice. However, after taking everything into consideration, I ultimately settled on the 1995 campaign. En route to earning Associated Press NFL Offensive Player of the Year honors and his first league MVP trophy, Favre completed 63 percent of his passes, finished second in the league with a passer rating of 99.5, his best mark as a member of the Packers, threw only 13 interceptions, and led all NFL quarterbacks with 38 touchdown passes and a career-high 4,413 yards passing, with his exceptional performance also gaining him recognition as the winner of the Bert Bell Award as the NFL Player of the Year.

Memorable Moments/Greatest Performances

Replacing Don Majkowski behind center for the first time on September 20, 1992, Favre led the Packers to their first win of the young season by completing 22 of 39 passes, for 289 yards and two touchdowns, with his stellar play enabling Green Bay to overcome a 17–3 deficit to Cincinnati heading into the fourth quarter and defeat the Bengals by a score of 24–23. Displaying his ability to lead his team back from adversity, Favre led the Packers on a pair of late scoring drives, tossing TD passes of five yards to Sterling Sharpe and 35 yards to Kitrick Taylor, with the game-winning throw to Taylor coming in the final minute of regulation.

Favre threw three touchdown passes for the first time in his career later in the year, leading the Packers to a 38–10 victory over the Detroit Lions on December 6, 1992, by completing TD passes of 65 and nine yards to Sterling Sharpe, and another of nine yards to Harry Sydney. He finished the game 15-of-19, for 214 yards.

Favre topped that performance on October 24, 1993, tossing four touchdown passes to Sterling Sharpe during a 37–14 win over the Tampa Bay Buccaneers, with his TD throws covering 7, 30, 10, and 32 yards. He finished the contest 20-of-35, for 268 yards.

Favre again torched the Tampa Bay secondary on September 25, 1994, leading the Packers to a lopsided 30–3 victory over the Buccaneers by completing 30 of 39 pass attempts for 306 yards and three touchdowns, with the longest of his TD passes being a 20-yarder to Ed West.

In a game in which he also passed for 321 yards and two touchdowns, Favre gave the Packers a dramatic 21–17 victory over the Atlanta Falcons on December 18, 1994, by scoring the game-winning touchdown with only seconds remaining in regulation.

During a 27–24 Monday night win over the Chicago Bears on September 11, 1995, Favre hooked up with Robert Brooks on a 99-yard scoring play, the longest pass completion in franchise history. He finished the game with 312 yards passing and three TDs.

Favre had another big day against Chicago two months later, leading the Packers to a 35–28 victory over the Bears on November 12, 1995, by completing 25 of 33 pass attempts, for 336 yards and five touchdowns, with his longest TD pass being a 44-yarder to Brooks.

Favre had an extremely efficient afternoon against Cincinnati on December 3, 1995, hitting on 31 of 43 pass attempts for 339 yards and three touchdowns during a 24–10 win over the Bengals.

Favre completed all four of his TD passes during the first half of a 34–23 victory over the New Orleans Saints on December 16, 1995, with the longest of those being a 40-yard connection with Robert Brooks.

Favre again threw four TD passes during a 34–3 win over Tampa Bay in the 1996 regular-season opener, with three of those going to tight end Keith Jackson, one of which covered 51 yards.

Favre accomplished the feat once more on November 3, 1996, leading the Packers to a 28–18 win over Detroit by completing 24 of 35 passes, for 281 yards and four TDs, including a 65-yard scoring strike to Don Beebe.

Favre tossed five touchdown passes in a game for the second time in his career during a 38–32 victory over the Vikings on September 21, 1997, hooking up twice with Antonio Freeman and once each with Robert Brooks, Terry Mickens, and Mark Chmura.

Although he also threw three interceptions during the contest, Favre ended up leading the Packers to a 37–30 win over the Carolina Panthers on September 27, 1998, by passing for 388 yards and five touchdowns, including a pair of TD tosses to Derrick Mayes.

Favre led the Packers to a dramatic 28–24 come-from-behind victory over the Raiders in the 1999 regular-season opener by throwing two late touchdown passes, with the second of those going to Jeff Thomason with just 11 seconds remaining in regulation. He finished the game with 333 yards passing, four touchdowns, and three interceptions.

Favre provided further heroics two weeks later, giving the Packers a 23–20 win over the Vikings on September 26, 1999, by tossing a 23-yard touchdown pass to Corey Bradford with just 12 seconds left in the fourth quarter.

Favre again came up big in the clutch for the Packers on October 10, 1999, giving them a 26–23 Sunday night win over Tampa Bay by completing a 21-yard TD pass to Antonio Freeman with just 1:05 left in regulation. He finished the game with two touchdown throws, no picks, and a season-high 390 yards passing.

Favre turned in one of his most efficient performances during a 31–23 win over the defending NFL champion Baltimore Ravens on October 14, 2001, completing 27 of 34 pass attempts, for 337 yards and three touchdowns.

Favre had a huge game against Jacksonville on December 3, 2001, leading the Packers to a 28–21 Monday night win over the Jaguars by throwing for 362 yards and three touchdowns, while also running six yards for the game-winning score with just 1:30 left in regulation.

Favre thrived against Detroit both times the Packers faced the Lions in 2002, leading Green Bay to a 37–31 win on September 22 by passing for

357 yards and three touchdowns, before throwing for 351 yards and two touchdowns during a lopsided 40–14 victory on November 10.

Favre also had a big game against Chicago on October 7, 2002, leading the Packers to a 34–21 win over the Bears by passing for 359 yards and three touchdowns, with one of those being an 85-yard connection with Donald Driver.

Favre led the Packers to a 38–21 victory over San Diego on December 14, 2003, by throwing for 278 and four touchdowns, with his last three TD passes coming within a span of 7½ minutes in the final period.

Although Favre and the Packers ended up losing a 45–31 shootout to Peyton Manning and the Colts on September 26, 2004 (Manning passed for 393 yards and five touchdowns), the Green Bay quarterback acquitted himself extremely well, throwing for 360 yards and four TDs, with the longest of those being a 79-yard connection with Javon Walker.

Favre again threw four TD passes during a 34–31 win over the Vikings on November 14, 2004, hooking up with Javon Walker, Tony Fisher, Bubba Franks, and William Henderson once each.

Favre followed that up by passing for 383 yards and one touchdown during a come-from-behind 16–13 win over the Houston Texans that the Packers trailed by 10 points heading into the fourth quarter, with the big play being a 24-yard scoring strike to Donald Driver.

The Packers spent Christmas Eve 2004 recording a 34–31 victory over the Minnesota Vikings, with Favre throwing for 365 yards and three touchdowns. Green Bay won the game on a 29-yard field goal by Ryan Longwell as time expired.

Favre led the Packers to a 31–24 win over the Lions on September 24, 2006, by completing 25 of 36 pass attempts for 340 yards and three touchdowns, including a 75-yard hookup with Greg Jennings.

Favre completed another long TD pass during a 23–17 win over the Vikings on November 12, 2006, collaborating with Donald Driver on an 82-yard scoring play just before halftime. He finished the game with 347 yards passing and two touchdowns.

Favre threw for 369 yards and three touchdowns during a 31–24 victory over the San Diego Chargers on September 23, 2007, with one of his TD passes being a 57-yard connection with Greg Jennings early in the fourth quarter that put the Packers ahead to stay.

Favre made history one week later, when, during a 23–16 win over the Minnesota Vikings on September 30, 2007, he hooked up with Greg Jennings on a 16-yard scoring play that gave him the 421st touchdown pass of his career, putting him one ahead of Dan Marino as the NFL's all-time leader in that category.

After hooking up with James Jones on a 79-yard scoring play earlier in the contest, Favre gave the Packers a 19–13 overtime win over the Denver Broncos on October 29, 2007, by completing an 82-yard TD pass to Greg Jennings on the first play from scrimmage in OT.

Favre led the Packers to a 34–0 rout of the Vikings on November 11, 2007, by completing 33 of 46 pass attempts for 351 yards and three touchdowns, with two of his TD tosses going to Ruvell Martin and the other to Donald Lee.

Favre had his last big game for the Packers on November 22, 2007, when he led them to a 37–26 win over the Lions by passing for 381 yards and three touchdowns.

Yet, Favre turned in the most memorable performance of his career nearly four years earlier, on December 22, 2003, when he led the Packers to a 41–7 manhandling of the Oakland Raiders just one day after his father passed away. Starting the Monday night contest in Oakland with a heavy heart, Favre performed brilliantly before an international television audience, throwing four touchdown passes in the first half, and finishing the game 22-of-30, for 399 yards and four TDs. Commenting on his decision to play afterwards, Favre said, "I knew that my dad would have wanted me to play. I love him so much, and I love this game. It's meant a great deal to me, to my dad, to my family, and I didn't expect this kind of performance. But I know he was watching tonight." Following the game's conclusion, Favre went to his father's funeral in Pass Christian, Mississippi. He later won an ESPY Award for his performance that evening.

NOTABLE ACHIEVEMENTS

- Passed for more than 3,000 yards 16 straight times, topping 4,000 yards on five occasions.
- Threw more than 30 touchdown passes eight times.
- Completed more than 60 percent of passes 11 times, topping 65 percent twice.
- Posted touchdown-to-interception ratio of better than 2–1 five times.
- Posted quarterback rating above 90.0 eight times.
- Led NFL quarterbacks in: pass completions twice; passing yards twice; touchdown passes four times; pass completion percentage once; and fourth-quarter comebacks once.
- Finished second in NFL in: pass completions four times; passing yards once; touchdown passes three times; completion percentage once; passer rating twice; and fourth-quarter comebacks twice.

- Holds NFL records for most: pass attempts (10,169); pass completions (6,300); passes intercepted (336); games started (298); and consecutive games started (297).
- Ranks second in NFL history with 71,838 yards passing and 508 touchdown passes.
- Holds Packers career records for most: pass attempts (8,754); pass completions (5,377); yards passing (61,655); touchdown passes (442); seasons played (16); games played (255); and consecutive games played (255).
- Ranks second in Packers history in passer rating (85.8) and completion percentage (61.4).
- Holds Packers record for longest pass completion (99 yards to Robert Brooks vs. Chicago on 9/11/95).
- Seven-time division champion (1995, 1996, 1997, 2002, 2003, 2004, and 2007).
- Two-time NFC champion (1996 and 1997).
- Super Bowl XXXI champion.
- 12-time NFC Offensive Player of the Week.
- 1995 Associated Press NFL Offensive Player of the Year.
- Three-time Associated Press NFL MVP (1995, 1996, and 1997).
- Two-time NFL Players Association MVP (1995 and 1996).
- Two-time Bert Bell Award winner as NFL Player of the Year (1995 and 1996).
- 2007 *Sports Illustrated* Sportsman of the Year.
- Nine-time Pro Bowl selection (1992, 1993, 1995, 1996, 1997, 2001, 2002, 2003, and 2007).
- Three-time First-Team All-Pro (1995, 1996, and 1997).
- Three-time Second-Team All-Pro (2001, 2002, and 2007).
- Five-time First-Team All-NFC selection (1995, 1996, 1997, 2002, and 2003).
- NFL 1990s All-Decade Team.
- Pro Football Hall of Fame All-1990s Second Team.
- Pro Football Reference All-2000s Second Team.
- #4 retired by Packers.
- Number 82 on the *Sporting News*' 1999 list of 100 Greatest Players in NFL History.
- Number 20 on NFL Films' 2010 list of 100 Greatest Players in NFL History.
- Elected to Pro Football Hall of Fame in 2016.

3

FORREST GREGG

Hailed by Vince Lombardi in his book *Run To Daylight* as "the finest player I ever coached," Forrest Gregg spent 14 of his 15 NFL seasons in Green Bay, establishing himself during that time as one of the greatest offensive linemen in league history. Anchoring the Packers' offensive line from his right tackle position, Gregg proved to be an integral part of a running attack that averaged 151.3 yards per game and 2,051 yards a season during the Lombardi years. Considered by his coaches and peers to be "the perfect offensive lineman," Gregg helped the Packers win six Western Conference championships, five NFL titles, and two Super Bowls, earning in the process nine Pro Bowl selections, eight All-Pro nominations, and a spot on the Packers 50th Anniversary Team. And, following the conclusion of his playing career, Gregg received the additional honors of being named to the NFL 1960s All-Decade Team and the NFL's 75th Anniversary All-Time Team, and being inducted into the Pro Football Hall of Fame.

Born in Birthright, Texas, on October 18, 1933, Alvis Forrest Gregg attended Sulphur Springs High School, where his outstanding play on the gridiron earned him a football scholarship from Southern Methodist University in Texas. Excelling on both sides of the ball while at SMU, Gregg twice earned All–Southwest Conference honors, prompting the Packers to select him in the second round of the 1956 NFL Draft, with the 20th overall pick.

Gregg spent his rookie campaign playing on special teams and serving as a backup offensive lineman, before missing the entire 1957 season while serving in the military. Garnering significantly more playing time upon his return to the Packers in 1958, Gregg established himself as one of the team's most reliable players, beginning a string of 13 consecutive seasons in which he appeared in every game. However, Gregg didn't truly blossom into a star until Vince Lombardi assumed control of the team the following year. Inserted at starting right tackle full-time, Gregg emerged as one of the league's top linemen, earning Pro Bowl honors for the first of six straight

Vince Lombardi called Forrest Gregg "the finest player I ever coached."
Courtesy of MearsOnlineAuctions.com

times, while also making Second-Team All-Pro. With the Packers winning the Western Conference championship in 1960, Gregg took another step forward, earning First-Team All-Pro honors for the first time in his career. And, as the Packers continued to establish themselves as the league's dominant team in subsequent seasons, the accolades continued to roll in for Gregg, who made First-Team All-Pro six straight times, from 1962 to 1967.

Although somewhat undersized at 6'4" and 250 pounds, Gregg emerged as the league's premier player at his position by learning how to out-finesse the larger defensive ends who typically sought to overpower their opponents. With most NFL teams inserting their top pass-rusher at left defensive end in those days, Gregg spent countless hours studying film and learning his opponents' weaknesses and tendencies, so much so that he already knew their every move by the time he lined up against them. As a result, Gregg presented serious problems to even the very best defensive linemen in the league, including Deacon Jones of the Los Angeles Rams, who said of his frequent foe, "Forrest Gregg—look at the coordination of his feet and hands, which is the sign of a great lineman. When you get into

Gregg, his arm reach, the way he positioned himself, his actions from left to right—the guy was just fantastic!"

In addition to his excellent technique, Gregg possessed outstanding athleticism and tremendous determination that enabled him to flawlessly execute the famed Packer "Power Sweep," with Jones noting, "His movements would cause you a lot of problems. The way he drove you out of that hole. He was the best drive-blocker I ever saw. . . . He was fundamentally sound coming off the football . . . I had to really get ready to play a guy like Forrest. I had to put in a lot of work."

Jones added, "He's not like some tackles, you know, I hit them upside the head with those hands and I'm done with them. You know, they're not gonna' be much of a problem that day. Not him. Forrest Gregg, you gotta' fight for 60 minutes . . . It ain't gonna' get no better than that. It ain't gonna' get no tougher than that."

In discussing the pride he took in his run blocking, Gregg commented, "They say you don't get much recognition on the offensive line, but there is a lot of satisfaction if you know you're doing your job and the coaches know it. Our backs always knew they didn't make those long runs by themselves."

After helping the Packers win three consecutive NFL titles and two Super Bowls between 1965 and 1967, Gregg remained in Green Bay three more years, continuing his then–franchise record 187 consecutive games played streak. Dealt to the Cowboys following the conclusion of the 1970 campaign, Gregg ended his playing career in Dallas, announcing his retirement after he earned his sixth NFL championship ring as a member of the Cowboys in 1971. Still considered to be one of the greatest offensive tackles ever to play the game, Gregg received a number 28 ranking in the *Sporting News'* 1999 list of the 100 Greatest Football Players in NFL History, placing him behind only Anthony Munoz and John Hannah among all offensive linemen.

A true student of the game, Gregg entered into a career in coaching after he retired as an active player, spending two years serving as an assistant in San Diego and Cleveland, before taking over as head coach of the Browns in 1975. After being relieved of his duties in Cleveland at the end of 1977, Gregg coached the Cincinnati Bengals from 1980 to 1983, before returning to Green Bay, where he led the Packers to an overall record of 25-37-1 between 1984 and 1987. Choosing to leave Green Bay in January 1988, Gregg spent two seasons coaching at his alma mater, SMU, before assuming the role of athletic director at that institution for the next four years. Following his stint at SMU, Gregg remained away from the game for more than a decade, before he accepted the position of vice president of football operations with the Canadian Football League's Ottawa Renegades in 2005. After serving in that capacity for a brief period of time, Gregg retired to Colorado Springs, Colorado, where he currently lives. Diagnosed with Parkinson's disease in October 2011, Gregg now struggles with the illness thought to be brought on by the many concussions he suffered while playing football in high school, college, and the NFL.

PACKERS CAREER HIGHLIGHTS

Best Season

With Gregg earning First-Team All-Pro honors seven times, any number of seasons could be identified as the finest of his career. However, Gregg perhaps accomplished his greatest feat in 1965, when, due to a rash of injuries that created a crisis on the Packers' offensive line, he spent time at both his normal right tackle position and at left guard, performing so well at each post that one major wire service named him All-NFL at tackle, while another named him to its first team at guard.

Memorable Moments/Greatest Performances

As an offensive lineman, Gregg usually found himself living vicariously through the accomplishments of others, with one of his finest moments coming on October 22, 1961, when the Packers amassed 467 yards of total offense during a 33–7 win over the Minnesota Vikings, with 241 of those coming on the ground.

Gregg and the rest of the Green Bay offensive line again dominated the opposition on November 11, 1962, helping the Packers compile 628 yards of total offense, including 294 on the ground, during a 49–0 blowout of the Philadelphia Eagles.

Yet, when asked what he considered to be his most memorable moment as a player, Gregg spoke of Vince Lombardi, saying, "The greatest experience I had as a player was playing for Vince Lombardi and playing in Super Bowl I." Recalling the significance of that first Super Bowl, Gregg went on to say, "We played the Kansas City Chiefs in Super Bowl I, and we went in thinking we would win that game. And we did. Had we not won, we would have felt like we let down what was at that time the National Football League. It was a very rewarding thing to have won that game and be on that team that played in the first Super Bowl."

Gregg earned nine Pro Bowl selections and eight All-Pro nominations during his time in Green Bay.
Courtesy of RMYAuctions.com

NOTABLE ACHIEVEMENTS

- Tied for fourth in Packers history in seasons played (14).
- Ranks sixth in Packers history in games played (187).
- Played in 187 consecutive games.
- Six-time Western Conference champion (1960, 1961, 1962, 1965, 1966, and 1967).
- Five-time NFL champion (1961, 1962, 1965, 1966, and 1967).
- Two-time Super Bowl champion (I and II).
- Nine-time Pro Bowl selection (1959, 1960, 1961, 1962, 1963, 1964, 1966, 1967, and 1968).

- Seven-time First-Team All-Pro (1960, 1962, 1963, 1964, 1965, 1966, and 1967).
- 1959 Second-Team All-Pro.
- Five-time All–Western Conference First-Team selection (1959, 1962, 1963, 1965, and 1967).
- NFL 1960s All-Decade Team.
- Pro Football Hall of Fame All-1960s Team.
- Pro Football Reference All-1960s First Team.
- Named to Packers 50th Anniversary Team in 1969.
- Named to NFL's 75th Anniversary All-Time Team in 1994.
- Number 28 on the *Sporting News'* 1999 list of 100 Greatest Players in NFL History.
- Number 54 on NFL Films' 2010 list of 100 Greatest Players in NFL History.
- Elected to Pro Football Hall of Fame in 1977.

4

RAY NITSCHKE

The face of the Packers defense for more than a decade, Ray Nitschke spent his entire 15-year career in Green Bay, establishing himself during that time as one of the most feared and respected players in the NFL. Anchoring the Green Bay defense from his middle linebacker position, Nitschke served as the team's emotional leader on that side of the ball, with his physical style of play, aggressiveness, and sheer ferocity inspiring his teammates and intimidating the opposition. One of only six Packer players to have his number retired (#66), Nitschke helped lead Green Bay to six Western Conference championships, five NFL titles, and victories in the first two Super Bowls, with his exceptional play earning him five All-Pro selections and spots on the Packers 50th Anniversary Team, the NFL's 50th Anniversary Team, and the league's 75th Anniversary Team. Nitschke's other honors include being named the NFL's greatest linebacker of all time in 1969 and being elected to the Pro Football Hall of Fame in 1978.

Born in Elmwood Park, Illinois, on December 29, 1936, Raymond Ernest Nitschke grew up without much parental supervision, being raised by his two older brothers after his father died in a car accident in 1940 and his mother lost her life due to a blood clot nine years later. Enraged by the loss of both his parents at such a young age, Nitschke took out his frustrations on the other neighborhood boys, with whom he engaged in frequent fist-fights. A poor student, Nitschke played fullback on one of Proviso East High School's three football teams as a freshman, before his low grades made him academically ineligible to compete as a sophomore. However, after improving his scores, Nitschke went on to star in multiple sports his final two years at Proviso East, excelling as a quarterback and safety on the gridiron, while also proving to be a standout pitcher and left fielder on the diamond.

Subsequently offered $3,000 to sign with MLB's St. Louis Browns, Nitschke instead chose to accept a football scholarship from the University of Illinois, where he continued to conduct himself in a somewhat atypical manner off the playing field, smoking, drinking heavily, and fighting at

Ray Nitschke anchored the Packers defense for 15 seasons from his middle linebacker position.
Courtesy of Laughead Studios

the drop of a hat. Nevertheless, he emerged as an elite player on both sides of the ball for the school's football team, excelling at fullback on offense, while also establishing himself as one of the best linebackers in all of college football on defense.

Having grown up on the outskirts of Chicago, Nitschke entered the 1958 NFL Draft hoping to be chosen by his beloved Bears. However, he instead ended up going to the Packers, who selected him in the third round, with the 36th overall pick. Nitschke garnered a significant amount of playing time as a rookie in 1958, although his first NFL season proved to be a dismal one, with the Packers posting a league-worst record of 1-10-1. But things began to look up after Vince Lombardi assumed control of the team the following year, with the Packers compiling a record of 7-5 that gave them their first winning mark in more than a decade.

The 1959 campaign provided just a small taste of what lay ahead, as the Packers subsequently emerged as an NFL powerhouse, winning six of the next eight Western Conference titles and five of the next eight league championships under Lombardi. And, as they established themselves as the "Team of the 1960s," Nitschke served as the driving force behind their strong showing on defense. Commenting on Nitschke's gradual rise to stardom, teammate Jerry Kramer noted, "He was just happy to be there the first couple of years, but he got this desire to be perfect, and you could see him make tackles, and they weren't perfect. He'd get up and kick the ground and be upset with himself for not making a perfect tackle. So, he developed a quest for perfection and excellence after a while."

The 6'3", 235-pound Nitschke, who became known for his ability to deliver hard hits to the opposition, explained his approach to his chosen profession by saying, "My father died when I was three, my mother when I was 14, so I took it out on all the kids in the neighborhood. What I like about this game is the contact, the man-to-man, the getting-it-out-of-your-system." He then added, "I'm not the biggest guy or the strongest guy either. I have to make up for lack of size with aggressiveness. I've always learned that the best way to play the game is to hit your opponent a little harder than he hits you. It's self-preservation."

Reflecting back on the manner in which Nitschke treated his own teammates during practice, Jerry Kramer claimed, "It didn't matter if you were in shorts and T-shirts, you always buckled your hat when you went close to Raymond because he was gonna' hit you."

Fellow Packers linebacker Dave Robinson added, "Ray's tackles and hits fired up our entire defense. He was a great tackler and arrived at the ball with the most ferocity. Remember, if you played defense for coach Lombardi, you had to be a good tackler. We practiced tackling twice a week—the NFL was a lot different back then."

Bears tight end Mike Ditka, who engaged in many physical battles with Nitschke, expressed his respect for his former adversary when he stated, "The toughest guy I ever played against was Ray Nitschke . . . he was a physical, tough guy, and he was a great football player. . . . The thing about Nitschke is that he played the game with passion. We had a lot of wars, based on mutual respect. He knocked the crap out of me, and I knocked the crap out of him. We went after each other, but it was clean. Neither one of us backed down from anyone."

Meanwhile, Chicago center Mike Pyle said, "I can say playing against Ray Nitschke shortened my career dramatically. I had great respect for Nitschke. I thought he was one of the greatest linebackers to play the game. Raymond hit awfully hard, but he wasn't a dirty player."

Yet, even though Nitschke, whose teammate Bart Starr claimed was strong enough "to throw a ball 100 yards at times, and 80 yards like it was nothing," built much of his reputation on his strength, toughness, and ability to defend against the run, he also possessed superior athletic ability that enabled him to excel in pass coverage as well, with his 25 career interceptions tying him for first place all-time among Packer linebackers. Nitschke also recorded a franchise-record 23 fumble recoveries over the course of his career.

After helping the Packers win their first NFL title under Lombardi in 1961, Nitschke emerged as arguably the league's best linebacker the following year, when he earned All-Pro honors for the first time by recording a career-high four interceptions and four fumble recoveries for a Packers team that repeated as league champions. He also made All-Pro in four of the next five seasons, as the Packers claimed three more NFL titles.

Nitschke's superb play for the NFL's foremost team earned him the respect and admiration of players and coaches throughout the league, with legendary head coach George Allen stating, "Nitschke was one of those special players who did things others didn't do. When I was with the Bears, we named one of our defenses '47 Nitschke' because it was copied from the way Ray played a certain situation. Naming a defense after a player is a pretty high compliment in my book."

Dave Robinson praised his longtime teammate when he said, "Pound for pound, there's never been a linebacker that's come close to Ray Nitschke. . . . He wasn't just a linebacker who sat back in the middle and hit people. He had great range and athletic ability, and I think people forget that—unless you played against him. Nitschke helped make those Packers teams great. He's in the Hall of Fame for a reason."

Although the media tended to portray Nitschke as something of a brute, he actually took a cerebral approach to his job, revealing, "I studied. I really prepared myself. I practiced hard, and I was always ready. There wasn't anything that happened on the field that I wasn't prepared for."

Over time, Nitschke also lost much of the anger he carried inside him during his youth, as Jerry Kramer noted when he said, "He quit drinking. Then he found a woman that loved him. Then he found a team that loved

Nitschke earned spots on both the NFL's 50th and 75th Anniversary Teams.
Courtesy of MearsOnlineAuctions.com

him. And he was able to accept the love of that team and give it back. And Raymond became a totally different person off the field. He was the same junkyard dog on the field, but, off the field, he was a beautiful human being. He turned into one of the most considerate, thoughtful, polite, caring, loving human beings I've ever known."

Nitschke remained with the Packers long after their dynasty ended, announcing his retirement during training camp in 1973. In addition to recovering more fumbles than any other player in team history, Nitschke ranks among the franchise's all-time leaders in seasons played (15) and games played (190). Aside from being named the greatest linebacker in the history of the league in 1969, Nitschke received a number 18 ranking from the *Sporting News* when that publication listed its 100 Greatest Players in NFL History in 1999, making him the second-highest-rated Packers player (behind only Don Hutson) and the third-highest-rated linebacker (behind only Lawrence Taylor and Dick Butkus). NFL Films also accorded him a number 47 ranking on its 2010 list of the 100 greatest players ever to perform in the league.

Following his retirement, Nitschke owned an automobile dealership in Green Bay, appeared in several TV commercials, and even made a few movie appearances, with the most notable of those being his role as a vicious prison guard in the Burt Reynolds film *The Longest Yard*. Nitschke also remained close to the Packers, often attending their practices and traveling to many of their road games. In fact, in the middle of the team's successful 1997 NFL title run, Reggie White revealed that Nitschke made certain that his successors played with the same intensity he had when he said, "Ray Nitschke, Willie Davis, Bart Starr, they come around. Nitschke, he's really intense. He'll come over and smack you in the face and say, 'You can't lose this game.' He's like a coach, but after a while you say, 'Ray, you got to stop smacking me.'"

Nitschke passed away at the age of 61, on March 8, 1998, after he suffered a heart attack while driving to the home of a family friend in Venice, Florida. Shortly thereafter, a poll of former Packer players and coaches conducted by the *Milwaukee Journal-Sentinel* listed him as the fourth-best player in franchise history, ranking him behind only Don Hutson, Brett Favre, and Bart Starr.

CAREER HIGHLIGHTS

Best Season

It could be argued that Nitschke played his best ball for the Packers in 1962, when he helped lead them to the NFL title by establishing career-high marks in interceptions (4) and fumble recoveries (4). But he earned consensus First-Team All-Pro honors for the only time in his career in 1966, when he led the Packers to the second of their three consecutive league championships by anchoring a defense that surrendered just 163 points to the opposition all season, making that his most impactful campaign.

Memorable Moments/Greatest Performances

Nitschke scored two defensive touchdowns during his career, with the first of those coming during a 41–7 rout of the expansion Dallas Cowboys on November 13, 1960, when he returned one of his two interceptions of the day 43 yards for a TD.

Nitschke recorded another pick-six during a 27–17 win over the Detroit Lions on October 8, 1967, returning an interception 20 yards for the only other touchdown of his career.

An exceptional big-game player, Nitschke intercepted a Y. A. Tittle pass during the Packers' 37–0 trouncing of the Giants in the 1961 NFL title game, while also anchoring a Green Bay defense that limited New York to only 130 yards of total offense, including just 31 yards on the ground.

Nitschke again proved to be a thorn in the side of the Giants in the following year's NFL championship game, leading the Packers to a 16–7 victory by deflecting a pass that resulted in an interception by fellow line-backer Dan Currie and recovering two fumbles, one of which thwarted a New York drive that had reached the Green Bay 10 yard line, with his exceptional all-around play earning him game MVP honors.

Nitschke turned in another outstanding performance against the Browns in the 1965 NFL championship game, with teammate Herb Adderley recalling one particular play he made during the Packers' 23–12 win over their Eastern Conference counterparts: "The play Nitschke made in the 1965 championship was as big as any play he made that year. Jim Brown came out of the backfield (in the third quarter) and Nitschke knocked the ball down in the end zone. Brown ran down the hash mark 20, 30 yards and Nitschke was right there with him. If Nitschke doesn't make that play in the end zone, it could be a whole different ballgame."

Nitschke also excelled in each of the first two Super Bowls, contributing six tackles and a sack to Green Bay's victory over Kansas City in Super Bowl I, and leading the Packer defense with nine tackles against Oakland in Super Bowl II.

Nitschke experienced one of his most memorable moments in his final regular-season game with the Packers, when, during a 30–20 win over the New Orleans Saints on December 17, 1972, he recorded the only pass reception of his career, gaining 34 yards on a catch he made after the Saints blocked an attempted field goal by Green Bay placekicker Chester Marcol.

Yet, shortly before he passed away, Nitschke revealed that he considered Green Bay's 21–17 victory over Dallas in the 1967 NFL championship game to be the most memorable of his career, stating:

The Ice Bowl was the culmination of the Lombardi era in Green Bay. We were going for our third championship. The Cowboys were an up-and-coming team approaching greatness. But you always took the field hearing Lombardi's voice in your mind. He taught us how to win under any conditions. He taught us you're always in the game. He told us it's 60 minutes long. . . . But, as the game went on, the field got icier and icier, and all my toes blistered up. I didn't even think about my feet. I didn't realize until a couple of hours after the game that I had frostbite. . . . But the ones I felt sorry for were the fans. Coming out of the tunnel onto the field, I looked up and saw the stadium was filled. I thought, "If they came out in this weather, I'll give it my best shot."

NOTABLE ACHIEVEMENTS

- Scored two defensive touchdowns during career on interception returns.
- Missed only four games in first 13 seasons.
- Finished second in NFL with four fumble recoveries in 1962.
- Holds Packers career record for most fumble recoveries (23).
- Ranks among Packers career leaders with 25 interceptions (tied—12th) and 385 interception-return-yards (13th).
- Ranks among Packers all-time leaders with 15 seasons played (3rd) and 190 games played (4th).
- Six-time Western Conference champion (1960, 1961, 1962, 1965, 1966, and 1967).
- Five-time NFL champion (1961, 1962, 1965, 1966, and 1967).
- Two-time Super Bowl champion (I and II).
- 1962 NFL Championship Game MVP.
- 1964 Pro Bowl selection.
- Two-time First-Team All-Pro (1964 and 1966).
- Three-time Second-Team All-Pro (1962, 1965, and 1967).
- 1965 All–Western Conference First-Team selection.
- NFL 1960s All-Decade Team.
- Pro Football Hall of Fame All-1960s Team.
- Pro Football Reference All-1960s First Team.
- #66 retired by Packers.
- Named to Packers 50th Anniversary Team in 1969.
- Named to NFL's 50th Anniversary Team in 1969.

- Named to NFL's 75th Anniversary All-Time Team in 1994.
- Number 18 on the *Sporting News'* 1999 list of 100 Greatest Players in NFL History.
- Number 47 on NFL Films' 2010 list of 100 Greatest Players in NFL History.
- Elected to Pro Football Hall of Fame in 1978.

5

AARON RODGERS

A tremendously gifted athlete who possesses a powerful throwing arm, excellent mobility, superb pocket-presence, and outstanding decision-making ability, Aaron Rodgers has excelled at quarterback for the Packers ever since he replaced Brett Favre behind center, enabling the franchise to move seamlessly into a new era. Over the course of the last 10 seasons, Rodgers has passed for more than 4,000 yards and thrown more than 30 touchdown passes six times each, leading the Packers to six division titles, one NFC championship, and one Super Bowl victory in the process. In addition to earning six trips to the Pro Bowl and three All-Pro nominations with his exceptional play, Rodgers has twice gained recognition as the NFL's Most Valuable Player and the NFC's Offensive Player of the Year. With Rodgers still performing at an elite level in his mid-30s, he seems destined to claim an even higher spot on this list by the time his playing career comes to an end, perhaps even moving past the man he succeeded as quarterback in Green Bay.

Born in Chico, California, on December 2, 1983, Aaron Charles Rodgers lived a somewhat nomadic existence as a youngster, moving with his family to Ukiah, California, and then to Beaverton, Oregon, before returning to Chico in 1997. Wherever he lived, though, Rodgers rooted passionately for the San Francisco 49ers and his favorite player, Joe Montana. An outstanding athlete himself, Rodgers excelled at both football and baseball while attending Pleasant Valley High School, proving to be particularly proficient on the gridiron, where he started for two years at quarterback, passing for a total of 4,421 yards during that time, and setting a single-season school record by throwing for 2,303 yards as a senior.

Drawing little interest from Division I programs due to his unimposing 5'10", 165-pound frame, Rodgers briefly considered quitting football and studying for law school as his final days at Pleasant Valley High approached. However, after declining an invitation from the University of Illinois to compete for a scholarship as a walk-on, Rodgers elected to enroll at nearby

Aaron Rodgers has won two NFL MVP awards while leading the Packers to six division titles and one NFL championship.
Courtesy of Keith Allison

Butte Community College, where he spent his freshman year leading the Roadrunners to a 10-1 record and the NorCal Conference championship by throwing 26 touchdown passes. Discovered by California Golden Bears head coach Jeff Tedford while competing for Butte, Rodgers subsequently received a scholarship offer to attend the University of California, where he spent the next two years, before deciding to forego his final season of college eligibility.

Although Rodgers, who had grown to 6'2" tall and 220 pounds by the time he declared himself eligible for the 2005 NFL Draft, received good grades from pro scouts, who referred to him as a "talented, strong-armed junior who combines arm strength, mechanics, and delivery to make all the throws," he ended up slipping to the tail end of the first round due to concerns over his small college background. Finally selected by the Packers with the 24th overall pick, Rodgers entered the NFL with a huge chip on his shoulder, aiming to prove that 23 other teams had made a huge mistake.

Rodgers, though, had to wait three long years before he made his point, because he spent the 2005 to 2007 campaigns languishing on the bench behind Brett Favre. Finally claiming the starting job for himself in 2008, Rodgers did not disappoint, finishing the season with 4,038 yards passing, 28 touchdown passes, a completion percentage of 63.6, a passer rating of 93.8, 207 yards rushing, and four rushing touchdowns. He followed that up with four straight outstanding seasons, compiling the following numbers during that time:

YEAR	YARDS PASSING	TD PASSES	INTS	COMP PCT	PASSER RATING
2009	4,434	30	7	64.7	103.2
2010	3,922	28	11	65.7	101.2
2011	4,643	45	6	68.3	**122.5**
2012	4,295	39	8	67.2	**108.0**

By throwing for 4,434 yards in 2009, Rodgers became the first quarterback in NFL history to surpass 4,000 yards in each of his first two years as a starter. Rodgers's passer rating of 122.5 in 2011 established a new single-season NFL record, while his 4,643 yards through the air and 45 TD passes both set new single-season franchise records. In addition to leading the league in passer rating twice, Rodgers ranked among the leaders in passing yards, touchdown passes, and completion percentage all four years, finishing second in TD passes in both 2011 and 2012. Rodgers earned Pro Bowl honors in 2009, 2011, and 2012, All-Pro honors in 2011 and 2012, and recognition as the league's Most Valuable Player in 2011. He also led the Packers to the NFL championship in 2010, earning Super Bowl XLV MVP honors by passing for 304 yards and three touchdowns during Green Bay's 31–25 victory over Pittsburgh.

Blessed with as much physical talent as perhaps anyone who has ever played the position of quarterback in the NFL, Rodgers has a very strong throwing arm and tremendous accuracy that enable him to fit the ball into the tightest of windows. Possessing outstanding touch on his passes as well, Rodgers, claims Packers head coach Mike McCarthy, "is definitely the best at throwing the deep ball that I've had the opportunity to work with." Capable of standing in the pocket and staring down a pass rush, or darting around until he finds an open receiver, Rodgers throws the ball extremely well on the move, with his mobility also allowing him to rush for 2,670 yards and 25 touchdowns over the course of his career. Commenting on Rodgers's rare combination of skills, veteran NFL coach Vic Fangio suggests, "He throws it just as good as anybody, if not better than anybody, and he's got all the elusiveness that goes with it. And he's got good guys to throw it to, so they're a hard operation to stop."

Rodgers's keen understanding of the game and superb leadership ability make him even more difficult to contend with. Coach McCarthy notes, "He's got total command of the huddle."

Former Packers wideouts Greg Jennings and Donald Driver attested to Rodgers's ability to provide leadership to his teammates, with Jennings commenting, "Aaron's the ultimate leader," and Driver saying, "I love him to death. He's probably one of the best team leaders I've ever seen."

And, as for Rodgers's grasp of the game, Jeff Tedford, his college coach, states, "I can't even begin to tell you how sharp he is, and how well he retains things. He is a student of the game. He loves it. He submerges himself in it. He doesn't just memorize things. He understands concepts."

Yet, former Packers teammate Aaron Kampman expresses the belief that Rodgers has never allowed football to totally consume him, suggesting, "He's got a perspective on life that football is his profession, it's not his life. It doesn't define, ultimately, who he is. I think he grasps and understands that. It's a key component to who he is."

Rodgers continued his exceptional play through the first half of the 2013 season, leading the Packers to a 5-2 record by passing for 2,536 yards and completing 17 touchdown passes, before fracturing his left clavicle during a 27–20 loss to the Chicago Bears on November 4. With Rodgers out of action the next two months, the Packers slumped badly, compiling a record of just 2-4-1 during that time. However, he returned for the regular-season finale, helping the Packers capture their third consecutive division title by throwing for 318 yards and two touchdowns during a dramatic 33–28 come-from-behind victory over the Bears that they won on a 48-yard TD pass from Rodgers to Randall Cobb with just 38 seconds remaining in regulation.

Rodgers has passed for more than 4,000 yards and thrown more than
30 touchdown passes six times each as a member of the Packers.
Courtesy of Mike Morbeck

Fully healthy by the start of the ensuing campaign, Rodgers had one
of his finest all-around seasons, earning Pro Bowl, All-Pro, and NFL MVP
honors by passing for 4,381 yards, throwing 38 touchdown passes and just
five interceptions, completing 65.6 percent of his passes, and finishing second in the league with a passer rating of 112.2. Rodgers earned Pro Bowl
honors in each of the next two seasons as well, performing particularly
well in 2016, when he ranked among the league leaders with 4,428 yards

passing, a completion percentage of 65.7, and a passer rating of 104.2, while topping the circuit with 40 touchdown passes and throwing only seven interceptions. Rodgers appeared headed for another banner year in 2017, before a hit from Anthony Barr during a 23–10 loss to Minnesota in Week 6 fractured his right collarbone, forcing him to undergo surgery during which he had 13 screws inserted into his neck and shoulder. Although Rodgers returned to action against the Panthers on December 17 in an effort to salvage Green Bay's season, his attempt proved futile, as Carolina's 31–24 victory over the Packers ended their playoff aspirations. Subsequently put back on injured reserve for the final two weeks of the season, Rodgers concluded the campaign with just 1,675 yards passing and 16 touchdown passes.

With Rodgers expected to return to full health by the start of the 2018 season, the Packers have high hopes that they will be able to capture their sixth division title in eight years. Rodgers will begin the season with career totals of 38,502 yards passing, 313 touchdown passes, and only 78 interceptions. He has also completed 65.1 percent of his passes and compiled a passer rating of 103.8 over the course of his career, with the last figure representing an NFL record. Rodgers also holds league marks for the best touchdown-to-interception ratio (4.013) and the lowest interception percentage (1.6). Only time will tell how much Rodgers adds to his legacy before his playing career comes to an end.

CAREER HIGHLIGHTS

Best Season

Although Rodgers posted extraordinary numbers in several other seasons as well, particularly in 2014, when he earned league MVP honors for the second time by passing for 4,381 yards and 38 touchdowns, while also throwing only five interceptions, the 2011 campaign would have to be considered his finest. In addition to establishing career-best marks in passing yards (4,643), touchdown passes (45), and completion percentage (68.3), Rodgers threw just six picks and led the league with a passer rating of 122.5, which set a new single-season NFL record. Meanwhile, his 4,643 yards passing established a new single-season franchise record, with his fabulous performance earning him numerous individual accolades, including NFC Offensive Player of the Year and NFL MVP honors, and recognition by the Associated Press as the Athlete of the Year.

Memorable Moments/Greatest Performances

Rodgers excelled in just his second career start, leading the Packers to a 48–25 victory over the Detroit Lions on September 14, 2008, by passing for 328 yards and three touchdowns, with his longest completion of the day being a 62-yard connection with Greg Jennings.

Rodgers gave the Packers a 21–15 Sunday night win over the Chicago Bears in the opening game of the 2009 regular season by completing a 50-yard touchdown pass to Greg Jennings with just 1:11 left in the fourth quarter.

Rodgers led the Packers to a lopsided 26–0 victory over the Lions on October 18, 2009, by completing 29 of 37 pass attempts, for 358 yards and two touchdowns, one of which came on a 47-yard hookup with James Jones on the opening possession of the game.

Rodgers again feasted off the Detroit secondary a few weeks later, celebrating Thanksgiving Day 2009 by completing 28 of 39 passes, for 348 yards and three touchdowns, during a 34–12 win over the Lions.

Although the Packers ultimately lost to the Pittsburgh Steelers by a score of 37–36 on December 20, 2009, Rodgers performed brilliantly throughout the contest. Going head-to-head with Pittsburgh quarterback Ben Roethlisberger, who finished the day with 503 yards passing and three TD passes, Rodgers threw for 383 yards, ran for one touchdown, and completed three TD passes, with one of those being an 83-yard connection with Greg Jennings. Particularly effective in the final period, Rodgers led the Packers to 22 fourth-quarter points, although their late rally came up just a bit short.

Rodgers performed exceptionally well in his first playoff start, passing for 423 yards and four touchdowns during a 51–45 overtime loss to the Arizona Cardinals in the 2009 NFC wild card game. Displaying his ability to overcome adversity, Rodgers led the Packers back from a 21-point third-quarter deficit and a 14-point fourth-quarter deficit by throwing four second-half touchdowns, before Arizona won the game less than two minutes into the overtime session when Karlos Dansby recovered a Rodgers fumble following a sack and returned the ball 17 yards for the winning touchdown.

Rodgers turned in an outstanding effort against his former mentor, Brett Favre, when he led the Packers to a lopsided 31–3 victory over the Minnesota Vikings on November 21, 2010, by throwing for 301 yards and four touchdowns, three of which went to Greg Jennings.

Rodgers earned NFC Offensive Player of the Week honors for the first time for his performance during a 34–16 win over the San Francisco 49ers on December 5, 2010, throwing for 298 yards and three touchdowns, with one of his TD passes being a 57-yard completion to Greg Jennings and another being a 61-yard connection with Donald Driver.

After sitting out the previous game with an injury, Rodgers made a triumphant return to the Packer lineup on December 26, 2010, passing for 404 yards and four touchdowns during a 45–17 blowout of the New York Giants, with his longest TD pass of the day being an 80-yard connection with Jordy Nelson midway through the first quarter.

Rodgers performed brilliantly during the Packers' 48–21 victory over the Atlanta Falcons in their 2010 NFC divisional playoff game matchup, completing 31 of 36 passes, for 366 yards and three touchdowns, and running for another score.

Rodgers gained a measure of revenge against Ben Roethlisberger and the Steelers for the earlier defeat he suffered at their hands by passing for 304 yards and three touchdowns during Green Bay's 31–25 win over Pittsburgh in Super Bowl XLV.

Rodgers had a tremendous all-around game versus the Denver Broncos on October 2, 2011, leading the Packers to a convincing 49–23 victory by running for two scores and passing for 408 yards and four touchdowns.

Rodgers followed that up with another superb effort one week later, throwing for 396 yards and two touchdowns during a 25–14 win over the Atlanta Falcons on October 9, with his 70-yard strike to James Jones late in the third quarter putting the Packers ahead to stay.

Rodgers exhibited his ability to perform well under pressure on December 4, 2011, when he calmly led the Packers downfield for a last-second, game-winning 31-yard field goal by Mason Crosby less than one minute after the Giants tied the score at 35–35 on an Eli Manning touchdown pass to Hakeem Nicks and a subsequent two-point conversion. Rodgers finished the game with 369 yards through the air and four touchdown passes.

Rodgers threw five touchdown passes for the first time in his career during a 35–21 win over the Chicago Bears on Christmas Day 2011, with his longest completion of the day being a 55-yard scoring strike to Jordy Nelson. He finished the game with 283 yards passing.

Although the Packers surrendered 446 yards through the air to Drew Brees during a 28–27 win over the Saints on September 30, 2012, they emerged victorious due to the pinpoint passing of Rodgers, who finished the game with 319 yards passing and four touchdowns.

Rodgers led the Packers to a 42–24 victory over the Houston Texans on October 14, 2012, by passing for 338 yards and a career-high six touchdowns, with three of his TD tosses going to Jordy Nelson, two to James Jones, and another to Tom Crabtree.

Rodgers followed that up with another strong outing against St. Louis, throwing for 342 yards and three touchdowns during a 30–20 win over the Rams on October 21, with his longest completion of the day being a 39-yard scoring strike to Randall Cobb.

Rodgers turned in one of his finest performances on September 15, 2013, when he led the Packers to a 38–20 victory over the Washington Redskins by completing 34 of 42 pass attempts, for a career-high 480 yards and four touchdowns.

Returning to action after missing the previous seven games with an injury, Rodgers gave the Packers a dramatic 33–28 win over the Bears in the 2013 regular-season finale by completing a 48-yard touchdown pass to Randall Cobb with only 38 seconds left in the fourth quarter.

During a 55–14 rout of the Bears on November 9, 2014, Rodgers passed for 315 yards and tied his career-high by throwing six touchdown passes, all of which came in the first half. Green Bay's longest scoring play of the game ended up being a 73-yard connection between Rodgers and Jordy Nelson.

After passing for 341 yards and three touchdowns during a 53–20 manhandling of the Philadelphia Eagles two weeks earlier, Rodgers led the Packers to a 26–21 win over the New England Patriots on November 30, 2014, by throwing for 368 yards and two touchdowns, one of which came on a 45-yard hookup with Jordy Nelson just before halftime.

Rodgers led the Packers to a 38–28 victory over the Kansas City Chiefs on September 28, 2015, by passing for 333 yards and five touchdowns, completing three of those to Randall Cobb, one to Ty Montgomery, and another to James Jones.

Rodgers once again displayed his ability to overcome adversity on December 3, 2015, when he led the Packers back from a 20–0 third-quarter deficit and a 23–14 fourth-quarter deficit by running for a 17-yard touchdown with just over three minutes remaining in regulation, before completing a 61-yard "Hail Mary" TD pass to Richard Rodgers into the end zone on the game's final play that gave the Packers a dramatic 27–23 come-from-behind win over the Detroit Lions.

Although the Packers ended up losing their 2015 divisional playoff matchup with Arizona by a score of 26–20 in overtime, Rodgers again performed miracles, sending the game into OT by hitting Jeff Janis with a 41-yard Hail Mary TD pass on the final play of regulation.

Rodgers keyed a 38–25 win over the Minnesota Vikings on Christmas Eve 2016 by running for one score and passing for 347 yards and four touchdowns.

Rodgers came up big for the Packers in the 2016 regular-season finale, giving them the division title by throwing for 300 yards and four touchdowns during a 31–24 victory over Detroit.

Rodgers subsequently led the Packers to a 38–13 win over the New York Giants in the 2016 NFC wild card game by passing for 364 yards and four touchdowns, with one of those coming on another miraculous Hail Mary pass, this one going to Randall Cobb from 42 yards out just before halftime.

Rodgers provided further heroics during the Packers' 34–31 victory over Dallas in a 2016 divisional playoff game, passing for 355 yards and two touchdowns, and setting up Mason Crosby's game-winning 51-yard field goal as time expired by hitting tight end Jared Cook on a third-and-20 sideline completion with just three seconds remaining in regulation.

Rodgers once again drove a dagger into the hearts of the Cowboys and their fans on October 8, 2017, earning NFC Offensive Player of the Week honors for the 16th time by leading the Packers on a nine-play, 75-yard touchdown drive late in the fourth quarter that gave them a 35–31 victory over Dallas. The drive culminated with a 12-yard touchdown pass to Davante Adams with only 11 seconds left on the clock.

NOTABLE ACHIEVEMENTS

- Has passed for more than 4,000 yards six times, topping 3,800 yards two other times.
- Has thrown more than 30 touchdown passes six times, topping 40 TD passes twice.
- Has completed more than 65 percent of passes seven times.
- Has posted touchdown-to-interception ratio of better than 4–1 five times.
- Has posted passer rating above 100.0 eight times.
- Has rushed for more than 300 yards four times.
- Has averaged more than five yards per carry five times.

- Has led NFL quarterbacks in: touchdown passes once; passer rating twice; and interception percentage twice.
- Has finished second in NFL in: touchdown passes twice; passer rating once; completion percentage once; and interception percentage twice.
- Holds NFL career records for: highest passer rating (103.8); best touchdown-to-interception ratio (4.013); and lowest interception percentage (1.6).
- Ranks among NFL career leaders with 313 touchdown passes (10th) and pass completion percentage of 65.1 (7th).
- Holds NFL single-season records for highest passer rating (122.5 in 2011) and best touchdown-to-interception ratio with at least 500 pass attempts (7.6 in 2014).
- Holds NFL record for most touchdown passes in a half (6).
- Holds Packers career records for: highest completion percentage (65.1); highest passer rating (103.8); best touchdown-to-interception ratio (4.013); and lowest interception percentage (1.6).
- Ranks second in Packer history in: pass attempts (4,895); pass completions (3,188); yards passing (38,502); and touchdown passes (313).
- Holds Packers single-season records for most yards passing (4,643 in 2011) and most touchdown passes (45 in 2011).
- Shares Packers single-game records for most yards passing (480 vs. Washington on 9/15/13) and most touchdown passes (6—twice).
- Six-time division champion (2007, 2011, 2012, 2013, 2014, and 2016).
- 2010 NFC champion.
- Super Bowl XLV champion.
- Super Bowl XLV MVP.
- 16-time NFC Offensive Player of the Week.
- Four-time NFC Offensive Player of the Month.
- Two-time NFC Offensive Player of the Year (2011 and 2014).
- Two-time FedEx Air NFL Player of the Year (2010 and 2014).
- Two-time Associated Press NFL MVP (2011 and 2014).
- Two-time NFL Players Association MVP (2011 and 2014).
- 2011 Bert Bell Award winner as NFL Player of the Year.
- 2011 Associated Press Athlete of the Year.
- Six-time Pro Bowl selection (2009, 2011, 2012, 2014, 2015, and 2016).
- Two-time First-Team All-Pro (2011 and 2014).
- 2012 Second-Team All-Pro.

6

HERB ADDERLEY

One of only three players in pro football history to play on six world championship teams, Herb Adderley won his first five NFL titles with the Packers during the 1960s, before earning his final championship ring as a member of the Dallas Cowboys in 1971. Excelling at left cornerback for the Packers for nine seasons after starring in college as a running back, Adderley proved to be perhaps the finest cover corner of his time, annually ranking among the league leaders in interceptions and interception-return yards, while also doing an outstanding job of returning kickoffs. Recording a total of 39 interceptions during his time in Green Bay, Adderley led the Packers in picks five times, en route to establishing himself as one of the franchise's all-time leaders in interceptions, interception-return yards, and defensive touchdowns scored. Along the way, Adderley earned five Pro Bowl selections, six All-Pro nominations, spots on the NFL 1960s All-Decade Team and the Packers 50th Anniversary Team, and a place in the Pro Football Hall of Fame.

Born in Philadelphia, Pennsylvania, on June 8, 1939, Herbert Allen Adderley starred in multiple sports while attending Northeast High School, earning All-City honors in football, basketball, and baseball, before accepting a football scholarship from Michigan State University. Spending his college career playing for the legendary Duffy Daugherty, Adderley excelled at running back for the Spartans, earning All–Big Ten Conference honors as a senior after leading the team in rushing yards once and pass receptions twice.

Selected by the Packers in the first round of the 1961 NFL Draft, with the 12th overall pick, Adderley arrived in Green Bay hoping to win a starting job in the offensive backfield. But, with future Hall of Famers Paul Hornung and Jim Taylor firmly entrenched at the two running back spots, Adderley spent much of his rookie season riding the bench and returning kickoffs. However, after expressing an interest in moving to the defensive side of the ball, Adderley received his big break during the season's second

Herb Adderley starred on all five Vince Lombardi championship teams during the 1960s.
Courtesy of RMYAuctions.com

half when starting cornerback Hank Gremminger suffered an injury that sidelined him for the remainder of the year.

Proving to be a natural at his new position, the 6'1", 205-pound Adderley performed so well at corner that he forced Gremminger to shift to safety the following year. After recording the first interception of his career during the latter stages of the 1961 campaign, Adderley earned First-Team All-Pro honors his second year in the league by picking off seven passes, which he returned for 132 yards and one touchdown. Adderley also returned one kickoff for a touchdown, with his exceptional play helping the Packers win their second straight NFL title. Commenting on Adderley's successful transition to cornerback, Vince Lombardi remarked, "I was too stubborn to switch him to defense until I had to. Now, when I think of what Adderley means to our defense, it scares me to think of how I almost mishandled him."

Although the Packers failed to repeat as NFL champions in either of the next two seasons, Adderley continued to perform magnificently at left cornerback, amassing a total of nine interceptions and 142 interception-return yards, en route to earning Pro Bowl and All-Pro honors both years. Using his speed, quickness, athleticism, and marvelous instincts to blanket the league's top receivers, Adderley soon became a favorite of Coach Lombardi, with the All-Pro cornerback relating the following story: "Lombardi had certain players who he'd call into his office and talk to; others he'd talk to on the field or in the locker room. One thing I remember he said to me. . . . He said I was the best cornerback he'd ever seen. In front of the whole team he said I was the best athlete . . . I'll always remember that."

Agreeing with Lombardi's assessment, former Packers teammate Jesse Whittenton said during a 2010 interview, "Herb was such a great athlete and a hard worker. Herb was a tough, hard-nosed player with a lot of speed and great instincts . . . and a very sound tackler who took great pride in it. He was such a natural on defense that I almost forgot that he came to us as a running back."

A key member of Green Bay's championship teams of 1965, 1966, and 1967, Adderley recorded a total of 14 interceptions over the course of those three seasons, earning in the process Pro Bowl and All-Pro honors all three years. Performing particularly well in 1965, Adderley picked off six passes, which he returned for a league-leading 175 yards and three touchdowns.

In discussing his longtime teammate, Jerry Kramer stated, "Oh boy, Herbie was a real talent. He was such a gifted athlete. His body was sculpted. Herbie had brains as well, and he knew how to read the opposing quarterbacks."

Kramer then added, "One of my biggest memories of Herbie was in the 'Ice Bowl' when he was covering Bob Hayes. Hayes would come out of the huddle when he was not involved in the pattern with his hands tucked inside of his pants. When Hayes was in the pattern, he had his hands out, hanging down at his side. Herb picked that up immediately. He also had an interception in the first half of that game. Obviously, turnovers are always important in that type of game."

Adderley's nose for the football gave him the ability to turn a game around in an instant, prompting opposing quarterbacks to often avoid throwing to his side of the field, as Bart Starr noted when he said, "After a few years, opponents just quit challenging him."

More than just an outstanding ball-hawk, Adderley employed a physical style of play that made him a strong defender against the run as well. In

Adderley excelled as both a cornerback and a kickoff returner during his time in Green Bay.
Courtesy of RMYAuctions.com

addressing Adderley's run-stopping skills, Packers left-side linebacker Dave Robinson said, "Herb used to tell me that, if I took care of the guard, he'd make the tackle. He was a sure tackler who delivered quite a blow. He didn't miss many tackles, and I'm talking about going against Hall of Famers like Jim Brown and Gale Sayers."

Adderley's excellence in all phases of the game prompted Jerry Kramer to claim that he had only one rival among NFL cornerbacks at the time, with Kramer suggesting, "Herb was right alongside Dick 'Night Train' Lane. Those two were in a class by themselves. They were head and shoulders above the other cornerbacks in the league, I felt."

Although the Packers' mediocre performance in 1968 and 1969 prevented Adderley from earning Pro Bowl or All-Pro honors either year, he remained one of the league's top corners, amassing a total of eight interceptions over the course of those two seasons, while leading the NFL with 169 interception-return yards in 1969. Yet, despite his strong play, Adderley left Green Bay following the conclusion of the 1969 campaign due to a strained relationship with Vince Lombardi's successor, Phil Bengtson. After requesting a trade to another team, Adderley found himself headed to Dallas, where he spent his final three years in the league playing for the rival Cowboys. He left the Packers having recorded 39 interceptions, 795 interception-return yards, 13 fumble recoveries, and seven defensive touchdowns as a member of the team. Adderley also returned two kickoffs for touchdowns, averaged 25.7 yards per return, and accumulated 3,080 yards on kickoff returns during his time in Green Bay, with the last figure placing him third in team annals.

After joining the Cowboys, Adderley contributed significantly to Dallas teams that captured consecutive NFC titles in 1970 and 1971 and their first league championship in the second of those campaigns. Combining with Mel Renfro to form arguably the NFL's top cornerback tandem, Adderley made an extremely favorable impression on Renfro, who later said, "I admired his play, and I kind of tried to think like him and get my own interceptions. When I saw him on film, the thing I noticed about Herb was his ability to take advantage of a quarterback's weakness. . . . He had a way of shuffling his feet and putting himself in position to make the interception. . . . They call them shut-down cornerbacks these days. Herb was that kind of guy."

But, with Adderley showing signs of slowing down in 1972, the Cowboys traded him to the Los Angeles Rams during the subsequent offseason, prompting the 34-year-old cornerback to announce his retirement. Adderley ended his career with 48 interceptions, 1,046 interception-return yards, 14 fumble recoveries, seven defensive touchdowns, and two special-team touchdowns, with his extraordinary play eventually earning him a number 45 ranking on the *Sporting News'* 1999 list of the 100 Greatest Players in NFL History. Although Adderley won his sixth NFL title while playing for the Cowboys, his heart remained in Green Bay, with the Hall of Fame cornerback being quoted in a revised edition of Jerry Kramer's memoir *Instant Replay* as saying, "I'm the only man with a Dallas Cowboys Super Bowl ring who doesn't wear it. I'm a Green Bay Packer."

Following his retirement, Adderley returned to Philadelphia to broadcast games for Temple University and the Philadelphia Eagles. He also coached as an assistant at Temple and with the Philadelphia Bell of the World Football League under head coach Willie Wood, who once said of his former Packers teammate, "God didn't make a whole lot of Herb Adderleys."

PACKERS CAREER HIGHLIGHTS

Best Season

Adderley had a tremendous all-around year for the Packers in 1962, earning the first of his four First-Team All-Pro selections by recording a career-high seven interceptions, which he returned for 132 yards and one touchdown, recovering four fumbles, and returning one kickoff for a touchdown. However, he performed slightly better in 1965, earning consensus First-Team All-Pro honors for the first of two straight times by picking off six passes, leading the league with 175 interception-return yards and three touchdown interceptions, picking off another pass in the playoffs, and recovering three fumbles.

Memorable Moments/Greatest Performances

After intercepting one pass during the regular season, Adderley recorded one of the four picks the Packers made against Y. A. Tittle during their 37–0 win over the Giants in the 1961 NFL title game.

Taking his game up a notch in his second full season, Adderley picked off a pair of Fran Tarkenton passes during the Packers' convincing 34–7 win over the Minnesota Vikings in the opening game of the 1962 campaign.

Adderley recorded the first pick-six of his career on September 30, 1962, when he punctuated a 49–0 victory over the Chicago Bears by intercepting a pass in the fourth quarter and returning the ball 50 yards for a TD.

Adderley turned apparent defeat into victory on October 7, 1962, when, with the Packers trailing Detroit by a score of 7–6 in the final minute of regulation, he picked off a Milt Plum pass near midfield and returned the ball 30 yards, to set up a last-second, 26-yard game-winning field goal by Paul Hornung.

Adderley turned in an outstanding all-around effort against Baltimore on November 18, 1962, leading the Packers to a 17–13 win over the Colts by recording an interception and returning a kickoff 103 yards for a touchdown.

Adderley scored his second special-teams touchdown during a 42–10 thrashing of the Los Angeles Rams on October 6, 1963, when he returned the opening kickoff 98 yards for a TD.

Adderley made another big play on special teams the following week, when, with the Packers clinging to a slim 30–28 lead over the Vikings late in the fourth quarter, he blocked a potential game-winning field goal by Minnesota, which teammate Hank Gremminger subsequently returned 80 yards for the clinching touchdown.

Excelling on defense as well in 1963, Adderley picked off Johnny Unitas twice during a 34–20 win over the Colts on October 27, 1963.

Adderley scored the Packers' first points of the 1965 campaign, when, during a lopsided 41–9 victory over the Pittsburgh Steelers in the regular-season opener, he intercepted a pass in the second quarter and returned the ball 34 yards for a touchdown.

Adderley again lit the scoreboard the following week, when he helped the Packers defeat Baltimore by a score of 20–17 by picking off a Johnny Unitas pass in the second quarter and returning the ball 44 yards for Green Bay's first touchdown of the game.

Adderley recorded his third pick-six of the year in the 1965 regular-season finale, returning an interception of a John Brodie pass 13 yards for a TD during a 24–24 tie with the 49ers.

Adderley scored the fifth defensive touchdown of his career during a 56–3 blowout of the expansion Atlanta Falcons on October 23, 1966, increasing the Packer lead to 35–3 in the third quarter, when he returned an interception 68 yards for a TD.

Adderley again scored just a little over one year later, when, during a 31–23 win over the St. Louis Cardinals on October 30, 1967, he picked off a Jim Hart pass and returned the ball 12 yards for a touchdown.

Adderley scored the final touchdown of his career on October 26, 1969, when he punctuated a 28–10 win over the Atlanta Falcons by recording an 80-yard interception return in the fourth quarter.

Adderley proved to be a huge factor in the 1967 NFL championship game, otherwise known as the Ice Bowl, picking off a pass and combining with the elements to hold speedster Bob Hayes to just three catches for 16 yards.

Adderley subsequently scored the first defensive touchdown in Super Bowl history, when he put the finishing touches on a 33–14 win over the Raiders in Super Bowl II by intercepting a Daryle Lamonica pass intended for Fred Biletnikoff and returning the ball 60 yards for a TD that increased the Packer lead to 33–7.

NOTABLE ACHIEVEMENTS

- Recorded at least five interceptions in a season four times.
- Accumulated more than 100 interception-return yards four times.
- Returned seven interceptions for touchdowns during career.

- Returned two kickoffs for touchdowns.
- Led Packers in interceptions five times.
- Led NFL in: interception-return yards twice; touchdown interceptions twice; and non-offensive touchdowns twice.
- Finished second in NFL with four fumble recoveries in 1962.
- Finished third in NFL in interceptions twice and average yards per kickoff return once.
- Holds Packers single-season record for most touchdown interceptions (three, in 1965).
- Ranks among Packers career leaders with: 39 interceptions (3rd); 795 interception-return yards (2nd); seven touchdown interceptions (tied—2nd); seven defensive touchdowns (tied—2nd); 3,080 kick-off-return yards (3rd); and 25.7 kickoff-return average (tied—7th).
- Five-time Western Conference champion (1961, 1962, 1965, 1966, and 1967).
- Five-time NFL champion (1961, 1962, 1965, 1966, and 1967).
- Two-time Super Bowl champion (I and II).
- Five-time Pro Bowl selection (1963, 1964, 1965, 1966, and 1967).
- Four-time First-Team All-Pro (1962, 1963, 1965, and 1966).
- Two-time Second-Team All-Pro (1964 and 1967).
- Six-time All–Western Conference First-Team selection (1963, 1964, 1966, 1967, 1968, and 1969).
- NFL 1960s All-Decade Team.
- Pro Football Hall of Fame All-1960s Team.
- Pro Football Reference All-1960s First Team.
- Member of AFL-NFL 1960–1984 All-Star Team.
- Named to Packers 50th Anniversary Team in 1969.
- Number 45 on the *Sporting News'* 1999 list of 100 Greatest Players in NFL History.
- Number 64 on NFL Films' 2010 list of 100 Greatest Players in NFL History.
- Elected to Pro Football Hall of Fame in 1980.

7

JIM TAYLOR

One of the toughest, most competitive men ever to play in the National Football League, Jim Taylor established himself as the symbol of offensive power during his time in Green Bay, combining with Paul Hornung to give the Packers the most potent running attack in the league. A throwback to an earlier era, Taylor ran with unmatched fury, dishing out as much punishment to opposing defenders as he received from them. The only running back other than Jim Brown to lead the NFL in rushing between 1957 and 1965, Taylor accomplished the feat in 1962, when he gained more than 1,000 yards on the ground for the third of five straight times. Taylor also scored more than 10 touchdowns five times, led the league in scoring once, and finished second to Brown in rushing on four separate occasions, retiring in 1967 as the NFL's second-leading all-time rusher. Taylor, who now ranks second in Packers' history in yards gained on the ground, continues to hold the career and single-season franchise records for most rushing touchdowns, with his superb play helping the Packers win five Western Conference championships, four NFL titles, and one Super Bowl. A five-time Pro Bowl selection, six-time All-Pro, and one-time league MVP, Taylor later received the additional honors of being named to the NFL 1960s All-Decade Team, the Packers 50th Anniversary Team, and the Pro Football Hall of Fame. Recognized for his excellence by his peers, Taylor received high praise from fellow Hall of Famers Jim Parker, John Mackey, and Bob Lilly, each of whom rated him among the top 10 players they ever saw. Meanwhile, Sam Huff and Merlin Olsen both ranked him as the second toughest player they ever played against.

Born in the middle of the Great Depression in Baton Rouge, Louisiana, on September 20, 1935, James Charles Taylor delivered newspapers as a young boy to help his widowed mother make ends meet. Although Taylor did not play football until his junior year at Baton Rouge High School, he excelled in multiple sports, with Bat Gourrier, his high school track coach, recalling years later, "Jim could have played anything and been good at it. If

Jim Taylor rushed for more than 1,000 yards five straight times.
Courtesy of MearsOnlineAuctions.com

you stuck a tennis racket in his hand, he would have been great. If someone bought him a set of golf clubs, he could out-do you in that, too. He was just a natural as an athlete."

After getting his start on the gridiron as a 5'9", 155-pound defensive back, Taylor shifted to running back in his senior year, when he added 15 pounds of muscle to his frame. Explaining why it took him so long to participate in football, Taylor said, "I didn't like the game. I didn't think I was big enough. I don't like anything unless I do it really well."

Choosing to remain close to home after fielding scholarship offers from several different colleges, Taylor signed to play football for Louisiana State University, where he spent just one year, before his struggles in the classroom forced him to transfer to Hines Junior College in Raymond, Mississippi. However, after improving his grades, Taylor returned to LSU, where he established himself as one of the nation's top running backs, leading the SEC in scoring in both 1956 and 1957, while rushing for a total of 1,314 yards. Commenting on Taylor's brilliant play his final two years in college, LSU head coach Paul Dietzel stated, "With the ball under his arm, Jimmy Taylor was the best running back I've ever coached. He was just so versatile."

With Taylor having earned First-Team All-America honors as a senior, the Packers made him the 15th overall pick of the 1958 NFL Draft, selecting him in the second round, ahead of other future stars Dan Currie, Ray Nitschke, and Jerry Kramer, who they tabbed later in the draft. Used sparingly as a rookie, Taylor gained only 247 yards on the ground and scored just one touchdown for a Packers team that compiled a league-worst record of 1-10-1. However, with the arrival of Vince Lombardi the following year, Taylor gradually assumed a far more prominent role, eventually earning the starting fullback job after beginning the season as the team's short-yardage back. Although Taylor rushed for only 452 yards over the course of the 1959 campaign, he ranked among the league leaders with eight touchdowns, scoring six of those on the ground and two more through the air. Emerging as a full-fledged star in 1960, Taylor began an exceptional five-year run during which he ranked second only to the great Jim Brown among NFL running backs, compiling the following numbers during that time:

YEAR	RUSHING YARDS	RECEIVING YARDS	RUSHING TDS	TOTAL TDS
1960	1,101	121	11	11
1961	1,307	175	15	16
1962	**1,474**	106	19	19
1963	1,018	68	9	10
1964	1,169	354	12	15

Taylor earned NFL MVP honors in 1962, when, in addition to leading the league with a career-high 1,474 yards rushing, he topped the circuit with 1,580 yards from scrimmage, 114 points scored, and 19 rushing touchdowns, the highest single-season mark in franchise history. He also finished second to Brown in rushing in each of the other four years, amassed more than 1,400 yards from scrimmage two other times, and averaged at least five yards per carry on three separate occasions, earning in the process Pro Bowl and All-Pro recognition all five years. More importantly, the Packers captured the Western Conference title in each of the first three seasons, also winning the NFL championship in both 1961 and 1962.

Running behind a formidable offensive line that included outstanding pulling guards Jerry Kramer and Fuzzy Thurston, Taylor helped perfect the famous "Packer Sweep," which served as an integral part of the team's offense throughout the 1960s. Meanwhile, the powerful Taylor combined with the extremely agile Paul Hornung to form a running tandem that Green Bay fans affectionately referred to as "Thunder and Lightning."

Although the 6-foot, 215-pound Taylor possessed only average size for a fullback, he proved to be arguably the most physical runner in the game, developing a reputation as one of the toughest and meanest players in the NFL. Listed by former quarterback Bobby Layne as one of "Pro Football's 11 Meanest Men" in a 1964 article that appeared in *Sport* magazine, Taylor sought out contact on every play, choosing to run over defenders, rather than run away from them. Extremely difficult to tackle, Taylor fought for every extra yard, adhering to a philosophy he described thusly: "Football is a contact sport. You've got to make them respect you. You've got to punish tacklers. You've got to deal out more misery than the tacklers deal out to you. . . . You got to enjoy punishment because you are going to deliver so much of it, and you are going to get so much of it. . . . If you are prepared, you don't really feel the punishment during the game."

Taylor's fierce competitiveness earned him the respect and admiration of teammates and opponents alike, with Ray Nitschke stating, "Taylor was in a class by himself. In 15 years with the pros, he's one of the toughest men I ever played against—and we were on the same team. He'd hurt you when you'd tackle him. He was as hard as a piece of granite. He had such strong legs."

Max McGee commented, "He liked to hit people. He's got a body that was built for hitting people."

Bill Curry, who spent two seasons blocking for Taylor from his center position, said, "Jim Taylor was unbelievable. He was a fierce, fierce competitor. When anybody tackled him, it was an insult. And, if he bit them, or punched them in the groin, or pushed their face in the mud, fine."

Boyd Dowler added, "Usually, a running back breaks the line of scrimmage, he looks for the end zone. Jimmy looked for the first safety he could run over."

In describing Taylor's running style, opposing coach George Allen said, "He ran with his elbows almost as much as his legs He'd lower his shoulders and swing his forearm out in front of him and flail away with his elbows and hurt people as he ran through them."

Yet, despite his extremely physical style of play, Taylor remained relatively injury-free over the course of his career, missing only two games his final eight years in the league. Crediting his longtime teammate's good health to his rigorous workout regimen, Jerry Kramer suggested, "He was an incredibly well-conditioned athlete. Probably the best-conditioned athlete, or one of the best, in the league. . . . He was a weight-lifter and a bodybuilder. He had a mind-set that he needed to punish the defense. Normally, the defense is always trying to make guys on offense get stung with their hits, while Jimmy thought it should be the exact opposite."

Taylor's attitude caused him to develop intense personal rivalries with some of the league's top defenders, most notably New York Giants middle linebacker Sam Huff, who said of his frequent foe, "He was always shooting his mouth off on the field. He'd tell me, 'Yeah, you're just a big talker.' He brought the best out in you. He was an unusual player, a great player, but an agitator . . . I did everything I could to that sonofabitch."

Meanwhile, Taylor's competitiveness caused him to develop a different sort of rivalry with Jim Brown, to whom he usually came out second-best in individual comparisons made between the two men. Yet, while the bigger, faster, and shiftier Brown possessed more talent than Taylor, the latter almost always gained more yards and scored more touchdowns when the two men played against each other. In discussing the running styles of his two greatest adversaries, Sam Huff noted, "The impact of meeting Taylor after five yards is greater than meeting Brown at the same point. Brown is strong, but he doesn't shock you like Taylor does. Brown would rather slide off to the side and keep going."

Vince Lombardi provided a more succinct assessment, stating, "Jim Brown will give you that leg and then take it away from you. Jim Taylor will give it to you and then ram it through your chest!"

Taylor's physical style of play finally began to take its toll on him in 1965, when he ran for just 734 yards and four touchdowns, while also averaging less than four yards per carry for the first time in six years. Nevertheless, he proved to be a significant contributor during the postseason, helping the Packers win the first of their three consecutive NFL titles by rushing for 156 yards and amassing 205 yards from scrimmage against Baltimore and Cleveland in the playoffs. Taylor followed that up with a solid 1966 campaign, when, in addition to rushing for 705 yards and four

Taylor retired as the NFL's second-leading all-time rusher.
Courtesy of MearsOnlineAuctions.com

touchdowns, he made a career-high 41 receptions for 331 yards and two TDs, giving him more than 1,000 yards from scrimmage for the sixth and final time in his career.

The 1966 season ended up being Taylor's last in Green Bay. Subsequently left unprotected by the Packers in the NFL Expansion Draft, Taylor joined the New Orleans Saints, with whom he spent one season before announcing his retirement prior to the start of the 1968 campaign. Taylor ended his career with 8,597 yards rushing, 83 rushing touchdowns, and an average of 4.4 yards per carry. He also caught 225 passes for 1,756 yards and 10 touchdowns, giving him 10,353 yards from scrimmage and 93 total touchdowns. In his nine years with the Packers, Taylor rushed for 8,207 yards, gained another 1,505 yards on 187 pass receptions, and scored 91 touchdowns, with his 81 rushing TDs representing the highest total in team annals. He also continues to rank among the franchise's all-time leaders in rushing yards (2nd), yards from scrimmage (4th), all-purpose yards (4th), total touchdowns scored (2nd), and rushing average (2nd).

Following his retirement, Taylor became a successful businessman, briefly serving as commissioner of the United States Rugby League, before moving on to other pursuits. Remaining in peak condition long after his playing career ended, Taylor participated in the Superstars competition in 1977 and finished fourth in 1979. As late as 2000, at the age of 65, Taylor stayed in shape by jogging five to six miles daily. Now in his 80s, Taylor currently lives in Baton Rouge, Louisiana, with his wife, Helen.

PACKERS CAREER HIGHLIGHTS

Best Season

Taylor had a huge year for the Packers in 1961, finishing second in the NFL with 1,307 yards rushing and 1,482 yards from scrimmage, leading the league with 16 touchdowns, and finishing third in the circuit with 96 points scored and a rushing average of 5.4 yards per carry. However, he performed even better the following season, setting a new league mark by scoring 19 touchdowns, leading the NFL with 1,474 yards rushing, 1,580 yards from scrimmage, and 114 points scored, and finishing second in the league with a rushing average of 5.4 yards per carry. By beating out Jim Brown for the rushing title, Taylor became just the third player in NFL history to lead the league in both rushing yards and total points scored, joining Brown and Steve Van Buren in an extremely select group. In addition to earning him First-Team All-Pro honors for the only time in his career, Taylor's extraordinary play prompted the Associated Press to name him NFL Player of the Year and the Newspaper Enterprise Association to accord him league MVP honors.

Memorable Moments/Greatest Performances

Although the Packers lost their October 19, 1958, meeting with the Washington Redskins by a score of 37–21, Taylor scored the first touchdown of his career on a 31-yard pass reception from quarterback Babe Parilli.

Taylor topped the 100-yard mark for the first time in the final game of the 1958 season, gaining 137 yards on 22 carries during a 48–21 loss to the 49ers, with his aggressive running style eliciting cheers from the fans in attendance at San Francisco's Kezar Stadium.

Taking that momentum with him into the 1959 regular-season opener, Taylor helped the Packers record a 9–6 victory over the Bears in Vince Lombardi's debut as head coach by scoring the game's only touchdown on a 5-yard run in the fourth quarter. He finished the contest with 98 yards on 22 carries.

Taylor keyed a 28–9 victory over the Detroit Lions on October 2, 1960, by carrying the ball 26 times for 151 yards and one touchdown.

Taylor led a 41–7 rout of the expansion Dallas Cowboys on November 13, 1960, by carrying the ball 15 times for 121 yards and three touchdowns, with his scoring plays covering 28, 4, and 23 yards.

Taylor starred again during a 41–13 dismantling of the Chicago Bears on December 4, 1960, scoring one touchdown and gaining 140 yards on 24 carries.

Taylor followed that up six days later by carrying the ball 27 times for a season-high 161 yards during a 13–0 win over the San Francisco 49ers.

Taylor proved to be the Packers' most potent offensive weapon during their 17–13 loss to the Philadelphia Eagles in the 1960 NFL title game, rushing for 105 yards and gaining another 46 yards on six pass receptions.

Taylor led the Packers to a convincing 49–17 victory over the Cleveland Browns on October 15, 1961, by carrying the ball 21 times for 158 yards and four touchdowns, with two of his TD runs covering 26 and 45 yards.

Taylor turned in an exceptional performance against the Giants on December 3, 1961, carrying the ball 27 times for a career-high 186 yards and two touchdowns during a 20–17 Packer win.

Taylor led the Packers to a 49–0 rout of the Bears on September 30, 1962, by carrying the ball 17 times for 126 yards and three touchdowns.

Averaging nearly 10 yards per carry on the day, Taylor rushed for a season-high 164 yards during a 48–21 win over the Minnesota Vikings on October 14, 1962.

Taylor nearly matched that total one week later, gaining 160 yards on the ground and scoring on runs of 16 and 25 yards during a 31–13 victory over the 49ers on October 21, 1962.

Taylor rushed for 124 yards and scored four touchdowns for the second time in his career on November 4, 1962, in leading the Packers to a lopsided 38–7 win over the Chicago Bears.

Taylor again scored four touchdowns the following week, gaining 141 yards on the ground and recording four short TD runs during a 49–0 trouncing of the Philadelphia Eagles.

Taylor led the Packers to a 33–14 victory over the Pittsburgh Steelers on November 3, 1963, by carrying the ball 30 times for 140 yards and one touchdown.

During a 30–7 win over the Detroit Lions on November 8, 1964, in which he gained 145 yards on 19 carries, Taylor recorded a career-long 84-yard touchdown run in the opening quarter that represented the longest run from scrimmage in the NFL the entire year.

Taylor helped the Packers forge a 24–24 tie with the Los Angeles Rams in the final game of the 1964 regular season by carrying the ball 17 times for a season-high 165 yards and one touchdown, with his 1-yard TD run late in the fourth quarter tying the score. Taylor also gained another 56 yards on four pass receptions.

Sport magazine named Taylor the most outstanding player of the 1965 NFL championship game after he gained 96 yards on the ground during the Packers' 23–12 win over the Browns.

Yet, Taylor turned in the most memorable performance of his career in the 1962 NFL title game, with the determination he displayed during the Packers' 16–7 victory over the Giants on Yankee Stadium's frozen turf coming to define his mental and physical toughness. Although Taylor gained just 85 yards on 31 carries, he scored Green Bay's lone touchdown on a seven-yard run in the second quarter and imposed his will against the league's best defense, with Steve Sabol, who filmed the game with his father for NFL Films, later describing the events that transpired on the field that day:

> The lasting image of that game in my mind is the ferocity and anger of Jim Taylor . . . his barely restrained rage as he ran with the ball. Taylor just got the shit kicked out of him all day long . . . There was all this trash-talking between him and especially Sam Huff . . . Tons of profanity when they tackled him. I had never experienced anything like that.

Withstanding a tremendous amount of punishment throughout the contest, Taylor required six stitches at halftime to close a gash on his elbow and spent much of the game swallowing blood after biting his tongue while being tackled by Huff in the first quarter. Commenting on the tenacity his adversary exhibited, Huff said afterwards, "Taylor isn't human. No human being could have taken the punishment he got today."

After the game, Taylor described the incident: "I never took a worse beating on a football field. The Giants hit me hard, and then I hit the ground hard. I got it both ways. This was the toughest game I've ever played . . . I just rammed it down their throats by letting my running do my talking. They couldn't rattle me . . . I think Huff hit me with his elbow after a tackle. Anyway, I cut my tongue of all things." Making Taylor's performance even more heroic is the fact that he played the entire game 15 pounds under his normal body weight, learning two weeks later that he entered the contest suffereing from hepatitis.

Teammate Jerry Kramer provided further insight into the physical abuse that Taylor endured, revealing years later, "In the '62 title game, the Giant defense beat the hell out of him. Jimmy had a great game, even as the Giants were piling on whenever they could or hitting after the whistle. On the plane going home, Jimmy was playing cards with us with his coat on, and his hands were still trembling. But he never said anything about how bad he was hurting or complained one bit."

NOTABLE ACHIEVEMENTS

- Rushed for more than 1,000 yards five times, topping 1,300 yards twice.
- Surpassed 1,000 yards from scrimmage six times, topping 1,500 yards twice.
- Rushed for more than 10 touchdowns four times.
- Scored more than 10 touchdowns five times.
- Scored more than 100 points once (114 in 1962).
- Averaged more than five yards per carry three times.
- Caught more than 40 passes once (41 in 1996).
- Amassed more than 300 receiving yards twice.
- Led NFL in: rushing yardage once; rushing touchdowns twice; touchdowns scored twice; points scored once; yards from scrimmage once; and carries twice.
- Finished second in NFL in: rushing yardage four times; rushing touchdowns three times; yards from scrimmage once; yards per rushing attempt once; and carries four times.
- Finished third in NFL in: touchdowns scored once; points scored once; and yards per rushing attempt twice.
- Led Packers in rushing seven straight times.
- First NFL player to rush for more than 1,000 yards in a season five straight times.
- Retired as NFL's second-leading all-time rusher.
- Holds Packers single-season record for most rushing touchdowns (19 in 1962).
- Holds Packers career record for most rushing touchdowns (81).
- Ranks among Packers career leaders with: 8,207 yards rushing (2nd); 9,712 yards from scrimmage (4th); 9,898 all-purpose yards (4th); 91 touchdowns (2nd); and 4.53-yard rushing average (2nd).

- Five-time Western Conference champion (1960, 1961, 1962, 1965, and 1966).
- Four-time NFL champion (1961, 1962, 1965, and 1966).
- Super Bowl I champion.
- 1962 NFL MVP.
- Five-time Pro Bowl selection (1960, 1961, 1962, 1963, and 1964).
- 1962 First-Team All-Pro.
- Five-time Second-Team All-Pro (1960, 1961, 1963, 1964, and 1966).
- Six-time All–Western Conference First-Team selection (1960, 1961, 1962, 1963, 1964, and 1966).
- NFL 1960s All-Decade Team.
- Pro Football Hall of Fame All-1960s Team.
- Pro Football Reference All-1960s First Team.
- Named to Packers 50th Anniversary Team in 1969.
- Elected to Pro Football Hall of Fame in 1976.

8

BART STARR

One of only two quarterbacks in NFL history to lead his team to as many as five league championships, Bart Starr accomplished the feat between 1961 and 1967, a period during which he served as the Packers' unquestioned leader. An extremely cerebral player who guided Green Bay's offense with calm and precision, Starr proved to be the perfect quarterback to work under Vince Lombardi, gaining his coach's trust with his intelligence, leadership skills, and ability to excel under pressure. A two-time Super Bowl MVP, Starr compiled the highest postseason passer rating of any quarterback in NFL history, en route to leading the Packers to an overall postseason record of 9-1. And, even though Starr's passing ability has been questioned by some, he ended his 16-year playing career with the highest completion percentage of any signal-caller in league history. Starr's all-around excellence earned him four Pro Bowl selections, three All-Pro nominations, one league MVP award, spots on the NFL 1960s All-Decade Team and the Packers 50th Anniversary Team, a place in the Pro Football Hall of Fame, and a number 41 ranking on the *Sporting News*' 1999 list of the 100 Greatest Players in NFL History.

Born in Montgomery, Alabama, on January 9, 1934, Bryan Bartlett Starr experienced a considerable amount of adversity in his youth, losing his younger brother to tetanus at the age of 12 and sharing a somewhat contentious relationship with his father—a career military man who exerted constant pressure on him to develop a mean streak. As a result, young Bart grew increasingly introverted as a teenager, rarely displaying his emotions to anyone.

Yet, despite his difficult childhood, Starr gradually emerged as a leader on the football field while attending local Sidney Lanier High School, earning All-State and All-America honors in his senior year for his outstanding play at quarterback. Subsequently courted by several colleges, Starr eventually elected to enroll at the University of Alabama, where he spent just

Bart Starr led the Packers to five NFL championships.
Courtesy of RMYAuctions.com

one season starting behind center due to a back injury he suffered during a hazing incident prior to the start of his junior year.

Although Starr accomplished very little during his college career, the Packers made him the 200th overall pick of the 1956 NFL Draft when they selected him in the 17th round, after Alabama basketball coach Johnny Dee recommended him to his friend, Green Bay personnel director Jack Vainisi. Starr subsequently spent his first four years in Green Bay competing for playing time with Tobin Rote and Babe Parilli, serving as Rote's backup in 1956, before starting a total of only 23 games over the course of the next three seasons, during which time he threw 17 touchdown passes and 29 interceptions, in leading the Packers to an overall record of just 7-15-1 in games he started.

Despite his struggles on the playing field, Starr made a favorable impression on new Packers head coach Vince Lombardi in 1959, with Lombardi later noting in his book, *Run to Daylight*, "At our quarterback meetings, even though he was not first-string, he could repeat almost verbatim everything we had discussed the previous three days, and that meant he had a great memory, dedication, and desire." Further impressed by Starr's mechanics, arm-strength, pocket-presence, ball-handling techniques, and decision-making ability, all of which he discovered through countless hours of watching film, Lombardi became convinced that the young quarterback possessed the qualities necessary to become a top signal-caller. Choosing to put his faith in Starr, Lombardi made the 26-year-old Alabama native his starting quarterback in 1960, after which the latter went on to lead the Packers to the Western Conference title. Earning the first of his three straight trips to the Pro Bowl, Starr concluded the 1960 campaign with 1,358 yards passing and a 57 percent pass-completion rate that placed him third in the league rankings. He followed that up by leading the Packers to the NFL championship in each of the next two seasons, when, starting every game behind center, he compiled an overall record of 24-4 during the regular season and a perfect 2-0 mark in the playoffs. After ranking among the league leaders with 2,418 yards passing, 16 touchdown passes, a 58.3 pass-completion percentage, and a passer rating of 80.3 in 1961, Starr earned All-Pro honors for the first time the following year by throwing for a career-high 2,438 yards, finishing second in the league with a passer rating of 90.7, and topping the circuit with a pass-completion percentage of 62.5.

Blessed with an extremely high football IQ, Starr impressed his teammates with his intelligence and ability to run the Packers' offense without much assistance from the coaching staff, with center Ken Bowman recalling, "Back then, the quarterbacks called their own plays. Lombardi would put together the game plan and go through situations with Bart. But, once the game started, rarely did coach Lombardi send somebody in there with a play."

In speaking of his longtime teammate, wide receiver Boyd Dowler said, "He [Starr] was a good athlete, but not a wonderful athlete, but the things that he did, and that was from the shoulders up, the neck up, a lot of those things, you can't put a number on that."

In addressing the 6'1", 197-pound Starr's other intangible qualities, Bowman stated, "Johnny Unitas probably had a better arm than Bart, but I don't think anybody had more strength of character, mental strength, or will to win. Whatever it took to win the game, he was willing to do."

Firmly believing that an outstanding signal-caller needed to be able to do much more than just throw the football well, Starr suggested, "The quarterback's job is to be a coach on the field. I'd say there are three things a quarterback must have. One, he's got to have the respect of his teammates. Two, his authority must be unquestioned. And three, his teammates must be willing to go to the gates of hell with him."

However, it took some time for Starr to establish himself as the Packers' unquestioned leader on the field because he first had to earn the complete trust and respect of Vince Lombardi. A stern taskmaster who demanded perfection from his players, Lombardi berated Starr in front of his teammates several times during their early days together. Weary of the abuse, Starr finally called his head coach aside one day and told him that if he expected the other players to accept the young quarterback as their leader, he needed to treat him with respect in their presence. Admiring Starr's forthrightness and spirit, Lombardi never again scolded him in public, saving any criticisms he might have had for private conversations between the two men.

Although the Packers failed to win the NFL title in either 1963 or 1964, Starr continued his solid play, performing especially well in the second of those campaigns, when he earned his second All-Pro nomination by passing for 2,144 yards, throwing 15 touchdown passes and only four interceptions, completing 60 percent of his passes, and leading the league with a passer rating of 97.1. Starr then led the Packers to three consecutive league championships and an overall record of 31-9-2 between 1965 and 1967, claiming league MVP honors in 1966, when he passed for 2,257 yards, threw 14 TD passes and just three interceptions, and led all NFL quarterbacks with a pass-completion percentage of 62.2 and a passer rating of 105. Displaying his ability to perform well under pressure, Starr led Green Bay to a perfect 7-0 playoff record over the course of those three campaigns, throwing for a combined 452 yards and three touchdowns in the first two Super Bowls, en route to earning game MVP honors both times.

Yet, even though the Packers created an NFL dynasty during the 1960s, the relatively modest numbers that Starr typically compiled limited the amount of personal recognition he received. Heading a balanced attack, Starr never threw as many as 300 passes or passed for more than 2,438 yards in any single season, helping to create the illusion that he possessed only average passing ability. In fact, some football pundits insist that Starr was merely an average quarterback who benefited from playing for the game's greatest coach, on the league's best team. But, most knowledgeable football people are aware of the impact that Starr made in Green Bay, and how important he was to the success of the team. Bill Curry, who snapped the

Starr earned Super Bowl MVP honors twice.
Public domain (Wikipedia)

ball to Starr from his center position for two years, suggested, "People have forgotten about Starr's big-play ability because the Packers were grind-it-out, run-the-football teams, and Bart's image was firmly planted as the staid executioner of the Vince Lombardi run-first offense. So, Bart Starr would call a fourth-and-one play-action pass and throw it for a touchdown, and the most daring kind of play, and people would simply forget it the next day because that was not his image."

Curry then added, "When he went with play-action, very often it was for huge plays. And, very often, a Packer game, or even a Packer season, would turn on a phenomenal execution of a fake, of a play-action, by Bart Starr at a time when the team couldn't move the ball, and the team would go on to win, and go on to win championships."

Starr also drew praise from Boyd Dowler, who said, "One of the best things about Bart was his consistency, his concentration, his total dedication to what he was doing . . . I played every game Bart played for coach Lombardi, and he was never any different."

Guard Fuzzy Thurston spoke of the confidence that Starr instilled in his teammates, claiming that, every time he stepped into the huddle, "ten other players believed the team was going to score. That's just the way he was, the feeling he inspired in everybody."

Meanwhile, Ray Nitschke stated, "Bart Starr utilized everything God gave him. He rose to the challenge. His best games were in the big games."

After leading the Packers to their third straight NFL title in 1967, Starr remained in Green Bay for another four years, before announcing his retirement following the conclusion of the 1971 campaign. He ended his playing career with 24,718 yards passing, 152 touchdown passes and 138 interceptions, a pass-completion percentage of 57.4 that ranked as the best in NFL history at the time, and a passer rating of 80.5 that placed him second only to Otto Graham among NFL quarterbacks. Over the course of 16 NFL seasons, Starr led the Packers to an overall record of 94-57-6, with the team compiling a mark of 73-22-4 in games he started behind center between 1960 and 1967.

Honored at a testimonial reception held at the Brown County Veterans Memorial Arena in Green Bay on October 17, 1970, Starr received high praise from President Richard Nixon, who said during the festivities:

> We honor him as a very great practitioner of his profession, the proud profession of professional football. And, as we honor him for that, we honor him not only for his technical skill but, as I've indicated, also for something that is just as important: his leadership qualities, his character, his moral fiber. . . . But I think the best way that I can present Bart Starr to his friends is to say very simply that the 60s will be described as the decade in which football became the number one sport in America, in which the Packers were the number one team, and Bart Starr was proudly the number one Packer.

After retiring as an active player, Starr spent one season serving as the Packers' quarterbacks coach under Dan Devine, before joining the CBS broadcast booth for two years. He then replaced Devine as head coach when the latter left for Notre Dame at the end of 1974, remaining in that post for the next nine seasons, during which time the Packers posted a disappointing overall record of 52-76-2. Dismissed in favor of former teammate Forrest Gregg following the conclusion of the 1983 campaign, Starr has remained away from the game ever since. Now in his mid-80s, Starr has experienced numerous health problems the past few years, including ischemic stroke, hemorrhagic stroke, a mild heart attack, seizures, and a broken hip. Nevertheless, Bart Starr's name remains a magical one in the city of Green Bay, and around the NFL, with the league naming an award after him. The Bart Starr Award is presented annually to an NFL player of outstanding character.

Starr, who once said, "The true measure of success is what you've contributed to your community and your nation. I've tried to live a life pleasing to my family and my God," received further confirmation of his strong moral fiber in Jerry Kramer's book, *Distant Replay*, with Kramer writing of his longtime teammate, "On the surface, Bart came as close to perfection as any man I ever met—perfection as a quarterback and as a human being. Bart never said he was perfect, but he did say he tried to be."

Internet football analyst Allen Barra wrote, "The best quarterback in pro football history isn't Joe Montana or Johnny Unitas or Otto Graham or Dan Marino or John Elway. If, by best, you mean most likely to win championships, then the man you want behind center is Bart Starr."

CAREER HIGHLIGHTS

Best Season

Starr performed extremely well for the Packers in 1962, leading them to a regular-season record of 13-1 and earning Second-Team All-Pro honors by passing for a career-high 2,438 yards, finishing second in the league with a passer rating of 90.7, and leading all NFL quarterbacks with a pass completion percentage of 62.5 and a pass interception percentage of 3.2. However, he had his finest all-around season in 1966, when the Associated Press, United Press International, and Newspaper Enterprise Association all accorded him league MVP honors after he passed for 2,257 yards, threw 14 touchdown passes and only three interceptions, and finished first among NFL quarterbacks with a pass completion percentage of 62.2, pass interception percentage of 1.2, and career-best passer rating of 105.0.

Memorable Moments/Greatest Performances

Starr threw the first touchdown pass of his career in his first start, when he connected with Billy Howton from 39 yards out during a 17–16 loss to the San Francisco 49ers on November 18, 1956.

Starr posted his first victory as a starting quarterback in the NFL on November 22, 1959, when he led the Packers to a 21–0 win over the Washington Redskins by completing 11 of 19 pass attempts for 120 yards and two touchdowns.

Starr led the Packers to a 41–13 pasting of the Chicago Bears on December 4, 1960, by completing 17 of 23 pass attempts for 227 yards and two touchdowns, with his TD tosses going to Paul Hornung from 17 yards out and Max McGee from 46 yards out.

Although Starr threw only nine passes during a 35–21 victory over the Los Angeles Rams in the final game of the 1960 regular season, he completed eight of them, finishing the contest with 201 yards passing and two touchdowns. After tossing a 57-yard TD pass to Max McGee, Starr collaborated with Boyd Dowler on a career-long 91-yard scoring play.

Starr had another extremely efficient afternoon on October 15, 1961, when he led the Packers to a 49–17 rout of the Cleveland Browns by completing 15 of 17 passes for 272 yards and one touchdown, with that being a 45-yard strike to Max McGee.

Starr went over 300 yards passing for the first time in his career two weeks later, when, during a 28–10 win over the Minnesota Vikings on October 29, 1961, he completed 18 passes for 311 yards and two touchdowns, hooking up with Jim Taylor from eight yards out and Max McGee from 23 yards out.

Starr reached another first on November 12, 1961, when he led the Packers to a 31–28 victory over the Chicago Bears by tossing three touchdown passes for the first time in his career, collaborating with Paul Hornung on a 34-yard scoring play, and hooking up with Ron Kramer on scoring plays that covered 53 and 8 yards.

Although limited to just 17 pass attempts in the 1961 NFL title game, Starr performed well, completing 10 of those for 164 yards and three touchdowns, in leading the Packers to a convincing 37–0 victory over the Giants.

Starr turned in his finest performance of the 1962 campaign on October 14, when he led the Packers to a 48–21 win over the Vikings by completing 20 of 28 pass attempts for 297 yards and three touchdowns, with the longest of those being a 55-yard connection with Max McGee.

Starr passed for a season-high 306 yards during a 21–17 win over the 49ers in the final game of the 1963 regular season, collaborating with Boyd Dowler on a pair of scoring plays that covered 53 and 50 yards.

Starr threw four touchdown passes for the first time in his career on November 1, 1964, when he led the Packers to a lopsided 42–13 victory over Minnesota by hooking up with both Max McGee and Jim Taylor twice. Starr finished the game with 186 yards through the air and a superb passer rating of 140.3.

Starr led the Packers to a memorable 31–21 come-from-behind win over the Lions on October 17, 1965, when, with Detroit holding a 21–3 lead at halftime, he threw three touchdown passes and ran for another score in the second half, finishing the game with 301 yards through the air. All three of Starr's TD passes came in the third quarter, with the longest of those being a 77-yard strike to Carroll Dale.

Starr turned in another notable performance three years later, when he led the Packers to a 28–17 victory over the previously undefeated Dallas Cowboys on October 28, 1968, by passing for 260 yards and four touchdowns, with one of those going to Carroll Dale, another to Boyd Dowler, and the final two to tight end Marv Fleming.

An exceptional big-game player over the course of his career, Starr performed extremely well during the Packers' 34–27 win over Dallas in the 1966 NFL championship game, completing 19 of 28 passes for 304 yards and four touchdowns, including a 51-yard strike to Carroll Dale.

Starr followed that up by completing 16 of 23 passes for 250 yards and two touchdowns, in leading the Packers to a 35–10 victory over Kansas City in Super Bowl I, earning in the process game MVP honors.

Starr once again earned Super Bowl MVP honors the following year, when he passed for 202 yards and one touchdown during the Packers' 33–14 win over the Oakland Raiders in Super Bowl II, with his TD pass being a 62-yard connection with Boyd Dowler in the second quarter.

Yet, Starr is most famous for a run he made in the 1967 NFL championship game, otherwise known as the Ice Bowl, that gave the Packers their third consecutive league title. With the Packers trailing the Dallas Cowboys by a score of 17–14 late in the fourth quarter, Starr navigated the ball down to the Dallas 1-yard line. However, with the icy field conditions making it difficult to execute quick-hitting running plays, two straight handoffs to Green Bay running backs left the Packers still seeking the go-ahead touchdown. With only 16 seconds remaining in regulation, Starr consulted with coach Vince Lombardi on the sideline and suggested that he try to sneak the ball into the end zone instead of handing it off. Calling a "35 wedge" in the huddle, which was a play designed for running back Chuck Mercein, Starr, unbeknownst to his teammates, kept the ball himself and pushed his way into the end zone, giving the Packers a 21–17 win in arguably the most famous game in football history.

NOTABLE ACHIEVEMENTS

- Passed for more than 2,000 yards five times.
- Completed more than 60 percent of passes four times, topping 65 percent once (66.1 in 1966).
- Posted touchdown-to-interception ratio of better than 3-to-1 twice.
- Posted quarterback rating above 90.0 four times, topping 100.0-mark twice.
- Led NFL quarterbacks in: completion percentage four times; passer rating four times; interception percentage three times; game-winning drives once; and fourth-quarter comebacks twice.
- Finished second in NFL in: passer rating once; completion percentage twice; and interception percentage once.
- Finished third in NFL in completion percentage once.
- Holds NFL record for highest career postseason passer rating (104.8).
- Retired with highest completion percentage (57.4) of any quarterback in NFL history.
- Holds Packers record (tied) for most seasons played (16).
- Ranks third in Packers history for most games played (196).
- Ranks among Packers career leaders with: 3,149 pass attempts (3rd); 1,808 pass completions (3rd); 24,718 yards passing (3rd); 152 touchdown passes (3rd); 57.4 completion percentage (3rd); and passer rating of 80.5 (3rd).
- Six-time Western Conference champion (1960, 1961, 1962, 1965, 1966, and 1967).
- Five-time NFL champion (1961, 1962, 1965, 1966, and 1967).
- Two-time Super Bowl champion (I and II).
- Two-time Super Bowl MVP (I and II).
- 1966 NFL MVP.
- Four-time Pro Bowl selection (1960, 1961, 1962, and 1966).
- 1966 First-Team All-Pro.
- Two-time Second-Team All-Pro (1962 and 1964).

- Two-time All–Western Conference First-Team selection (1961 and 1966).
- NFL 1960s All-Decade Team.
- Pro Football Hall of Fame All-1960s Team.
- #15 retired by Packers.
- Named to Packers 50th Anniversary Team in 1969.
- Number 41 on the *Sporting News'* 1999 list of 100 Greatest Players in NFL History.
- Number 51 on NFL Films' 2010 list of 100 Greatest Players in NFL History.
- Elected to Pro Football Hall of Fame in 1977.

9

WILLIE DAVIS

Once asked to describe the attributes of a great player, Vince Lombardi said, "You look for speed, agility and size. You may get two of these qualities in one man and, when you have three, you have a great player. In Willie Davis, we have a great one. For a big man, 6'3" and 240 pounds, he has excellent agility, and he has great sincerity and determination."

Combining all those outstanding attributes, Willie Davis served as the prototype for the modern-day defensive end. Anchoring the Packers' defensive line for 10 seasons from his left end position, Davis wreaked havoc on opposing offenses, terrorizing quarterbacks with his exceptional pass-rush skills, while also doing a superb job of defending against the run. Extremely durable as well, Davis made 138 straight starts for the Packers, continuing in the process his career-long string of 162 consecutive games played. One of the most respected players in the game, Davis earned five Pro Bowl selections and six All-Pro nominations during his time in Green Bay, en route to also earning spots on the Pro Football Hall of Fame All-1960s Team and the Packers 50th Anniversary Team. A member of all five Vince Lombardi NFL championship teams, Davis received the additional honors of being accorded a number 69 ranking on the *Sporting News'* 1999 list of the 100 Greatest Players in NFL History and being inducted into the Pro Football Hall of Fame in 1981.

Born in Lisbon, Louisiana, on July 24, 1934, William Delford Davis came from humble beginnings, growing up in a poor, small town in Arkansas, where he attended Booker T. Washington High School. After enrolling at Grambling State University following his graduation, Davis spent his college career on the gridiron playing for legendary head coach Eddie Robinson, performing well enough at that small black college that the Cleveland Browns selected him in the 15th round of the 1956 NFL Draft, with the 181st overall pick. Davis then sat out the entire 1957 campaign, before appearing in every game for the Browns in each of the next two seasons, with Cleveland head coach Paul Brown switching him back and

Willie Davis starred at left defensive end for the Packers for 10 seasons.
Courtesy of www.ClaremontShows.com

forth between offense and defense. Unable to reach his full potential with the Browns due to the manner in which they used him, Davis welcomed a trade to the Green Bay Packers, who acquired him for backup wide receiver A. D. Williams prior to the start of the 1960 campaign.

Inserted at left defensive end full-time upon his arrival in Green Bay, Davis soon emerged as one of the Packers' best players after being told by head coach Vince Lombardi, "With your quickness, you can be a great pass rusher. I want you to know that you're going to make it there, or you won't make this ball club."

Davis did indeed make it at his new position, using his size, speed, strength, and agility to dominate his opponent at the line of scrimmage. A relentless pass rusher, Davis gave opposing quarterbacks nightmares, applying constant pressure to top signal-callers such as Johnny Unitas, Y. A. Tittle, and Fran Tarkenton. Commenting on his ability to rush the quarterback, Davis said, "I think I was an aggressive player that generated major pursuit. I used to chase down plays and do things that I was blessed with the speed and ability to do."

Although Davis played in an era when the NFL did not keep an official record of defensive statistics such as tackles and sacks, John Turney, a member of the Professional Football Researchers Association, reports that the defensive end had well in excess of 100 sacks during his time in Green Bay, "possibly more than 120," including a minimum of over 40 between 1963 and 1965. Davis himself is quoted as saying, "I would think I would have to be the team's all-time leader in sacks. I played 10 years and I averaged in the 'teens in sacks for those 10 years. I had 25 one season. (Paul) Hornung just reminded me of that the other day."

Much more than just a pass-rusher, though, Davis also did an outstanding job of defending against the run, with Hall of Fame running back Bobby Mitchell stating:

> The thing that I was impressed with was his ability to turn that tackle loose and run down a running back from the far end. We hadn't seen a lot of that from ballplayers. He could move from his set position so quickly that he never got the full blow from the offensive guy coming at him, so he very seldom got pancaked. All of that was a part of making him great because he could slip and slide away from some of the big linemen who were coming at him. He could move so quick that he'd get into position to make those tackles. He could run down people.

Mitchell also considered Davis to be an extremely cerebral player, noting, "Willie was one of those guys that you thought intelligence first. He exuded it all the time. You'd hear about it from other ballplayers because they were very much aware of Willie's smarts."

An opportunistic player as well who had a knack for making big plays, Davis scored two touchdowns, recorded two safeties, and recovered 22 fumbles during his career, with the last figure representing the second-highest total in franchise history.

Davis never missed a game his entire NFL career.
Courtesy of ClaremontShows.com

Davis's varied skill set made him a key contributor to Packer teams that won six Western Conference championships, five NFL titles, and two Super Bowls during his time in Green Bay. Serving as the Packers' defensive captain his last several years with the team, Davis set an example for his teammates by appearing in 138 straight games between 1960 and 1969, extending in the process his string of 162 consecutive games played as a pro.

But, with Lombardi gone and the Packers struggling on the field, an aging Davis elected to announce his retirement in 1969. Honored by the Packers, who held a Willie Davis Day on December 21, 1969, Davis proclaimed, "Basically, my whole career has been proving a point—that I can play football with guys that came from bigger colleges; that I can play football against the best football players from anywhere; that I can carve my niche."

Davis, whose effervescent personality earned him the nickname "Dr. Feelgood" among his teammates, subsequently used his intelligence, leadership ability, and positive outlook to embark on an extremely successful business career following his retirement from football. After working as a color commentator on NFL telecasts for NBC during the early 1970s, Davis, who earned his bachelor's degree in math and industrial arts while at Grambling, and later earned his master's degree in business administration from the University of Chicago while playing in the NFL, gradually rose to become one of the most prominent businessmen in America. In addition to owning several radio stations across the nation and operating his own Willie Davis Distributing Company, Davis has sat on the board of directors of several Fortune 500 companies. He also served as the director of the 1984 Olympic Committee in Los Angeles, and, in 1994, be became the second black member of the Packers Board of Directors. Yet, with all the success he has experienced in the business world, Davis, now in his mid-80s, has never forgotten the man who served as his greatest inspiration, often saying that, whenever he went into a sales meeting, the words and lessons of Vince Lombardi went with him.

PACKERS CAREER HIGHLIGHTS

Best Season

Because the NFL did not keep an official record of sacks and tackles until well after Davis retired, there is no way of knowing with any degree of certainty which season proved to be his most dominant. However, with closest estimates indicating that Davis compiled a minimum of 40 sacks between 1963 and 1965, including 25 in one of those years, we'll identify 1965 as his finest season because he earned consensus First-Team All-Pro honors, recorded one of his two career interceptions, and recovered two fumbles.

Memorable Moments/Greatest Performances

Davis scored the first points of his career during a convincing 41–13 victory over the Bears on December 4, 1960, when he recovered a fumble in the end zone on special teams, giving the Packers an early 10–0 lead.

Davis scored his only defensive touchdown during a 26–14 loss to the Lions on November 22, 1962, when he recovered a fumble in the end zone.

Davis recorded the first of his two career safeties on October 6, 1963, when he gave the Packers a 9–7 lead over the Los Angeles Rams late in the first quarter of a game they ultimately won by a score of 42–10 by tackling quarterback Roman Gabriel in the end zone.

Davis again lit the scoreboard during a 23–0 win over the Falcons on October 1, 1967, when he brought down quarterback Randy Johnson in the end zone for a safety, recording in the process one of the eight sacks the Packers registered against Atlanta on the day.

Excelling in each of Green Bay's first two Super Bowl victories, Davis recorded 1½ sacks of Len Dawson during the Packer's 35–10 win over the Chiefs in Super Bowl I, before bringing down Daryle Lamonica three times during their 33–14 win over Oakland in Super Bowl II.

NOTABLE ACHIEVEMENTS

- Scored two touchdowns during career (one on defense and one on special teams).
- Recorded two safeties during career.
- Played in 138 consecutive games for Packers.
- Tied for second in Packers history with 22 fumble recoveries.
- Six-time Western Conference champion (1960, 1961, 1962, 1965, 1966, and 1967).
- Five-time NFL champion (1961, 1962, 1965, 1966, and 1967).
- Two-time Super Bowl champion (I and II).
- Five-time Pro Bowl selection (1963, 1964, 1965, 1966, and 1967).
- Five-time First-Team All-Pro (1962, 1964, 1965, 1966, and 1967).
- 1963 Second Team All-Pro.
- NFL 1960s All-Decade Team.
- Pro Football Hall of Fame All-1960s Team.
- Pro Football Reference All-1960s First Team.
- Named to Packers 50th Anniversary Team in 1969.
- Number 69 on the *Sporting News'* 1999 list of 100 Greatest Players in NFL History.
- Number 86 on NFL Films' 2010 list of 100 Greatest Players in NFL History.
- Elected to Pro Football Hall of Fame in 1981.

10

JAMES LOFTON

One of the most athletically gifted wide receivers in the history of the game, James Lofton used his blinding speed, good size, and soft hands to emerge as arguably the NFL's premier player at his position during the first half of the 1980s. Leading the Packers in pass receptions and receiving yards in each of his nine seasons as a member of the team, Lofton caught more than 50 passes seven times and amassed more than 1,000 receiving yards five times while wearing the Green and Gold, en route to establishing himself as the franchise's all-time leader in both categories by the time he left Green Bay at the end of 1986. Still holding down one of the top spots in every major pass-receiving category more than three decades after he played his last game for the Packers, Lofton currently ranks fourth in team annals in pass receptions (530) and second in receiving yards (9,656), with his stellar play for the Packers between 1978 and 1986 earning him seven Pro Bowl selections and four All-Pro nominations. Continuing to perform at an elite level after he left Green Bay, Lofton ended his playing career with more receiving yards than any other player in NFL history, earning in the process a spot on the NFL 1980s All-Decade Team and a place in the Pro Football Hall of Fame.

Born in Fort Ord, California, on July 5, 1956, James David Lofton attended George Washington High School in Los Angeles, California, where, in addition to excelling in football as a quarterback and safety, he starred in track as a sprinter and long-jumper. After accepting a track scholarship from Stanford University, Lofton put together a brilliant college career in which he won the long jump at the 1978 NCAA Track and Field Championships with a wind-aided leap of 26 feet, 11¾ inches, while also qualifying for a berth in the 100, 200, and 400-meter dashes, posting a personal-best time of 20.5 seconds in the second event. Also performing exceptionally well on the gridiron while at Stanford, Lofton earned Second-Team All-America honors as a senior in 1977 by making 57 receptions for 1,010 yards and 14 touchdowns.

Selected by the Packers with the sixth overall pick of the 1978 NFL Draft, Lofton made an immediate impact in Green Bay, earning a spot on the NFL All-Rookie Team and his first trip to the Pro Bowl by making 46 receptions for 818 yards and six touchdowns. He followed that up with another strong performance in 1979, catching 54 passes, amassing 968 receiving yards, and scoring four touchdowns, before beginning an exceptional six-year run during which he established himself as one of the very best receivers in all of football. Surpassing 1,000 receiving yards in all but the strike-shortened 1982 campaign, Lofton compiled the following numbers the other five years:

YEAR	RECS	RECEIVING YARDS	TD RECS
1980	71	1,226	4
1981	71	1,294	8
1983	58	1,300	8
1984	62	1,361	7
1985	69	1,153	4

Lofton ranked among the NFL leaders in receiving yards each season, placing as high as second in 1981. He also topped the circuit in average yards per reception twice, leading the league with marks of 22.4 yards and 22.0 yards per catch in 1983 and 1984, respectively, with his outstanding play earning him four All-Pro nominations and six straight Pro Bowl selections.

The 6'3", 192-pound Lofton proved to be the Randy Moss of his era in many ways, with his size, speed, and agility making him a matchup nightmare for any opposing defensive back. Able to blow past defenders with his 4.3 speed and long, graceful stride, Lofton often found himself so wide open that he had to slow down to gather in his quarterback's pass.

In discussing Lofton's ability to separate himself from his defender, New England Patriots cornerback Raymond Clayborn commented, "He's got, like, this afterburner. It seems the longer he goes, the faster he gets."

Meanwhile, Packers tight end Paul Coffman said, "I've always envied him. He's a gazelle, while I'm one of those guys about whom they always said, 'If he could run, he could play in the NFL.'"

Lofton also knew how to use his size to his advantage, proving to be an expert at getting his long frame in front of his defender and then quickly turning upfield in one motion. If he did have a weakness, though, it was

James Lofton led the Packers in pass receptions and receiving yards in each of his nine seasons in Green Bay.
Courtesy of ClaremontShows.com

his unwillingness to go underneath and catch the short pass, because he considered himself to be a thoroughbred whose primary function was to attack corners deep.

Although Lofton compiled slightly less impressive numbers in 1986, he still managed to catch 64 passes, amass 840 receiving yards, and score four touchdowns, becoming in the process just the 14th player in league history to top 500 career receptions. After establishing himself as Green Bay's all-time leader in receiving yardage the previous season, Lofton moved ahead of Don Hutson into first place on the team's all-time pass receiving list with his 64 catches in 1986.

Yet, in spite of Lofton's outstanding on-field performance, he experienced a considerable amount of turmoil away from the playing field during his time in Green Bay. After having an earlier charge of sexual assault against him dismissed due to a lack of evidence, Lofton found himself being accused of a similar act some two years later, when an exotic dancer claimed in 1986 that he forced her to perform a sexual act on the stairs of a local nightclub. Although Lofton, the married father of three children, ended up being found innocent in a court of law, the alleged incident did irreparable damage to his reputation, prompting the Packers to trade him to the Los Angeles Raiders for a pair of future draft picks during the subsequent offseason when local sponsors threatened to cut their ties with the organization.

Reflecting back on the Packers' decision to deal him to the Raiders, Lofton said, "They just thought it would be tough for me to stay there. And, with the stance that they took, perhaps that I was guilty before I was proven innocent by suspending me, I don't know if they were covering their tracks or doing what they felt was best for them."

Lofton left Green Bay with career totals of 530 receptions, 9,656 receiving yards, 49 touchdown catches, and 9,901 yards from scrimmage, all of which place him among the Packers' all-time leaders. He also ranks fourth in franchise history with an average of 18.22 yards per reception. Extremely durable as well, Lofton missed just one game in his nine seasons with the Packers, failing to appear in only the final game of the 1986 campaign after being suspended by the team.

After leaving the Packers, Lofton spent two years in Los Angeles, playing his best ball for the Raiders in 1987, when he made 41 receptions for 880 yards and five touchdowns. From Los Angeles, Lofton moved on to Buffalo, where he helped the Bills capture three straight AFC championships, earning his final trip to the Pro Bowl in 1991 by catching 57 passes, amassing 1,072 receiving yards, and making eight touchdown receptions. Displaying a high level of professionalism during his time in Buffalo, Lofton later drew praise from Bills head coach Marv Levy, who said, "He was a true gentleman and a great leader. There was no showboat in him, no hot dog in him. He did everything with class."

After helping the Bills win their third consecutive conference title in 1992, Lofton split the ensuing campaign between the Philadelphia Eagles and the Los Angeles Rams, before announcing his retirement at season's end. He concluded his playing career with 764 receptions, a then–NFL record 14,004 receiving yards, 75 TD receptions, and 76 total touchdowns.

Lofton ended his career with more receiving yards than any other player in NFL history.
Public domain (Wikipedia)

Since retiring as an active player, Lofton has remained close to the game, serving as a color analyst and sideline reporter for NFL coverage on Westwood One radio broadcasts from 1999 to 2001, before becoming the wide receiver coach for the San Diego Chargers in 2002. After six years in that post, Lofton spent one season serving the Raiders in a similar capacity, before spending the next eight years back at Westwood One, where he became a member of the *Sunday Night Football* broadcast team. Lofton moved to a television position on the *NFL on CBS* in 2017.

PACKERS CAREER HIGHLIGHTS

Best Season

Lofton played his best ball for the Packers from 1980 to 1985, surpassing 58 receptions and 1,100 receiving yards in all but one of those six seasons, with the only exception being the strike-shortened 1982 campaign. It could be argued that Lofton had his greatest season in 1984, when, in addition to making 62 receptions, scoring seven touchdowns, and leading the league with an average of 22 yards per catch, he established career-high marks in receiving yards (1,361) and yards from scrimmage (1,443). Nevertheless, the 1981 campaign would have to be considered Lofton's finest all-around season, because, in addition to making a career-high eight touchdown catches, he made 71 receptions and finished second in the NFL with 1,294 receiving yards, earning in the process his lone First-Team All-Pro selection.

Memorable Moments/Greatest Performances

Lofton made a huge impact in just his second game as a pro, helping the Packers record a 28–17 victory over the New Orleans Saints on September 10, 1978, by making three receptions, all of which went for touchdowns. Amassing a total of 107 receiving yards on the day, Lofton teamed up with David Whitehurst on scoring plays that covered 42, 47, and 18 yards.

Lofton helped lead the Packers to a 14–9 win over the Cincinnati Bengals on October 5, 1980, by making eight catches for 114 yards and one touchdown.

Although the Packers lost their October 19, 1980, matchup with the Cleveland Browns by a score of 26–21, Lofton had another big game, making eight receptions for 136 yards and one touchdown—a 26-yard connection with Lynn Dickey early in the fourth quarter that gave Green Bay a 21–13 lead at the time.

Lofton torched the San Francisco defensive secondary for eight catches and 146 receiving yards during a 23–16 win over the 49ers on November 9, 1980.

Although the Packers suffered a 27–21 defeat at the hands of the Giants one week later, Lofton had a huge game, making eight catches for a season-high 175 yards and one touchdown.

Lofton once again starred in defeat on September 13, 1981, making eight receptions for 179 yards during a 31–17 loss to the Atlanta Falcons.

Although Lofton made only two catches during a 31–27 loss to the Detroit Lions on October 25, 1981, one of them went for a 75-yard touchdown, marking his longest reception of the season.

Lofton helped lead the Packers to a 35–23 victory over the Minnesota Vikings on November 29, 1981, by making seven receptions for 159 yards and one touchdown, with that being a 47-yard hookup with Lynn Dickey early in the fourth quarter.

Lofton made the pivotal play of a 27–19 Monday night win over the Giants on September 20, 1982, when, with the Packers trailing by a score of 19–7 in the third quarter, he completely changed the momentum of the contest by scoring on an 83-yard end-around that brought his team to within one touchdown of New York. The Packers went on to score 20 unanswered points, with Lofton finishing the game with four catches for 101 yards and that one rushing TD.

Lofton again exhibited his blinding speed during a 38–7 victory over the Atlanta Falcons on December 26, 1982, collaborating with Lynn Dickey on scoring plays that covered 80 and 57 yards, with his 80-yard reception representing the longest of his career.

Although the Packers exited the 1982 postseason tournament after suffering a 37–26 loss to the Dallas Cowboys in the second round of the playoffs, Lofton acquitted himself extremely well against "America's Team," making five receptions for 109 yards and scoring two touchdowns, with one of those coming on a 71-yard run early in the fourth quarter that cut the Dallas lead to four points.

Lofton had a big game against Houston in the 1983 regular-season opener, helping to lead the Packers to a 41–38 overtime victory over the Oilers by making eight catches for 154 yards and one touchdown, which came on a 74-yard hookup with Lynn Dickey in the fourth quarter that gave Green Bay a 38–31 lead with only minutes remaining in regulation. The Packers eventually won the game in OT on a 42-yard field goal by Jan Stenerud.

Lofton followed that up with another huge effort during the Packers' 25–21 loss to the Pittsburgh Steelers in Week 2 of the 1983 campaign, making five catches for 169 yards, and connecting with Dickey on scoring plays that covered 71, 73, and 12 yards.

Although the Packers lost to the Atlanta Falcons in overtime by a score of 47–41 on November 27, 1983, Lofton once again starred in defeat, making seven catches for 161 yards and one touchdown.

Even though his extraordinary effort went for naught, Lofton turned in his finest individual performance during a 17–14 Monday night loss to the Denver Broncos on October 15, 1984, reaching career highs with 11 catches and 206 receiving yards, while also hooking up with Lynn Dickey on a 54-yard scoring play in the fourth quarter.

Lofton helped lead the Packers to a 43–10 rout of the Detroit Lions on October 6, 1985, by making 10 receptions for 151 yards.

NOTABLE ACHIEVEMENTS

- Surpassed 50 receptions seven times, topping 60 catches five times and 70 catches twice.
- Surpassed 1,000 receiving yards five times, topping 1,200 yards on four occasions.
- Made eight touchdown receptions twice.
- Averaged more than 20 yards per reception twice.
- Led NFL in yards-per-catch twice.
- Finished second in NFL with 1,294 receiving yards in 1981.
- Finished third in NFL with 1,300 receiving yards in 1983.
- Led Packers in pass receptions and receiving yards nine straight times (1978–1986).
- Ranks among Packers career leaders with: 530 pass receptions (4th); 9,656 receiving yards (2nd); 9,901 yards from scrimmage (3rd); 49 touchdown receptions (8th); and average of 18.22 yards per reception (4th).
- Missed just one game in nine seasons with Packers, appearing in 136 consecutive games.
- 1982 division champion.
- Retired in 1993 with more receiving yards (14,004) than any other player in NFL history.
- Named to 1978 NFL All-Rookie Team.
- Seven-time Pro Bowl selection (1978, 1980, 1981, 1982, 1983, 1984, and 1985).
- 1981 First-Team All-Pro.
- Three-time Second-Team All-Pro (1980, 1982, and 1983).
- Three-time First-Team All-NFC selection (1980, 1981, and 1982).
- Three-time Second-Team All-NFC selection (1983, 1984, and 1985).
- NFL 1980s All-Decade Team.
- Pro Football Hall of Fame All-1980s Second Team.
- Pro Football Reference All-1980s First Team.
- Elected to Pro Football Hall of Fame in 2003.

11

WILLIE WOOD

One of the finest defensive backs of his era, Willie Wood spent his entire 12-year NFL career in Green Bay, appearing in every game the Packers played during that time. An exceptional ball-hawk who also developed a reputation as one of the league's hardest hitters, Wood recorded 48 interceptions and 699 interception-return yards from his free safety position over the course of his career, with those figures placing him second and third, respectively, in team annals. An outstanding punt returner as well, Wood holds franchise marks for most punt returns and punt-return yards, with his exceptional all-around play helping the Packers win six Western Conference championships, five NFL titles, and two Super Bowls during the 1960s. Along the way, Wood earned eight Pro Bowl selections, seven All-Pro nominations, spots on the NFL 1960s All-Decade Team and the Packers 50th Anniversary Team, and a place in the Pro Football Hall of Fame.

Born in Washington, DC, on December 23, 1936, William Vernell Wood spent his early years being raised by his single mother in the rough inner-city of the nation's capital, where he used his exceptional athletic ability to escape poverty. Excelling in both football and basketball while attending Armstrong High School, Wood headed west after he accepted an athletic scholarship from Coalinga Junior College in southern California. After earning junior college All-America honors for his performance on the gridiron as a freshman, Wood transferred to the University of Southern California, where he spent the next three years starting at quarterback and safety for the Trojans, becoming in the process the first African-American signal-caller in the history of the Pacific Coast Conference.

Remaining undaunted after going undrafted by all 13 NFL teams following his graduation in 1960 due to concerns over his size (he stood 5'10" tall and weighed only 170 pounds) and an injury to his collarbone that forced him to miss several games his final two years at USC, Wood wrote letters to several pro teams requesting a tryout. With only the Packers responding, Wood headed for Green Bay, where he earned a roster spot as

Willie Wood earned eight trips to the Pro Bowl and seven
All-Pro selections during his time in Green Bay.
Courtesy of MearsOnlineAuctions.com

a backup defensive back and punt returner on the Packers' 1960 Western
Conference championship team.

After bulking up to 190 pounds, Wood laid claim to the starting free
safety job in his sophomore campaign of 1961, helping the Packers win
their first NFL title under Vince Lombardi by recording a team-leading five
interceptions and five fumble recoveries, while also returning two punts for
touchdowns. Establishing himself as one of the NFL's premier players at his
position in 1962, Wood earned Second-Team All-Pro honors and his first
Pro Bowl selection by leading the league with nine interceptions, which he
returned for a total of 132 yards. After another strong performance the following year, Wood began a string of seven consecutive Pro Bowl selections

and six straight All-Pro nominations in 1964, twice recording as many as six interceptions in a season.

Wood's football acumen and experience as a quarterback in college helped make him an expert at reading opposing offenses, contributing greatly to his lofty interception totals. But, in addition to gaining a reputation as one of the league's top pass defenders, Wood became known as a fierce, devastating hitter who Vince Lombardi called the team's surest tackler. Known to flip Cleveland's powerful, 230-pound Hall of Fame running back Jim Brown with crushing tackles at the knees on numerous occasions, Wood drew praise from former teammate and fellow safety Tom Brown, who said, "What a ferocious tackler he was. He didn't wrap his arms around people, he came in and dove at your legs and flipped you over a couple of times."

In speaking of his longtime teammate, Willie Davis told the *Los Angeles Times* in 2007, "He used to go down low and really hit the big guys to take them down. There was never a tree too big for Willie to chop down."

An outstanding team leader as well who inspired the other men around him, Wood, claimed Jerry Kramer, was the only member of the Packers that Ray Nitschke feared. Speaking with the *Milwaukee Journal Sentinel* in 2008, Kramer revealed that Green Bay's ferocious middle linebacker often said that he was not afraid of Vince Lombardi. But Kramer added, "He said he was scared of Willie. Nitschke said he hated to miss a tackle because Willie would give him this withering look."

Also respected for his toughness, durability, and ability to play through injury, Wood never missed a game in his 12 seasons with the Packers, playing in 166 consecutive regular-season contests. In discussing what he considered to be one of his greatest attributes, Wood suggested, "Determination probably was my trademark. I was talented, but so were a lot of people. I'd like people to tell you I was the toughest guy they ever played against."

Wood's consecutive games played streak came to an end following the conclusion of the 1971 campaign when he announced his retirement. In addition to his 48 interceptions and 699 interception-return yards, Wood ended his career with 16 fumble recoveries, 1,391 punt-return yards, and two punt-return TDs. He also returned two interceptions for touchdowns.

After retiring as an active player, Wood entered into a career in coaching, spending three seasons serving as defensive backs coach for the San Diego Chargers, before becoming the defensive coordinator of the Philadelphia Bell of the World Football League in 1975. Wood later served as an assistant under former Packers teammate Forrest Gregg on the coaching staff of the Canadian Football League's Toronto Argonauts, before briefly taking over as head coach after Gregg departed for Cincinnati following the

In addition to excelling on defense, Wood amassed more yards returning punts than anyone else in franchise history.
Courtesy of ClaremontShows.com

conclusion of the 1979 campaign. By serving as head man in Toronto for most of the next two seasons, Wood became the first black head coach in professional football.

Relieved of his duties in Toronto after the Argonauts got off to an 0-10 start in 1981, Wood tried unsuccessfully to find a coaching job in the NFL, with his son, Andre, later revealing, "The thing is, my dad never wanted to leave football. He needed a stable way to make a living. But I know he would have stayed in the NFL coaching track had he been asked to. But he wasn't." As a result, Wood went to school, got his contractor's license in Washington and Maryland, and opened his own mechanical contracting business in Washington, which he called Wood Mechanical Systems.

Unfortunately, Wood subsequently began experiencing physical problems that have confined him to a wheelchair for much of the last two decades. After undergoing cervical spine surgery, two replacements of the same knee, and hip replacement surgery, Wood moved into an assisted living facility in his hometown of Washington, DC, where he currently resides. Robbed of many of his cognitive functions by the dementia that has engulfed him the last several years, the 81-year-old Wood spends most of his time sitting in a wheelchair listening to jazz and 1950s doo-wop. Although he occasionally goes out in public to sign autographs, he sometimes falls asleep at those events or has to be reminded whom he is with.

CAREER HIGHLIGHTS

Best Season

Although Wood only earned Second-Team All-Pro honors in 1962, he played the best ball of his career for the Packers that year, earning his first Pro Bowl nomination by leading the league with nine interceptions, which he returned for 132 yards, while also finishing second in the circuit with an average of 11.9 yards per punt return and a total of 273 punt-return yards.

Memorable Moments/Greatest Performances

Wood, who scored two touchdowns on special teams during his career, did so for the first time during a 30–10 win over the 49ers on September 24, 1961, when he put the Packers ahead to stay early in the second quarter by returning a punt 39 yards for a TD.

Wood accomplished the feat again just two weeks later, contributing to a lopsided 45–7 victory over the Baltimore Colts on October 8, 1961, by intercepting a pass and returning a punt 72 yards for a touchdown.

Wood turned in an outstanding all-around performance in the opening game of the 1962 campaign, picking off a pair of Fran Tarkenton passes and returning two punts for 68 yards during a 34–7 win over the Minnesota Vikings.

Wood made a big play for the Packers during their 16–7 victory over the New York Giants in the 1962 NFL championship game, making a touchdown-saving tackle on a kickoff return.

Although the Packers suffered a 27–17 defeat at the hands of the Los Angeles Rams on October 25, 1964, Wood recorded the first pick-six of his career, intercepting a Roman Gabriel pass and returning the ball 42 yards for a touchdown.

Wood crossed the opponent's goal line for the final time in his career on October 16, 1966, when he clinched a 17–0 victory over the Bears by returning an interception 20 yards for a touchdown in the fourth quarter.

Wood helped the Packers record a 14–10 victory over the Baltimore Colts on December 10, 1966, by picking off Johnny Unitas twice.

Wood intercepted more than one pass in a game for the final time on October 12, 1970, when he recorded two of the four picks the Packers made against San Diego quarterbacks John Hadl and Marty Domres during a 22–20 win over the Chargers.

However, Wood made the biggest play of his career in Super Bowl I, when his third-quarter interception and subsequent 50-yard return to the Kansas City 5-yard line helped the Packers break open a close contest. The Packers, who led by a score of 14–10 at the time, went on to score 21 unanswered points, giving them a 35–10 victory over the AFL champions. Commenting on Wood's interception of Len Dawson's pass following the conclusion of the contest, Vince Lombardi said, "That was the steal of the game . . . Willie Wood at his finest."

NOTABLE ACHIEVEMENTS

- Recorded at least five interceptions in a season five times.
- Accumulated more than 100 interception-return yards twice.
- Returned two interceptions for touchdowns during career.
- Returned two punts for touchdowns during career.
- Led Packers in interceptions five times.
- Led NFL in: interceptions once; punt-return touchdowns once; and punt-return average once.
- Finished second in NFL in: fumble recoveries once; punt-return yards three times; and punt-return average twice.
- Finished third in NFL with six interceptions in 1965.
- Never missed a game entire career.

- Holds NFL record for most consecutive starts by a safety (166).
- Holds Packers career records for most punt returns (187) and punt-return yards (1,391).
- Ranks among Packers career leaders with: 48 interceptions (2nd); 699 interception-return yards (3rd); 16 fumble recoveries (tied—5th); 166 games played (10th); and 166 consecutive games played (4th).
- Six-time Western Conference champion (1960, 1961, 1962, 1965, 1966, and 1967).
- Five-time NFL champion (1961, 1962, 1965, 1966, and 1967).
- Two-time Super Bowl champion (I and II).
- Eight-time Pro Bowl selection (1962, 1964, 1965, 1966, 1967, 1968, 1969, and 1970).
- Five-time First-Team All-Pro (1964, 1965, 1966, 1967, and 1969).
- Two-time Second-Team All-Pro (1962 and 1968).
- Six-time All–Western Conference First-Team selection (1962, 1965, 1967, 1968, 1970, and 1971).
- NFL 1960s All-Decade Team.
- Pro Football Hall of Fame All-1960s Team.
- Pro Football Reference All-1960s First Team.
- Named to Packers 50th Anniversary Team in 1969.
- Elected to Pro Football Hall of Fame in 1989.

12

REGGIE WHITE

Considered by many football experts to be the greatest defensive end in the history of the game, Reggie White earned more individual accolades over the course of his 15-year NFL career than any other player ever to man the position. A first-ballot Pro Football Hall of Fame inductee, White earned 13 consecutive Pro Bowl nominations, 13 All-Pro selections, two NFL Defensive Player of the Year trophies, a spot on the NFL's 75th Anniversary All-Time Team, and a number 22 ranking on the *Sporting News'* 1999 list of the 100 Greatest Players in NFL History. The only player ever to record double-digit sack totals in nine consecutive seasons, White retired in 2000 with 198 career sacks, the highest total in league history at the time. Although White spent most of his peak seasons with the Philadelphia Eagles, he still had enough left by the time he arrived in Green Bay in 1993 to register a total of 68½ sacks over the course of the next six seasons, earning in the process six trips to the Pro Bowl, five All-Pro nominations, and recognition as the NFL Defensive Player of the Year for a second time. More importantly, White helped lead the Packers to two conference championships and one NFL title, while simultaneously changing the culture in Green Bay, which subsequently became a much more desirable destination for impending free agents.

Born in Chattanooga, Tennessee, on December 19, 1961, Reginald Howard White spent his early years being raised by his unwed mother, before being placed with his grandmother, Mildred Dodd, at the age of eight. After lettering in football, basketball, and track and field at Howard High School, White, who became an ordained minister at the age of 17, accepted an athletic scholarship from the University of Tennessee. Acquiring the nickname "The Minister of Defense" while in college, White set school records for most sacks in a career (32) and in a season (15). Performing particularly well as a senior in 1983, White recorded 100 tackles (72 solo), nine tackles for loss, and 15 sacks, en route to earning SEC Player of the Year and consensus All-America honors.

Reggie White earned Pro Bowl honors in each of his six seasons with the Packers.
Courtesy of MearsOnlineAuctions.com

Subsequently selected by the Memphis Showboats in the 1984 USFL Territorial Draft, and by the Philadelphia Eagles with the fourth overall pick of the 1984 NFL Supplemental Draft, White chose to remain close to home and signed a five-year deal to play for the Showboats. However, after registering a total of 23½ sacks in his two years in Memphis, White signed with the Eagles when the USFL folded following the conclusion of the 1985 campaign.

White ended up spending eight years in Philadelphia, establishing himself during that time as one of the most dominant defensive players in NFL history. Recording double-digit sacks in each of those eight seasons from his left end position, White brought down opposing quarterbacks behind the line of scrimmage 124 times in 121 games, earning in the process seven trips to the Pro Bowl and six First-Team All-Pro nominations. Particularly dominant in 1987, White gained recognition as the NFL Defensive Player of the Year by recording a league-leading and career-high 21 sacks in only 12 games.

Almost impossible to block one-on-one due to his size, strength, and quickness, the 6'5", 291-pound White typically found himself being engaged by multiple blockers. But, no matter how opposing teams tried to slow him down, White invariably forced them to alter their approach by creating havoc in the offensive backfield. In discussing how he prepared himself mentally to play against White, longtime New York Giants quarterback Phil Simms offered, "You didn't worry about going over your game plan. I truly would sit on my stool in the locker room going, 'OK now. Hang in there. Alright. You know, hang in there. It's going to be rough. Just, you know, come on, hang.' You had to give yourself a pep talk to be tough enough to endure what was going to happen, because it always did happen."

Simms then added, "He was the greatest, he was the most talented person I ever played against in the league, and you know I'm putting some unbelievable players in that category."

Simms and the rest of the quarterbacks in the NFC East undoubtedly breathed a huge sigh of relief when the 31-year-old White signed a four-year, $17 million free agent deal with the Packers following the conclusion of the 1992 campaign, after claiming that God told him to go to Green Bay. The first big-name free agent to switch teams, White made an enormous impact in his first year with the Packers, recording 13 sacks and 79 tackles, while also establishing himself as the team's vocal and spiritual leader.

Subsequently called "the cornerstone and foundation" of the Packers by the team's late defensive coordinator, Fritz Shurmur, White also drew praise from head coach Mike Holmgren, who attempted to put the star defensive end's 1993 performance in perspective by saying, "He made us a better football team—no question about it. We went from 23 on defense to two, with no noticeable dramatic personnel changes, except for one man. . . . One man changed your offensive thinking for the entire game."

As much as White contributed to the Packers on the playing field and in the locker room, he also helped change the attitude held toward the city of Green Bay throughout the league, particularly among black players, as team president Bob Harlan noted when he said, "Everyone thought the last place he would sign was Green Bay, and it was monumental because, not only did he sign, but he recruited for Green Bay and got guys like Sean

Jones to come here. He sent a message to the rest of the NFL that Green Bay was a great place to play."

Former NFL center Jamie Dukes, who White recruited for the Packers, recalled, "When I talked to Reggie, he said in that Reggie voice, 'Quit playing games and come win some football games.' Reggie saw all these positives about Green Bay that no one knew about. It was an oasis to play football. . . . There is no question, had Reggie not gone to Green Bay to make Green Bay cool, that wouldn't have happened. Prior to that, Green Bay wasn't on the menu of places you wanted to go."

Keith Jackson, who signed with the Packers as a free agent in 1995 after earlier spending four seasons playing with White in Philadelphia, agreed with Dukes's assessment, stating, "Reggie saw Green Bay as an opportunity to go somewhere where the people are super fans. And, when you lose a game, there's nobody screaming at you saying you're a bum. The media is reporting the facts and not trying to create controversy. It was actually an oasis to play football, and you really concentrated on being a football player."

Jackson then added, "You ask anybody that played there long enough, and they will tell you Green Bay was the best thing that happened to their careers. But nobody really wanted to see until Reggie said, 'God sent me to Green Bay.'"

Continuing to perform well in each of the next two seasons, White recorded eight sacks in 1994, before earning NFC Defensive Player of the Year honors the following season by registering a team-leading 12 sacks. He then recorded 8½ sacks during the championship campaign of 1996, before getting to Patriots quarterback Drew Bledsoe three times during Green Bay's 35–21 win over New England in Super Bowl XXXI.

Recalling the overall contributions that White made to the Packers' first NFL championship in nearly three decades, Mike Holmgren said, "Reggie was special, and he made Sean Jones special. He made Santana Dotson special. He made Gilbert Brown special. All those big guys that played up front, someone was gonna' be singled up because you had Reggie White on your side. . . . We had Favre leading the offense, but Reggie was the guy that kind of put it all together for us and allowed us to get to the Super Bowl . . . Reggie was a special player—one of the greatest players of all time."

White spent two more years with the Packers, recording 11 sacks for Green Bay's 1997 NFC championship team, before earning NFL Defensive Player of the Year honors for the second time in 1998 by finishing second in the league with 16 sacks. Choosing to announce his retirement at season's end, White ended his time in Green Bay with a total of 68½ sacks, which currently places him third in team annals. He also recorded 301 tackles

White retired with more career sacks than anyone else in NFL history.
Courtesy of MearsOnlineAuctions.com

(239 unassisted), one interception, 14 forced fumbles, and eight fumble recoveries.

After remaining away from the game for one year, White elected to come out of retirement and sign with the Carolina Panthers, for whom he recorded 5½ sacks in 2000, before retiring for good following the conclusion of the campaign. White ended his NFL career with 198 sacks, which leaves him second only to Bruce Smith in league history. However, his 23½ sacks as a member of the USFL's Memphis Showboats gives him a total of 221½ sacks as a professional, making him pro football's all-time sacks leader. White also recorded more than 1,100 tackles, intercepted three passes, forced 33 fumbles, and recovered 20 others, two of which he returned for touchdowns.

Unfortunately, White did not live long after his playing career ended, succumbing to cardiac arrhythmia on the morning of December 26, 2004, just one week after he celebrated his 43rd birthday. The Medical Examiner's Office subsequently speculated that the pulmonary sarcoidosis and sleep apnea from which White had suffered for years likely caused his death.

Upon learning of his passing, NFL commissioner Paul Tagliabue said, "Reggie White was a gentle warrior who will be remembered as one of the greatest defensive players in NFL history. Equally impressive as his achievements on the field was the positive impact he made off the field and the way he served as a positive influence on so many young people."

Mike Holmgren paid tribute to White by stating, "First of all, he was just a wonderful player. Then, as a person, he was just the best. He was one of the leaders, along with Brett Favre, of our football team in Green Bay. I'm a better person for having been around Reggie White."

Johnny Majors, who coached White at the University of Tennessee, commented, "He was one of the greatest players who ever put on a uniform at his position. I once referred to him as the Tony Dorsett of defensive linemen. There's never been a better one."

Brett Favre expressed his admiration for his former teammate by saying, "I had the utmost respect for Reggie White as a player. He may have been the best player I've ever seen, and he certainly was the best I've ever played with or against."

Choosing to waive the usual five-year waiting period, the Pro Football Hall of Fame opened its doors to White at its next induction ceremonies, admitting him posthumously in 2006.

In assessing his playing career, White once said, "The thing that I know, and everyone else knows, is that no one can ever take my accomplishments away. My goal as a football player was to be the best to ever play my position. I believe I've reached my goal." You will not find any disagreement with that statement here.

PACKERS CAREER HIGHLIGHTS

Best Season

It could be argued that White made his greatest overall impact in Green Bay in 1993, because, in his first year with the Packers, he helped transform their defense into one of the league's best by recording 13 sacks and 79 tackles. Nevertheless, the 1998 campaign is generally considered to be his finest as a member of the organization. En route to earning consensus First-Team All-Pro honors and recognition as the NFL's Defensive Player of the Year, White forced four fumbles and finished second in the league with 16 sacks, his highest total in 10 years.

Memorable Moments/Greatest Performances

White had a huge game against Denver on October 10, 1993, leading the Packers to a 30–27 victory over the Broncos by sacking John Elway three times.

White recorded two of the seven sacks the Packers registered against Jim Harbaugh during a 17–3 win over the Chicago Bears on October 31, 1993.

White earned NFC Defensive Player of the Week honors for the first of three times as a member of the Packers on November 14, 1993, when he tackled New Orleans quarterback Wade Wilson behind the line of scrimmage twice during a 19–17 win over the Saints.

White led a stifling Green Bay defense to a 28–0 shutout of the Los Angeles Raiders on December 26, 1993, by recording 2½ of the eight sacks the Packers registered against Raider quarterbacks Vince Evans and Jeff Hostetler.

With the Packers making their first playoff appearance in 11 years in the 1993 NFC wild card game, White helped lead the Packers to a 28–24 victory over the Lions by sacking Detroit quarterback Erik Kramer twice.

White recorded his only interception as a member of the Packers during a 31–10 win over the Seattle Seahawks on September 29, 1996, picking off a Rick Mirer pass and subsequently returning the ball 46 yards to the Seattle 21-yard line.

White contributed to a 13–7 victory over the Tampa Bay Buccaneers on October 27, 1996, by recording a sack and setting up a Chris Jacke field goal with a blocked punt.

White had another big game against Tampa Bay on September 13, 1998, earning NFC Defensive Player of the Week honors by sacking quarterback Trent Dilfer three times during a 23–15 victory over the Buccaneers.

White earned that distinction for the final time in his career on November 1, 1998, when he recorded three of the nine sacks the Packers registered against Steve Young during a 36–22 win over the San Francisco 49ers.

Still, there is little doubt that White experienced his finest moment as a member of the Packers when he helped lead them to a 35–21 victory over New England in Super Bowl XXXI by sacking Patriots quarterback Drew Bledsoe three times.

NOTABLE ACHIEVEMENTS

- Finished in double digits in sacks four times.
- Recorded 79 tackles in 1993.
- Finished second in NFL with 16 quarterback sacks in 1998.
- Led Packers in sacks five times.
- Ranks third in Packers history with 68½ career sacks.
- Ranks second in NFL history with 198 career sacks.
- Three-time division champion (1995, 1996, and 1997).
- Two-time NFC champion (1996 and 1997).
- Super Bowl XXXI champion.
- Three-time NFC Defensive Player of the Week.
- 1995 Associated Press NFC Defensive Player of the Year.
- 1998 Associated Press NFL Defensive Player of the Year.
- Six-time Pro Bowl selection (1993, 1994, 1995, 1996, 1997, and 1998).
- Two-time First-Team All-Pro (1995 and 1998).
- Three-time Second-Team All-Pro (1994, 1996, and 1997).
- Five-time First-Team All-NFC selection (1993, 1994, 1995, 1996, and 1998).
- NFL 1980s All-Decade Team.
- Pro Football Hall of Fame All-1980s First Team.
- NFL 1990s All-Decade Team.
- Pro Football Hall of Fame All-1990s First Team.
- Pro Football Reference All-1990s First Team.
- #92 retired by Packers.
- Named to NFL's 75th Anniversary All-Time Team in 1994.
- Number 22 on the *Sporting News'* 1999 list of 100 Greatest Players in NFL History.
- Number seven on NFL Films' 2010 list of 100 Greatest Players in NFL History.
- Elected to Pro Football Hall of Fame in 2006.

13

PAUL HORNUNG

The first man to win the Heisman Trophy, be selected with the first overall pick of the NFL Draft, be named the league's Most Valuable Player, and gain induction into both the Professional and College Football Halls of Fame, Paul Hornung perhaps contributed more than anyone else to the success the Packers experienced their first few seasons under Vince Lombardi. An extremely versatile player who excelled as both a runner and a receiver, Hornung also did an outstanding job of blocking for backfield mate Jim Taylor, delivering the halfback option pass with accuracy, and driving the ball through the uprights as Green Bay's placekicker—a role he assumed in six of his nine years with the Packers. A three-time NFL scoring champion, Hornung had a "nose for the end zone," scoring at least 10 touchdowns in a season twice, more than 100 points in a season three times, and at least four touchdowns in a game on two separate occasions. In addition to earning 1961 NFL MVP honors with his superb all-around play, Hornung earned two trips to the Pro Bowl and three All-Pro selections, helping the Packers win five Western Conference championships, four NFL titles, and one Super Bowl in the process. And, following the conclusion of his playing career, the man who became known as "The Golden Boy" for his good looks and seemingly charmed life received the additional honors of being named to both the NFL 1960s All-Decade Team and the Packers 50th Anniversary Team.

Born in Louisville, Kentucky, on December 23, 1935, Paul Vernon Hornung first displayed his exceptional all-around athletic ability while attending local Bishop Benedict Joseph Flaget High School, lettering four years each in football, baseball, and basketball. Although Paul "Bear" Bryant subsequently recruited him to play for the University of Kentucky in nearby Lexington, Hornung instead elected to enroll at the University of Notre Dame, where he spent his sophomore season of 1954 serving as a backup fullback. Moved to halfback and safety the following year, Hornung emerged as one of the finest players in the nation, amassing 1,215 yards of

Paul Hornung teamed up with Jim Taylor to give the Packers the NFL's top running-back tandem during the early 1960s.
Courtesy of RMYAuctions.com

total offense and scoring six touchdowns. After being shifted to quarterback prior to the start of his senior year, Hornung performed so well that he ended up winning the Heisman Trophy, even though the Fighting Irish finished the season just 2-8. Accumulating 1,337 yards of total offense, Hornung led his team in passing, rushing, scoring, kickoff and punt returns, and punting. An outstanding defender as well, Hornung also led the Irish in passes broken up and placed second on the team in interceptions and tackles made, establishing himself in the process as arguably the greatest all-around player in the school's rich history.

Having graduated from Notre Dame with a degree in business, Hornung subsequently became the first overall pick of the 1957 NFL Draft when the Packers tabbed him with a bonus selection. After experiencing so much individual success in college, Hornung began his professional career in somewhat ignominious fashion, spending his first two seasons in Green Bay serving as placekicker and part-time fullback for a Packers team that compiled an overall record of just 4-19-1. However, following the arrival of Vince Lombardi in 1959, the fortunes of Hornung and the Packers both changed dramatically.

Assigned the role of starting halfback by Lombardi, Hornung teamed up with fullback Jim Taylor the next few seasons to give the Packers the NFL's top running-back tandem. With Hornung functioning as "Mr. Outside" and Taylor as "Mr. Inside," the Packers placed in the league's top three in rushing six straight times, ranking number one in the circuit on three separate occasions. Running effectively behind arguably the league's best offensive line, Hornung and Taylor ran Lombardi's "Packer Sweep" to perfection, blocking for one another and catching passes out of the backfield as well. Proving to be particularly versatile, the 6'2", 210-pound Hornung emerged as a triple-threat on offense, excelling as a runner, receiver, and occasional passer, while also consistently ranking among the league leaders in field goals made and field goal percentage. Playing his best ball for the Packers from 1959 to 1961, Hornung compiled the following numbers over the course of those three seasons:

YEAR	RUSH YDS	REC YDS	RUSH TDS	TOTAL TDS	POINTS
1959	681	113	7	7	**94**
1960	671	257	**13**	**15**	**176**
1961	597	145	8	10	**146**

In addition to leading the NFL in points scored all three years, Hornung annually ranked among the league leaders in rushing touchdowns and total touchdowns scored, topping the circuit in each of those categories as well in 1960. He also completed five touchdown passes during that time, with his fabulous all-around play earning him two Pro Bowl selections, three consecutive All-Pro nominations, and NFL MVP and Player of the Year honors in 1961. Meanwhile, after improving their record to 7-5 in the first of those campaigns, the Packers claimed the Western Conference title in 1960 and the NFL championship the following year.

Hornung's outstanding play in all phases of the game, which once prompted Vince Lombardi to call him "the most versatile man who ever played the game," earned him the undying respect and admiration of his head coach, who author George Sullivan quoted in his book, *The Great Running Backs*, as saying, "You have to know what Hornung means to this team. I have heard and read that he is not a great runner, or a great passer, or a great field-goal kicker, but he led the league in scoring for three seasons. In the middle of the field, he may be only slightly better than an average ballplayer, but, inside the 20-yard line, he is one of the greatest I have ever seen. He smells that goal line."

Bart Starr also greatly appreciated everything Hornung brought to the team, suggesting, "I'm not sure enough people realize how talented this man was. Not only was he a Heisman Trophy winner, he was an excellent runner, he was an excellent blocker, he was a great pass receiver, he threw our option pass very, very well, and he was an outstanding kicker. Everything we called on him to do, he excelled at."

Even President John F. Kennedy held Hornung in extremely high esteem. Called into active duty during the 1961 season, Hornung ended up missing two games, although his weekend passes allowed him to play most Sundays. But, with the NFL championship game vs. the New York Giants rapidly approaching, his availability for that contest remained uncertain. Placing a call to the president, Vince Lombardi arranged with his friend to grant Hornung Christmas leave from the Army, after which Kennedy said, "Paul Hornung isn't going to win the war on Sunday, but the football fans of this country deserve the two best teams on the field that day." Hornung went on to lead the Packers to a 37–0 thrashing of the Giants by scoring 19 points, on one rushing touchdown, three field goals, and four PATs. Recalling the inspiration that Hornung provided to his teammates that day, Henry Jordan told Michael O'Brien in the latter's Lombardi biography entitled *Vince*, "When Paul got that leave from the Army and walked into that locker room, you could just feel the confidence grow in that room."

Extremely popular off the field as well, Hornung developed a reputation during his time in Green Bay as a real ladies' man who John M. Ross once described in *America Weekly* as a "205-pound Adonis who constantly runs the risk of becoming the first player in history to be carried triumphantly from the field on the soft shoulders of a shrieking female horde." Availing himself of the city's nightlife, Hornung frequently found himself being fined by Vince Lombardi for rules infractions, even though the Packers' head coach perhaps felt closer to him than any other member of the team. Despite being a Victorian at heart, Lombardi secretly admired the brazenness and tremendous self-confidence that the town's most eligible bachelor displayed with members of the opposite sex. Lombardi also appreciated Hornung's leadership ability, which he often exhibited by taking the team's younger players with him on his speaking engagements and then splitting his fee with them. More than anything, though, Lombardi admired Hornung for his performance, dedication, and ability to excel under pressure, which the latter addressed when he said, "This game is more mental than physical. . . . It's the guys who are right mentally who come out on top. It's the guys who don't make the big mistakes who win. Maybe that's why I do well in big games. When the pressure's on, guys get tight. By my very nature, I'm a loose character. . . . In the big games, I make less mistakes than some other guy."

Those very same qualities endeared Hornung to his Packer teammates, with Jerry Kramer writing in his book, *Distant Replay*, "Paul was always the star of our team. We all loved Paul." Kramer then added, "He became what he had to be to make us successful. Paul could do it all, and he did love to score—both on the field and off it."

However, Hornung's penchant for high-living ultimately proved to be his undoing. After appearing in only nine games in 1962 due to an assortment of injuries, Hornung suffered the indignity of being suspended from football indefinitely by NFL commissioner Pete Rozelle in April 1963 for betting on NFL games and associating with undesirable persons. He subsequently missed the entire 1963 season, before being reinstated prior to the start of the 1964 campaign, with Lombardi's constant lobbying of Rozelle contributing greatly to his return. In exchange for Lombardi's efforts, Hornung agreed not to have anything to do with gambling, to stay out of Las Vegas, and to forego attending the Kentucky Derby, which he typically frequented every year.

Unfortunately, Hornung never regained his earlier form after he returned to the Packers in 1964, rushing for only 914 yards and scoring just 18 touchdowns over the course of the next three seasons. Plagued by injuries much of the time, Hornung spent most of 1965 and 1966 coming off the bench, although he did manage to gain 635 yards from scrimmage and score eight touchdowns in the first of those campaigns, with five of his TDs coming during a late-season victory over the Baltimore Colts that helped the Packers clinch the Western Conference title. After Hornung sat out Super Bowl I with a pinched nerve in his neck, the Packers, thinking that no team would want an injured player, left him unprotected in the

Hornung, seen here with Bart Starr, led the NFL in scoring three straight times.
Courtesy of LegendaryAuctions.com

1967 NFL Expansion Draft. However, the New Orleans Saints selected him, bringing his 10-year stay in Green Bay to an end. Although Hornung initially intended to join the Saints, a subsequent medical examination revealed that the nerve injury to his neck represented a serious threat to his permanent health. Told by doctors that continued play might result in paralysis, Hornung chose to retire, ending his career with 3,711 yards rushing, 50 rushing touchdowns, an average of 4.2 yards per carry, 130 receptions, 1,480 receiving yards, 12 receiving touchdowns, 383 yards passing, five touchdown passes, 66 field goals, 190 successfully converted point-after attempts, and 760 points scored, with the last figure representing the fifth-highest total in franchise history. Hornung also ranks among the Packers' all-time leaders in rushing yardage (9th), rushing touchdowns (3rd), and total touchdowns (5th).

Following his playing days, Hornung began a career in broadcasting, serving as an analyst for Notre Dame and other college games. He also made several wise real estate investments in the Louisville area and abandoned his bachelor lifestyle, marrying twice—once in 1967 and again in 1980. Hornung, whose earlier neck injury left him with limited use of his right arm, currently suffers from dementia, likely brought on by the multiple concussions he incurred during his career. In summing up his legacy, Hornung once said, "I was very fortunate. I don't look back and say I was a special type of player. I think I did okay. I don't have many regrets, but I think you get to the point after you quit that, after a while, you're done being a celebrity. You don't want it anymore. Sometimes you wish you weren't Paul Hornung. Still, it's been pretty nice being Paul Hornung."

PACKERS CAREER HIGHLIGHTS

Best Season

Hornung performed brilliantly for the Packers in 1961, earning NFL MVP honors and his second consecutive First-Team All-Pro selection by gaining 597 yards on the ground and another 145 yards on 15 pass receptions, scoring 10 touchdowns, and leading the league with 146 points scored. However, he compiled better overall numbers the previous season, when he gained a career-best 928 yards from scrimmage, led the league with 13 rushing touchdowns, 15 total touchdowns, and 176 points scored, successfully converted 15 field goal attempts and all 41 of his extra-point attempts, and completed a pair of touchdown passes, thereby having a hand in 188 of the 332 total points the Packers scored on the year. Hornung's 176 points remained an NFL record until LaDainian Tomlinson tallied 186 points for the San Diego Chargers in 2006.

Memorable Moments/Greatest Performances

Hornung rushed for more than 100 yards for the first time in his career during a 21–20 win over the 49ers on October 11, 1959, carrying the ball 28 times for 138 yards and one touchdown.

Hornung displayed his tremendous versatility during a 38–20 win over the Los Angeles Rams on December 6, 1959, carrying the ball 11 times for

74 yards, throwing touchdown passes of 26 and 30 yards to Boyd Dowler, and kicking a 23-yard field goal.

Hornung led the Packers to a 36–14 victory over the 49ers in the 1959 regular-season finale by carrying the ball 15 times for 83 yards and three touchdowns, with the longest of those being a 13-yard scamper.

Although the Packers lost their November 20, 1960, matchup with the Rams by a score of 33–31, Hornung starred in defeat, rushing for 47 yards and two touchdowns, catching two passes for another 45 yards, completing an 18-yard TD pass to Boyd Dowler, and kicking a 12-yard field goal.

Hornung once again exhibited the totality of his game during a 41–13 victory over the Bears on December 4, 1960, rushing for 68 yards, gaining another 32 yards on three pass receptions, scoring a pair of touchdowns, and successfully converting field goal attempts of 21 and 41 yards.

Hornung gave the Packers all the offense they needed to defeat the 49ers 13–0 on December 10, 1960, scoring all 13 of their points on a 28-yard run and a pair of field goals, while gaining 86 yards on the ground and another 25 yards on four pass receptions.

Hornung turned in arguably the finest all-around performance of his career on October 8, 1961, when he scored a franchise-record 33 points during a 45–7 blowout of the Baltimore Colts. In addition to scoring four touchdowns during the contest, with one of those coming on a season-long 54-yard run, Hornung successfully converted one field goal attempt and six extra points, carried the ball 11 times for 111 yards, and caught three passes for 28 yards.

Hornung turned in another superb all-around effort a few weeks later, leading the Packers to a 31–28 win over the Bears on November 12, 1961, by carrying the ball 22 times for 94 yards and one touchdown, making a 34-yard TD reception, and kicking a 51-yard field goal.

Hornung set an NFL championship game scoring record in 1961, when he tallied 19 points during the Packers' lopsided 37–0 victory over the New York Giants. In addition to carrying the ball 20 times for a game-high 89 yards and one touchdown, Hornung caught three passes for 47 yards and kicked three field goals and four extra points.

Continuing his brilliant all-around play in 1962, Hornung led the Packers to a convincing 34–7 victory over the Minnesota Vikings in the regular-season opener by carrying the ball 10 times for 67 yards and three touchdowns, completing a 41-yard pass to Boyd Dowler, and successfully converting two field goal attempts and four extra points, scoring in the process a total of 28 points.

Hornung also proved to be a huge factor in the final game of the 1962 regular season, collaborating with Bart Starr on a career-long 83-yard touchdown reception during the Packers' 20–17 win over the Rams.

Yet, Hornung turned in one of his most memorable performances during the latter stages of his career, ironically doing so in a game he didn't even expect to start. With the Packers facing the Baltimore Colts in a showdown for first place in the NFL Western Conference on December 12, 1965, Hornung, who scored just three touchdowns in the season's first 12 games after assuming a backup role, found himself starting alongside Jim Taylor in the Green Bay backfield. Rising to the occasion, the former Heisman Trophy winner set a franchise record by scoring five touchdowns, in leading the Packers to a 42–27 victory. In addition to rushing for three scores, Hornung hooked up with Bart Starr on a pair of long TD receptions that covered 50 and 65 yards. Although Hornung's five touchdowns ended up being overshadowed somewhat by the six TDs Gale Sayers tallied for the Bears against San Francisco later that same day, they helped the Packers lay claim to the Western Conference title. Hornung again starred during Green Bay's 23–12 win over Cleveland in the NFL championship game, carrying the ball 18 times for 105 yards and one touchdown.

NOTABLE ACHIEVEMENTS

- Rushed for more than 10 touchdowns once (13 in 1960).
- Scored more than 10 touchdowns twice.
- Scored more than 100 points three times.
- Averaged more than 4.5 yards per carry four times, topping five yards per carry once (5.3 in 1957).
- Amassed more than 250 receiving yards twice.
- Led NFL in: rushing touchdowns once; touchdowns scored once; and points scored three times.
- Finished second in NFL in field goals made once and field goal percentage twice.
- Finished third in NFL with eight rushing touchdowns in 1961.
- Led Packers in rushing twice.
- Holds NFL records for most games with at least 30 points scored (2) and most games with at least 25 points scored (3).
- Holds Packers single-game record for most points scored (33 vs. Baltimore Colts on 10/8/61).

- Holds Packers single-season record for most points scored (176 in 1960).
- Ranks among Packers career leaders with: 3,711 yards rushing (9th); 50 rushing touchdowns (3rd); 62 touchdowns scored (tied—6th); and 760 points scored (5th).
- Five-time Western Conference champion (1960, 1961, 1962, 1965, and 1966).
- Four-time NFL champion (1961, 1962, 1965, and 1966).
- Super Bowl I champion.
- 1961 NFL MVP.
- 1961 Bert Bell Award winner as NFL Player of the Year.
- Named Outstanding Player of 1961 NFL Championship Game.
- Two-time Pro Bowl selection (1959 and 1960).
- Two-time First-Team All-Pro (1960 and 1961).
- 1959 Second-Team All-Pro.
- Two-time All–Western Conference First-Team selection (1960 and 1961).
- NFL 1960s All-Decade Team.
- Pro Football Hall of Fame All-1960s Team.
- Named to Packers 50th Anniversary Team in 1969.
- Elected to Pro Football Hall of Fame in 1986.

14

JIM RINGO

—   —

enerally considered to be the finest center of his era, Jim Ringo spent 11 of his 15 NFL seasons in Green Bay, earning Pro Bowl and All-Pro honors seven times each during that time. Persevering through perhaps the most difficult period in franchise history, Ringo survived the dark days of the 1950s to serve as a captain on the Packers' first two championship teams under Vince Lombardi. Relying on his intelligence, intensity, and quickness, Ringo overcame his relative lack of size to establish himself as one of the most important members of a Packers team that captured three straight Western Conference titles and two consecutive NFL champion-ships during the early 1960s, earning in the process spots on the NFL 1960s All-Decade Team and the Packers 50th Anniversary Team. And, after being traded to the Eagles, Ringo continued his outstanding play in Philadelphia, earning three more Pro Bowl selections and two more All-Pro nominations. Yet, ironically, it is for the manner in which he left Green Bay that Ringo is best remembered.

Born in Orange, New Jersey, on November 21, 1931, James Stephen Ringo grew up some 56 miles west, in the town of Phillipsburg, where he starred in football while attending Phillipsburg High School. After earning All-State honors as a center in his senior year of 1948, Ringo accepted an athletic scholarship from Syracuse University, which he entered still two months shy of his 18th birthday. Standing 6'1" tall and weighing less than 200 pounds upon his arrival at the Syracuse campus, Ringo nevertheless proved to be a capable two-way player for the Orangemen, performing well enough on both sides of the ball to be chosen by the Packers in the seventh round of the 1953 NFL Draft, with the 80th overall pick.

Still weighing only 211 pounds by the time he arrived at the Packers' training camp in Grand Rapids, Minnesota, Ringo soon became discour-aged by the much larger men he found himself competing against and the camp's militaristic rules, prompting him to return home. However, after being chastised by the members of his family, who told him, in his own

Jim Ringo proved to be the NFL's top center of his day, earning Pro
Bowl and All-Pro honors seven times each as a member of the Packers.
Courtesy of RMYAuctions.com

words, that "they didn't want a quitter," Ringo returned to the Packers, with
whom he eventually earned a roster spot, spending his rookie campaign
serving as a backup to starting center Dave Stephenson.

Having bulked up to more than 225 pounds during the subsequent
offseason, Ringo laid claim to the starting center job in 1954, beginning in
the process a string of 14 straight seasons in which he started every game at
that position for his team. Although the Packers remained one of the NFL's
worst clubs the next few years, compiling an overall record of just 18-41-1

from 1954 to 1958, Ringo gradually emerged as one of the league's top centers, earning consecutive trips to the Pro Bowl and his first two All-Pro selections in 1957 and 1958.

The situation in Green Bay changed dramatically once Vince Lombardi assumed control of the team in 1959, with the Packers subsequently establishing themselves as an NFL powerhouse. Commenting on the impact Lombardi made, Ringo stated, "Everything was completely different. This man came in a complete unknown and turned everything around. The man was just one of the greatest coaches you'll ever find; a great philosopher and a great man."

With Lombardi building his offense around Ringo, who weighed 235 pounds by the time his new coach arrived, the team's center flourished, earning Pro Bowl and consensus First-Team All-Pro honors five straight times from 1959 to 1963 after being named co-captain. Using his speed, mobility, football intelligence, and outstanding technique to dominate his opponents, Ringo proved to be an ideal blocker for Lombardi's famous power sweep. Quick on his feet, good with his hands, and blessed with tremendous balance, Ringo also excelled in pass protection, with former teammate Willie Davis once commenting, "What tenacity he had as a center in the NFL. Probably, no one was better."

Doing a superb job of picking off the middle linebacker on plays up the middle or burying the defensive tackle on sweeps, Ringo also drew praise from Coach Lombardi, who stated on one occasion, "A bigger man might not be able to make the cut-off blocks on our sweeps the way Jim does. The reason Ringo's the best in the league is because he's quick and he's smart. He runs the offensive line, calls the blocks, and he knows what every lineman does on every play."

Ringo's exceptional blocking helped lead the Packers to consecutive NFL titles in 1961 and 1962, with the center later noting, "That experience was just incredible. To be a champion in a community that small was something else. No matter where you went, somebody knew you. You'd walk down the street and people would say hi and want to talk about the Packers."

Yet, despite his tremendous popularity and outstanding play on the field, Ringo found himself headed for Philadelphia following a bizarre series of events that allegedly took place prior to the start of the 1964 campaign. According to teammate Jerry Kramer's account in his book *Instant Replay*, Ringo enlisted the services of an agent to negotiate a new contract for him with Vince Lombardi. Upset over being introduced to a player's agent for the first time, Lombardi asked the agent to step outside for five minutes,

Ringo anchored the Packers' offensive line on their first two
championship teams under Vince Lombardi.
Courtesy of MearsOnlineAuctions.com

after which he informed him that he needed to talk to the Eagles instead,
because he had just traded Ringo to Philadelphia.

However, over the years, it has been suggested that there is little truth to
the story. With the Packers also sending fullback Earl Gros to Philadelphia
in a deal that netted them linebacker Lee Roy Caffey and a first-round draft
pick in return, it seems likely that Lombardi had actually been negotiating
that trade with the Eagles for some time. Furthermore, Ringo himself once
said, "I didn't have an agent. They were only for the elite players back then.

I really don't know how that story got going. Sometimes people create their own stories and such fallacies are not good things." Nevertheless, Ringo attained a certain level of immortality as a result.

After leaving the Packers, Ringo, who started 126 consecutive regular-season games as a member of the team, spent his final four years in the league with the Eagles, starting another 56 straight games with them during that time. Looking back at the trade that sent him to Philadelphia, Ringo stated, "My life was back on the East Coast. So it was nice to get back there. I commuted back and forth every day and never had to move out of the house. It was ideal for me."

Choosing to announce his retirement following the conclusion of the 1967 campaign after earning three more Pro Bowl selections and a pair of Second-Team All-Pro nominations as a member of the Eagles, Ringo went on to serve on the coaching staffs of the Los Angeles Rams, Buffalo Bills, Chicago Bears, New England Patriots, and New York Jets, experiencing his greatest success in Buffalo, where he helped build the dominant offensive line that eventually became known as "The Electric Company." Elected to the Pro Football Hall of Fame in 1981, Ringo retired from football seven years later, after which he moved to Chesapeake, Virginia. Ringo, who suffered from Alzheimer's disease later in life, died of pneumonia on November 19, 2007, just two days shy of his 76th birthday. Following his passing, Hall of Fame resident/executive director Steve Perry wrote, "As Vince Lombardi once observed, Jim epitomized the toughness and determination needed to not only play the center position, but to become one of the game's most dominant offensive linemen of his era."

PACKERS CAREER HIGHLIGHTS

Best Season

Although Ringo earned consensus First-Team All-Pro honors five straight times from 1959 to 1963, he turned in his most notable performance for the Packers in 1957, when, despite playing for a team that concluded the campaign with a record of just 3-9 and spending the better part of five weeks being hospitalized for mononucleosis, only being released to play on weekends, he earned Pro Bowl and All-Pro honors for the first time in his career.

Memorable Moments/Greatest Performances

Serving as the team's offensive captain for much of his time in Green Bay, Ringo anchored an offensive line that enabled Packer running backs to gain a season-high 255 yards on the ground during a 28–9 win over the Detroit Lions on October 2, 1960.

Ringo also excelled against the Giants in the 1961 NFL title game, helping the Packer offense amass a total of 345 yards, 181 of which came on the ground.

NOTABLE ACHIEVEMENTS

- Played in 126 consecutive games.
- Three-time Western Conference champion (1960, 1961, and 1962).
- Two-time NFL champion (1961 and 1962).
- Seven-time Pro Bowl selection (1957, 1958, 1959, 1960, 1961, 1962, and 1963).
- Six-time First-Team All-Pro (1957, 1959, 1960, 1961, 1962, and 1963).
- 1958 Second-Team All-Pro.
- Five-time All–Western Conference First-Team selection (1958, 1959, 1960, 1961, and 1962).
- NFL 1960s All-Decade Team.
- Pro Football Hall of Fame All-1960s Team.
- Pro Football Reference All-1950s Second Team.
- Pro Football Reference All-1960s First Team.
- Named to Packers 50th Anniversary Team in 1969.
- Elected to Pro Football Hall of Fame in 1981.

15

HENRY JORDAN

The fifth member of Vince Lombardi's defense to be inducted into the Pro Football Hall of Fame, Henry Jordan joined former teammates Herb Adderley, Willie Davis, Ray Nitschke, and Willie Wood in Canton after spending 11 seasons anchoring the middle of Green Bay's defensive line. Joining the Packers in 1959 after spending the previous two years in Cleveland, Jordan contributed mightily to the success Lombardi's squad experienced during the 1960s, using his speed, strength, and determination to excel in the trenches. Although often overlooked in favor of some of his more glamorous teammates, Jordan helped lead the Packers to six Western Conference championships, five NFL titles, and two Super Bowl wins, earning in the process four Pro Bowl selections and six All-Pro nominations. Jordan's strong play at right tackle also earned him spots on the Packers 50th Anniversary Team in 1969 and the NFL's 75th Anniversary All-Time Team in 1994.

Born in Emporia, Virginia, on January 26, 1935, Henry Wendell Jordan starred on the gridiron while attending Warwick High School. Following his graduation in 1953, he enrolled at the University of Virginia, where he excelled in multiple sports, serving as captain of the Cavaliers' football team as a senior, while also earning All-America honors in wrestling by winning the ACC Championship and finishing runner-up in the heavyweight class of the 1957 NCAA Championships.

Subsequently selected by Cleveland in the fifth round of the 1957 NFL Draft, with the 52nd overall pick, Jordan spent his first two years in the league serving the Browns as a backup defensive tackle and special teams player, before being acquired by the Packers for a fourth-round draft pick prior to the start of the 1959 campaign in one of Vince Lombardi's first moves as general manager and head coach. Immediately inserted at right defensive tackle upon his arrival in Green Bay, Jordan soon became a fixture at that post, starting 134 out of a possible 136 contests over the course of the next 10 seasons.

Henry Jordan's superior play on the interior of Green Bay's defensive line earned him four trips to the Pro Bowl and six All-Pro nominations. Courtesy of RMYAuctions.com

Strong and quick, the 6'2", 248-pound Jordan used his wrestling background to gain leverage against his opponent, as teammate Jerry Kramer noted when he said, "If you would start guessing with Henry, you would get in trouble. He was so damn quick. He was a little like Artie Donovan in that he would read you a little bit and give you a move and go. . . . Plus Henry was a NCAA wrestling champ, or close to it, at Virginia, so he used the things that made him a great wrestler when he got to the NFL. Things like strength and quickness, plus using leverage at the right time."

Kramer added, "Henry was a very bright fellow. He had extreme quickness. He was small for a defensive tackle, but he had great quickness, and he survived on his quickness. He was also pretty strong, but his quickness was outstanding."

Jordan missed only two games his first 10 years with the Packers.
Courtesy of RMYAuctions.com

Jordan used his quickness and intelligence to establish himself as one of the NFL's top defensive tackles, earning four trips to the Pro Bowl and five consecutive First-Team All-Pro selections between 1960 and 1966. Helping the Packers win five NFL titles during his time in Green Bay, Jordan made huge contributions to a defense that allowed just 10.5 points per game to the opposition in 1962, and another that surrendered only 11.6 points per game to their opponents in 1966.

Excelling against both the run and the pass, Jordan drew praise from Baltimore Colts Hall of Fame offensive lineman Jim Parker, who claimed, "After I play Green Bay, my ankles hurt all week. I had to stay on the balls of my feet against Henry because I never knew what he was going to do next. Other tackles don't have Henry's moves."

Fellow Hall of Famer Willie Davis, who spent 10 seasons playing alongside Jordan on Green Bay's defensive line, discussed the qualities that made his longtime teammate so successful, stating, "Jordan had the good quickness as an inside rusher, but he very seldom overpowered someone. He would just kind of slither through a crack or, almost off a movement of quickness, he was able to penetrate. He was very slender, and he could take a seam and split two offensive linemen. . . . He had very big and strong legs, and I think, once he was able to split two guys, he was able to really power his way between them."

Extremely popular with his teammates, Jordan also became known for his sense of humor and quick wit during his time in Green Bay, with two of his most notable quips focusing on Vince Lombardi, of whom he said, "He treats us all alike—like dogs," and "When Lombardi says, 'Sit down,' I don't look for a chair."

Unfortunately, after Jordan missed just two games his first 12 years in the league, injuries limited him to only five contests in 1969, prompting him to announce his retirement prior to the start of the ensuing campaign. In addition to his four Pro Bowl selections and six All-Pro nominations, Jordan earned All–Western Conference First-Team honors three times during his time in Green Bay.

Following his retirement, Jordan moved to Milwaukee, where he helped oversee Wisconsin's popular annual music festival Summerfest. Seven years later, on February 21, 1977, he died of a heart attack he suffered following a workout at the Milwaukee Athletic Club. After collapsing in a restroom at the facility, Jordan had oxygen and heart massage administered to him, to no avail. He was only 42 years old at the time of his passing.

PACKERS CAREER HIGHLIGHTS

Best Season

Jordan earned Pro Bowl and First-Team All-Pro honors for the first time in 1960, when he finished second in the NFL with a career-high five fumble recoveries. He earned another trip to the Pro Bowl and consensus First-Team All-Pro honors for one of two times in 1963, when he once again ranked among the league leaders with four fumble recoveries. Nevertheless, Jordan made a greater overall impact in both 1962 and 1966, when he helped anchor a Packers defense that surrendered fewer than 12 points per game to the opposition both years. Because Jordan made First-Team All-Pro in the first of those campaigns and only earned a spot on the Second Team in the other, we'll identify 1962 as his finest all-around season.

Memorable Moments/Greatest Performances

Jordan scored the only touchdown of his career during a 45–21 win over the Dallas Cowboys on November 29, 1964, when he recovered a fumble and rumbled 60 yards for a TD in the second quarter.

In addition to anchoring a defense that surrendered just 37 yards on the ground to the Giants all day, Jordan contributed to the Packers' lopsided 37–0 victory over New York in the 1961 NFL championship game by tipping a Y. A. Tittle pass into the arms of Ray Nitschke, whose interception led to Green Bay's second TD of the game.

Jordan came up with another big play during the Packers' 23–12 win over the Browns in the 1965 NFL title tilt, blocking a third-quarter field goal attempt by Cleveland's Lou Groza.

Continuing to excel in postseason play in 1966, Jordan sacked Don Meredith once during the Packers' victory over Dallas in the NFL championship game, before recording another 1½ sacks, making six tackles, and tipping a pass that Willie Wood intercepted during their win over Kansas City in Super Bowl I.

Jordan again starred in the playoffs the following year, recording 3½ sacks of Los Angeles quarterback Roman Gabriel during the Packers' 28–7 victory over the Rams in the battle for the 1967 Western Conference championship.

NOTABLE ACHIEVEMENTS

- Scored one defensive touchdown during career on a fumble return.
- Finished second in NFL with five fumble recoveries in 1960.
- Finished third in NFL with 60 fumble-return yards in 1964.
- Ranks fourth in Packers history with 20 fumble recoveries.
- Six-time Western Conference champion (1960, 1961, 1962, 1965, 1966, and 1967).
- Five-time NFL champion (1961, 1962, 1965, 1966, and 1967).
- Two-time Super Bowl champion (I and II).

- Named Outstanding Lineman of 1961 Pro Bowl.
- Four-time Pro Bowl selection (1960, 1961, 1963, and 1966).
- Five-time First-Team All-Pro (1960, 1961, 1962, 1963, and 1964).
- 1966 Second Team All-Pro.
- Three-time All–Western Conference First-Team selection (1961, 1962, and 1963).
- Pro Football Reference All-1960s First Team.
- Named to Packers 50th Anniversary Team in 1969.
- Named to NFL's 75th Anniversary All-Time Team in 1994.
- Elected to Pro Football Hall of Fame in 1995.

16

— JERRY KRAMER —

The man who delivered perhaps the most famous block in NFL history, Jerry Kramer earned a permanent place in Packers lore when he led Bart Starr into the end zone for the winning touchdown in the closing moments of the 1967 NFL championship game. Yet, even though that single play made a household name out of someone who manned one of the most anonymous positions in professional sports, Kramer accomplished a great deal more over the course of his 11-year career, all of which he spent with the Packers. A three-time Pro Bowler and six-time All-Pro, Kramer served as a key figure in Green Bay's ascension to elite status among NFL teams, with his exceptional lead blocking helping the Packers win six Western Conference championships, five NFL titles, and two Super Bowls. Generally considered to be one of the finest pulling guards in league history, Kramer also earned spots on the NFL 1960s All-Decade Team, the Packers 50th Anniversary Team, the NFL's 50th Anniversary Team, and, finally in 2018, 45 years after he first became eligible for induction, a place in the Pro Football Hall of Fame.

Born in Jordan, Montana, on January 23, 1936, Gerald Louis Kramer moved with his parents and five siblings from northern Utah to northern Idaho at the age of 10. After settling with his family in the city of Sandpoint, Kramer attended Sandpoint High School, where he starred on the gridiron, prompting the University of Idaho to offer him a football scholarship. Excelling as an offensive lineman under head coach Skip Stahley while in college, Kramer subsequently found himself being selected by the Packers in the fourth round of the 1958 NFL Draft, with the 39th overall pick.

Although Kramer appeared in every game for the Packers as a rookie in 1958, he didn't start any of them, serving the team primarily as a reserve who played mostly on special teams. However, with Vince Lombardi taking over as head coach the following year, Kramer laid claim to the starting right guard job, which he retained for the remainder of his career.

Jerry Kramer spent his entire 11-year career in Green Bay.
Courtesy of MearsOnlineAuctions.com

Struggling somewhat with his confidence his first season under Lombardi, Kramer experienced the usual highs and lows of any first-year, full-time starter in 1959. But, under Lombardi's constant prodding and cajoling, Kramer soon realized his full potential, earning First-Team All-Pro honors for the first of five times in 1960 after helping the Packers capture the Western Conference title. In addressing the outstanding performance of his right guard, Lombardi said, "Jerry Kramer did not know how good he was when he first joined the Green Bay Packers. You'd be surprised how much confidence a little success will bring."

Hampered by a badly injured ankle in 1961, Kramer started only eight games, preventing him from earning any postseason honors. But he appeared in the Pro Bowl and made First-Team All-Pro in each of the next two seasons, when, in addition to doing an outstanding job of protecting quarterback Bart Starr and blocking for running backs Jim Taylor, Paul Hornung, Tom Moore, and Elijah Pitts, he served as the Packers' primary placekicker, leading the NFL in field goal percentage in 1962, before finishing fourth in the league with 91 points scored the following year.

Standing 6'3" tall and weighing 245 pounds, Kramer possessed only average size for an offensive lineman of the day. However, his speed and quickness enabled him to excel as a downfield blocker, making him particularly effective in escorting running backs around end when the Packers chose to run their famous "Power Sweep." Praising Kramer in a 1969 article that appeared in the *Chicago Tribune*, Vince Lombardi proclaimed, "Jerry Kramer is the best guard in the league. Some say the best in the history of the game."

After being diagnosed at the Mayo Clinic with actinomycosis during the early stages of the 1964 campaign, Kramer ended up starting just two games, contributing to the Packers' failure to win their third league championship in four years. However, a return to full health the following year enabled Kramer to begin a string of four straight seasons in which he started every game at right guard for the Packers. And, over the course of those four seasons, he appeared in one Pro Bowl and earned three All-Pro nominations, helping the Packers claim three more NFL titles in the process. Experiencing his finest moment in the final seconds of 1967's Ice Bowl, Kramer helped give the Packers a dramatic 21–17 victory over the Cowboys when he drove Dallas defensive tackle Jethro Pugh into the end zone from the 1-yard line, enabling Bart Starr to cross the goal-line with the winning score. Kramer's memorable block led to the release of his first book, the best-selling *Instant Replay*, a season-long diary that chronicled the life of a professional football offensive lineman.

Having undergone 22 surgeries during his 11 years in the league, Kramer decided to retire after the Packers finished just 6-7-1 under new head coach Phil Bengtson in 1968. In addition to his outstanding blocking as an offensive lineman, Kramer successfully converted 29 out of 54 field goal attempts and 90 out of 95 extra-point attempts over the course of his career, scoring a total of 177 points in the process.

Kramer delivered the most famous block in NFL history in the Ice Bowl.
Courtesy of MearsOnlineAuctions.com

Shortly after Kramer retired, he began work on a second book, which he called *Farewell to Football*. Kramer also briefly worked as a color commentator on CBS NFL telecasts, before editing the book, *Lombardi: Winning Is the Only Thing*, following the passing of the legendary coach in 1970. The last work presented a collection of reminiscences of Lombardi from coaches, players, friends, and family members that Kramer interviewed. After remaining out of the spotlight for the next several years, Kramer released *Distant Replay* in 1985, a book that updated the whereabouts of the members of the Packers' Super Bowl I championship team following a team reunion at Lambeau Field one year earlier.

Although Kramer, who now lives in Boise, Idaho, took great pride in being named to both the Packers 50th Anniversary Team and the NFL's 50th Anniversary Team one year after he retired as an active player, football's ultimate honor continued to elude him until 2018, when the Pro Football Hall of Fame finally opened its doors to him, thereby validating the earlier endorsement provided by legendary defensive tackle Merlin Olsen, who once said, "There is no question in my mind that Jerry Kramer has Hall of Fame credentials. Respect is given grudgingly in the trenches of the NFL, and Jerry has earned my respect as we battled eye to eye in the pits on so many long afternoons." The 82-year-old Kramer entered Canton 50 years after he played his last game for the Packers.

CAREER HIGHLIGHTS

Best Season

Kramer had his finest all-around season for the Packers in 1963, when, doubling as the team's placekicker, he finished fourth in the league in field goals made (16) and points scored (91), earning in the process his second consecutive trip to the Pro Bowl and consensus First-Team All-Pro honors for one of two times.

Memorable Moments/Greatest Performances

Kramer earned a game ball for his performance during the Packers' 16–7 win over the Giants in the 1962 NFL championship game, when, in addition to doing an outstanding job at right guard, he recovered a fumble and scored 10 points, successfully converting one extra point and field goal attempts of 26, 29, and 30 yards on a frozen field at Yankee Stadium.

Kramer had his finest day as a placekicker on November 3, 1963, going a perfect 4-for-4 on field goal attempts during a 33–14 victory over the Pittsburgh Steelers, with the longest of his kicks traveling 37 yards.

Kramer and the rest of the Packers offensive line had a sensational day against Cleveland in the 1965 NFL title game, opening up gaping holes for running backs Jim Taylor and Paul Hornung, in helping the Packers record a 23–12 victory over the Browns. Playing on a snowy and muddy Lambeau Field, Kramer and fellow guard Fuzzy Thurston proved to be particularly effective, serving as the driving forces behind Green Bay's legendary power sweep that enabled the Packers to gain a total of 204 yards on the ground.

Hornung scored the game's final touchdown on one of those power sweeps, with Kramer leading the way by blocking both the middle linebacker and the right cornerback.

Still, there is little doubt that the play for which Kramer is remembered most occurred two years later, in the NFL championship game that came to be known as the Ice Bowl. With the Packers trailing Dallas by a score of 17–14 in the game's closing moments and a berth in Super Bowl II at stake, Green Bay tried unsuccessfully to run the ball into the Dallas end zone from the 1 yard line on consecutive plays. After calling their final timeout with just 16 seconds left in the contest, the Packers turned to Bart Starr, who, behind a double-team block on Cowboys defensive tackle Jethro Pugh by Kramer and center Ken Bowman, snuck the ball into the end zone for the game-winning score. Discussing the play in his classic football book, *Instant Replay*, Kramer wrote:

> Bart called the "hut" signal. Jethro was on my inside shoulder, my left shoulder. I came off the ball as fast as I ever have in my life. I slammed into Jethro hard. All he had time to do was raise his left arm. He didn't even get it up all the way, and I charged into him. His body was a little high, the way we'd noticed in the movies, and, with Bowman's help, I moved him outside. Willie Townes, next to Jethro, was down low, very low. He was supposed to come in low and close to the middle. He was low, but he didn't close. He might have filled the hole, but he didn't, and Bart churned into the opening and stretched and fell and landed over the goal-line.

The play, which subsequently became known simply as "The Block" in Green Bay, remains one of the most famous in NFL history.

NOTABLE ACHIEVEMENTS

- Led NFL with field goal percentage of 81.8 in 1962.
- Finished fourth in NFL with 16 field goals made and 91 points scored in 1963.
- Six-time Western Conference champion (1960, 1961, 1962, 1965, 1966, and 1967).
- Five-time NFL champion (1961, 1962, 1965, 1966, and 1967).
- Two-time Super Bowl champion (I and II).

- Three-time Pro Bowl selection (1962, 1963, and 1967).
- Five-time First-Team All-Pro (1960, 1962, 1963, 1966, and 1967).
- 1968 Second-Team All-Pro.
- Three-time All–Western Conference First-Team selection (1963, 1966, and 1967).
- NFL 1960s All-Decade Team.
- Pro Football Hall of Fame All-1960s Team.
- Pro Football Reference All-1960s First Team.
- Named to Packers 50th Anniversary Team in 1969.
- Named to NFL's 50th Anniversary Team in 1969.
- Elected to Pro Football Hall of Fame in 2018.

17

CLAY MATTHEWS

Born with football in his blood, Clay Matthews has followed in the footsteps of his father, former NFL linebacker Clay Matthews Jr., and uncle, Pro Football Hall of Fame offensive lineman, Bruce Matthews, in carving out an extremely successful career for himself on the gridiron. An exceptional all-around athlete with superior pass-rushing skills, Matthews has led the Packers in sacks in seven of his nine years in the league, bringing down opposing quarterbacks behind the line of scrimmage a franchise-record 81 times. A consummate team player who has done whatever the coaching staff has asked of him throughout his career, Matthews has assumed numerous roles on defense the past several seasons, manning all three linebacker positions at different times. In all, Matthews has contributed to teams that have won five division titles, one NFC championship, and one Super Bowl during his time in Green Bay, earning in the process six Pro Bowl selections, three All-Pro nominations, and recognition as the 2010 NFC Defensive Player of the Year.

Born in Northridge, California, on May 14, 1986, William Clay Matthews III attended Agoura High School in Agoura Hills, California, where he proved to be a late bloomer on the football field, failing to start until his senior year, when he finally began to develop physically. Subsequently garnering interest only from Division-I FCS schools and local community colleges, Matthews elected to try to make a name for himself at the University of Southern California, where he ended up spending his collegiate career starring on special teams for head coach Pete Carroll after first entering the program as a walk-on student athlete. Granted a full athletic scholarship prior to the start of the 2006 season, Matthews went on to win three straight Special Teams Player of the Year awards. He also served the Trojans as a backup outside linebacker for two years, before finally earning a starting job as a senior.

Although Matthews started for the Trojans at linebacker for just that one season, he performed so well after committing to weight training and

Clay Matthews has recorded more sacks than anyone else in franchise history.
Courtesy of Mike Morbeck

conditioning programs early that year that the Packers selected him in the first round of the 2009 NFL Draft, with the 26th overall pick. Spending most of his rookie season starting at right-outside linebacker, Matthews led the team with 10 sacks and 45½ quarterback pressures, while also recording 51 tackles, deflecting seven passes, and recovering three fumbles, one of which he returned for the first touchdown of his career. In addition to earning Pro Bowl honors and recognition as the NFC Defensive Rookie of the Year with his outstanding play, Matthews drew praise from Packers outside linebacker coach and former All-Pro Kevin Greene, who said of his protégé, "He has a set of skills that I have not seen in an outside linebacker. Clay has a set of skills that I didn't have. He has another gear I didn't have. He's better than Kevin Greene was."

Performing even better after he moved to left-outside linebacker in 2010, Matthews finished fourth in the league with 13½ sacks, made 59 tackles, and recorded the first pick-six of his career, earning in the process his second straight trip to the Pro Bowl, First-Team All-Pro honors, and recognition as the NFC Defensive Player of the Year. Matthews accomplished all he did despite playing the second half of the season with a stress fracture in his lower leg. Constantly double-teamed in pass protection the following year, Matthews recorded just six sacks. Nevertheless, his 55 tackles, three forced fumbles, nine pass deflections, team-high 53½ quarterback pressures, and three interceptions, one of which he returned 38 yards for a touchdown, later prompted Matthews to identify the 2011 campaign as his finest overall season.

Hampered by injuries in each of the next two seasons after returning to the right side of Green Bay's defense, Matthews missed four games in 2012 with a pulled hamstring and another five contests the following year with a broken thumb. Yet, he still managed to earn Pro Bowl and Second-Team All-Pro honors in the first of those campaigns by finishing fifth in the league with 13 sacks, before recording 7½ sacks in 2013.

Possessing outstanding size and strength, the 6'3", 255-pound Matthews often employs a "bull-rush" to overpower his opponent. However, his quickness and agility also enable him to apply pressure to opposing quarterbacks by outmaneuvering the larger offensive linemen who attempt to block him. Matthews's tremendous athleticism, which has allowed him to play both middle and outside linebacker during his time in Green Bay, once prompted him to proclaim, "I don't think there's a position on this field I couldn't play."

A fierce competitor with a burning desire to win, Matthews takes great pride in his performance, stating, "I don't just want to go out there and do my job—I want to excel at it. I hold myself to a high standard. I expect to make plays that alter the game, and, if I don't, I hold myself accountable."

Alternating between middle and outside linebacker during games in 2014, depending on the play call, Matthews helped lead the Packers to their fourth consecutive division title by recording 11 sacks, one interception, and a career-high 71 tackles, forcing two fumbles, and defensing nine passes, earning in the process Pro Bowl and Second-Team All-Pro honors. Playing middle linebacker exclusively the following year to help compensate for the Packers' defensive shortcomings, Matthews recorded only 6½ sacks.

Matthews has excelled at all three linebacker positions during his time in Green Bay.
Courtesy of Mike Morbeck

Nevertheless, he managed to earn his sixth Pro Bowl selection by making 66 tackles and intercepting one pass, while serving as the centerpiece of Green Bay's defense. After being limited by injuries to just 12 games, five sacks, and 24 tackles in 2016, Matthews rebounded somewhat in 2017 to record 8½ sacks and 44 tackles, with his 8½ sacks making him the Packers' all-time official sacks leader.

In addition to his franchise-record 81 sacks, Matthews has recorded 452 tackles (338 solo), six interceptions, 14 forced fumbles, five fumble recoveries, and three defensive touchdowns as a member of the Packers. Although the 32-year-old linebacker appears to be approaching the latter stages of his career, he still seems to have a few good years left, making it quite possible for him to raise himself to an even higher position in these rankings before his time in Green Bay comes to an end.

CAREER HIGHLIGHTS

Best Season

Although Matthews considers the 2011 campaign to be his finest all-around season, he turned in his most dominant performance for the Packers the previous year, when he recorded 59 tackles, 55 quarterback pressures, and a career-high 13½ sacks, returned an interception 62 yards for a touchdown, and forced two fumbles. In addition to earning First-Team All-Pro honors for the only time in his career with his exceptional play, Matthews gained recognition as the 2010 NFC Defensive Player of the Year and the *Sporting News* NFL Defensive Player of the Year. He also finished a close second to Pittsburgh's Troy Polamalu in the Associated Press NFL Defensive Player of the Year voting.

Memorable Moments/Greatest Performances

Matthews scored the first touchdown of his career in the second quarter of a 30–23 loss to the Minnesota Vikings on October 5, 2009, when he forced Adrian Peterson to fumble, scooped up the loose ball, and returned it 42 yards for a TD.

Matthews earned NFC Defensive Player of the Week honors for the first of four times for his performance during a 27–14 win over the Baltimore Ravens in Week 13 of the 2009 campaign, when he recorded six tackles, two sacks, and a forced fumble.

Matthews recorded multiple sacks for the first time in his career during a lopsided 26–0 victory over the Detroit Lions on October 18, 2009, when he brought down Daunte Culpepper behind the line of scrimmage twice.

Matthews had a huge game against Philadelphia in the 2010 regular-season opener, recording three sacks, seven tackles, and one forced fumble during a 27–20 win over the Eagles.

Matthews followed that up with another exceptional performance against Buffalo in Week 2, earning NFC Defensive Player of the Week honors for the second time by recording three sacks and five tackles during a 34–7 rout of the Bills.

Matthews again gained recognition as the NFC Defensive Player of the Week for his performance during a 45–7 blowout of the Dallas Cowboys on November 7, 2010. After sacking Dallas quarterback Jon Kitna earlier in the contest, Matthews put the finishing touches on the victory by intercepting a Kitna pass and returning it 62 yards for his second career touchdown.

Matthews continued his outstanding play in the 2010 postseason, recording 3½ sacks and forcing one fumble during the Packers' successful run to the NFL championship. Making perhaps the biggest play of his career in Super Bowl XLV, Matthews forced a game-changing fumble by Rashard Mendenhall, when he brought down the Pittsburgh running back on the first play of the fourth quarter, with the ball on the Packers 33-yard-line and the Steelers driving to take the lead. Retaining their four-point advantage after Desmond Bishop scooped up the loose ball, the Packers went on to record a 31–25 victory that brought them their fourth Super Bowl title.

Matthews helped lead the Packers to a 38–35 win over the Giants on December 4, 2011, by sacking Eli Manning once and picking off one of his passes early in the second quarter and returning the ball 38 yards for a touchdown.

Matthews led an assault on Chicago quarterback Jay Cutler on September 13, 2012, when he recorded 3½ of the seven sacks the Packers registered during a 23–10 victory over the Bears.

Matthews had another big game against Chicago on November 9, 2014, when he recorded a sack and 11 tackles (nine unassisted) during a 55–14 thrashing of the Bears.

Matthews earned NFC Defensive Player of the Week honors for the fourth time later that year, when he recorded 2½ sacks and six tackles during a 20–3 win over Tampa Bay on December 21, 2014.

Matthews made history on September 28, 2017, when he brought down Chicago quarterback Mike Glennon behind the line of scrimmage during a 35–14 victory over the Bears, becoming in the process the Packers' all-time sacks leader.

NOTABLE ACHIEVEMENTS

- Has scored three defensive touchdowns during career.
- Has finished in double digits in sacks four times.
- Has led Packers in sacks seven times.
- Holds Packers career record for most sacks (81).
- Five-time division champion (2011, 2012, 2013, 2014, and 2016).
- 2010 NFC champion.
- Super Bowl XLV champion.
- 2009 NFC Defensive Rookie of the Year.
- Four-time NFC Defensive Player of the Week.
- September 2010 NFL Defensive Player of the Month.
- 2010 NFC Defensive Player of the Year.
- 2010 *Sporting News* NFL Defensive Player of the Year.
- Finished second in 2010 Associated Press NFL Defensive Player of the Year voting.
- 2010 Butkus Award winner.
- Six-time Pro Bowl selection (2009, 2010, 2011, 2012, 2014, and 2015).
- 2010 First-Team All-Pro.
- Two-time Second-Team All-Pro (2012 and 2014).

18

BOBBY DILLON

Choosing to announce his retirement just one year after Vince Lombardi took over as head coach in Green Bay, Bobby Dillon never had an opportunity to share in the glory the Packers experienced during the 1960s. As a result, he has been largely forgotten by recent generations of Packer fans. Nevertheless, Dillon established himself during his eight years in Green Bay as one of the finest defensive backs in franchise history. The Packers' all-time leader in interceptions and interception-return yards, Dillon led the team in picks in each of his first seven seasons, retiring with the second-most interceptions in NFL history. Recording as many as nine interceptions in a season three times, Dillon also ranks among the franchise's all-time leaders with five defensive touchdowns, with his superb play at free safety earning him four Pro Bowl selections, five All-Pro nominations, and spots on the Pro Football Reference All-1950s Team and the Packers 50th Anniversary Team. Amazingly, Dillon accomplished all he did despite playing his entire career with vision in just one eye.

Born in Temple, Texas, on February 23, 1930, Bobby Dan Dillon suffered a series of accidents as a child that left him completely blind in his left eye. Detailing the events that transpired, Dillon recalled:

> We lived on a farm. The first thing that I remember—I was like five or six years old—my dad was doing something, and I got a piece of metal in my eye. The doctor removed it and it caused a little cataract to grow. They removed that. Then, when I was nine years old, I was helping some people move, and I was wearing glasses. Another little boy my age accidentally hit me in the face with a board and broke my glasses, cutting the white part of the eye. The eye started deteriorating and, by the time I was 10 years old, it would not dilate, and it was hurting my sight. So, when I was 10, they decided to take it out. At that time, it was a glass eye.

Bobby Dillon starred for the Packers during the 1950s, accumulating more interceptions and interception-return yards over the course of the decade than anyone else in franchise history.
Courtesy of Sportsmemorabilia.com

Dillon also revealed that his impaired vision prevented him from playing football until he enrolled at local Temple High School, disclosing, "My parents wouldn't let me play football. My older brother had played, and I always wanted to, but they didn't think it was a good idea. So, I didn't play in junior high. Finally, when I was 15 years old, I really wanted to badly, and they said, 'Go out for spring training if you want to.' I made the starting lineup and played three years in high school."

Following his graduation from Temple High, Dillon continued to play football at the University of Texas, where he earned All-America honors as a defensive back and kick-returner. Although the Packers subsequently selected him in the third round of the 1952 NFL Draft, with the 28th overall pick, Dillon seriously considered pursuing a different career because he had a job in construction waiting for him back home. Recalling the decision that faced him at the time, Dillon said, "I was late for training camp already because of the (college) all-star game, and I had decided I wasn't going to play, so I called the Packers. (Packers scout) Jack Vainisi called me back and convinced me to play by offering me $500 a year more. My first contract was $6,500 a year, which was pretty high for a rookie. The top players back then made $10,000. I had a degree in accounting, so that sounded pretty good to me for five months of work."

Immediately inserted into the starting defensive backfield upon his arrival in Green Bay, Dillon had a solid rookie campaign, leading the Packers in interceptions for the first of seven straight times with four picks. Improving upon his performance the following year, Dillon finished fifth in the league with nine interceptions, which he returned for a total of 112 yards and one touchdown. Dillon then earned All-Pro honors for the first of five straight times in 1954 by ranking among the league leaders with seven interceptions and 111 interception-return yards.

In discussing his quick adaptation to the pro game despite his physical malady, Dillon said, "It's just the way it was, so it never bothered me when I was playing. I returned punts when I was at Texas, so I think it happened at a young enough age that I made an adjustment without knowing any different."

Dillon also revealed that the men he competed with and against in the NFL treated him very much like any other player, recalling:

> There wasn't any big deal made about it. The only adjustment I made was that I learned to have my head on a swivel. Those guys would look for you from the blind side. Everybody knew I had only one eye. In fact, Bobby Layne was playing at Detroit and he'd come by and say, "You one-eyed son of a bitch. I'll get you today." He'd laugh. What I should have done was take the eye out and wear a patch. That would have gotten me a lot more publicity for one thing, and it would have been a lot safer.

Continuing to establish himself as one of the NFL's top defensive backs in 1955, Dillon earned his first of four consecutive Pro Bowl selections by finishing second in the league with nine interceptions, while also ranking third in the circuit with 153 interception-return yards. He followed that up in 1956 by picking off seven passes, which he returned for a league-leading 244 yards and one touchdown. Dillon then earned Pro Bowl and First-Team All-Pro honors for the final two times in 1957 and 1958 by amassing a total of 15 interceptions and 314 interception-return yards, returning two of those picks for touchdowns.

With most teams during the 1950s using their best athletes on defense at the two safety positions, Dillon described how his role differed from that of the modern-day safety:

I had cover responsibility. When we played the Chicago Bears, they had an end, Harlon Hill, and, no matter where he went, I went with him. I played him man every game we ever played and had good success. Elroy Hirsch, I covered man-to-man; Tom Fears, after Elroy left. Every time we played Baltimore, I played Raymond Berry man-to-man. Val Joe (Walker) would move over to my position and strong left, the cornerback, would move over to the other safety position and I'd take his corner. We didn't change personnel, we'd just move them over.

Having intercepted a total of 51 passes his first seven years in the league, Dillon later marveled at how he recorded so many picks, stating, "I don't know how I got so many. It amazes me because we played 12 games and, back then, if a team threw 20 or 25 times, that was a lot. When I was in the middle of it, I didn't know how many I had. Then they started writing that I had more than anyone who had played in Green Bay. My last year, I only had one interception, but, for the first six games, no one threw a pass to a guy I was guarding."

In discussing his longtime teammate, Dave Hanner said, "He and Willie Wood were the two best safeties we ever had here. Old Bobby was smart. And he was tough. He'd get knocked out a couple times a game, but he'd come right back. Return punts with one eye, and he did a good job. When Lombardi came here, he talked about Bobby being the best defensive back in the league at that time."

In spite of the success he experienced in 1958, Dillon initially planned to retire at season's end, disclosing years later, "After the '58 season, we had a terrible year and it wasn't any fun playing. And I wasn't making any money. I had a job with a company (in Temple, Texas) that was small then, but it looked like it had a good future. So, I told the Packers I wasn't coming back, and I told them in February. So, it wasn't like a last-minute deal. They traded for Emlen Tunnell knowing I wasn't going to be there."

However, with the regular season fast approaching, the Packers and their new head coach, Vince Lombardi, convinced Dillon to return for at least one more year. Although Green Bay ended up posting a winning record (7-5) for the only time in Dillon's career in 1959, the 29-year-old safety elected to call it quits at season's end, finishing his career with 52 interceptions, which placed him second only to Emlen Tunnell in NFL history at the time. Dillon also amassed a total of 976 interception-return yards, which places him first in team annals as well.

Dillon retired with the second most interceptions of any player in
NFL history.
Courtesy of Sportsmemorabilia.com

Dillon later admitted that he decided to retire even though things in
Green Bay appeared to be heading in the right direction at the time, noting, "There was a good nucleus on that team when I left. There were good
players before Lombardi got there, but no leadership. We could have been
9-3 his first year, but we didn't know how to win, yet. I could see they were
going to get a lot better, quickly."

Yet, Dillon never regretted retiring when he did, stating, "I had some
calls from other teams after I left, but, when I quit, I quit. I didn't look
back on it."

Dillon, who had started working the previous offseason for a grow-ing company, Wilsonart, which manufactured kitchen countertops in his hometown of Temple, Texas, added, "The money wasn't all that good in the NFL in those days, the company was growing fast, and they wanted me to come and work for them full-time. It was something I couldn't resist. It's not a decision I've ever regretted, though I regret not playing on a cham-pionship team."

Dillon ended up working for the company now known as Wilsonart International for 36 years, during which time it expanded into a global leader for countertops, surfaces, and adhesives, with facilities around the world. Dillon, who assumed the role of president during his final decade with the company, also spent his final two years there serving as chairman and chief executive officer, before retiring to private life in 1995.

CAREER HIGHLIGHTS

Best Season

Although Dillon recorded nine interceptions three times, he compiled his most impressive overall numbers for the Packers in 1956, when, in addi-tion to picking off seven passes, he led the NFL with a career-high 244 interception-return yards, earning in the process First-Team All-Pro honors from four different news sources and a spot on the Associated Press's "offi-cial" Second-Team squad. However, Dillon had his finest all-around season in 1957, when he earned consensus First-Team All-Pro honors for one of three times by ranking among the league leaders with nine interceptions and 180 interception-return yards.

Memorable Moments/Greatest Performances

Dillon scored the first of his five career touchdowns during a 21–21 tie with the Chicago Bears on November 8, 1953, when he picked off a George Blanda pass and returned it 49 yards for the game's opening score.

Dillon recorded his second pick-six on October 30, 1954, when he returned an interception 59 yards for a TD during a 37–14 win over the Philadelphia Eagles.

Dillon helped the Packers defeat the Baltimore Colts by a score of 38–33 on October 14, 1956, when he returned an interception 42 yards for a touchdown in the third quarter, increasing Green Bay's lead to 38–26.

Although the Packers lost their November 17, 1957, meeting with the Los Angeles Rams by a score of 31–27, Dillon recorded the fourth touchdown of his career during the contest, returning an interception 55 yards for a TD.

Dillon lit the scoreboard for the final time in his career during a 34–20 loss to the Chicago Bears in the 1958 regular-season opener, scoring the Packers' first touchdown of the season early in the first quarter when he picked off an Ed Brown pass and returned it 37 yards for a TD.

Dillon again performed brilliantly in defeat on Thanksgiving Day 1953, when he set a franchise record (later tied by Willie Buchanon) by recording four interceptions during a 34–15 loss to the Detroit Lions, picking off Bobby Layne twice and Tom Dublinski another two times.

NOTABLE ACHIEVEMENTS

- Returned five interceptions for touchdowns during career.
- Recorded nine interceptions in a season three times.
- Amassed more than 100 interception-return yards six times, topping 200 yards once (244 in 1956).
- Led NFL with 244 interception-return yards in 1956.
- Finished second in NFL with nine interceptions in 1955.
- Finished third in NFL in interception-return yards twice and non-offensive touchdowns once.
- Led Packers in interceptions seven times.
- Holds Packers single-game record for most interceptions (four vs. Detroit on 11/26/53).
- Holds Packers career records for most interceptions (52) and most interception-return yards (976).
- Ranks among Packers career leaders with five touchdown interceptions (tied-3rd) and five defensive touchdowns (tied—4th).
- Retired with second-most interceptions in NFL history.
- Four-time Pro Bowl selection (1955, 1956, 1957, and 1958).
- Four-time First-Team All-Pro (1954, 1955, 1957, and 1958).
- 1956 Second-Team All-Pro.
- Three-time All–Western Conference First-Team selection (1956, 1957, and 1958).
- Pro Football Reference All-1950s Second Team.
- Named to Packers 50th Anniversary Team in 1969.

19

STERLING SHARPE

H is career cut short by a serious neck injury suffered during the latter stages of the 1994 campaign, Sterling Sharpe has yet to gain induction into the Pro Football Hall of Fame. Nevertheless, Sharpe made an enormous impact on the Packers and the NFL as a whole during his time in Green Bay, gaining widespread acclaim as one of the league's premier wide receivers by topping the circuit in pass receptions three times, receiving yards once, and touchdown receptions twice. En route to setting new franchise records for most career receptions (since broken) and most catches and TD catches in a single season, Sharpe led the Packers in receptions and receiving yards in each of his seven seasons, becoming in 1993 the first player in NFL history to catch as many as 100 passes in consecutive seasons. Sharpe also amassed more than 1,000 receiving yards five times and made at least 10 touchdown receptions on four separate occasions, with his exceptional play earning him five trips to the Pro Bowl, three All-Pro nominations, and five All-NFC selections.

Born in Chicago, Illinois, on April 6, 1965, Sterling Sharpe grew up in Glennville, Georgia, where he developed a reputation as an outstanding all-around athlete at Glennville High School, starring in basketball and track, while also excelling as a quarterback, running back, and linebacker on the gridiron. Following his graduation, Sharpe enrolled at the University of South Carolina, where he earned All-America honors by setting school records for most career receptions (169) and receiving yards (2,497).

Recalling the unique skill set that Sharpe exhibited during his college days, Gamecocks radio analyst Tommy Suggs said, "He seemed to be full-speed at one step. He had a burst that you just don't see from a lot of players. Plus, he had physical size. And he had a tremendous awareness of where he was on the field and where everybody else was all the time. That's what made him so good on kickoff returns and running after the catch."

Sharpe also drew praise from former Gamecocks safety Brad Edwards, another All-American who ended up playing 10 seasons in the NFL.

Sterling Sharpe led the Packers in receptions and receiving yards seven
straight times.
Courtesy of PristineAuction.com

Reflecting back on what it was like facing Sharpe in practice, Edwards
offered, "I would line up there in practice in one-on-one drills and try to
go against him. And I'd get beat every single day. You talk about needing
thick skin. I'd just keep jumping in there and getting hammered by the guy.
He absolutely made me so much of a better football player. I'd get into a
regular game, and nobody's as good as the guy I'd been going against every
day in practice."

Edwards added, "You always knew he was a great athlete, but you
could see the evolution in his productivity and his performance as it began
to happen. That senior year in 1987, he was absolutely one of the top five,
if not higher, best football players in the country. He did things that we'd
look back at on video and say, 'Who can do that?' He would make moves
downfield and make catches, and you just would go, 'How many people in
this country can do that at the level he's doing it?'"

Sharpe's extraordinary play at the collegiate level prompted the Packers to select him with the seventh overall pick of the 1998 NFL Draft. Making an immediate impact upon his arrival in Green Bay, Sharpe started all 16 games as a rookie, leading the team with 55 receptions and 791 receiving yards. He followed that up with a brilliant sophomore campaign in which he earned Pro Bowl and First-Team All-Pro honors by leading the NFL with 90 receptions, while also finishing second in the league with 1,423 receiving yards and 12 touchdown catches. In compiling those numbers, Sharpe broke Don Hutson's franchise records for most receptions and receiving yards in a season. Sharpe continued to perform at an elite level in each of the next two seasons, earning his second straight trip to the Pro Bowl in 1990 by making 67 receptions for 1,105 yards and six touchdowns, before catching 69 passes and amassing 961 receiving yards the following year.

Yet, as well as Sharpe played in 1990 and 1991, he proved to be even more productive the next three seasons after new head coach Mike Holmgren installed the West Coast Offense in Green Bay. Ideally suited to that system, Sharpe expressed his satisfaction with the team's new offensive scheme when he said, "I've had a chance to line up all over the field, and that makes it hard to double me. And, if you get open, they will get you the ball. As a receiver, you can't help but love it." Teaming up with Brett Favre to form arguably the league's most dynamic passing combination, Sharpe compiled the following numbers over the course of the next three seasons:

YEAR	RECS	RECEIVING YARDS	TD RECS
1992	108	1,461	13
1993	112	1,274	11
1994	94	1,119	18

By leading the NFL in receptions, receiving yards, and touchdown catches in 1992, Sharpe became just the sixth player in league history to top the circuit in all three categories in the same season, joining Ray Flaherty (1932), Don Hutson (1936, 1941–1944), Elroy Hirsch (1951), Raymond Berry (1959), and Jerry Rice (1990) on an extremely exclusive list. Sharpe's 108 catches also established a new single-season NFL record, a mark that he broke the very next year when he led the league with 112 receptions, making him the first player ever to reach triple digits in that category two straight times. Meanwhile, Sharpe's 18 touchdown receptions in 1994 represented the second-highest total in league history at the time, with only

Sharpe holds single-season franchise records for most receptions and most TD catches.
Courtesy of PristineAuction.com

Jerry Rice (22 in 1987) having caught more TD passes in a single season. Sharpe's brilliant play earned him Pro Bowl honors in each of those three seasons and First-Team All-Pro recognition in both 1992 and 1993.

In addition to his size and strength, the 6-foot, 207-pound Sharpe possessed good speed and great moves that enabled him to get open against anyone. He also had terrific hands and never shied away from going over the middle to make difficult catches in heavy traffic. Known for his toughness, Sharpe started every game for the Packers from 1988 to 1994, playing through numerous injuries that included broken ribs, pulled hamstrings, and turf toe. Considering himself to be an extension of his home stadium, Sharpe stated, "Lambeau Field is Old School. You play when you're hurt, you play in the cold, you play in the mud, you play when the field conditions are nowhere near their best, and you go out there and you perform because you're a professional. Every time I think of Lambeau Field, that's football to me."

Unfortunately, Sharpe's "Old School" mentality eventually proved to be his undoing. After injuring his neck in the next-to-last game of the 1994 regular season, Sharpe did further damage to himself by starting the following week, helping the Packers advance to the playoffs by making nine receptions for 132 yards and three touchdowns during a 34–19 victory over the Tampa Bay Buccaneers. Unable to appear in either of Green Bay's post-season contests, Sharpe discovered during the subsequent offseason that the severity of his injury would make it impossible for him to continue playing. Announcing his retirement following the conclusion of the 1994 campaign, Sharpe ended his career with 595 receptions, 8,134 receiving yards, 65 touchdown receptions, and 66 total touchdowns scored, all of which place him among the franchise's all-time leaders.

Because Sharpe's injury forced him to retire two years before the Packers defeated New England in Super Bowl XXXI, his younger brother, Shannon, gave him the first of the three Super Bowl rings he won, noting the huge impact that Sterling made on his life by saying, "The two people who influenced me the most, good or bad, are Sterling and my grandmother. Everything I know about being a man, about football, everything I know about sports, pretty much in life, is because of those two people."

After retiring as an active player, Sharpe accepted a studio position, working as an NFL analyst at ESPN, NBC, and, currently, the NFL Network.

CAREER HIGHLIGHTS

Best Season

Sharpe had a tremendous year for the Packers in 1989, earning Pro Bowl and First-Team All-Pro honors for the first time by leading the NFL with 90 receptions, while also finishing second in the league with 1,423 receiving yards and 12 touchdown receptions. He also performed brilliantly in his final season, concluding the 1994 campaign with 94 catches, 1,119 receiving yards, and a league-leading 18 TD catches, a single-season franchise record. However, Sharpe had his finest all-around season in 1992, when he became just the sixth player in NFL history to win the Triple Crown for receivers by topping the circuit with 108 receptions, 1,461 receiving yards, and 13 TD catches, establishing in the process a new league mark (since broken) for most catches in a season.

Memorable Moments/Greatest Performances

Sharpe topped 100 receiving yards for the first time in his career during a 19–9 loss to the Detroit Lions on November 20, 1988, finishing the contest with eight catches for 124 yards.

Sharpe reached another milestone during the latter stages of a 30–14 loss to the Lions two weeks later, scoring the first touchdown of his career on a 24-yard connection with quarterback Randy Wright. He finished the game with six catches for 71 yards and that one TD.

With the Packers having spotted New Orleans a 24–7 halftime lead on September 17, 1989, Sharpe completed a furious second-half comeback by hauling in a 3-yard TD pass from quarterback Don Majkowski in the final minute of regulation that gave Green Bay an unlikely 35–34 victory. Sharpe finished the game with eight catches for 107 yards and one touchdown.

Although the Packers lost their matchup with the Los Angeles Rams the following week by a score of 41–38, Sharpe starred in defeat, making eight catches for 164 yards and one TD.

Sharpe contributed to a 31–13 win over Dallas on October 8, 1989, by making six receptions for 132 yards and one touchdown, which came on a season-long 79-yard catch-and-run that put the Packers ahead to stay midway through the fourth quarter.

Sharpe proved to be the difference in a 20–19 victory over the Minnesota Vikings on November 26, 1989, making 10 catches for 157 yards, and scoring both Packer touchdowns on pass plays that covered 34 and nine yards.

Sharpe again provided most of the offensive firepower during a 17–16 win over Tampa Bay the following week, making eight receptions for 169 yards, and scoring Green Bay's only two touchdowns on pass plays that covered 21 and 55 yards.

Sharpe turned in his finest performance of the 1990 campaign on November 18, when he helped lead the Packers to a 24–21 victory over the Phoenix Cardinals by making 10 catches for 157 yards and one touchdown, which came on a 54-yard hookup with Don Majkowski.

Sharpe performed heroically during a 34–24 loss to the Buffalo Bills on November 10, 1991, making eight receptions for 133 yards and one touchdown, with that being a 58-yard connection with Mike Tomczak midway through the third quarter that momentarily put the Packers ahead by a score of 21–17.

Although Sharpe caught just two passes from Brett Favre during a 17–3 win over the Pittsburgh Steelers on September 27, 1992, one of them went for a 76-yard touchdown in the second quarter that put the Packers ahead to stay.

Sharpe starred in defeat on November 8, 1992, making a career-high 11 catches for 160 yards during a 27–7 loss to the Giants.

Sharpe earned NFC Offensive Player of the Week honors for the first of three times for his performance during a 28–13 victory over the Los Angeles Rams in Week 16 of the 1992 campaign, when he made eight receptions for 110 yards and a pair of second-quarter touchdowns that covered 17 and 16 yards.

Sharpe again torched the Los Angeles defensive secondary during a 36–6 win over the Rams in the 1993 regular-season opener, making seven catches for 120 yards, and scoring the Packers' first touchdown of the year on a 50-yard hookup with Brett Favre in the first quarter.

En route to earning NFC Offensive Player of the Week honors for the second time, Sharpe led the Packers to a 37–14 victory over the Tampa Bay Buccaneers on October 24, 1993, by making 10 receptions for 147 yards and a career-high four touchdowns, scoring on pass plays that covered 7, 30, 10, and 32 yards.

Sharpe helped lead the Packers to a 28–24 win over the Detroit Lions in their first playoff game in 11 years by making five catches for 101 yards and three touchdowns in the 1993 NFC wild card game, with the last of his TDs being a 40-yard connection with Brett Favre late in the fourth quarter that provided the margin of victory.

Although the Packers lost their November 24, 1994, meeting with the Dallas Cowboys by a score of 42–31, Sharpe had a huge game, making nine receptions for 122 yards and four touchdowns, with his scoring plays covering 1, 36, 30, and 5 yards.

Sharpe made his last NFL game a memorable one, helping the Packers advance to the playoffs as a wild card by catching nine passes for 132 yards and three touchdowns during their 34–19 win over Tampa Bay in the 1994 regular-season finale. Hooking up with Brett Favre on scoring plays that covered 6, 22, and 6 yards, Sharpe earned NFC Offensive Player of the Week honors for the third time in his career.

NOTABLE ACHIEVEMENTS

- Surpassed 100 receptions twice, topping 90 catches two other times.
- Surpassed 1,000 receiving yards five times, topping 1,400 yards twice.
- Made more than 10 touchdown receptions four times.
- Scored more than 100 points once (108 in 1994).
- Led NFL in: pass receptions three times; receiving yards once; and touchdown receptions twice.
- Finished second in NFL in: receiving yards once; touchdown receptions once; and touchdowns scored once.
- Finished third in NFL in receiving yards once and touchdown receptions once.
- Led Packers in pass receptions and receiving yards seven straight times (1988–1994).
- Holds Packers single-season records for most pass receptions (112 in 1993) and most touchdown receptions (18 in 1994).
- Holds share of Packers record for most touchdown receptions in one game (4—twice).
- Ranks among Packers career leaders with: 595 pass receptions (2nd); 8,134 receiving yards (3rd); 8,206 yards from scrimmage (6th); 8,276 all-purpose yards (7th); 65 touchdown receptions (3rd); and 66 total touchdowns scored (5th).
- Never missed a game in seven seasons with Packers, appearing in 112 consecutive games.
- First player in NFL history to surpass 100 receptions in consecutive seasons (1992 and 1993).
- Three-time NFC Offensive Player of the Week.
- Five-time Pro Bowl selection (1989, 1990, 1992, 1993, and 1994).
- Three-time First-Team All-Pro (1989, 1992, and 1993).
- Three-time First-Team All-NFC selection (1989, 1992, and 1993).
- Two-time Second-Team All-NFC selection (1990 and 1994).

20

CLARKE HINKLE

One of the most versatile players in NFL history, Clarke Hinkle spent 10 seasons in Green Bay and excelled in every facet of the game. Leading the Packers in rushing seven times between 1932 and 1941, Hinkle ended his playing career with more yards gained on the ground than any other running back in league history. And, even though Hinkle rushed for a total of only 3,860 yards, he continues to rank seventh in team annals in that category, as of this writing. An outstanding defender as well, Hinkle developed a reputation during his time in Green Bay as one of the league's hardest hitters and surest tacklers, striking fear into his opponents with his aggressive style of play from his middle linebacker position. Hinkle also contributed to the Packers on special teams, serving as their primary kicker for most of his career, and as their punter for his final three seasons, with his excellent all-around play helping the Packers win three Western Conference championships and two NFL titles. Meanwhile, Hinkle's stellar play on both sides of the ball earned him three Pro Bowl selections, nine All-Pro nominations, spots on the Pro Football Hall of Fame All-1930s Team and the NFL's 75th Anniversary All-Time Two-Way Team, and a place in the Pro Football Hall of Fame.

Born in Toronto, Ohio, on April 10, 1909, William Clarke Hinkle attended local Toronto High School, before enrolling at Bucknell University, where he set numerous school records on the gridiron, including most touchdowns in one game (eight versus Dickinson in 1929). In addition to scoring a total of 37 touchdowns from 1929 to 1931, Hinkle starred for the Bisons on defense, with Carl Snavely, his college coach, later calling him, "Without a doubt, the greatest defensive back I have ever seen or coached."

After earning All-America honors as a fullback and linebacker by leading Bucknell to a record of 6-0-3 in his senior year of 1931, Hinkle elected to sign with the Packers, with whom he ended up spending his entire NFL career. Establishing himself as the team's starting fullback as a rookie in 1932, the 5'11", 202-pound Hinkle rushed for 331 yards and three

Clarke Hinkle ended his career as the NFL's all-time leading rusher.
Courtesy of RMYAuctions.com

touchdowns, en route to earning Second-Team All-Pro honors for the first of three straight times. He subsequently totaled 1,045 yards rushing and eight touchdowns over the course of the next three seasons, before helping the Packers capture the NFL title in 1936 by rushing for 476 yards and five touchdowns, while also averaging a career-high 4.8 yards per carry.

Often compared to Bronko Nagurski, his counterpart on the arch-rival Chicago Bears, Hinkle served as a triple threat on offense, displaying an ability to run, pass, and kick with the league's best throughout his career. Quick and powerful, Hinkle proved to be extremely difficult to bring down, typically inflicting a considerable amount of punishment on his tackler. Once called "the greatest all-around fullback ever to play in the National Football League" by Curly Lambeau, Hinkle also drew praise from Cecil Isbell, who said of his longtime teammate, "He did not have the brute power of Nagurski because he did not have Bronk's size. But he had the knack you see today in a runner like Jim Taylor of exploding at the point of impact. He was a compact runner, and he had the same kind of balance Taylor has—he could take the shock of a tackle, bounce sideways, and keep going. And he never quit. He wanted to win more than anyone I ever saw."

Halfback Herm Schneidman, who played in the Green Bay backfield with Hinkle from 1935 to 1939, added, "I think he liked to hit people any chance he could. Clarke was a great football player who could do a lot of things well . . . and he played nearly 60 minutes of every game. . . . He was our workhorse on offense and then was our top defensive man. He relished hitting people and was a great tackler. If he got his hands on the ball carrier, they were going down."

An intimidating defender who ranked with the league's hardest hitters, Hinkle gained a reputation as one of the few players powerful enough to bring down Bronko Nagurski one-on-one. In fact, Hinkle once hit the 230-pound fullback so hard that he broke his nose and cracked two of his ribs, with Nagurski stating years later, "They said I was hard to tackle, but here was a guy [Hinkle] who didn't have too much trouble."

Extremely intense, Hinkle got so psyched up for a game that he played it in a fury, flying all over the field hitting people and yelling at the opposition, while also trying to instill the same level of intensity in his teammates. Commenting on Hinkle's maniacal behavior after watching film of Don Hutson and Bronko Nagurski in an effort to determine how the two legendary Hall of Famers might fare in the modern game, widely acclaimed *Sports Illustrated* pro football writer Paul Zimmerman said in 1989, "As I was watching the early footage of Hutson, another figure kept emerging— Hinkle. . . . Bronko was a great name, and Nagurski was bigger. But Hinkle . . . he was an iron man. He played like a maniac."

Continuing his string of four consecutive First-Team All-Pro selections in 1937, Hinkle ranked among the league leaders with 552 yards rushing, 668 yards from scrimmage, and 57 points scored, while also topping the circuit with five rushing touchdowns and seven total touchdowns. He followed that up with another strong performance in 1938, earning First-Team All-Pro honors for the final time by scoring seven touchdowns and leading the league with a career-high 58 points scored.

Hinkle rivaled Chicago's Bronko Nagurski as the finest fullback of his era.
Courtesy of RMYAuctions.com

Hinkle remained with the Packers for another three years, scoring five touchdowns for their 1939 NFL championship team, and leading the league in field goals made in both 1940 and 1941, before retiring at the age of 32 to enter the Coast Guard following the outbreak of World War II. In addition to rushing for 3,860 yards during his career, Hinkle gained another 537 yards on 49 pass receptions, giving him a total of 4,397 yards from scrimmage. He also intercepted three passes and scored 44 touchdowns, with his 35 rushing TDs representing the fifth-highest total in franchise history. Meanwhile, Hinkle's 3,860 yards rushing remained a league record until 1949, when Philadelphia's Steve Van Buren surpassed it.

After being named to the Packers All-Time Team in both 1946 and 1957, Hinkle gained entrance into the Pro Football Hall of Fame in 1964, with his induction speech ironically being delivered by his greatest rival, Bronko Nagurski, whose respect he earned through the years with his ability, hard work, and dedication to his profession. Hinkle later received the additional distinction of having the Packers' outdoor practice field named after him, with the team honoring him in that fashion in 1997, nine years after he passed away in Steubenville, Ohio, at the age of 79, on November 9, 1988.

Although somewhat biased, Curly Lambeau once expressed his admiration for Hinkle by ranking him ahead of Bronko Nagurski and Ernie Nevers as the greatest fullback of his time, suggesting, "The greatest of them is Hink. Nagurski was a terrific runner who could hit you like a truck. Nevers, a great all-around boy, played his heart out whether the Cardinals were ahead, 40–0, or behind, 40–0. But no fullback ever played all-around football like Hinkle. No guy ever gave more to his team. No guy, not even Nevers, loved it more."

CAREER HIGHLIGHTS

Best Season

Hinkle had one of his finest statistical seasons in 1936, when he helped lead the Packers to the NFL title by rushing for 476 yards, scoring five touchdowns, and averaging a career-best 4.8 yards per carry. However, he performed even better the following year, finishing second in the league with a career-high 552 yards rushing and topping the circuit with seven touchdowns. Over the course of that 1937 campaign, Hinkle scored a touchdown in six consecutive games, a feat that only Don Hutson and Paul Hornung have since bettered among Packer players.

Memorable Moments/Greatest Performances

Hinkle gave the Packers a 15–10 win over the Portsmouth Spartans on October 9, 1932, by scoring his first career touchdown on a 22-yard run in the fourth quarter.

A little over two years later, on October 21, 1934, Hinkle hauled in a career-long 69-yard TD pass from Arnie Herber during a 15–0 victory over the Chicago Cardinals.

Hinkle proved to be the difference in a 13–6 win over the Philadelphia Eagles in the 1935 regular-season finale, kicking a 39-yard field goal and putting the Packers ahead to stay with a 47-yard touchdown run in the third quarter.

Hinkle recorded the longest run of his career during a 21–10 win over the Chicago Bears on November 1, 1936, when, after being met at the line of scrimmage by Bronko Nagurski, who knocked him into the Green Bay backfield, he regained his bearings and took off around end for a 59-yard touchdown run.

Hinkle scored three touchdowns in one game for the only time in his career during a 28–7 victory over the Chicago Cardinals on November 10, 1940, hauling in a 12-yard TD pass from Arnie Herber and scoring twice on short runs.

However, the most memorable play of Hinkle's career took place during a 14–7 loss to the Chicago Bears on September 24, 1933, when he forced the seemingly indestructible Bronko Nagurski to leave the game with a hit of epic proportions. With Hinkle prepared to punt the ball to the Bears on third down, he chose instead to take off for the right sideline in an effort to gain the yardage necessary to allow the Packers to retain possession of the ball. Hotly pursued by Nagurski, who had the angle on him, Hinkle surprised his adversary by heading back toward the middle of the field. With Nagurski closing in, Hinkle pivoted and threw his shoulder into Nagurski's face, breaking his nose and fracturing two of his ribs. Although woozy himself, Hinkle rose from the turf and returned to the Packer huddle. Meanwhile, after rising to his feet, a dazed Nagurski had to be helped to the sidelines, where he spent the remainder of the game.

NOTABLE ACHIEVEMENTS

- Rushed for more than 500 yards once (552 in 1937).
- Surpassed 600 yards from scrimmage once (668 in 1937).
- Averaged more than 4.5 yards per carry once (4.8 in 1936).
- Averaged more than 40 yards per punt twice.
- Led NFL with five rushing touchdowns and seven total touchdowns in 1937.
- Led NFL in: scoring once; field goals made twice; and field goal percentage twice.

- Finished second in NFL in: rushing yardage once; rushing touchdowns twice; and scoring once.
- Finished third in NFL in: rushing touchdowns three times; total touchdowns once; yards from scrimmage once; all-purpose yards once; and field goal percentage twice.
- Led Packers in rushing yardage seven times.
- Ranks among Packers career leaders with 3,860 yards rushing (7th) and 35 rushing touchdowns (5th).
- Retired as NFL's all-time leading rusher.
- Three-time Western Conference champion (1936, 1938, and 1939).
- Two-time NFL champion (1936 and 1939).
- Three-time Pro Bowl selection (1938, 1939, and 1940).
- Four-time First-Team All-Pro (1935, 1936, 1937, and 1938).
- Five-time Second-Team All-Pro (1932, 1933, 1934, 1939, and 1941).
- NFL 1930s All-Decade Team.
- Pro Football Hall of Fame All-1930s Team.
- Named to Packers All-Time Team in 1946 and 1957.
- Named to Packers All–Iron Man Era Team in 1976.
- Named to NFL's 75th Anniversary All-Time Two-Way Team in 1994.
- Elected to Pro Football Hall of Fame in 1964.

21

CHARLES WOODSON

One of the finest defensive backs in NFL history, Charles Woodson resurrected his somewhat disappointing career after he joined the Packers in 2006, establishing himself over the course of the next seven seasons as the greatest free agent signing in franchise history, aside from Reggie White. After injuries and a somewhat apathetic attitude prevented him from reaching his full potential his first eight years in Oakland, Woodson emerged as arguably the league's most versatile defensive weapon during his time in Green Bay, with his size, speed, and superb instincts giving him the ability to play any position in the defensive backfield. Assuming numerous roles on defense between 2006 and 2012, Woodson recorded a total of 38 interceptions, which ties him for the fourth most in Packers history. Returning nine of those picks for touchdowns, Woodson also holds franchise records for most touchdown interceptions and most defensive touchdowns scored (10). Woodson's stellar play, which helped lead the Packers to three division titles, one conference championship, and one NFL title, earned him four Pro Bowl selections, four All-Pro nominations, recognition as the 2009 NFL Defensive Player of the Year, and a spot on the NFL 2000s All-Decade Team.

Born in Fremont, Ohio, on October 7, 1976, Charles C. Woodson attended Ross High School, where he starred in multiple sports, excelling as a point guard in basketball, a sprinter and long jumper in track and field, and a running back in football. Ending his high school career on the gridiron with school records for most rushing yards (3,861) and most points scored (466), Woodson earned numerous individual accolades as a senior, being named Ohio's "Mr. Football" and a High School All-American by both *USA Today* and *Parade* magazine. Subsequently recruited by several colleges as a running back, Woodson ultimately decided to enroll at the University of Michigan, where he ended up making a name for himself on defense.

Although Woodson also returned punts and occasionally played wide receiver during his three years at Michigan, he built his reputation primarily on his defensive play, starting 34 straight games for the Wolverines at

Charles Woodson resurrected his career in Green Bay.
Courtesy of Mike Morbeck

cornerback, en route to earning three All–Big Ten First-Team selections and two Chevrolet Defensive Player of the Year awards. Performing particularly well as a junior in 1997, Woodson became the only primarily defensive player to win the Heisman Trophy award after leading the Wolverines to an undefeated season and a share of the National Championship, with his brilliant play also earning him consensus First-Team All-America honors, recognition as the Big Ten Defensive Player of the Year, and the Bronko

Nagurski Trophy, presented annually to college football's best defensive player.

Feeling that he had nothing left to prove at the collegiate level, Woodson declared himself eligible for the 1998 NFL Draft, with the Oakland Raiders subsequently selecting him in the first round, with the fourth overall pick. Making an immediate impact upon his arrival in Oakland, Woodson earned Pro Bowl and NFL Defensive Rookie of the Year honors in 1998 by intercepting five passes, which he returned for 118 yards and one touchdown. Continuing to perform well in each of the next three seasons, Woodson earned three more trips to the Pro Bowl and two All-Pro nominations. Yet, despite the early success he experienced in Oakland, Woodson remained something of a disappointment to the Raiders and their fans, failing to live up to the lofty expectations they had for him when he first came out of college. After intercepting a total of only six passes from 1999 to 2001, Woodson found himself being plagued by injuries in three of the next four seasons, enabling him to record just six more interceptions, while simultaneously developing a reputation for falling asleep during meetings, rarely studying film, and spending many a night out on the town. Finally losing patience with Woodson after a broken leg sidelined him for the final 10 games of the 2005 campaign, the Raiders chose not to offer him a new contract when he became a free agent at season's end.

With Woodson's injury history and declining production scaring off most potential suitors, Green Bay became the only viable option for him, prompting him to sign a seven-year, $52 million contract with the Packers. Yet, even though Woodson accepted Green Bay's offer, he did so somewhat reluctantly, recalling years later, "I wasn't happy that day. I wasn't happy whatsoever. I wasn't sold on coming here, but there were really no other options."

Woodson added, "Everything—organization, nightlife, the whole thing—just being in Green Bay. The talk is always this is no place for a black man, and that's just how it was."

In assessing the Packers' signing of Woodson, *ESPN.com* writer Len Pasquarelli wrote at the time, "In terms of name value, Woodson is clearly the Packers' most significant offseason addition. Whether his game still lives up to Woodson's name, however, is questionable, at least based on the last two seasons."

However, Woodson's move to Green Bay ended up being a blessing in disguise for him, as former Raiders teammate Rich Gannon suggested when he said, "Green Bay was a career-saver for Charles. He was an elite talent in Oakland, but he was never held accountable. He practiced the way he wanted to and played the way he wanted to. There wasn't the discipline and structure that he needed."

Gannon also stated, "There was never any question about his talent. I remember competing against him at training camp, and he was ridiculous. When he went to Green Bay, it was like a guy like Randy Moss going to the Patriots. You've got structure and discipline around you, and you've got to be a certain way and perform. . . . There was this evolution where he became a completely different person, working with young players, being very unselfish."

Fellow Heisman Trophy winner Tim Brown, who also spent time with Woodson in Oakland, expressed similar sentiments, saying, "The maturity factor and the realization that, 'Hey, this is my last stop,' was enough for him to step up and do things the right way."

Brown then added that he was surprised to see Woodson looking bigger and stronger when he saw him in 2007, noting, "He said he was lifting weights. In seven years, I never saw him lift a weight in Oakland. He'd ride the bike and that was about it."

Woodson's new attitude, hard work, and newfound dedication to his profession ended up paying huge dividends for both him and the Packers. After finishing third in the league with eight interceptions in 2006, Woodson helped the Packers advance to the NFC championship game the following year by picking off four passes and scoring two touchdowns on defense. He then began a string of four straight seasons in which he earned Pro Bowl and All-Pro honors, recording a total of 25 interceptions during that time, seven of which he returned for touchdowns. Performing particularly well in 2009, Woodson made First-Team All-Pro for the second time in his career and earned NFL Defensive Player of the Year honors by leading the league with nine interceptions, which he returned for 179 yards and three touchdowns.

Developing into much more than just an outstanding cover corner during his time in Green Bay, Woodson gradually evolved into one of the league's most complete players, with Packers defensive coordinator Dom Capers making good use of his exceptional all-around ability. Used by Capers at different times as a cornerback, safety, linebacker, and slot defender, the 6'1", 200-pound Woodson displayed a tremendous amount of versatility, drawing praise from Capers, who said, "He has the combination you look for. He has the size and the physical tools to play the position. The thing I like is that he's a smart player. . . . Not only does he have good football instincts, but he understands the game. He gives you the flexibility where you can move him around."

Packers cornerbacks coach Joe Whitt Jr. also held Woodson in extremely high esteem, stating, "He's a Hall of Fame player. I tell my other guys, 'Don't look at Woodson now. He has the ability to do some things other guys just can't do.'"

Whitt added, "Probably the thing that I respect about his game more than most is he truly loves the game. That's why he plays so hard, and he plays with so much passion. He's not doing it for the money. He could really care less about it. He does it because he's a very prideful man, and he loves to play. . . . It bothers him when people don't think he's the best. It really bothers him. He goes out there and tries to prove he's the absolute best at what he does."

Emerging as a true team leader in Green Bay, Woodson received the distinction of being named defensive co-captain in 2010—a role he took quite seriously. After breaking his collarbone while diving successfully to defend a pass late in the first half of Super Bowl XLV, Woodson gave an impassioned speech to his teammates at halftime, before cheering them on from the sidelines during the second half of a 31–25 victory over Pittsburgh.

After recording 74 tackles and leading the league with seven interceptions in 2011, Woodson moved to strong safety the following year to help compensate for the loss of Nick Collins, who suffered what proved to be a career-ending neck injury the previous season. However, Woodson ended up missing the final nine games of the campaign after breaking his collarbone again during a 30–20 win over the St. Louis Rams in Week 7, prompting the Packers to release him at the end of the year to clear salary cap space. In addition to picking off 38 passes and scoring a franchise-record 10 defensive touchdowns during his time in Green Bay, Woodson amassed 568 interception-return yards, recorded 462 tackles and 11½ sacks, and accumulated a total of 631 yards on 75 punt returns.

Bemoaning the loss of Woodson following his departure, Joe Whitt commented, "It was sort of unfair to the guys who followed him because we wanted Charles Woodson–type play, and there's only one of him in the world. We might've tried to do some things that were sort of outside of our character, trying to create that position. He's a once-in-a-lifetime player, and you can't replace him."

After being released by the Packers, Woodson returned to Oakland, where he spent his final three seasons playing safety for the Raiders. Recording 10 more interceptions and scoring one more touchdown during that time, Woodson retired following the conclusion of the 2015 campaign with career totals of 65 interceptions, 966 interception-return yards, 13 defensive touchdowns, 1,205 tackles, 33 forced fumbles, 18 fumble

Woodson holds franchise records for most touchdown interceptions and most defensive touchdowns scored.
Courtesy of Mike Morbeck

recoveries, and 20 sacks, with his 11 touchdown interceptions representing the second-highest total in NFL history. Shortly thereafter, Woodson joined ESPN's *Sunday NFL Countdown* program, taking over the position previously held by Keyshawn Johnson.

Although Woodson spent just seven of his 18 NFL seasons in Green Bay, he continues to hold the city he once frowned upon close to his heart, stating long after he left the Packers, "I'm always going to feel connected to the city. There's always going to be love between me and Green Bay. . . . It's special. I spent seven years in Green Bay. A lot of good times, a lot of great years . . . I guess you never know until you give something a try."

PACKERS CAREER HIGHLIGHTS

Best Season

Woodson had a tremendous year for the Packers in 2008, earning Pro Bowl and Second-Team All-Pro honors by finishing second in the NFL with seven interceptions, two of which he returned for touchdowns, while also ranking among the league leaders with 169 interception-return yards, making 62 tackles, and recording a career-high three sacks. However, he performed even better the following year, leading the league with nine picks and three touchdown interceptions, amassing a career-high 179 interception-return yards, defensing 21 passes, forcing four fumbles, and recording two sacks and 81 tackles (63 solo), en route to gaining recognition as the 2009 NFL Defensive Player of the Year. In discussing Woodson's brilliant play over the course of the campaign, Green Bay defensive coordinator Dom Capers said, "I've said it before, he's had two or three games that I can't imagine any defensive player in the league having better games. I think it speaks volumes when he was player of the month in September and came back and got player of the month again in November." By also being named NFC Defensive Player of the Month in December, Woodson became the only player to receive the award three times in one season.

Memorable Moments/Greatest Performances

Woodson scored the first of his franchise-record 10 defensive touchdowns during a 34–24 victory over the Miami Dolphins on October 22, 2006, when he put the Packers ahead to stay early in the third quarter by returning an interception 23 yards for a TD.

Woodson earned NFC Defensive Player of the Week honors for the first of four times on October 14, 2007, when he picked off a pass and recovered a Santana Moss fumble, which he returned 57 yards for the go-ahead touchdown in a 17–14 win over the Washington Redskins.

Woodson made another huge play three weeks later, when he sealed a 33–22 victory over the Kansas City Chiefs in the game's final minute by returning an interception 46 yards for a TD.

Woodson contributed to a 48–25 win over the Detroit Lions in Week 2 of the 2008 campaign by recording a pair of interceptions, the second of which he returned 41 yards for a touchdown.

Although the Packers lost to Tampa Bay two weeks later by a score of 30–21, Woodson recorded another pick-six during the contest, giving Green Bay a 21–20 lead early in the fourth quarter by returning an interception 62 yards for a touchdown.

Woodson again lit the scoreboard during a 31–24 loss to Cincinnati in Week 2 of the 2009 campaign, when he picked off a Carson Palmer pass and returned the ball 37 yards for a TD.

Woodson performed brilliantly against Dallas on November 15, 2009, earning NFC Defensive Player of the Week honors for the second time by recording nine tackles, a sack, two forced fumbles, and an interception during a 17–7 victory over the Cowboys, with his superb all-around effort making him the first player in NFL history to have a sack, two forced fumbles, and an interception in the same game.

Woodson turned in another exceptional effort against Detroit less than two weeks later, when he helped lead the Packers to a 34–12 win over the Lions on Thanksgiving by making seven tackles, forcing a fumble, recording a sack, and intercepting a pair of Matthew Stafford passes, the second of which he returned 38 yards for Green Bay's final touchdown of the game. Woodson also blanketed Calvin Johnson throughout the contest, limiting him to just two catches for 10 yards, with his superb play once again earning him NFC Defensive Player of the Week honors.

Woodson scored the last of his three touchdowns in 2009 in the regular-season finale, returning an interception 45 yards for a TD during a convincing 33–7 victory over the Arizona Cardinals.

Woodson had a huge game against Detroit on October 3, 2010, leading the Packers to a 38–26 victory over the Lions by recording 11 tackles and scoring what proved to be the game-winning touchdown early in the third quarter, when he picked off a Shaun Hill pass and subsequently returned the ball 48 yards for a TD.

Woodson scored his final touchdown as a member of the Packers during a 49–23 rout of the Denver Broncos on October 2, 2011, when he returned an interception 30 yards for a TD.

NOTABLE ACHIEVEMENTS

- Recorded at least seven interceptions four times.
- Surpassed 100 interception-return yards twice.
- Led NFL in interceptions twice and touchdown interceptions once.
- Finished second in NFL in: interceptions once; touchdown interceptions once; and non-offensive touchdowns once.
- Finished third in NFL in: interceptions once; interception-return yards once; and fumble return yards once.
- Led Packers in interceptions four times.
- Holds Packers career records for most touchdown interceptions (9) and most defensive touchdowns scored (10).
- Ranks among Packers career leaders with 38 interceptions (tied—4th) and 568 interception-return yards (5th).
- Ranks among NFL's all-time leaders with: 65 interceptions (5th); 966 interception-return yards (12th); 11 touchdown interceptions (2nd); and 13 non-offensive touchdowns (5th).
- Three-time division champion (2007, 2011, and 2012).
- 2010 NFC champion.
- Super Bowl XLV champion.
- 2009 Associated Press NFL Defensive Player of the Year.
- Four-time NFC Defensive Player of the Week.
- Four-time NFC Defensive Player of the Month.
- Four-time Pro Bowl selection (2008, 2009, 2010, and 2011).
- Two-time First-Team All-Pro (2009 and 2011).
- Two-time Second-Team All-Pro (2008 and 2010).
- NFL 2000s All-Decade Team.
- Pro Football Hall of Fame All-2000s First Team.
- Pro Football Reference All-2000s Second Team.

22

DAVE ROBINSON

A n exceptional all-around linebacker who defended equally well against the run and the pass, Dave Robinson spent 10 seasons in Green Bay, combining with Ray Nitschke and Lee Roy Caffey to form one of the finest linebacking trios of the 1960s. Big, strong, and agile, Robinson did an outstanding job of stuffing the run and pursuing ball-carriers, while also excelling in pass coverage, with his 21 career interceptions tying him for third-place all-time among Packer linebackers. An outstanding clutch performer who had a knack for making big plays, Robinson helped lead the Packers to three NFL championships and two Super Bowl victories, earning in the process three Pro Bowl selections, two All-Pro nominations, and spots on the NFL 1960s All-Decade Team and the Packers 50th Anniversary Team. And, long after he retired, Robinson finally received the well-deserved honor of being inducted into the Pro Football Hall of Fame.

Born in Mount Holly, New Jersey, on May 3, 1941, Richard David Robinson attended Moorestown High School, where he starred in both football and basketball. After accepting a scholarship offer from Penn State University, Robinson spent three years excelling on both sides of the ball for the Nittany Lions, starring as a tight end on offense and an end on defense. Performing particularly well as a senior in 1962, Robinson earned First-Team All-America honors and recognition as the College Player of the Year from the Newark Athletic Club and the College Lineman of the Year from the Philadelphia Sports Writers Association.

Subsequently selected by the Packers in the first round of the 1963 NFL Draft, with the 14th overall pick, and the San Diego Chargers in the third round of the 1963 AFL Draft, with the 17th overall pick, Robinson elected to play for the Packers after he learned that the Chargers intended to trade his AFL rights to the Buffalo Bills. Moved from defensive end to outside linebacker upon his arrival in Green Bay, Robinson spent his rookie campaign backing up Dan Currie and playing on special teams, before laying claim to the starting left linebacker job his second year in the league.

Remaining in that post for the next nine seasons, Robinson served as a key member of a Green Bay defense that ranked among the NFL's best for most of the 1960s, establishing himself during that time as one of the league's most versatile linebackers. Blessed with outstanding size and speed, the 6'3", 245-pound Robinson used his length and quickness to apply pressure to opposing quarterbacks. Meanwhile, his strength helped make him a force against the run. And, in spite of his size, Robinson possessed the agility and athleticism to stay with the league's top tight ends in pass coverage, with Chicago's Mike Ditka calling him "as reliable as they come." In fact, Robinson recorded a total of 12 interceptions for Green Bay's championship teams of 1965, 1966, and 1967, with his five picks in 1966 tying cornerback Bob Jeter for the team lead, and his 12 picks over the course of those three seasons representing the highest total compiled by any linebacker in the league.

Commenting on his ability to excel in pass coverage, Robinson noted, "You see the guys today, the tight ends today, they push off the linebackers and they drag up. They didn't do that against me. I have a picture where I picked one against Mike Ditka, who did it very well."

Robinson added, "Every day, we worked with the backs in coverage. I had to cover Gale Sayers and Jim Brown, one-on-one. I remember one time I ran 40 or 50 yards down the field with Gale Sayers and intercepted the ball. In Chicago, for that matter."

As for the problems Robinson presented to opposing offenses in the passing game, San Francisco head coach Jack Christiansen said, "Trying to pass over Robinson, with his arms and reaction, is like trying to pass over the Empire State building."

In praising his longtime teammate, Willie Davis, who combined with Robinson and cornerback Herb Adderley to form an elite threesome on the left side of Green Bay's defense, stated, "With him as the left outside linebacker and me as the left defensive end, we lined up next to each other for a lot of years, and I never played with someone that was more knowledgeable. In many ways, he kind of set the pattern for a linebacker in Green Bay for a while . . . I would say that the greatest thing about him was how physical he was. I can tell you right now, there wasn't a tight end that didn't have great respect for Dave."

Expressing similar sentiments toward Robinson, Herb Adderley proclaimed, "Dave Robinson is as good or better than any outside linebacker in the Hall of Fame, including Bobby Bell or Jack Ham."

In addition to his other attributes, Robinson proved to be extremely durable over the course of his career, playing in all 14 games in eight of his

Dave Robinson combined with Ray Nitschke and Lee Roy
Caffey to give the Packers the finest linebacking trio of
their time.
Courtesy of MearsOnlineAuctions.com

10 seasons with the Packers and appearing in 127 out of a possible 140
regular-season contests.

After earning three Pro Bowl selections, four First-Team All-Conference
nominations, and two All-Pro selections between 1966 and 1969, Robinson
suffered the only major injury of his career in 1970, when he tore his Achil-
les tendon, limiting him to just four games. Although he performed well
for the Packers after he returned to the team the following year, Robinson

Robinson's 21 interceptions tie him for third-place all-time among Packer linebackers.
Courtesy of MearsOnlineAuctions.com

spent the next two seasons feuding with new head coach Dan Devine, who he later called his worst coach at any level—high school, college, or pros. Traded to the Washington Redskins by Devine following the conclusion of the 1972 campaign, Robinson spent his final two seasons in Washington and recorded six more interceptions, one of which he returned 28 yards for the only touchdown of his career. Choosing to announce his retirement in August 1975, Robinson ended his career with 27 interceptions, 449 interception-return yards, and 12 fumble recoveries, nine of which came as a member of the Packers.

Following his playing days, Robinson, who spent his offseasons working for the Schlitz Brewery in Milwaukee, took a full-time job at Schlitz, where he remained until 1984, when he started his own beer distributorship in Akron, Ohio. After semi-retiring in 2001, Robinson spent five years working in sales for an artificial turf company, before officially retiring in 2006. Five years later, Robinson survived a bout with colon cancer that changed his outlook on life, prompting him to later tell reporters, "I am here for a purpose."

After failing to gain admission to the Pro Football Hall of Fame for nearly 40 years, Robinson finally received football's ultimate honor in 2013, when the members of the seniors committee nominated him for induction. Upon learning of his election, Robinson said, "I wasn't surprised as much as I was just relieved. If I didn't make it this time, I didn't know what I was going to do. . . . You can't get back on as a senior candidate. I'm 71 years old. I would never be back. This would be my one last shot." He then added, "When you wait a long time, you gain a great deal of appreciation for what it really means to get in the Hall of Fame. I was 14 years old when I started playing football, and this is it. I can't go any higher."

PACKERS CAREER HIGHLIGHTS

Best Season

Robinson played his best ball for the Packers from 1965 to 1967, a period during which he earned two Pro Bowl selections and his lone First-Team All-Pro nomination by recording 12 interceptions, the highest total amassed by any NFL linebacker. Although Robinson established career-high marks with 141 interception-return yards in 1965 and five interceptions in 1966, he earned consensus First-Team All-Pro honors for the only time in 1967, prompting me to identify that as his finest season.

Memorable Moments/Greatest Performances

Robinson made one of the biggest plays of his career in the next-to-last game of the 1965 regular season, when, with the Packers holding a slim 14–13 lead over Baltimore late in the first half and the Colts in possession of the ball deep in Green Bay territory, he intercepted a short swing pass thrown by backup quarterback Gary Cuozzo, which he returned 87 yards to the Colts 10 yard line. The Packers subsequently scored a touchdown that gave them a 21–13 lead at the half and went on to win the contest by a score of 42–27, enabling them to clinch a playoff berth.

Robinson again proved to be a thorn in the side of the Colts during a late-season matchup between the two teams the following year, clinching a 14–10 victory and the Western Conference title for the Packers by recovering a Johnny Unitas fumble deep in Green Bay territory in the closing moments.

Yet, Robinson will always be remembered most fondly by the fans of Green Bay for the play he made against Dallas in the closing moments of the 1966 NFL championship game that helped preserve a 34–27 win over the Cowboys. With Dallas in possession of the ball on the Green Bay 2 yard line, Don Meredith rolled to his right looking for an open receiver on fourth down. However, Robinson applied tremendous pressure to Meredith, draping himself all over the Dallas quarterback as he heaved a desperation pass into the end zone that safety Tom Brown picked off for the game-clincher that gave the Packers their second straight NFL title.

NOTABLE ACHIEVEMENTS

- Intercepted five passes in 1966.
- Finished third in NFL with 141 interception-return yards in 1965.
- Tied for third all-time among Packers linebackers with 21 career interceptions.
- Three-time Western Conference champion (1965, 1966, and 1967).
- Three-time NFL champion (1965, 1966, and 1967).
- Two-time Super Bowl champion (I and II).
- 1967 Pro Bowl MVP.
- Three-time Pro Bowl selection (1966, 1967, and 1969).
- 1967 First-Team All-Pro.
- 1968 Second-Team All-Pro.
- Four-time All–Western Conference First-Team selection (1966, 1967, 1968, and 1969).
- NFL 1960s All-Decade Team.
- Pro Football Hall of Fame All-1960s Team.
- Named to Packers 50th Anniversary Team in 1969.
- Elected to Pro Football Hall of Fame in 2013.

23

DONALD DRIVER

One of the most beloved players in Packers history, Donald Driver spent his entire 14-year NFL career in Green Bay, catching more passes for more yards during that time than any other player in franchise history. Surpassing 70 receptions and 1,000 receiving yards seven times each, Driver led the Packers in both categories on multiple occasions, en route to also setting a franchise record for the most consecutive games with at least one catch. Extremely durable as well, Driver missed just nine games his final 13 years in the league, appearing in more contests over the course of his career than anyone else in team annals, excluding Brett Favre. Driver's consistently outstanding play, which earned him three Pro Bowl selections, helped lead the Packers to six division titles, one conference championship, and one NFL title.

Born in Houston, Texas, on February 2, 1975, Donald Jerome Driver grew up in abject poverty with his mother and five siblings, living out of a U-Haul truck for a period of time after a collection agency confiscated his family's possessions following the divorce of his parents. Forced to spend many nights in motel rooms that his mother purchased with food stamps, young Donald and his older brother Marvin III began stealing cars and selling drugs during their teenage years to make ends meet, with Driver telling *USA Today* years later, "You try to do anything you can to provide for your family." Driver's life finally began to turn around, though, when he moved in with his grandmother at the age of 14.

Excelling in multiple sports while attending Milby High School in Houston, Driver lettered four times each in football, baseball, basketball, and track, gaining a considerable amount of notoriety for his performance on the gridiron, where he starred as a wide receiver, defensive back, and kickoff returner. Continuing to compete in football and track after enrolling at Alcorn State University in Mississippi, Driver earned conference "Athlete of the Year" honors five times, concluding his college career with 88 receptions for 1,993 yards, while also recording personal bests of 2.30

Donald Driver ranks second in franchise history in games played.
Courtesy of Mike Morbeck

meters in the high jump, 15.62 meters in the triple jump, and 7.75 meters in the long jump.

Despite the tremendous athletic prowess that Driver displayed in college, he lasted until the seventh round of the 1999 NFL Draft, when the Packers finally claimed him with the 213th overall pick. Considered a long-shot to make the team when he arrived at his first training camp, Driver made an extremely favorable impression on everyone in attendance with his daring and determination, with then–Packers GM Ron Wolf recalling, "He was just fearless, so you knew right away, if we nurture this, we have something really special here—if he doesn't kill himself first. Obviously, we didn't realize the steps this young fellow would take, but we didn't draft players to fail. We drafted players we thought would have an opportunity to make our team, and Donald did more than that."

Looking back at his initial impression of the 6-foot, 188-pound Driver, former Packers defensive back Darren Sharper said:

> My first memory of Donald was when he was the seventh-round pick in 1999, and we didn't know who he was. I remember a practice when he was a rookie and I was already a starter, and I was covering him in the slot. I wasn't worried about him at all, and so, when Brett threw the ball, it looked like it was thrown too far, and I thought for sure it'd be an incompletion. Out of nowhere, Driver makes this flying, one-handed catch against me. It was incredible. In that training camp, he just made play after play after play, and you could just tell that, with how hard he worked and the skills that he had, he was just special.

Driver's dedication and resolve ended up earning him a roster spot, after which he spent his first three seasons in Green Bay serving as a backup, making just 37 receptions for 520 yards and three touchdowns during that time. However, he assumed a far more prominent role after the Packers released Antonio Freeman prior to the start of the 2002 campaign, rapidly emerging as Brett Favre's favorite target. Establishing himself as the Packers' go-to guy on offense, Driver earned Pro Bowl honors his first year as a starter by leading the team with 70 receptions, 1,064 receiving yards, and nine touchdown catches. He then posted a somewhat less impressive stat-line in 2003 (52 catches, 621 yards, and 2 TDs) after suffering a scary neck injury against Minnesota in the regular-season opener that forced him to leave a nearly silent Lambeau Field on a stretcher. Subsequently asked by his wife to retire, Driver recalled telling her, "I don't think God's done with us yet. If I can recover from this, let's just see where God takes us. Eleven years later, He took us to places we never thought we would go."

Fully recovered by the start of the 2004 campaign, Driver began an outstanding six-year run during which he compiled the following numbers:

YEAR	RECS	RECEIVING YARDS	TD RECS
2004	84	1,208	9
2005	86	1,221	5
2006	92	1,295	8
2007	82	1,048	2
2008	74	1,012	5
2009	70	1,061	6

By topping 70 receptions and 1,000 receiving yards six straight times, Driver became the first Packers player to accomplish the feat. In the process of doing so, he also broke Sterling Sharpe's franchise record for most pass receptions and surpassed James Lofton as the team's all-time leader in receiving yardage. Driver ranked among the league leaders in receptions twice and receiving yards three times during that period, earning Pro Bowl honors in both 2006 and 2007. Meanwhile, his bright smile, infectious laugh, and consistency on the playing field made him extremely popular with his teammates and the hometown fans.

In expressing his admiration for his former teammate, Darren Sharper said, "The thing about Driver is that he was a complete receiver; he was stronger than he looked, a guy that could go across the middle, take some hits, and still have enough balance that he would be able to shed defenders and make big plays. When I got to Minnesota and he made some plays against us, I could tell that he had matured into a complete, premier receiver for that team, and that he was a guy that was going to do that for a long time."

Brett Favre praised his longtime teammate by stating:

Donald was a tremendous player. He overcame great odds to make the team when he first joined us and, as has been well documented, extreme challenges while he was growing up. He was dependable and productive for the Packers. Even though some of the big plays we had together come to mind, it really is the way he could make guys miss that stands out to me, like the long touchdown he had just before halftime in Minnesota (in 2006). He also was a big reason we won the division at the Metrodome in '04. I have great memories of playing with Donald. He was a great teammate—he was very likeable in the locker room. That he could go from a seventh-round draft choice to the Packers' all-time leading receiver is a real tribute to him.

Driver also gradually emerged as a quiet leader during his time in Green Bay, serving as a positive influence on the younger receivers who joined the team during the latter stages of his career. In discussing Driver, James Jones commented:

He was one of the hardest-working players I have ever seen. A lot of guys, when they get to stardom, they tend to relax and not care as much about their craft and getting better. Every year I played with Donald Driver, he was striving to get better every season. He was at every practice. Mike McCarthy would tell him, "You can go ahead and relax at this practice," and he would not miss one. As a young guy, watching that truly helped me become a better professional and a better player. He was one of the coolest teammates to be around. He was always full of fun, always wanting to help other people get better on the field no matter what. He was just a leader.

Jordy Nelson added, "He was a playmaker. That is the first thing that comes to my mind when I think of him on the field—all the amazing catches he would make, the one-handed catches. He could just make plays. He would be practicing every single day, wouldn't take a day off no matter how many years he had been here."

Driver also drew praise from Vikings defensive end Jared Allen, who suggested, "Donald was one of those players that you always had to be aware of as a defense no matter where he was on the field. He put pressure on defensive linemen to get to the quarterback quickly because, if you didn't, Donald would find a way to get open."

Driver spent three more years in Green Bay, seeing his playing time gradually diminish during that time, before announcing his retirement following the conclusion of the 2012 campaign while appearing as a guest on ESPN2's *Mike and Mike in the Morning* show. He ended his career with 743 receptions, 10,137 receiving yards, 61 TD catches, and 62 total touchdowns scored (he also ran for one touchdown). The Packers subsequently held a public retirement ceremony for Driver in the Lambeau Field Atrium that hundreds of fans attended. Speaking to the assembled mass, Driver stated, "You know, even though I feel that I can still play the game, God has made the answer clear to me. Retirement is now. I have to retire as a Green

Driver holds franchise records for most pass receptions and most receiving yards.
Courtesy of Mike Morbeck

Bay Packer. I've always said that I never want to wear another uniform—but always the green and gold."

Driver, who vividly remembers his difficult childhood, remained active in the community throughout his playing career, making over 300 charitable appearances and creating with his wife, Betina, in 2001 the Donald

Driver Foundation, which offers assistance to ill children with unmanageable hospital bills, provides housing for the homeless, and donates to a variety of local charities. Since retiring as an active player, he has continued his charitable work by donating much of his time and efforts to such institutions as Children's Hospital of Wisconsin and Goodwill Industries. Driver has also authored three children's books and released his official memoir, *Driven*, which includes many personal stories about his impoverished childhood and his years with the Packers that he never shared before.

Driver, whose accomplishments often flew under the radar during his playing days (he never earned All-Pro honors), waxed philosophical when he said, "You never get recognition until you're dead and gone. So, maybe, when I'm dead and gone, someone will say, 'You know something . . . that man was a great player.'"

CAREER HIGHLIGHTS

Best Season

Driver performed extremely well for the Packers in both 2004 and 2005, totaling 170 receptions, 2,429 receiving yards, and 14 touchdowns over the course of those two campaigns. However, he had his finest all-around season in 2006, when he scored eight touchdowns and finished fifth in the league with 92 receptions and 1,295 receiving yards, establishing career-high marks in each of the last two categories.

Memorable Moments/Greatest Performances

Although the Packers suffered a heartbreaking 33–31 defeat at the hands of the Carolina Panthers on December 12, 1999, Driver recorded the first TD reception of his career during the contest, hooking up with Brett Favre on an 8-yard scoring play midway through the third period.

Driver had his breakout game on September 29, 2002, making five catches for 97 yards and two touchdowns during a 17–14 win over Carolina, with his 22-yard TD reception with 4:10 remaining in regulation providing the margin of victory.

Driver followed that up by topping 100 receiving yards for the first time in his career, making four catches for 120 yards and one touchdown during a 34–21 Monday night win over the Chicago Bears, with his scoring play covering 85 yards.

Driver turned in an outstanding performance against Detroit on November 10, 2002, making a career-high 11 receptions for 130 yards during a lopsided 40–14 victory over the Lions.

Driver nearly equaled that mark on October 11, 2004, making 10 catches for 150 yards during a 48–27 loss to the Tennessee Titans.

Driver posted extremely similar numbers during a 16–13 win over the Houston Texans on November 21, 2004, making 10 receptions for 148 yards and one touchdown, which covered 24 yards.

Driver came up big in the clutch for the Packers during a 34–31 victory over the Minnesota Vikings on Christmas Eve 2004, making 11 catches for 162 yards and one touchdown, which came on a 3-yard grab that tied the score at 31–31 with just 3:34 remaining in regulation. The Packers subsequently won the game on a 29-yard Ryan Longwell field goal as time expired.

Driver made significant contributions to two of the Packers' four victories in 2005, making 10 receptions for 114 yards during their 33–25 win over Atlanta on November 13, before catching six passes for 118 yards during their 23–17 win over Seattle in the regular-season finale.

Driver had a huge game against Minnesota on November 12, 2006, making six catches for a career-high 191 yards and one touchdown during a 23–17 victory over the Vikings, with his TD being an 82-yard connection with Brett Favre late in the first half that put the Packers ahead to stay.

Driver turned in another outstanding effort against San Francisco on December 10, 2006, helping the Packers record a 30–19 win over the 49ers by making nine receptions for 160 yards and one touchdown, with his scoring play covering 68 yards.

Driver contributed to a 37–26 victory over the Detroit Lions on November 22, 2007, by making 10 catches for 147 yards.

Although the Packers ended up losing the 2007 NFC championship game to the Giants, Driver hooked up with Brett Favre on a 90-yard touchdown reception, the longest postseason play in franchise history.

Driver helped lead the Packers to a 31–21 win over Detroit in the 2008 regular-season finale by making six catches for 111 yards and one touchdown, which covered 71 yards.

Driver again torched the Detroit secondary on Thanksgiving Day 2009, making seven receptions for 142 yards and one touchdown during a 34–12 victory over the Lions, with his 68-yard connection with Aaron Rodgers leading to Green Bay's first touchdown.

NOTABLE ACHIEVEMENTS

- Surpassed 70 receptions seven times, topping 80 catches four times and 90 catches once.
- Surpassed 1,000 receiving yards seven times, topping 1,200 yards three times.
- Made nine touchdown receptions twice.
- Finished fifth in NFL in: pass receptions once; receiving yards once; and TD receptions once.
- Led Packers in pass receptions five times and receiving yards four times.
- Holds Packers record for most consecutive games with at least one pass reception (133).
- Holds Packers career records for most pass receptions (743) and most receiving yards (10,137).
- Ranks among Packers career leaders with: 10,354 yards from scrimmage (2nd); 10,363 all-purpose yards (2nd); 61 touchdown receptions (4th); 62 total touchdowns scored (tied—6th); 14 seasons played (tied—4th); and 205 games played (2nd).
- Six-time division champion (2002, 2003, 2004, 2007, 2011, and 2012).
- 2010 NFC champion.
- Super Bowl XLV champion.
- Three-time Pro Bowl selection (2002, 2006, and 2007).

24

MIKE MICHALSKE

One of the finest two-way linemen to play in the NFL during the league's formative years, Mike Michalske earned All-Pro honors in seven of his 10 NFL seasons, doing so five times as a member of the Packers from 1929 to 1935. Nicknamed "Iron Mike" for his stamina and durability, Michalske played all 60 minutes of almost every game during his time in Green Bay, missing only nine of 104 contests, with five of those coming after he sustained a career-ending back injury in his final season. Excelling as a guard on both sides of the ball, Michalske served as a key blocker on offense for the Packers' NFL championship teams of 1929, 1930, and 1931, opening up holes for the likes of Johnny (Blood) McNally and Bob Monnett, while also doing an outstanding job of defending against the run and applying pressure to opposing quarterbacks on defense. In addition to his numerous All-Pro selections, Michalske's stellar all-around play earned him spots on the NFL 1920s All-Decade Team and the Packers All–Iron Man Era Team, as well as eventual induction into the Pro Football Hall of Fame.

Born to German immigrant parents in Cleveland, Ohio, on April 24, 1903, August Mike Michalske starred in baseball, football, and basketball while attending local West Tech High School. Following his graduation from West Tech, Michalske enrolled at Penn State University, where he spent three years splitting his time on the gridiron between the guard, half-back, fullback, and tackle positions. After earning All-America honors as a senior in 1925, Michalske signed with the American Football League's New York Yankees, with whom he spent the next three seasons, remaining with them after they joined the National Football League in 1927. However, after making First-Team All-Pro as a guard in each of his first two NFL seasons, Michalske joined the Packers when the Yankees disbanded following the conclusion of the 1928 campaign.

Already considered to be the best guard in the National Football League by the time he arrived in Green Bay, Michalske helped the Packers win their first league championship in 1929 by performing magnificently on both

Mike Michalske starred on both sides of the ball for three Packer championship teams.
Courtesy of RMYAuctions.com

sides of the ball, earning in the process First-Team All-Pro honors for the third of five straight times. Speaking of Michalske at season's end, Chicago Cardinals fullback Ernie Nevers, a five-time All-Pro himself, rated him as the best player in the NFL, calling him a "wonder" and adding, "There's nobody like him on the college or professional field today." Continuing to perform at an elite level in each of the next two seasons, Michalske earned consensus First-Team All-Pro honors in 1930 and 1931 as well, with the Packers claiming the NFL title both years.

Combining with Cal Hubbard to anchor the Packers' offensive line from his left guard position, the 6-foot, 210-pound Michalske possessed a rare combination of speed, agility, and power, which he used to explode off the line and lead interference for the ball-carrier. Although Michalske lacked Hubbard's size, he proved to be the quicker and nimbler of the two, enabling him to succeed against opponents who often outweighed him by 20 or 30 pounds. Meanwhile, when the other team had the ball, Michalske used his quickness and elusiveness to pioneer both the blitz and an early version of modern linebacking play. Employing a knifing, slicing style on defense, Michalske had the ability to run plays down before they fully developed, often tailing the opposing guard from the opposite side and tackling the ball-carrier before he reached the line of scrimmage. Michalske also excelled at pressuring the quarterback, frequently disrupting passing plays with his pursuit of opposing signal-callers.

Michalske's other attributes included his extraordinary stamina and durability, as well as his intelligence and intricate knowledge of the sport. In addressing the first trait, Michalske said, "I didn't get hurt. Not until I injured my back in my last year. I played both ways—60 minutes almost every game." And, speaking of Michalske's grasp of the game, teammate Buckets Goldenberg stated, "Mike was not only a smart player, but he had a fine mind for football and a great interest in the game from all standpoints. He sold Lambeau on quite a few of his ideas."

Following the Packers' three-year championship run, Michalske remained with the team for another four seasons, earning Second-Team All-Pro honors in both 1934 and 1935, before retiring prior to the start of the 1936 campaign to become basketball coach and assistant football coach at Lafayette College. However, he chose to return to the Packers as a player-coach in 1937, appearing in six games with them, before suffering a back injury that ended his playing career. Officially announcing his retirement on August 8, 1938, Michalske left the game with two touchdowns and one safety to his credit, recording all of those as a member of the Packers.

Following his playing days, Michalske entered into a lengthy career in coaching that included stints with the Chicago Cardinals (1939), St. Norbert College (1940–1941), Iowa State University (1942–1946), the Baltimore Colts of the All-America Football Conference (1949), Baylor University (1950–1952), Texas A&M University (1953), and the

Michalske's superb all-around play earned him a spot on the NFL 1920s All-Decade Team and a place in the Pro Football Hall of Fame.
Courtesy of RMYAuctions.com

University of Texas (1954). He also remained close to the Packers, scouting for them in 1947, and continuing to file scouting reports on draft prospects while coaching in college and during his retirement. Moving to De Pere, Wisconsin, in his later years, Michalske lived until October 26, 1983, when he passed away at a Green Bay hospital at the age of 80.

Inducted into the Pro Football Hall of Fame in 1964, Michalske became the first guard to be so honored, with his contemporaries feeling strongly that he earned that distinction. Speaking of his former opponent more than a decade after Michalske retired, Hall of Fame quarterback Benny Friedman said, "I would put him down in my book as the best guard, bar none, I ever saw." Meanwhile, longtime Packers teammate Johnny (Blood) McNally proclaimed, "He was as great as any football player Green Bay ever had. He had very fast reflexes. He would start moving before his opponent. That was his chief asset, besides his tremendous fighting spirit."

PACKERS CAREER HIGHLIGHTS

Best Season

Michalske earned the first of his three consecutive First-Team All-Pro nominations as a member of the Packers in 1929, when he helped lead his new team to a 12-0-1 record and the NFL championship, contributing significantly to an offense that scored 198 points during the season, and to a defense that allowed the opposition a total of only 22 points. Nevertheless, with Michalske's exceptional blocking from his guard position helping the Packers score 291 points two years later (easily their highest total until 1942, when they scored 300 points), the 1931 campaign would have to be considered his finest season.

Memorable Moments/Greatest Performances

Michalske made the most memorable play of his career during a 6–2 win over the Chicago Bears on November 1, 1931, when he scored his team's only points on an 80-yard interception return for a touchdown.

Michalske once again proved to be the difference in the 1932 regular-season opener, when he led the Packers to a 15–7 victory over the Chicago Cardinals by recording a safety and recovering a fumble in the end zone for the second and final defensive touchdown of his career.

NOTABLE ACHIEVEMENTS

- Scored two defensive touchdowns during career (one interception return and one fumble return).
- Three-time NFL champion (1929, 1930, and 1931).
- Three-time First-Team All-Pro (1929, 1930, and 1931).
- Two-time Second-Team All-Pro (1934 and 1935).
- NFL 1920s All-Decade Team.
- Pro Football Hall of Fame All-1920s Team.
- Named to Packers All-Time Team in 1946 and 1957.
- Named to Packers All–Iron Man Era Team in 1976.
- Elected to Pro Football Hall of Fame in 1964.

25

─ LEROY BUTLER ─

The first defensive back in NFL history to record at least 20 career interceptions and 20 career sacks, LeRoy Butler overcame serious leg and foot problems that confined him to a wheelchair for much of his youth to eventually establish himself as one of the most durable players ever to take the field for the Packers. Appearing in more games than any other defensive back in franchise history (181), Butler spent his entire 12-year NFL career in Green Bay, missing a total of only four contests his first 11 years in the league. A sure tackler and hard hitter, Butler ranks third all-time on the Packers with 1,014 career tackles, bringing down opposing ball-carriers more than 100 times on three separate occasions from his strong safety position. Outstanding in pass coverage as well, Butler led the Packers in interceptions five times, with his stellar all-around play helping them win two conference championships and one NFL title. A four-time Pro Bowler, Butler also earned four All-Pro selections and a spot on the Pro Football Hall of Fame All-1990s First Team. Yet, he is perhaps remembered most by Packer fans for being the originator of the "Lambeau Leap."

Born in Jacksonville, Florida, on July 19, 1968, LeRoy Butler III suffered through a difficult childhood during which he spent much of his time either in a wheelchair or in leg braces while undergoing therapy to strengthen the bones in his pigeon-toed feet. At the age of eight after his sister accidentally knocked him out of his wheelchair, young LeRoy suddenly found himself able to walk without any difficulty. Butler subsequently went on to star in football while attending local Robert E. Lee High School, before enrolling at Florida State University, where he spent three seasons playing under head coach Bobby Bowden. Concluding his college career with 194 tackles and nine interceptions, Butler earned consensus All-America honors as a senior, prompting the Packers to select him in the second round of the 1990 NFL Draft, with the 48th overall pick.

Although Butler spent his first season in Green Bay serving as a backup and playing mostly on special teams, he managed to make an impact

LeRoy Butler led the Packers in interceptions five times and tackles once. Courtesy of BidAmi.com

whenever he took the field on defense, tying for the team lead with three interceptions. After laying claim to the starting right cornerback job the following year, Butler picked off another three passes and recorded 63 tackles, which placed him third on the club. However, he didn't truly hit his stride until the Packers moved him to his more natural position of strong safety in 1992, remaining at that post for the rest of his career. After intercepting one pass and registering 74 tackles in his first year at strong safety, Butler established himself as arguably the league's top player at that position over the course of the next few seasons, earning Pro Bowl and First-Team All-Pro honors four times between 1993 and 1998. Having one of his finest seasons for the Packers in 1993, Butler recorded more than 100 tackles for the first of three times and ranked among the NFL leaders with six interceptions and 131 interception-return yards, earning in the process his first trip to the Pro Bowl and his initial All-Pro selection. Butler also emerged as a tremendous fan favorite that year, when, after returning a recovered fumble 25 yards for a touchdown, he jumped into the stands behind the end zone to celebrate his score with the hometown fans, thereby inventing what eventually became known as the "Lambeau Leap."

Butler followed up his exceptional 1993 campaign with two more solid seasons, performing especially well in 1995, when he picked off five passes and once again brought down opposing ball-carriers more than 100 times. He then began a string of three straight seasons in which he earned Pro Bowl and All-Pro recognition, helping to lead the Packers to the 1996 NFL championship by finishing second on the team in tackles, recording a career-high 6½ sacks, and intercepting five passes, which he returned for 149 yards and one touchdown.

Serving as one of the cornerstones of Green Bay's defense for most of his career, the 6-foot, 197-pound Butler proved to be an outstanding team leader whose versatility made him a key contributor to Packer teams that advanced to the playoffs six straight times. Quick enough to cover wide receivers, while also being strong and aggressive enough to bring down running backs near the line of scrimmage, Butler annually ranked among the team leaders in interceptions and tackles, finishing first on the club in picks five times. Also capable of applying pressure to opposing quarterbacks via the blitz, Butler recorded at least three sacks in a season on three separate occasions. Extremely tough and durable as well, Butler started every game for six straight seasons at one point, appearing in every contest in 1997 despite being plagued by a badly torn bicep muscle the entire year. However, Butler perhaps made his greatest contributions to the Packers with his leadership and tremendous on-field presence. A consummate team player who restructured his contract on several occasions to help the Packers fit other players under the salary cap, Butler spent his last few seasons in Green Bay serving as a coach on the field, directing his teammates on where to line up, and shouting out instructions as to what they should look for on each play.

After earning Pro Bowl and First-Team All-Pro honors for the third consecutive time in 1998, Butler remained a fixture in the Green Bay defensive backfield for two more years, before a broken shoulder blade sustained while tackling Atlanta Falcons running back Jamal Anderson nine games into the 2001 campaign forced him to the sidelines for the remainder of the year, essentially bringing his playing career to an end. Choosing to announce

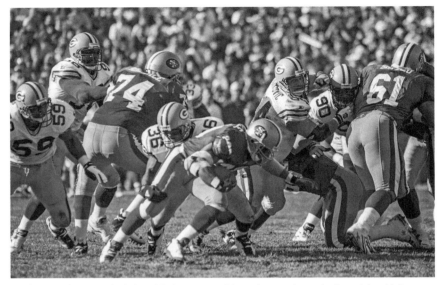

Butler (#36) recorded the third most tackles of any player in franchise history.
Courtesy of George A. Kitrinos

his retirement prior to the start of the 2002 season after learning that the shoulder had not healed properly, Butler ended his career with a total of 1,014 tackles, which places him third in team annals. He also ranks among the franchise's all-time leaders with 38 interceptions (tied for fourth), 533 interception-return yards (sixth), and 181 games played (seventh).

Since retiring as an active player, Butler has entered into a career in broadcasting, providing television and radio commentary on Packer games for Time Warner Cable Sports Channel and 105.7 The Fan. He has also co-authored several books, one of which, *The LeRoy Butler Story*, tells of his rise from childhood disability and the housing projects of Jacksonville, Florida, to NFL stardom.

CAREER HIGHLIGHTS

Best Season

Butler had an outstanding year for the Packers in 1993, earning Pro Bowl and First-Team All-Pro honors for the first time by recording a career-high six interceptions and 90 solo tackles, while also forcing two fumbles and recovering another, which he returned for a touchdown. However, he had his finest all-around season in 1996, earning First-Team All-Pro recognition for the first of three straight times by picking off five passes, which he returned for one touchdown and a total of 149 yards, recovering two fumbles, recording 87 tackles, and amassing a career-high 6½ sacks.

Memorable Moments/Greatest Performances

Butler helped lead the Packers to a 17–3 win over the Bears on October 31, 1993, by recording an interception and the first sack of his career.

Although the Packers suffered a 27–17 defeat at the hands of the Dallas Cowboys in the divisional round of the 1993 playoffs, Butler performed well in just his second postseason start, intercepting a pass and recovering a fumble.

Butler came up big for the Packers during a 35–28 win over the Bears on November 12, 1995, picking off a pass and recording a sack of Chicago quarterback Erik Kramer, with his interception deep in Green Bay territory with less than two minutes remaining in regulation helping to preserve the victory.

Butler picked off two passes in one game for the first time in his career during a 34–3 win over the Tampa Bay Buccaneers in the 1996 regular-season opener.

Butler contributed to a lopsided 42–10 victory over the San Diego Chargers two weeks later by recording another pair of interceptions, one of which he returned 90 yards for a touchdown.

Butler turned in an exceptional all-around effort against Tampa Bay on October 27, 1996, helping the Packers defeat the Bucs by a score of 13–7 by knocking down one pass, recording 1½ sacks, and making nine tackles.

Butler contributed significantly to a 38–32 win over the Vikings on September 21, 1997, by intercepting two passes and making a touchdown-saving tackle on Robert Smith at the Green Bay 6 yard line after the Minnesota running back reeled off a 50-yard run.

Butler picked off another two passes during a 20–10 victory over the Detroit Lions on November 2, 1997.

Butler again proved to be a thorn in the side of Detroit in the 1998 regular-season opener, scoring Green Bay's first touchdown of the campaign when he returned a recovered fumble 32 yards for a first-quarter TD that gave the Packers an early 10–0 lead in a game they went on to win by a score of 39–19.

Butler contributed to a 36–22 victory over the 49ers on November 1, 1998, by recording two sacks and one forced fumble.

Yet, the most memorable play of Butler's career took place during a 28–0 victory over the Los Angeles Raiders on December 26, 1993, when he invented the "Lambeau Leap." With the Packers hosting the Raiders and already up by a score of 14–0 early in the fourth quarter, Butler forced a fumble by Los Angeles running back Randy Jordan. After Reggie White scooped up the loose ball at the Raiders' 35-yard-line, he ran with it for 10 yards before lateraling it to Butler, who ran the remaining 25 yards for the first touchdown of his career. Seeking to share his joy with the home-town fans, Butler made a spontaneous leap into the arms of the fans in the south bleachers, inventing in the process the "Lambeau Leap," which wide receiver Robert Brooks later popularized by leaping completely into the stands following a touchdown.

NOTABLE ACHIEVEMENTS

- Scored three career defensive touchdowns (one interception return and two fumble returns).
- Recorded at least five interceptions four times.
- Surpassed 100 interception-return yards three times.
- Recorded 6½ sacks in 1996.
- Recorded more than 100 tackles three times.
- Led Packers in interceptions five times and tackles once.
- Ranks among Packers career leaders with: 1,014 total tackles (3rd); 735 unassisted tackles (5th); 38 interceptions (tied—4th); 533 interception-return yards (6th); and 181 games played (7th).
- First defensive back in NFL history to record at least 20 career sacks and 20 career interceptions.
- Three-time division champion (1995, 1996, and 1997).
- Two-time NFC champion (1996 and 1997).
- Super Bowl XXXI champion.
- 1996 Week 3 NFC Defensive Player of the Week.
- Four-time Pro Bowl selection (1993, 1996, 1997, and 1998).
- Four-time First-Team All-Pro (1993, 1996, 1997, and 1998).
- Four-time First-Team All-NFC selection (1993, 1996, 1997, and 1998).
- NFL 1990s All-Decade Team.
- Pro Football Hall of Fame All-1990s First Team.
- Pro Football Reference All-1990s First Team.

26

— AHMAN GREEN —

The Packers' all-time leading rusher, Ahman Green spent seven years in Green Bay, gaining more than 1,000 yards on the ground in all but one of those seasons. An explosive runner who is one of just two players in NFL history to have two touchdown runs of 90 or more yards, Green gained more yards rushing (6,848) and yards from scrimmage (9,036) than anyone else in the league from 2000 to 2004, establishing in the process franchise records for most yards rushing in a season (1,883) and in a game (218). Also excelling as a receiver coming out of the backfield, Green caught more than 50 passes four times and amassed more than 500 receiving yards twice, enabling him to also accumulate more yards from scrimmage and all-purpose yards than any other player in Packers' history. Green's exceptional all-around play helped lead the Packers to three division titles, earning him four Pro Bowl selections, one All-Pro nomination, and recognition as the 2003 NFC Offensive Player of the Year.

Born in Omaha, Nebraska, on February 16, 1977, Ahman Rashad Green attended Omaha North High School before transferring to Omaha Central, where, in addition to earning High School All-America and state Player of the Year honors in football as a senior, he competed in powerlifting and track and field, posting a personal-best time of 10.61 seconds in the 100-meter dash. Following his graduation from Omaha Central, Green chose to remain close to home and accepted an athletic scholarship from the University of Nebraska. Performing brilliantly for the Cornhuskers the next three seasons, Green helped lead them to a pair of national championships by rushing for 3,880 yards and 42 touchdowns, with his superb play earning him Freshman All-America honors and recognition as All–Big 12 Conference and a Second-Team All-American as a junior.

Choosing to forego his final year of college eligibility, Green entered the 1998 NFL Draft, where the Seattle Seahawks selected him in the third round, with the 76th overall pick. Stuck behind veteran running back Ricky Watters in Seattle, Green accomplished very little his first two years in the league, gaining just 329 yards on the ground and scoring only one touchdown. However, he finally received a reprieve on April 15, 2000, when the Seahawks dealt him and a fifth-round draft pick to the Packers for defensive back Fred Vinson and a sixth-round pick, in one of the best trades the Green Bay front office ever made. After earning the starting halfback job his first year in Green Bay, Green went on to compile the following numbers over the course of the next five seasons:

YEAR	RUSHING YARDS	RECEIVING YARDS	YARDS FROM SCRIMMAGE	TDS
2000	1,175	559	1,734	13
2001	1,387	594	1,981	11
2002	1,240	393	1,633	9
2003	1,883	367	2,250	20
2004	1,163	275	1,438	8

In addition to leading all NFL players in rushing yards and yards from scrimmage during that five-year period, Green set single-season franchise records with his 1,883 yards rushing, 2,250 yards from scrimmage, and 20 touchdowns in 2003, earning in the process recognition as NFC Offensive Player of the Year. He also averaged at least 4.5 yards per carry in four of those five seasons, posting a career-high mark of 5.3 in his banner year of 2003. Meanwhile, Green surpassed 50 receptions four times, making a career-best 73 catches in 2000, with his outstanding all-around play earning him Pro Bowl honors from 2001 to 2004, his lone All-Pro selection in 2001, and First-Team All-NFC honors in both 2001 and 2003.

Standing six feet tall and weighing 217 pounds, Green possessed the size and strength to run over people. However, his speed, quickness, and elusiveness also gave him the ability to run away from defenders, making him a threat to go the distance any time he touched the ball. Green exhibited his game-breaking ability on December 28, 2003, and October 24, 2004, when he scored on touchdown runs of 98 and 90 yards, respectively, making him just the second player in NFL history to record more than one TD run of at least 90 yards (Bo Jackson was the other).

Green's string of five straight seasons in which he ran for more than 1,000 yards came to an end in 2005, when he appeared in only five games due to injury. However, he once again topped the 1,000-yard mark in 2006,

Ahman Green's 8,322 yards rushing represents a franchise record.
Courtesy of George A. Kitrinos

rushing for 1,059 yards, gaining another 373 yards on 46 pass receptions, and scoring six touchdowns.

A free agent following the conclusion of the 2006 campaign, Green elected to sign with the Houston Texans, with whom he spent two injury-riddled seasons, rushing for only 554 yards and scoring just five touchdowns. Released by the Texans on February 10, 2009, Green re-signed with the Packers some eight months later to add depth to their depleted backfield. Assuming the role of a backup the final eight games of the season, Green rushed for 160 yards and one touchdown, before being released by the Packers at the end of the year. He left Green Bay having rushed for 8,322 yards and 54 touchdowns as a member of the team. Green also made 350 receptions for 2,726 yards and 14 touchdowns while playing for the Packers.

Unable to draw interest from any other NFL team, Green spent the 2010 season with the Omaha Nighthawks of the United Football League, before signing a two-year contract with the Montreal Alouettes of the

Canadian Football League on March 9, 2011. However, Green never appeared in a single game north of the border, retiring after an injured hamstring suffered on the second day of training camp prompted the Alouettes to release him.

Unfortunately, Green has run afoul of the law since retiring as an active player, being arrested at his Wisconsin home during the early morning hours of June 26, 2017, for allegedly slapping and shoving his 15-year-old daughter into a kitchen cabinet during a fight over household chores. According to the Brown County Sheriff's Office, deputies took Green into custody after his daughter fled the family's home and sought out a neighbor, claiming she had been abused. Green later partially corroborated his daughter's story, telling responding officers that he struck her over the head with an open hand and shoved her after she refused to clean the dirty dishes.

PACKERS CAREER HIGHLIGHTS

Best Season

Green had easily his finest season for the Packers in 2003, when, in addition to making 50 receptions for 367 yards and five touchdowns, he rushed for 15 touchdowns and a franchise-record 1,883 yards, with his 2,250 yards from scrimmage and 20 total touchdowns scored also establishing single-season franchise marks that still stand. Green finished second in the NFL in yards rushing, rushing touchdowns, and total touchdowns, with his fabulous performance earning him one of his two First-Team All-NFC nominations.

Memorable Moments/Greatest Performances

Green had his breakout game for the Packers on September 24, 2000, when he keyed a 29–3 victory over the Arizona Cardinals by carrying the ball 12 times for 93 yards, gaining another 49 yards on two pass receptions, and scoring his first touchdown as a member of the team on a 19-yard run.

Green went over 100 yards rushing for the first time in his career on November 19, 2000, when he gained 153 yards on 24 carries during a 26–24 win over the Indianapolis Colts.

Green helped lead the Packers to a 33–28 victory over the Minnesota Vikings on December 17, 2000, by carrying the ball 25 times for a season-high 161 yards, while also making four catches for 31 yards and one touchdown.

Green (#34) led all NFL players in rushing yards and yards from scrimmage from 2000 to 2004.
Courtesy of Mike Morbeck

Green began the 2001 campaign in style, leading the Packers to a convincing 28–6 win over the Lions in the regular-season opener by carrying the ball 17 times for 157 yards and two touchdowns, with his TD runs covering 31 and 83 yards.

Green turned in an outstanding all-around effort against Tampa Bay on November 4, 2001, catching six passes for 49 yards, carrying the ball 24 times for 169 yards, and scoring on a 63-yard run, in helping the Packers record a 21–20 victory over the Buccaneers that they won on a late 55-yard punt return TD by Allen Rossum.

Green starred again during a 30–7 victory over the Cleveland Browns on December 23, 2001, gaining 150 yards on the ground, with his longest run of the day being a 43-yard jaunt off left tackle that helped set up the Packers' final score early in the fourth quarter.

Green helped lead the Packers to a 37–34 overtime win over Atlanta in the 2002 regular-season opener by gaining 155 yards on 27 carries and making six receptions for another 42 yards.

Green rushed for 88 yards and three touchdowns during a lopsided 30–9 victory over the Washington Redskins on October 20, 2002, scoring on TD runs that covered 24, 2, and 8 yards.

Green provided much of the impetus for a 31–6 win over the Detroit Lions on September 14, 2003, by scoring on a 65-yard run on the Packers' second play from scrimmage. He finished the game with 23 carries for 160 yards and that one touchdown.

Green displayed his skills before a national television audience two weeks later, leading the Packers to a 38–23 Monday night win over the Chicago Bears on September 29, 2003, by carrying the ball 19 times for 176 yards and two touchdowns, with one of those being a 60-yard run on Green Bay's second offensive series of the game.

Green amassed nearly 200 yards of total offense during a 30–27 win over the Minnesota Vikings on November 2, 2003, gaining 137 yards on 21 carries, and catching five passes for another 52 yards and one touchdown, in leading the Packers to victory.

Although the Packers suffered a 17–14 defeat at the hands of the Philadelphia Eagles the following week, Green had another big game, carrying the ball 29 times for 192 yards, and scoring a pair of touchdowns, with one of those coming on a 24-yard pass reception and the other on a 45-yard run that put Green Bay ahead by a score of 14–10 with just over seven minutes remaining in the final period.

Green capped off his banner year of 2003 with an exceptional performance in the final game of the regular season, leading the Packers to a lopsided 31–3 victory over Denver by carrying the ball 20 times for a franchise-record 218 yards and two touchdowns, with one of those coming on a 98-yard scamper that represents the longest run from scrimmage in franchise history.

Although the Packers once again lost to Philadelphia by three points in the opening round of the postseason tournament, dropping a 20–17 decision to the Eagles, Green continued his outstanding play, carrying the ball 25 times for 156 yards.

Green turned in his finest performance of the ensuing campaign on October 24, 2004, when he led the Packers to a 41–20 win over the Dallas Cowboys by carrying the ball 15 times for 163 yards and two touchdowns, scoring one of those on a season-long 90-yard run.

NOTABLE ACHIEVEMENTS

- Rushed for more than 1,000 yards six times, topping 1,800 yards once (1,883 in 2003).
- Surpassed 1,500 yards from scrimmage four times, topping 2,000 yards once (2,250 in 2003).
- Rushed for at least 10 touchdowns twice.
- Scored more than 10 touchdowns three times, scoring 20 TDs in 2003.
- Scored more than 100 points once (120 in 2003).
- Averaged more than five yards per carry twice.
- Caught more than 50 passes four times, topping 70 receptions once (73 in 2000).
- Amassed more than 500 receiving yards twice.
- Finished second in NFL in: rushing yardage once; rushing touchdowns once; and touchdowns scored once.
- Finished third in NFL in yards from scrimmage twice.
- Led Packers in rushing six times.
- Holds Packers career records for most: yards rushing (8,322); yards from scrimmage (11,048); and all-purpose yards (11,244).
- Holds Packers single-season records for most: yards rushing (1,883 in 2003); yards from scrimmage (2,250 in 2003); and touchdowns scored (20 in 2003).
- Holds Packers single-game record for most yards rushing (218 vs. Denver on 12/28/2003).
- Ranks among Packers career leaders with 54 rushing touchdowns (2nd) and 68 touchdowns scored (3rd).
- Three-time division champion (2002, 2003, and 2004).
- 2003 NFC Offensive Player of the Year.
- Six-time NFC Offensive Player of the Week.
- Four-time Pro Bowl selection (2001, 2002, 2003, and 2004).
- 2001 Second-Team All-Pro.
- Two-time First-Team All-NFC selection (2001 and 2003).
- Pro Football Reference All-2000s Second Team.

27

JORDY NELSON

The Packers' top receiver for much of the last decade, Jordy Nelson combined with Aaron Rodgers during that time to form one of the NFL's most dynamic passing tandems. Surpassing 80 receptions three times and 1,200 receiving yards four times, Nelson led the Packers in each of those categories on four separate occasions, with his 1,519 receiving yards in 2014 representing the highest single-season total in franchise history. Ranking third in team annals in pass receptions and fifth in receiving yards, Jordan also recorded the second most touchdown receptions of any Packers player, with only the immortal Don Hutson having gathered in more TD passes. Nelson's outstanding play at wide receiver helped the Packers win five division titles, one conference championship, and one Super Bowl, earning him in the process one Pro Bowl selection and one All-Pro nomination.

Born in Manhattan, Kansas, on May 31, 1985, Jordy Ray Nelson grew up helping his father and older brother tend 200 head of Black Angus cattle and cultivate more than 1,000 acres of land on the family farm, working long hours before and after school every day. After enrolling at Riley County High School in Riley, Kansas, Nelson established himself as a star in multiple sports, excelling in basketball, football, and track and field, where, as a senior in 2003, he won state titles in Class 3A in the 100 meters, 200 meters, 400 meters, and long jump. Equally proficient on the gridiron, Nelson played quarterback for the Falcons as a senior, being named Flint Hills Player of the Year by the *Manhattan Mercury* after completing 62 percent of his passes for 1,029 yards and eight touchdowns, while also rushing for 1,572 yards and 25 touchdowns. Commenting on the exceptional speed that Nelson displayed during his high school years, Riley County head football coach Steve Wagner recalled, "We'd put the ball in his hands, and he would just take off. He was so fast. It's like the pads didn't slow him down."

Still, Nelson garnered interest from only in-state Division II schools Emporia State and Washburn, prompting him to walk on at Kansas State. In explaining his decision, Nelson said, "I didn't want to go to Washburn,

Jordy Nelson's 1,519 receiving yards in 2014 represent a single-season franchise record.
Courtesy of Gabriel Cervantes via Wikipedia

have a great career, and think, 'What if I went to K-State?' I didn't want any what-ifs."

Initially miscast as a free safety at Kansas State, Nelson struggled for two years, before emerging as a star in his senior year after being moved to wide receiver. In addition to making 122 receptions for 1,606 yards and 11 touchdowns, Nelson returned two punts for touchdowns and threw two TD passes, earning in the process consensus All-America honors, while also being named a finalist for the Biletnikoff Award, presented annually to the nation's top receiver.

In discussing Nelson, Penn State coach James Franklin, who served as offensive coordinator at Kansas State during that time, says, "There are stereotypes in football, especially at certain positions. Those stereotypes are wrong. A lot of people didn't want to give Jordy credit for being what he is—big, fast, and strong. I just know we wanted to get him the ball as often and in as many ways as possible."

Subsequently selected by the Packers in the second round of the 2008 NFL Draft, with the 36th overall pick, Nelson spent his first two seasons in Green Bay seeing a significant amount of action on special teams as a kickoff and punt-returner, while also backing up Donald Driver and Greg Jennings at wide receiver. Nevertheless, after making 33 receptions for 366 yards and two touchdowns as a rookie in 2008, Nelson amassed 1,045 all-purpose yards the following year, accumulating 725 of those as a return-man and the other 320 as a receiver.

Assuming the role of third wideout in 2010, Nelson posted more impressive numbers on offense, concluding the campaign with 45 receptions for 582 yards and two touchdowns. However, he didn't emerge as a true offensive threat until the following year, when he led the team with 68 catches, 1,263 receiving yards, and 15 touchdown receptions, with the last figure placing him third in the league rankings. Limited by injuries to just 12 games in 2012, Nelson failed to perform at the same lofty level, finishing the season with 49 receptions, 745 receiving yards, and seven TD catches. But a return to full health in 2013 enabled Nelson to earn unofficial First-Team All-Pro recognition from *Pro Football Focus* by making 85 receptions for 1,314 yards and eight touchdowns. He followed that up with another exceptional performance in 2014, earning Pro Bowl and official Second-Team All-Pro honors from the Associated Press by ranking among the league leaders with 98 receptions, a franchise-record 1,519 receiving yards, and 13 TD catches.

Certainly, Nelson's rise to elite status among NFL receivers could be attributed in large part to his physical gifts. Although somewhat slender at 6'3" and 217 pounds, Nelson has outstanding strength and knows how to use his size to his advantage. In addition to doing an excellent job of using his hands to fend off tight coverage at the line of scrimmage, he is expert at using his height and length to ward off defenders downfield. Nelson also possesses deceptive speed, often using his long stride to separate himself from opposing defensive backs. In discussing the qualities that have allowed Nelson to experience so much success deep downfield over the course of his career, Packers receivers coach Edgar Bennett credits his "great strength and combative hand technique to get off the line of scrimmage," quickly adding

Nelson ranks second only to Don Hutson in franchise history with 69 touchdown receptions.
Courtesy of Keith Allison

that "he's fast." Furthermore, once Nelson is free and running on deep routes, he is adept at keeping defenders behind him, denying their leverage to defend against the pass, and staying off the sideline, thereby giving Aaron Rodgers a window in which to throw.

Yet, Nelson attributes at least part of his tremendous productivity to another factor. When asked by the *Green Bay Press Gazette* if racial bias has contributed in any way to the success he has experienced as a pro, Nelson, who is known affectionately to many of his teammates as "White Lightning," replied, "Honestly, I think it has." Revealing that he and his teammates believe that the paucity of outstanding white receivers in the NFL causes many opponents to dismiss his abilities, Nelson stated, "As receivers, we've talked about it. I know [cornerbacks coach] Joe Whitt tells me all the time, when all the rookies come in, he gives them the heads up, telling them, 'Don't let him fool ya.' That's fine with me."

Former Packers teammate Greg Jennings corroborated Nelson's statements when he told that same newspaper, "They underestimate him. . . . Seriously, a lot of it has to do with the fact that guys look at him and say, 'Okay, yeah, he's the white guy, he can't be that good.' Well, he is that good. . . . Guys still underestimate Jordy's ability when he's standing in front of them. Honestly, I don't know what more they need to see. . . . It's easy for someone to say, 'Oh yeah, he's like one of those other white receivers.' He's not. I'm sorry. He's not."

Jennings then added, "You've got a quarterback [Aaron Rodgers] who can throw any receiver open at any given time if the receiver understands what he's supposed to do. And Jordy understands what he's supposed to do. Combine that with Jordy's skills, and what you get is a joy to watch."

Rodgers expressed his feelings on the matter when he said on his weekly *ESPN Milwaukee* radio show, "When you see Jordy out there, you think, 'Oh well, he's a white wide receiver. He won't be very athletic. I am not sure why he keeps sneaking up on guys.'"

After amassing more than 1,000 receiving yards in each of the previous two seasons, Nelson missed the entire 2015 campaign after he tore the ACL in his right knee during a preseason game against Pittsburgh. However, he returned the following year to make 97 receptions for 1,257 yards and lead the league with 14 TD catches, earning in the process NFL Comeback Player of the Year honors. With Rodgers missing much of 2017, Nelson experienced a precipitous drop-off in production, making only 53 receptions for 482 yards and six touchdowns. Nevertheless, with his 53 catches, he reached 550 for his career, moving him past James Lofton into third place on the Packers' all-time pass-receiving list. Nelson also ranks among the club's all-time leaders with 7,848 receiving yards (5th), 69 touchdown receptions (2nd), and 69 total touchdowns scored (3rd).

Nelson's subpar performance this past season convinced team management that the 33-year-old receiver's best days are behind him, prompting the Packers to release him during the early stages of the 2018 free-agent signing period. As of this writing, it remains to be seen with what team Nelson will continue his career. But wherever he winds up, he will bring with him the strong work ethic that once prompted former teammate Greg Jennings to describe him as "a hardworking farm boy," adding, "His physical skill set is second to none, but he's smart, he works at his craft, and he studies the game. He's a hardworking farm boy in his life, and he's a hardworking farm boy on the field."

CAREER HIGHLIGHTS

Best Season

Nelson performed exceptionally well for the Packers in 2011, amassing 1,263 receiving yards and scoring a career-high 15 touchdowns. He also had huge years in 2013 and 2016, making 85 receptions for 1,314 yards and eight touchdowns in the first of those campaigns, before leading the league with 14 TD catches and ranking among the leaders with 97 receptions and 1,257 receiving yards in the second. However, Nelson had his finest all-around season in 2014, when he earned Pro Bowl and All-Pro honors for the only time by scoring 13 touchdowns and establishing career-high marks in receptions (98) and receiving yards (1,519), with the last figure representing a single-season franchise record.

Memorable Moments/Greatest Performances

Nelson made the first touchdown reception of his career during a 48–25 win over the Detroit Lions on September 14, 2008, when he collaborated with Aaron Rodgers on a 29-yard scoring play.

Nelson amassed more than 100 receiving yards for the first time during a lopsided 45–17 victory over the Giants on December 26, 2010, making four receptions for 124 yards and one touchdown, with his scoring play coming on an 80-yard hookup with Aaron Rodgers.

Nelson turned in an outstanding effort against Pittsburgh in Super Bowl XLV, helping the Packers record a 31–25 win over the Steelers by making nine catches for 140 yards and one touchdown, which came on a 29-yard connection with Aaron Rodgers that gave the Packers an early 7–0 lead.

Although Nelson made just two receptions during a 24–3 win over the St. Louis Rams on October 16, 2011, one of them went for a career-long 93-yard touchdown, giving him a total of 104 receiving yards on the day.

Nelson made another big play against Tampa Bay on November 20, 2011, when his 40-yard TD reception with 2:55 left in the fourth quarter all but clinched a 35–26 victory over the Buccaneers. He finished the game with six receptions for 123 yards and two touchdowns.

Nelson had a huge game against Detroit in the 2011 regular-season finale, making nine receptions for 162 yards and three touchdowns during the Packers' 45–41 win over the Lions, with his scoring plays covering 7, 36, and 58 yards.

Nelson helped key a 42–24 victory over the Houston Texans on October 14, 2012, by making nine catches for 121 yards and three touchdowns, with the longest of those being a 41-yard TD grab on the Packers' first offensive series of the game.

Nelson starred again the following week, making eight receptions for 122 yards and one touchdown during a 30–20 win over the St. Louis Rams on October 21, 2012.

Nelson helped lead the Packers to a 44–31 victory over Minnesota on October 27, 2013, by making seven catches for 123 yards and two touchdowns, which covered 11 and 76 yards.

Nelson came up big in the 2013 regular-season finale, making 10 receptions for 161 yards during a 33–28 victory over the Chicago Bears that the Packers won on a last-minute touchdown pass from Aaron Rodgers to Randall Cobb.

Nelson made nine catches for a career-high 209 yards and one touchdown during a 31–24 win over the Jets on September 14, 2014, with his 80-yard connection with Aaron Rodgers late in the third quarter providing the margin of victory.

Nelson had another big game two weeks later, making 10 receptions for 108 yards and two touchdowns during a 38–17 win over the Bears on September 28, 2014.

Nelson again torched the Chicago secondary during a 55–14 blowout of the Bears on November 9, 2014, making six catches for 152 yards and two touchdowns, with his scoring plays covering 73 and 40 yards.

Nelson turned in another outstanding performance one month later, keying a 43–37 victory over the Atlanta Falcons on December 8, 2014, by making eight receptions for 146 yards and two touchdowns, with one of those covering 60 yards.

Although the Packers lost their November 13, 2016, meeting with the Tennessee Titans by a score of 47–25, Nelson amassed 126 receiving yards, scored one touchdown, and made a career-high 12 receptions during the contest.

Nelson helped the Packers record a 21–13 win over the Houston Texans on December 4, 2016, by making eight catches for 118 yards and one touchdown, which came on a 32-yard hookup with Aaron Rodgers early in the fourth quarter that put the Packers ahead to stay.

The Packers celebrated the holidays in 2016 with a 38–25 victory over Minnesota on Christmas Eve, with Nelson making nine receptions for 154 yards and two touchdowns during the contest.

NOTABLE ACHIEVEMENTS

- Surpassed 80 receptions three times, topping 90 catches twice.
- Surpassed 1,200 receiving yards four times, topping 1,500 yards once (1,519 in 2014).
- Surpassed 1,000 all-purpose yards six times.
- Surpassed 10 touchdown receptions three times.
- Led NFL with 14 touchdown receptions in 2016.
- Finished second in NFL with 13 touchdown receptions in 2014.
- Finished third in NFL with 15 touchdown receptions in 2011.
- Finished fourth in NFL in receiving yards once and touchdowns once.
- Finished fifth in NFL in pass receptions once and average yards per reception once.
- Led Packers in pass receptions four times and receiving yards four times.
- Holds Packers single-season record for most receiving yards (1,519 in 2014).
- Ranks among Packers career leaders with 550 pass receptions (3rd); 7,848 receiving yards (5th); 7,848 yards from scrimmage (7th); 9,280 all-purpose yards (5th); 69 touchdown receptions (2nd); 69 total touchdowns scored (3rd); and 416 points scored (9th).
- Five-time division champion (2011, 2012, 2013, 2014, and 2016).
- 2010 NFC champion.
- Super Bowl XLV champion.
- 2014 Pro Bowl selection.
- 2014 Second-Team All-Pro.
- 2016 Associated Press NFL Comeback Player of the Year.

28

— CAL HUBBARD —

The only man to be inducted into both the Major League Baseball Hall of Fame and the Pro Football Hall of Fame, Cal Hubbard has been described as the most feared lineman in the NFL during the league's early years. A mountain of a man who possessed exceptional speed and quickness for a man his size, Hubbard helped his teams capture four league championships in his first five years as a pro, winning one title with the New York Giants in 1927 and another three with the Packers from 1929 to 1931. Spending most of his peak years in Green Bay, Hubbard played for the Packers from 1929 to 1933, and, then again, in 1935, earning three consecutive First-Team All-Pro nominations as a member of the team. Meanwhile, the dominance that Hubbard displayed on both sides of the ball eventually earned him spots on the NFL 1920s All-Decade Team, the Packers 50th Anniversary Team, and the NFL's 75th Anniversary All-Time Two-Way Team. The members of the Hall of Fame Committee also chose to honor Hubbard in 1969 by naming him the NFL's Greatest Offensive Tackle of All-Time.

Born in a small farmhouse in Keytesville, Missouri, on October 31, 1900, Robert Calvin Hubbard won letters in four sports while attending Keytesville High School, excelling in baseball, football, basketball, and track. Already weighing more than 200 pounds at the age of 14, Hubbard aspired to attend the United States Military Academy at West Point from an early age. However, he had to abandon that dream when doctors discovered he had flat feet.

Following his graduation from Keytesville High, Hubbard enrolled at Chillicothe Business College in Chillicothe, Missouri, where he played football, while also continuing to work on his family farm and umpiring pickup baseball games in his spare time. Later transferring to Centenary College in Shreveport, Louisiana, Hubbard spent three seasons starring on the gridiron, becoming the school's first All-American. Hubbard continued his long journey to the pros after he transferred to Geneva College in Beaver

Cal Hubbard helped the Packers win the NFL title in each of his first three seasons in Green Bay.
Courtesy of CollectAuctions.com

Falls, Pennsylvania, concluding his college career at the rather advanced age of 26, in 1926. Making an extremely favorable impression on everyone who saw him perform at the collegiate level, the massive Hubbard, who stood somewhere between 6'2" and 6'5" tall, depending on the source, and weighed well in excess of 250 pounds, drew praise from former Geneva roommate, Pip Booth, who recalled that "Hubbard moved like a cat and always smashed into the ball-carrier with his face or chest. Once I saw him smash down the whole side of a defensive line by himself."

Signing with the New York Giants shortly before he celebrated his 27th birthday, Hubbard performed brilliantly as a rookie, earning First-Team All-Pro honors by helping the defense of the 1927 NFL champions limit opposing offenses to a total of just 20 points all season long. Yet, in spite of the early success he experienced in New York, Hubbard never felt comfortable there, prompting him to request a trade to the Packers the following year after he fell in love with Green Bay's small-town atmosphere during a 1928 road visit.

Dealt to the Packers for quarterback Al Bloodgood in the fall of 1929, Hubbard continued to perform at an elite level over the course of the next few seasons, dominating his opponent on both sides of the ball, in helping the Packers win their first three NFL titles. Named First-Team All-Pro in 1931, 1932, and 1933, Hubbard played tackle on both offense and defense for the Packers, after earlier spending much of his time in New York playing off the line on defense. In fact, Hubbard's unique combination of size and quickness enabled him to assume numerous spots along the defensive front throughout his career, making him, in many ways, a pioneer of the modern linebacker position. In discussing the freedom Hubbard's coaches gave him to freelance on defense, *New York Times* columnist Arthur Daley wrote, "On occasions, he'd even station himself as a widely spaced end and knock down most of the enemy line like a bowling ball spilling pins."

Daley also provided an account of how longtime New York Giants head coach Steve Owen, who once claimed Hubbard "could outrun any back in the league for 30 yards," described the massive lineman:

> According to Steve Owen—it was Hubbard who revolutionized defensive play. The seven-man line was the accepted defense until restless Cal discovered he was missing too much fun and too many tackles by staying anchored in one spot in the scrimmage line. Because he was so fast, he was able to stay back a few yards and either plug up the hole he had vacated or make tackles on the other side of the line. Thus, he became the first roving backer-up.

A bruising tackler as well, Hubbard drew praise from opposing quarterback Harry Newman, who suggested, "Green Bay had the most brutal lineman in the game, Cal Hubbard. He played tackle and was about 6'5" and maybe 270 pounds. He played with the same kind of intensity that Dick Butkus did later. We used to say of Cal that, even if he missed you, he still hurt you. When he tackled you, you remembered it. I do to this day."

Meanwhile, former Packers teammate Mike Michalske, who said Hubbard effectively carried up to 270 pounds, almost 70 more than the average NFL player at the time, described his fellow lineman as "a big man in a small world."

Perhaps even more effective on offense, Hubbard proved to be a powerful and agile blocker who has been credited with being the first man to pull out of the line and lead interference downfield.

Hubbard continued to wreak havoc on his opponents until 1934, when he announced his retirement to become line coach at Texas A&M.

The members of the Hall of Fame Committee named Hubbard the NFL's Greatest Offensive Tackle of All-Time in 1969.
Courtesy of RMYAuctions.com

However, after one year in that post, he decided to return to the Packers, with whom he spent the 1935 campaign doubling as a player and offensive line coach, before splitting the following season between the Giants and Pittsburgh Pirates, who later became the Steelers. Retiring for good at the end of 1936, Hubbard concluded his playing career having earned a total of five First-Team All-Pro selections, with three of those coming as a member of the Packers.

After leaving the NFL, Hubbard, who had spent the previous several offseasons umpiring minor-league baseball, became an umpire at the major-league level, continuing to function in that capacity until 1951, when he lost his depth perception after a pellet lodged in his right eye during a hunting accident, forcing him to retire from baseball officiating. Hubbard subsequently became the American League's supervisor of umpires, remaining in that position until 1969, when he retired to private life.

After spending the first few years of his retirement living in Milan, Missouri, Hubbard relocated to St. Petersburg, Florida, in 1976—the same year he received induction into the Baseball Hall of Fame for his contributions as an umpire. With the Pro Football Hall of Fame having opened its doors to him 13 years earlier, Hubbard became the only man to be so honored in both sports. Unfortunately, Hubbard passed away shortly thereafter, losing his battle with cancer on October 17, 1977, just two weeks shy of his 77th birthday.

Respected and admired by everyone he competed with and against, Hubbard drew praise from longtime New York Giants center and fellow Hall of Famer Mel Hein, who told author Richard Whittingham, "The greatest tackle I ever played against was Cal Hubbard."

Meanwhile, Bo McMillan, a college football legend who later became an NFL player and head coach, proclaimed just prior to his death in 1952, "The greatest player who ever lived was Cal Hubbard—lineman or back, college or professional."

PACKERS CAREER HIGHLIGHTS

Best Season

Although Hubbard performed magnificently for the Packers in 1931, earning the first of his three straight First-Team All-Pro nominations by dominating the opposition on both sides of the ball to such an extent that he helped Green Bay post a point differential of +204, he made his greatest overall impact two years earlier, when his stellar all-around play helped lead the Packers to their first NFL title. Along the way, Hubbard made huge contributions to a defense that surrendered only 22 points to the opposition all season long.

Memorable Moments/Greatest Performances

Even though Hubbard built his reputation primarily on his exceptional line play, he managed to score two touchdowns over the course of his career, with the first of those coming during a 37–7 victory over the Staten Island Stapletons on November 30, 1930, when he gathered in a short TD pass from Red Dunn.

Hubbard crossed the opponent's goal line for the only other time on September 29, 1935, when he returned an interception eight yards for a fourth-quarter touchdown that clinched a 16–7 win over the Giants.

NOTABLE ACHIEVEMENTS

- Caught one touchdown pass during career.
- Returned one interception for a touchdown during career.
- Three-time NFL champion (1929, 1930, and 1931).
- Three-time First-Team All-Pro (1931, 1932, and 1933).
- NFL 1920s All-Decade Team.
- Pro Football Hall of Fame All-1920s Team.
- Named to Packers 50th Anniversary Team in 1969.
- Named to Packers All–Iron Man Era Team in 1976.
- Named to NFL's 50th Anniversary All-Time Team in 1969.
- Named to NFL's 75th Anniversary All-Time Two-Way Team in 1994.
- Named NFL's Greatest Offensive Tackle of All-Time by Hall of Fame Committee in 1969.
- Elected to Pro Football Hall of Fame in 1963.

29

TONY CANADEO

One of only six Green Bay Packers to have his number retired by the team, Tony Canadeo established himself as one of the most versatile performers in franchise history over the course of his career. In addition to retiring as the Packers' all-time leading rusher, Canadeo proved to be an accomplished passer, punter, return man, and defender during his time in Green Bay, assuming each of those roles at different times as a member of the team. After beginning his career as a backup at several positions, Canadeo eventually emerged as one of the NFL's top running backs, becoming in 1949 just the third player in league history to rush for more than 1,000 yards in a season. Canadeo also ranked among the league's leading passers and return men in other seasons, with his outstanding all-around play extending to the defensive side of the ball, where he intercepted a total of nine passes. In the end, Canadeo's tremendous versatility enabled him to earn three All-Pro nominations, a spot on the NFL 1940s All-Decade Team, and a place in the Pro Football Hall of Fame.

Born in Chicago, Illinois, on May 5, 1919, Anthony Robert Canadeo learned to play football on the sandlots of Chicago while growing up on the city's northwest end. After attending Steinmetz High School, located in Chicago's Belmont Cragin neighborhood, Canadeo enrolled at Gonzaga University in Spokane, Washington, where he acquired the nickname the "Gray Ghost of Gonzaga" due to his prematurely graying hair. Starring in the offensive backfield for Gonzaga, Canadeo earned the distinction of being named "Outstanding Italian-American Athlete of 1939" by the National Italian-American Civic League.

Subsequently selected by the Packers in the ninth round of the 1941 NFL Draft, with the 77th overall pick, Canadeo arrived in Green Bay with few expectations surrounding him. Relegated to backup duty on both offense and defense his first year in the league, Canadeo spent his earliest days with the Packers serving as an understudy to starters Cecil Isbell and Clarke Hinkle in the offensive backfield, while also seeing limited action

In 1949, Tony Canadeo became just the third player in NFL history to gain more than 1,000 yards on the ground in a season.
Courtesy of RMYAuctions.com

as a defensive back. However, after rushing for only 137 yards, passing for just 54 more, scoring three touchdowns, and intercepting two passes as a rookie, Canadeo assumed a more prominent role in 1942. Although Isbell remained the Packers' starting quarterback, Canadeo saw significantly more playing time, passing for 310 yards and three touchdowns, gaining 272 yards on the ground, scoring three TDs, recording one interception on defense, amassing over 200 yards on special teams, and averaging just under 36 yards per punt.

With Isbell having announced his retirement following the conclusion of the 1942 campaign, Canadeo emerged as a triple-threat halfback for the Packers in 1943, earning his lone First-Team All-Pro selection by ranking among the league leaders with 489 yards rushing, 875 yards passing, and nine TD passes, while also scoring five touchdowns, intercepting two passes, and amassing 335 yards on kickoff and punt returns. However, just as Canadeo appeared to be hitting his stride, he missed almost all of the next two seasons while serving in the military during World War II, appearing in only three games in 1944, before missing the entire 1945 campaign.

Returning to the Packers in 1946 after spurning an offer to play in the rival All-America Football Conference, Canadeo assumed a heavier workload on offense than ever before. Establishing himself as one of the NFL's top running backs, Canadeo ranked among the league leaders in rushing in each of the next four seasons, amassing a total of 1,529 yards on the ground from 1946 to 1948, before rushing for 1,052 yards in 1949, when he joined Chicago's Beattie Feathers (1934) and Philadelphia's Steve Van Buren (1947 and 1949) as the only men in NFL history to surpass the 1,000-yard mark in a season. Canadeo also scored four touchdowns that year, earning in the process Second-Team All-Pro honors for the second straight time.

Though not particularly fast or elusive, Canadeo emerged as an elite runner primarily because of the determination and tenacity he displayed while carrying the football. And, even though Canadeo's 5'11", 190-pound frame made him just an average-size running back for his day, contemporary Jim Benton identified him as one of the three toughest players to tackle, ranking him alongside Frank Sinkwich and Steve Van Buren in that regard.

After celebrating his 31st birthday during the previous offseason, Canadeo shared running back duties with Billy Grimes in 1950, limiting him to only 247 yards on the ground, although he also scored four touchdowns and amassed 780 all-purpose yards, accumulating 411 of those on kickoff returns. Grimes, who led the team in rushing yards and touchdowns, later credited Canadeo for much of his success, stating, "Tony Canadeo is one of the toughest players I ever played with. He did a lot of blocking for me, and that helped me a lot."

Canadeo's opportunities to run with the football continued to diminish in each of the next two seasons, as he gained a total of only 322 yards on the ground in 1951 and 1952. Yet, he remained a key contributor on offense, establishing career-high marks in pass receptions (22) and receiving yards (226) in 1951, before announcing his retirement following the conclusion of the 1952 campaign. In addition to ending his career with a then–franchise-record 4,197 yards rushing, Canadeo caught 69 passes for 579 yards, scored 31 touchdowns, threw for 1,642 yards and 16 touchdowns, gained 513 yards on punt returns and 1,736 yards on kickoff returns, intercepted nine passes, averaged 37.1 yards per punt, and posted a rushing average of 4.1 yards per carry. Some 65 years after Canadeo played his last game for the Packers, he remains the fourth-leading rusher in franchise history. The Packers chose to honor him immediately after he left the NFL,

Canadeo retired as the Packers' all-time leading rusher.
Courtesy of RMYAuctions.com

retiring his number 3 in 1952, one season after Don Hutson's number 14 became the team's first officially retired number.

Continuing his association with the Packers long after he retired as an active player, Canadeo remained with the organization as a television analyst and a member of its executive committee for years, serving on the team's board of directors for more than three decades. After Canadeo passed away at the age of 84 on November 29, 2003, the Packers honored him for the remainder of that season by wearing a sticker on the back of their helmets that featured his number 3 inside a black football.

Following Canadeo's passing, *Milwaukee Journal Sentinel* sportswriter Tom Silverstein wrote, "Of all the players, coaches, and executives who left an imprint on the Packers organization, none did it for longer than the affable Canadeo."

Meanwhile, longtime Packers spokesman Lee Remmel said of Canadeo, "He was probably one of the best all-around players in Packer history. He could do just about anything. He was a good runner, a good blocker, a good returner, and a good receiver. . . . He was one of the toughest players the Packers have ever had, an extremely hard-nosed player."

CAREER HIGHLIGHTS

Best Season

Although Canadeo earned his lone First-Team All-Pro nomination in 1943 by rushing for 489 yards, scoring five touchdowns, averaging a career-high 5.2 yards per carry, and passing for 875 yards and nine touchdowns, he had his finest season in 1949, when he earned Second-Team All-Pro honors by finishing second in the league with a career-best 1,052 yards rushing and placing third in the circuit with an average of 5.1 yards per carry.

Memorable Moments/Greatest Performances

Canadeo led the Packers to a 24–7 win over the Cleveland Rams on September 21, 1941, by throwing an 18-yard TD pass to Joe Laws and scoring himself on a 3-yard run.

Canadeo again displayed his versatility on October 18, 1942, when he ran 50 yards for a touchdown and completed a 28-yard TD pass to Joe Laws during a convincing 45–28 victory over the Rams.

Canadeo tossed a career-high three touchdown passes during a 35–14 triumph over the Detroit Lions on October 10, 1943, connecting with Lou Brock from seven yards out, and collaborating with Andy Uram on scoring plays that covered 20 and 39 yards.

Canadeo turned in a tremendous all-around effort against the Giants on October 31, 1943, leading the Packers to a 35–21 victory by carrying the ball 18 times for 122 yards, including a 35-yard TD run, hauling in a 12-yard touchdown pass from Andy Uram, and completing a pair of TD passes to Don Hutson.

Although the Packers won only two games in 1949, Canadeo starred in both victories, carrying the ball 16 times for 100 yards and one touchdown during a 19–0 win over the New York Bulldogs on October 7, and toting the ball 21 times for 117 yards and one TD during a 16–14 victory over the Detroit Lions on October 30.

NOTABLE ACHIEVEMENTS

- Rushed for more than 500 yards twice, topping 1,000 yards once (1,052 in 1949).
- Amassed more than 200 receiving yards once (226 in 1951).
- Averaged more than 4.5 yards per carry five times, topping 5 yards per carry twice.
- Finished second in NFL with 1,052 yards rushing in 1949.
- Finished third in NFL in: rushing yardage once; yards from scrimmage once; yards per rushing attempt three times; and yards per kickoff return twice.
- Led Packers in rushing yardage five times.
- Third player in NFL history to rush for more than 1,000 yards in a season.
- Ranks fourth in Packers history with 4,197 yards rushing.
- 1944 NFL champion.
- 1943 First-Team All-Pro.
- Two-time Second-Team All-Pro (1948 and 1949).
- NFL 1940s All-Decade Team.
- Pro Football Hall of Fame All-1940s Team.
- #3 retired by Packers.
- Elected to Pro Football Hall of Fame in 1974.

30

BILL FORESTER

Originally drafted by the Packers as a defensive lineman, Bill Forester spent most of his first four seasons in Green Bay doing a creditable job at middle guard for one of the NFL's most porous defenses. However, after being shifted to linebacker his fifth year in the league, Forester gradually emerged as one of the circuit's top outside backers, earning Pro Bowl, All-Conference, and All-Pro honors four straight times for Packer teams that won three consecutive Western Conference titles and two straight NFL championships under Vince Lombardi. Displaying a nose for the football throughout his career, Forester intercepted 21 passes and recovered 15 fumbles in his 11 seasons with the Packers, with his 21 picks tying him for third all-time in franchise history among linebackers. Extremely intelligent as well, Forester drew praise from former teammate Bill Quinlan, who called him, "the smartest linebacker I ever knew." Also an outstanding leader, Forester spent his final seven seasons in Green Bay serving as defensive captain of a team that developed into an NFL powerhouse.

Born in Dallas, Texas, on August 9, 1932, George William Forester attended Woodrow Wilson High School, where he earned All-City and All-State honors as a fullback/linebacker for the Wildcats. After graduating from high school at only 16 years of age in 1949, Forester enrolled at Southern Methodist University (SMU), where he continued to star on the gridiron, earning All–Southwest Conference honors in his junior and senior years, while splitting his time between the linebacker and defensive tackle positions.

Subsequently selected by the Packers in the third round of the 1953 NFL Draft, with the 31st overall pick, Forester began his pro career as a defensive lineman, playing middle guard, a position that Chicago Bears Hall of Famer Bill George later helped transform into middle linebacker as many teams transitioned from 5-2 defenses to a 4-3 alignment. After spending his sophomore campaign of 1954 at left outside linebacker, Forester returned to middle guard, where he spent the next two seasons amassing a total of eight interceptions. Shifted permanently to right outside linebacker

Bill Forester starred at linebacker for Vince Lombardi's first two NFL
championship teams.
Courtesy of MearsOnlineAuctions.com

in 1957, Forester performed well at his new post after being named the
team's defensive captain, recording four interceptions and a career-high 79
interception-return yards. But, after spending the following year serving as
part of a four-man linebacker rotation that also included veteran Tom Bettis
and rookies Ray Nitschke and Dan Currie, Forester emerged as a star when
Vince Lombardi and his defensive coach Phil Bengtson arrived in 1959.

With Nitschke assuming the role of middle linebacker full time, Forester received more of an opportunity to use his outstanding athleticism
on the outside, enabling him to earn the first of his four consecutive Pro
Bowl selections. Although he stood 6'3" and weighed 237 pounds, Forester
had good speed and quickness, allowing him to excel in pass coverage. He

also tackled well and had great hands, which can be evidenced by his 21 career interceptions. Forester also did an excellent job of using his hands to separate himself from his blocker when defending against the run, with Chicago Bears tight end Mike Ditka recalling, "I remember Bill Forester well. He was a hard guy to block because he used his hands so well. Guys that used their hands well bothered me, because you couldn't put a good lick on them. They kept you away from the body."

Heralding Forester as an unsung player on the outstanding Packer defenses of the early 1960s, Ditka added, "Green Bay had a lot of great players on their defense when I played: guys like Herb Adderley, Ray Nitschke, Willie Davis, Willie Wood, Henry Jordan—all Hall of Famers. . . . Not everyone will get the recognition, but remember this: it takes 11 to make a defense. Bill Forester was one of them. He was a damn good football player."

Echoing Ditka's sentiments, longtime Packers teammate Forrest Gregg, who also played with Forester at SMU, stated, "At SMU, they played Bill at defensive tackle, defensive end, running back and linebacker. Bill was a very good all-around football player. He was pretty fast for a guy his size, with natural strength. He was smart and played the linebacker position well."

Gregg also shared a story about an encounter he had with Forester during a training camp scrimmage in his rookie season of 1956: "I was playing left tackle and Bill was the middle linebacker. I came inside, and my responsibility was to block Bill, and I caught him pretty good. He said, 'You'd better watch yourself, boy.' A few plays later we ran the same play, and Bill hit me so hard the first thing that hit the ground was the back of my head. I learned something: you don't mess with Bill."

Yet, Forester's greatest assets may well have been his intelligence and leadership ability, for which Lombardi praised him when he said in 1963, "There is no one on this club who is more quiet and self-contained. . . . He is highly intelligent and steady on and off the field, and his leadership is one of action rather than words. There is an aura of efficiency about him that the others respect and rise to."

Forester continued his outstanding play in 1960, earning All-Pro and All–Western Conference honors for the first of four straight times. Although the Packers lost the NFL title game to the Philadelphia Eagles, they won the next two league championships, with Forester's strong play and superb leadership proving to be key factors in the success they experienced during that time. Forester remained with the Packers until the end of 1963, when he announced his retirement at only 31 years of age. Expressing the belief that Forester might have retired somewhat prematurely, Pat Peppler, who served as Green Bay's personnel director from 1963 to 1971,

Forester earned Pro Bowl and All-Pro honors four times each as a member of the Packers.
Courtesy of PristineAuction.com

opined, "I think he could have still played the game. He was part of the old guard from the 1950s. When I arrived, he was near the end of his career and Lee Roy Caffey replaced him after he retired . . . Bill didn't get the national attention, but he had quite a career in Green Bay after those tough years in the 1950s." In addition to recording 21 interceptions and 15 fumble recoveries over the course of his career, Forester never missed a game, starting 138 consecutive contests for the Packers from 1953 to 1963.

Following his playing days, Forester and his family moved back to Dallas, where he ran a successful sporting goods business for decades before retiring from the business world. Forester passed away at the age of 74, on April 27, 2007.

CAREER HIGHLIGHTS

Best Season

Forester performed well for the Packers in 1957, recording four interceptions for the third straight season, while also establishing career-high marks in interception-return yards (79), fumble recoveries (4), and fumble-return yards (45). However, he played the best ball of his career under Vince

Lombardi's coaching staff from 1959 to 1962, earning four consecutive trips to the Pro Bowl and three straight First-Team All-Pro nominations. Although Forester failed to intercept a single pass in the last of those campaigns, he contributed significantly to a Green Bay defense that surrendered just 148 points to the opposition, earning in the process consensus First-Team All-Pro honors for the only time, and prompting me to identify 1962 as the finest season of his career.

Memorable Moments/Greatest Performances

Forester helped the Packers defeat the Detroit Lions by a score of 24–17 on Thanksgiving Day 1959 by recording a career-long 37-yard interception return.

Forester made a key play against San Francisco in the 1959 regular-season finale, when, with the score tied at 14–14 early in the third quarter, he shifted the momentum to Green Bay's side by tackling 49ers quarterback Y. A. Tittle in the end zone for a safety. The Packers subsequently went on to score another 20 unanswered points, giving them a 36–14 win over the 49ers and a record of 7-5 in Vince Lombardi's first year as head coach.

Forester turned in one of his finest performances against the Giants in the 1961 NFL title game, teaming up with fellow linebackers Ray Nitschke and Dan Currie to lead a Packer defense that created five turnovers, yielded just six first downs, and limited New York to just 150 yards of total offense during a convincing 37–0 victory.

NOTABLE ACHIEVEMENTS

- Intercepted 21 passes and recovered 15 fumbles during career.
- Intercepted four passes in three different seasons.
- Finished third in NFL with 45 fumble-return yards in 1957.
- Never missed a game entire career.
- Tied for eighth in Packers history with 15 fumble recoveries.
- Three-time Western Conference champion (1960, 1961, and 1962).
- Two-time NFL champion (1961 and 1962).
- Four-time Pro Bowl selection (1959, 1960, 1961, and 1962).
- Three-time First-Team All-Pro (1960, 1961, and 1962).
- 1963 Second-Team All-Pro.
- Four-time All–Western Conference First-Team selection (1960, 1961, 1962, and 1963).

31

CHARLEY BROCK

One of the best all-around players to perform for the Packers during the two-way era that extended from the earliest days of the NFL into the late-1940s, Charley Brock starred on both sides of the ball during his nine seasons in Green Bay, anchoring the Packers' offensive line from his center position, while also excelling as a linebacker on defense. Although often overlooked in the annual All-Pro voting in favor of New York's Mel Hein and Chicago's Clyde "Bulldog" Turner, who most people considered to be the league's top two players at both positions, Brock still managed to earn four All-Pro selections and three Pro Bowl nominations, while helping the Packers capture two league championships. Displaying a nose for the football throughout his career, Brock intercepted 20 passes and recovered 13 fumbles over the course of nine NFL seasons, even though the league did not begin keeping an official record of fumble recoveries until 1945—his seventh year in the league. Brock also scored four defensive touchdowns, with his outstanding play on both sides of the ball eventually earning him spots on the Pro Football Hall of Fame All-1940s Team and the Packers All–Iron Man Era Team.

Born in Columbus, Nebraska, on March 15, 1916, Charles Jacob Brock developed his football skills competing with and against his seven brothers on his family's farm. After starring on the gridiron while attending nearby Kramer High School, Brock enrolled at the University of Nebraska, where he established himself as one of the best two-way linemen in the nation, while simultaneously displaying his leadership ability by serving as team captain. After also captaining the West team in the 1939 East-West Shrine Game and the All-Stars in the 1939 College All-Star Game, Brock joined the Packers when they selected him in the third round of that year's NFL Draft, with the 24th overall pick. Commenting years later on Curly Lambeau's selection of Brock, former Packers' teammate Herm Schneidman said, "Curly liked to draft players from Minnesota, Notre Dame, Wisconsin, Nebraska—the big colleges in the Midwest."

Charley Brock starred at both center and linebacker for the Packers for nine seasons.
Courtesy of Heritage Auctions

Performing exceptionally well for the Packers as a rookie, Brock made an immediate impact in Green Bay, with Schneidman recalling, "You could tell Charley was going to be a player. He earned the respect of the coaches and his teammates with his play." Earning Pro Bowl honors his first year in the league, Brock helped lead the Packers to the NFL championship by starting at center on offense, while also contributing from his linebacker position on defense. Proving to be a key figure in the 1939 NFL title game, Brock intercepted two passes and made a touchdown-saving tackle during the Packers' 27–0 victory over the New York Giants. Continuing to excel in his sophomore campaign of 1940, Brock earned his second consecutive trip to the Pro Bowl, with *Collyers Eye Magazine* also naming him to its unofficial First-Team All-Pro squad.

Although somewhat undersized for a center at 6'2" and 207 pounds, Brock proved to be a rock on the Packers' offensive line, with Curly Lambeau admiring him for his competitiveness, toughness, and leadership. With his duties as a center in the single-wing offense requiring him to snap the ball to a tailback several yards behind him, Brock spent a considerable amount of time each day practicing that particular chore. However, his responsibilities went well beyond delivering the ball accurately to the back, because he also needed to lead the offensive charge off the line of scrimmage. Indeed, with the prevalent style of play at the time very much resembling loosely officiated mayhem, Brock broke his nose five times during interior line scrums.

Yet, as well as Brock played on offense, he excelled even more as a defender. In addition to intercepting 20 passes and making 13 officially recorded fumble recoveries, Brock scored four touchdowns on returns and specialized in stripping ball-carriers of the pigskin, often enabling Green Bay's offense to begin its drives in the opponent's territory.

Brock earned the last of his three Pro Bowl selections in 1942 by recording a career-high six interceptions, before making Second-Team All-Pro for the first of three times the following year, when he picked off four passes, which he returned for a total of 61 yards. After being named team captain prior to the start of the 1944 campaign, Brock helped lead the Packers to their sixth NFL title, earning in the process his second consecutive Second-Team All-Pro nomination. Later identifying 1944 as his favorite season, Brock recalled, "I don't think we had the personnel that year, but we had a bunch of boys who wanted to play football, and we won the championship with probably less talent than we had in other years." Brock followed that up with arguably his finest individual season, earning First-Team All-Pro honors for the only time in his career in 1945 by picking off four passes and leading the league with 122 interception-return yards, two defensive touchdowns, and 52 fumble-return yards.

Brock remained with the Packers for another two years, before announcing his retirement following the conclusion of the 1947 campaign. He ended his career having missed a total of only five games in his nine years in the league, with four of those resulting from an emergency appendectomy he underwent in the middle of the 1943 season.

Following his playing days, Brock spent one year serving as line coach at the University of Omaha, before coaching the Packers' defense for one season. He subsequently became a successful local businessman who

Brock helped the Packers defeat the Giants in the 1939 NFL title game by recording a pair of interceptions.
Courtesy of RMYAuctions.com

formed the Packer Alumni Association, for which he served as president for many years. After being elected to the Packers Hall of Fame in 1973, Brock lived another 14 years, passing away at the age of 71, on May 25, 1987.

CAREER HIGHLIGHTS

Best Season

Brock performed exceptionally well for the Packers in 1942, earning the last of his three Pro Bowl selections by finishing third in the NFL with a career-high six interceptions, while also returning one fumble for a touchdown. However, he had his finest all-around season in 1945, earning his lone First-Team All-Pro nomination by picking off four passes, recovering five fumbles, and leading the league with 122 interception-return yards, two touchdown interceptions, and 52 fumble-return yards.

Memorable Moments/Greatest Performances

Brock proved to be a dominant force on the line of scrimmage during a 45–28 win over the Cleveland Rams on October 18, 1942, anchoring an offensive line that helped the Packers produce 539 yards of total offense, 209 of which they gained on the ground.

Brock turned in a similarly impressive performance on the other side of the ball on November 18, 1945, serving as the central figure in a Packer defense that surrendered a total of just 48 yards to a combined Boston Yanks/Brooklyn Tigers squad during a 28–0 Green Bay win.

Brock, who scored four defensive touchdowns during his career, lit the scoreboard for the first time on November 12, 1939, when he returned an interception 42 yards for a TD during a 23–16 win over the Philadelphia Eagles.

Brock helped the Packers overcome a 10-point, fourth-quarter deficit to the Chicago Cardinals on October 4, 1942, by recovering a fumble and returning it 20 yards for the game-winning score of a 17–13 Green Bay victory.

Brock recorded the second pick-six of his career on October 7, 1945, when he punctuated a 57–21 mauling of the Detroit Lions with a 33-yard touchdown interception return in the fourth quarter.

Brock scored his fourth and final touchdown seven weeks later, when, during the third quarter of a 23–14 win over the Giants on November 25, 1945, he returned an interception 27 yards for a TD.

Yet, Brock is perhaps remembered most for two huge plays he made during Green Bay's 27–0 victory over New York in the 1939 NFL title game. After preventing the Giants from tying the score at 7–7 late in the first half by catching running back Tuffy Leemans from behind at the Green Bay 15 yard line, Brock intercepted a pass in the Packer end zone on the very next play. The Packers subsequently scored 20 unanswered points in the second half, giving them their fifth league championship, with Brock recording two of their six interceptions on the day.

NOTABLE ACHIEVEMENTS

- Intercepted 20 passes and recovered 13 fumbles during career.
- Scored four defensive touchdowns during career (three interception returns and one fumble return).
- Intercepted six passes in 1942.
- Amassed more than 100 interception-return yards once (122 in 1945).
- Led NFL in: interception-return yards once; fumble-return yards once; touchdown interceptions once; and non-offensive touchdowns twice.

- Finished second in NFL in fumbles recovered once.
- Finished third in NFL in interceptions once and fumbles recovered once.
- Two-time Western Conference champion (1939 and 1944).
- Two-time NFL champion (1939 and 1944).
- Three-time Pro Bowl selection (1939, 1940, and 1942).
- 1945 First-Team All-Pro.
- Three-time Second-Team All-Pro (1943, 1944, and 1946).
- NFL 1940s All-Decade Team.
- Pro Football Hall of Fame All-1940s Team.
- Named to Packers All-Time Team in 1946 and 1957.
- Named to Packers All–Iron Man Era Team in 1976.

32

GALE GILLINGHAM

The last member of the Vince Lombardi–led Packer squads to remain active with the team, Gale Gillingham spent his entire 10-year NFL career in Green Bay, starting every game in eight of his last nine seasons after unseating Fuzzy Thurston as the starter at left guard his second year in the league. Possessing a rare combination of power, speed, and technique, Gillingham established himself as one of the league's top offensive linemen, earning five Pro Bowl nominations and four All-Pro selections, with his outstanding blocking helping the Packers win their last two NFL titles under Lombardi. Long after his playing career ended, Gillingham remains one of the most unheralded players in franchise history.

Born in Madison, Wisconsin, on February 3, 1944, Gale Herbert Gillingham grew up on a farm in nearby Stoughton, before moving with his family to Little Falls, Minnesota, during his teenage years. After playing fullback for Little Falls High School's football team, Gillingham enrolled at the University of Minnesota, where he successfully transitioned to offensive and defensive tackle, performing so well at both posts that the Packers selected him in the first round of the 1966 NFL Draft, with the 13th overall pick.

Although Gillingham spent most of his first NFL season serving as a backup offensive guard and special-teams player, Jerry Kramer later revealed in his book *Distant Replay* that it soon became apparent to everyone that the talented rookie seemed destined to claim a starting spot for himself, writing:

Gilly was such a good kid, had such a good attitude, that none of us who had been on the offensive line for so long really resented his arrival. It was just the natural progression of life. Fuzzy [Thurston] was aging, slowing down a bit. Gilly was young and swift and strong. Of course, we all envied his youth and his speed and his vigor, and hated him for all the things we had lost. Until he showed up, Forrest [Gregg] and I had always been the fastest offensive linemen on the team. Suddenly, we no longer were.

Gale Gillingham starred at guard for the Packers for nine seasons.
Courtesy of MearsOnlineAuctions.com

Kramer went on to say, "Gilly was also a hell of a ballplayer, with great size and speed. I remember Forrest and I would always win our offensive line sprints all the time until Gilly became a starter. We just couldn't beat Gilly in our races, even when we tried to cheat a little bit. Finally, Forrest looked at me one day and said, 'We might as well give up, Jerry. We ain't going to beat him.'"

Taking over for Thurston as the team's starting left guard early in 1967 after the veteran hurt his knee in training camp, Gillingham began a string of five straight seasons in which he started every game for the Packers, performing exceptionally well for a Green Bay squad that captured its third consecutive NFL title. After spending one more year at left guard, Gillingham moved to the right side of the Packers' offensive line in 1969 following the retirement of Jerry Kramer. Continuing to excel at right guard, Gillingham earned three straight trips to the Pro Bowl and two All-Pro selections between 1969 and 1971, with Forrest Gregg later writing in his 2010 book entitled *Winning in the Trenches: A Lifetime of Football* that Bob Lilly told him that "Gale Gillingham was the best guard he'd ever played against."

The 6'3" Gillingham, who tipped the scales at 255 pounds at the beginning of his career but weighed closer to 275 pounds by the time he retired, had the ideal build for a guard. Thick and powerful, he helped pioneer the idea of using weights as a means of preparing oneself for the season, noting years later, "In Green Bay, at first hardly anybody lifted, so you didn't do much of anything during the season. But I always tried to hit it in the offseason."

Commenting on the advantage Gillingham's strength gave him over his opponents, Packers running back John Brockington said of his former teammate, "He was a beast. Gilly was a weightlifter. He pounded those weights. He was something else. Physical and fast. He was bigger. Mean. He played Mike Reid of Cincinnati in the third game of the year. He made Mike Reid [an All-Pro himself] look like a baby. Put somebody ordinary over Gilly and the guy had no chance. Gilly was going to pound him to death."

In discussing Gillingham's strength in his book *Distant Replay*, Jerry Kramer wrote, "Mike Reid of the Bengals said that Gillingham 'hit me so hard, I almost couldn't fall.'" Kramer added that Philadelphia Eagles standout middle linebacker Bill Bergey noted, "When you played football and you're concentrating and you get hit, it never hurts. When Gillingham hit me, it hurt."

Also blessed with exceptional speed and agility for a man his size, Gillingham excelled as a downfield blocker, with his explosiveness off the ball, outstanding balance, and ability to adjust to the movement of defenders in a split second making him particularly effective in helping the Packers run their famous power sweep. A good teammate and a fierce competitor as well, Gillingham drew praise from Packers trainer Domenic Gentile, who stated, "He was a high-intensity type player. He was such a perfectionist that, in his eyes, he had to be errorless at every practice. He could not stand mediocrity."

Gillingham's quest for perfection made it extremely difficult for him to accept the fact that the Packers compiled a winning record in just two of his final eight seasons. The 1972 campaign proved to be particularly disheartening for Gillingham, who suffered a season-ending injury to his right knee in Week 2 after foolishly being moved to defensive tackle by head coach Dan Devine. Although a healthy Gillingham performed extremely well for the Packers after he returned to the team the following year at his normal right guard position, earning Pro Bowl honors for the first of two straight times, the losing finally got the better of him, prompting him to sit out the entire 1975 campaign. Expressing his dissatisfaction with the team's

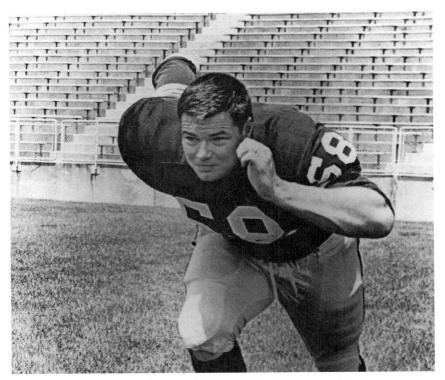

Gillingham earned NFL Offensive Lineman of the Year honors in 1970.
Courtesy of SportsMemorabilia.com

performance years later, Gillingham revealed, "The losing killed me. I was burned out and beat up, both mentally and physically."

With the Packers having denied his request to be traded to another team, Gillingham returned for one more season, before announcing his retirement at the end of 1976. He ended his career with five Pro Bowl selections, the highest total amassed by any guard in franchise history. Yet, despite his multiple trips to the Pro Bowl, Gillingham, according to his ex-teammates, remained disappointed in the years that followed that he never received the recognition he felt he deserved.

Following his playing days, Gillingham returned to Minnesota, where he spent more than two decades selling real estate, before retiring to private life in 2010. He lived just one more year, passing away on October 20, 2011, at the age of 67, after suffering a heart attack while lifting weights at his home in Little Falls.

CAREER HIGHLIGHTS

Best Season

Gillingham had an outstanding season for the Packers in 1971, gaining recognition as the NFC choice for the NFLPA/Coca-Cola Offensive Lineman of the Year. However, he performed even better the previous season, earning one of his two First-Team All-Pro selections and being named the inaugural winner of the Forrest Gregg Award as the NFL Offensive Lineman of the Year following the conclusion of the 1970 campaign.

Memorable Moments/Greatest Performances

Gillingham acquitted himself extremely well in his first full season as a starter, performing especially well during the 1967 postseason, when he neutralized star defensive tackles Roger Brown of the Rams, Bob Lilly of the Cowboys, and Tom Keating of the Raiders, in helping the Packers win their third consecutive NFL championship and second straight Super Bowl.

Gillingham and the rest of the Green Bay offensive line had a big day against Atlanta on October 26, 1969, helping Packer running backs gain a season-high 241 yards on the ground during a 28–10 win over the Falcons.

Gillingham had another huge game against Cincinnati on October 3, 1971, helping to pave the way for Packer running backs to rush for a season-high 256 yards, with John Brockington topping the 100-yard mark for the first time in his career.

Yet, when asked what he remembered most about his football career, Gillingham chose not to focus on one particular play or one specific game. Instead, he discussed the feelings of anticipation that engulfed him in the moments leading up to the opening kickoff of any contest, stating, "I love my kids dearly, but I have never been as close to people as I was every Sunday when I walked through that damn tunnel to the field. I thought so much of those guys walking with me, I didn't want to do anything to let them down. We would kill for each other. We would die for each other. We would do anything for each other."

NOTABLE ACHIEVEMENTS

- Two-time Western Conference champion (1966 and 1967).
- Two-time NFL champion (1966 and 1967).

- Two-time Super Bowl champion (I and II).
- Five-time Pro Bowl selection (1969, 1970, 1971, 1973, and 1974).
- Two-time First-Team All-Pro (1969 and 1970).
- Two-time Second-Team All-Pro (1968 and 1971).
- Four-time First-Team All-NFC selection (1970, 1971, 1973, and 1974).
- 1970 NFL Offensive Lineman of the Year.
- 1971 NFC Offensive Lineman of the Year.

33

ARNIE HERBER

The first in a long line of outstanding Packer quarterbacks, Arnie Herber served as the primary signal-caller in Green Bay for nearly a decade, helping lead the team to three Western Conference championships and two NFL titles. The best deep passer of his time, Herber threw for more than 1,000 yards twice, setting a new NFL record in 1936, when he amassed 1,239 yards through the air. Teaming up with Don Hutson to form the first great quarterback-receiver tandem in NFL history, Herber led the league in passing yards, touchdown passes, and passer rating three times each, en route to earning three All-Pro selections, a spot on the NFL 1930s All-Decade Team, and a place in the Pro Football Hall of Fame. Herber accomplished all he did even though his small hands forced him to alter his grip on the football so that he might deliver it with power and precision.

Born in Green Bay, Wisconsin, on April 2, 1910, Arnold Charles Herber grew up rooting for his hometown team, selling programs at Packers games as a youth, before starring in football and basketball at local Green Bay West High School. After enrolling at the University of Wisconsin, Herber spent one year playing on the school's freshman football team, before transferring to Regis College in Denver, Colorado, which dropped its football program following his sophomore campaign of 1929. With the onset of the Great Depression, the 20-year-old Herber dropped out of school and returned to Green Bay, where he briefly worked as a handyman in the Packers clubhouse until head coach Curly Lambeau offered him a spot on the team's roster after giving him a tryout early in 1930.

Joining a Packers team in the middle of a three-year championship run, Herber initially found himself being treated with disdain by the club's veteran players, who often called him "dummy." However, after seeing extremely limited action his first two years in the league, Herber earned the respect of his teammates in 1932, when he emerged as the NFL's top passer. Functioning primarily as a single-wing tailback in the famous Notre Dame Box formation, Herber earned his lone First-Team All-Pro selection

Arnie Herber teamed up with Don Hutson during the 1930s to form the NFL's first great quarterback-receiver tandem.
Courtesy of RMYAuctions.com

by leading the league with 639 yards passing and nine touchdown passes, while also rushing for 149 yards and one touchdown. He followed that up by throwing for 656 yards and finishing first in the league with a completion percentage of 40.3 in 1933, before leading all NFL quarterbacks with 799 yards passing, eight TD passes, a completion percentage of 36.5, and a passer rating of 45.1 in 1934. Herber then earned Second-Team All-Pro honors for the first of two straight times in 1935 by finishing second in the league with 729 yards passing and eight touchdown passes, six of which went to rookie wide receiver Don Hutson, with whom he combined to form the NFL's deadliest passing combination the next few seasons.

Excelling as a deep passer even though his short fingers and pudgy hands forced him to grip the oddly shaped ball used at that time with his thumb over the laces to prevent wobbling and impart spiraling action on his longer throws, Herber drew praise from Curly Lambeau, who said during a 1960s interview, "A lot of guys today can throw the ball as far, or maybe farther [than Herber], but none as well for distance. The guy was phenomenal."

Helping to pave the way for future generations of NFL quarterbacks to make better use of the deep pass as an offensive weapon, Herber greatly influenced the league's top two quarterbacks of the 1940s, Washington's Sammy Baugh and Chicago's Sid Luckman, who also became known for their ability to deliver the deep ball with accuracy. In addressing the strength of his arm, Herber stated, "Actually, the longest pass I ever threw in a game was 75 yards, against the St. Louis Gunners. Don Hutson caught the ball on the goal line."

Herber also developed a reputation for his toughness, coolness, and ability to excel under pressure. Choosing not to wear a helmet until 1938, Herber took a merciless beating in almost every game because he needed time for his receivers to get open downfield for his longer passes. Yet, he did not allow the physical abuse he endured to affect his performance, once re-entering a game shortly after he suffered a broken nose.

Herber's style of play and ability to throw the ball deep made him a perfect match for Don Hutson, with the two men emerging during the championship campaign of 1936 as the NFL's first truly dominant quarterback–wide receiver tandem. While Hutson led the league in every major pass-receiving category, Herber topped the circuit with a quarterback rating of 58.9, 11 touchdown passes, and 1,239 yards passing, with the last two figures establishing new league marks.

Hampered by injuries in each of the next two seasons, Herber posted far less impressive numbers. However, he returned to top form in 1939, leading the Packers to their fifth NFL title by passing for 1,107 yards and eight touchdowns, while also compiling a league-best quarterback rating of 61.6, averaging just under 40 yards per punt, and intercepting two passes on defense. Herber subsequently shared quarterback duties with Cecil Isbell in 1940, after which the Packers waived him prior to the start of the ensuing campaign. Choosing to announce his retirement, Herber ended his time in Green Bay with 6,749 yards passing, 66 touchdown passes, 90 interceptions, a completion percentage of 40.6, and a quarterback rating

Herber set a new NFL record in 1936 when he passed for 1,239 yards.
Courtesy of MearsOnlineAuctions.com

of 48.5. He also rushed for 201 yards and scored seven touchdowns, with three of those coming on runs, three on pass receptions, and one on an interception return.

Herber remained away from football for the next three years, during which time he attempted to enlist in the military to serve his country during World War II. But, after being rejected for his varicose veins, the 34-year-old Herber returned to the draft-depleted NFL as a member of the New York Giants, who coaxed him out of retirement in 1944. Although slower of foot and somewhat overweight, Herber managed to lead the Giants to a berth in the 1944 NFL title game, which they lost to the Packers by a score of 14–7. He remained in New York for one more year, before retiring for good following the conclusion of the 1945 campaign. Leaving the game with the reputation of being pro football's greatest long-distance passer, Herber retired with career totals of 8,041 yards passing, 81 touchdown passes, and 106 interceptions, a pass completion percentage of 40.9, and a quarterback rating of 50.1.

After being elected to the Pro Football Hall of Fame in 1966, Herber received the additional distinction in 1969 of being named to the Hall's All-1930s Team. He passed away just two months later, dying of cancer at only 59 years of age, on October 14, 1969.

PACKERS CAREER HIGHLIGHTS

Best Season

Herber had an outstanding all-around season in 1932, earning his lone First-Team All-Pro selection by leading all NFL quarterbacks with 639 yards passing and nine touchdown passes, rushing for a career-high 149 yards, running for one touchdown, and scoring another on an interception return. However, he played his best ball for the Packers in 1936, leading the league with a career-high 1,239 yards passing and 11 touchdown passes, while also topping the circuit with a quarterback rating of 58.9. Herber's exceptional play, which led the Packers to their fourth NFL title, earned him Second-Team All-Pro honors for the second straight season.

Memorable Moments/Greatest Performances

Herber began his pro career in style, tossing a 50-yard TD pass to Lavvie Dilweg during a 14–0 win over the Chicago Cardinals in the opening game of his rookie campaign of 1930.

Herber turned in an outstanding all-around effort against Staten Island on October 30, 1932, leading the Packers to a 26–0 victory over the Stapletons by throwing a pair of touchdown passes to Roger Grove and returning an interception 85 yards for another score.

Herber threw three touchdown passes for the first time in his career during a 21–0 win over the Boston Braves on November 13, 1932, with the longest of those being a 35-yard connection with Johnny (Blood) McNally.

Herber accomplished the feat again during a 41–0 dismantling of the Cincinnati Reds on October 14, 1934, connecting with Hank Bruder, Roger Grove, and Al Rose on scoring plays that covered 9, 11, and 25 yards, respectively.

Herber exhibited his arm strength when he completed an 83-yard touchdown pass to Don Hutson on the first play from scrimmage during a 7–0 win over the Chicago Bears on September 22, 1935. According to *True Sport*, Herber's pass traveled 66 yards in the air before it reached Hutson.

In Green Bay's next meeting with Chicago on October 27, 1935, Herber led the Packers to a 17–14 come-from-behind victory over the Bears by hitting Hutson with a pair of fourth-quarter TD passes that covered 69 and four yards.

Herber performed well in the 1936 NFL title game, completing six of his 14 pass attempts, for 129 yards and two touchdowns, in leading the Packers to a 21–6 win over the Boston Redskins. After hooking up with Don Hutson on a 48-yard TD pass in the first quarter, Herber completed an 8-yard touchdown pass to Milt Gantebein in the third period.

Herber found Hutson in the end zone three times during the 1938 regular-season opener, leading the Packers to a 26–17 win over the Cleveland Rams by hitting his favorite receiver with passes that covered 7, 53, and 18 yards.

The duo of Herber and Hutson struck once again during a 27–20 win over the Chicago Cardinals on October 8, 1939, collaborating on a 92-yard scoring play that remains one of the longest in franchise history.

NOTABLE ACHIEVEMENTS

- Returned one interception for a touchdown during career.
- Passed for more than 1,000 yards twice, setting new NFL record by passing for 1,239 yards in 1936.
- Led NFL quarterbacks in: pass completions three times; passing yardage three times; touchdown passes three times; completion percentage twice; and passer rating three times.
- Finished second in NFL in: pass completions twice; passing yardage once; touchdown passes once; and completion percentage once.

- Finished third in NFL in: passing yardage twice; touchdown passes once; and passer rating once.
- Ranks sixth in Packers history with 66 career touchdown passes.
- Three-time Western Conference champion (1936, 1938, and 1939).
- Four-time NFL champion (1930, 1931, 1936, and 1939).
- 1939 Pro Bowl selection.
- 1932 First-Team All-Pro.
- Two-time Second-Team All-Pro (1935 and 1936).
- NFL 1930s All-Decade Team.
- Pro Football Hall of Fame All-1930s Team.
- Elected to Pro Football Hall of Fame in 1966.

34

— **JOHN (BLOOD) MCNALLY** —

One of the most colorful and eccentric players to perform in the NFL during the formative period of the league's existence, John (Blood) McNally played for five different teams between 1925 and 1938, acquiring during that time the nickname "The Vagabond Halfback" for his off-the-field behavior and spontaneity. Blessed with a considerable amount of talent as well, Blood made more touchdown receptions and recorded more interceptions than any other NFL player prior to 1938, with his ability to score from anywhere on the field making him the most exciting and dynamic player of his time. Spending most of his peak seasons in Green Bay, Blood helped lead the Packers to their first four NFL championships, earning in the process a place in the Pro Football Hall of Fame and spots on the NFL 1930s All-Decade Team and the Packers All–Iron Man Era Team. Meanwhile, Blood's colorful personality and unconventional behavior made him perhaps the league's most recognizable figure until Don Hutson came along.

Born in New Richmond, Wisconsin, on November 27, 1903, John Victor McNally Jr. possessed unusual intelligence and a near photographic memory that enabled him to graduate from high school at only 14 years of age. Although McNally never played high school sports, he developed into an exceptional all-around athlete after he enrolled at St. John's University in Collegeville, Minnesota, earning letters in baseball, basketball, football, and track, before transferring to Notre Dame. Working for a Minneapolis newspaper while still in college, McNally and a friend, Ralph Hanson, heard they could make extra money by playing football for a local semi-pro team. Not wishing to lose his amateur standing, McNally, who still answered to the name John McNally at the time, decided to use a fake name during his tryout. Receiving the inspiration for his famous alias on the ride over to the team's practice facility, McNally recalled years later, "On the way there, we passed a theater on Hennepin Avenue, and up on the marquee I saw the name of the movie that was playing, *Blood and Sand* with Rudolph Valentino. Ralph was behind me on my motorcycle, and I turned my head

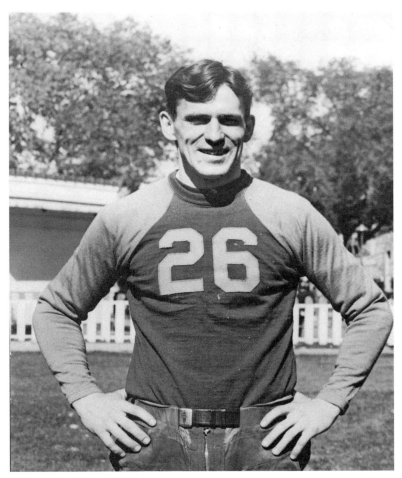

John (Blood) McNally proved to be the most colorful and exciting player
of his time.
Courtesy of RMYAuctions.com

and shouted, 'That's it. I'll be Blood and you be Sand.'" Although McNally
continued to use his given name outside of football, he subsequently
became known strictly as Johnny Blood on the playing field, explaining in
1936, "I've seen it written that my real name is John Blood McNally and I
just dropped the last part for pro football purposes, but that isn't so. I was
just John McNally until I decided to be Johnny Blood carrying a football."

Blood spent the next few seasons competing at the semi-pro level,
before beginning his professional career with the Milwaukee Badgers in
1925. After one year in Milwaukee, Blood split the next three years between

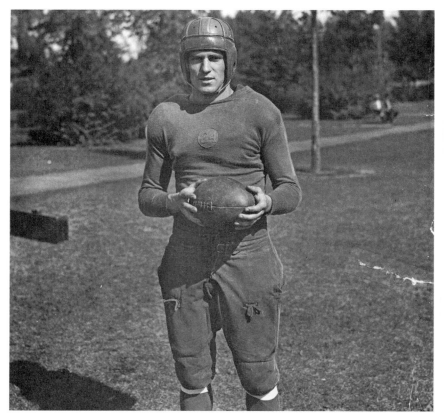

McNally caught more TD passes and recorded more interceptions than any
other NFL player prior to 1938.
Courtesy of RMYAuctions.com

the Duluth Eskimos (1926–1927) and the Pottsville Maroons (1928). With
the Maroons folding at the end of 1928, Blood signed with the Packers,
finally arriving in Green Bay shortly before he celebrated his 26th birthday.

Making an immediate impact on his new team, Blood helped lead the
Packers to their first NFL title in 1929 by finishing first on the club with
406 yards rushing, while also scoring five touchdowns. After contributing
to Green Bay's 1930 championship team by scoring another five TDs,
Blood led the Packers to their third straight NFL title in 1931 by scoring a
league-leading 84 points and 14 touchdowns.

Known for his speed, agility, and pass-catching ability, the 6'1", 188-
pound Blood proved to be equally effective on both sides of the ball. A
superb receiver with tremendous speed, sure hands, and great leaping

ability, Blood posed a scoring threat any time he got his hands on the ball, with legendary Chicago Bears head coach George Halas once stating, "The Packers had a lot of great players, but until Don Hutson came along, Johnny Blood was the one guy who could beat you with the one big play."

Hutson, himself, once said, "I never saw a fellow who could turn a ball game around as quickly as Johnny Blood."

Easily the league's most exciting player prior to the arrival of Hutson, Blood, according to unofficial and incomplete statistics provided by *The Football Encyclopedia*, scored 49 touchdowns, made 38 TD receptions (29 with the Packers), and accumulated 2,429 receiving yards over the course of his career, with the last two numbers surpassing the figures compiled by any other NFL player who competed primarily during the league's pre-statistical era. Meanwhile, in addition to being a hard and sure tackler on defense, Blood recorded an unofficial total of 40 interceptions, later deemed to be an NFL record at the time of his retirement.

Yet, as much as his on-field accomplishments brought him personal glory, Blood became equally well known for his behavior off the playing field, which made him a legend in his own time. The exploits of Blood that have been substantiated through the years include:

- Jumping across a narrow ledge six stories from the ground to gain access to a Los Angeles hotel room
- Fleeing an increasingly hostile towel fight with Packers end Lavvie Dilweg by climbing on top of a fast-moving train and crawling across car tops
- Playing almost an entire game with a collapsed kidney
- Having to be rescued by teammates while attempting chin-ups on the stern's flagpole of the ocean liner SS *Mariposa* while traveling across the Pacific Ocean for a barnstorming game in Hawaii
- Riding the blinds between trains on the way to training camp to avoid having to pay a fare
- Climbing down the face of a hotel in downtown Chicago to avoid curfew and recite poetry to the swooning women below

In discussing his somewhat atypical behavior, and why he made football his chosen profession, Blood (McNally) explained years later:

I wanted a life in which I could do something I enjoyed and still have leisure to do other things I enjoyed. Football was an escape, certainly, but an escape into something I enjoyed. In the off-season

I would ship out to the Orient as an ordinary seaman and enjoy the beauty of the Pacific Islands. Or I would winter on Catalina Island off the coast of Los Angeles. Understand, I was not afraid of work. I had sufficient energy that work did not bother me at all. I was a hard worker. To me, freedom did not mean being able only to do the non-difficult but, rather, to do what I chose to do. One winter in Catalina, I worked three shifts. I worked in the brickyard all day, making bricks. I worked the next eight hours in a gambling hall as a bouncer. And the next eight hours I "honeymooned" with a redhead.

But, while tales of drinking, romancing, and other excessive behavior provided Packer historians with material galore, Curly Lambeau found little amusement in his star player's extracurricular activities, with McNally telling the *Green Bay Press-Gazette* in 1983, "Curly didn't completely understand me. But I don't perfectly understand myself." As a result, even though Blood continued to perform well for the Packers in 1932 and 1933, Lambeau sold him to the Pittsburgh Pirates (now the Steelers) prior to the start of the 1934 campaign.

Blood subsequently spent one injury-riddled season in Pittsburgh, before he convinced Lambeau to re-sign him by performing well for a pair of semi-pro teams in a series of exhibition games the following September. Returning to the city of his greatest triumphs in 1935, Blood gained 115 yards on the ground, made a team-leading 25 receptions for 404 yards and three touchdowns, and scored another TD on an interception return, before amassing 212 yards from scrimmage and scoring three touchdowns for Green Bay's 1936 NFL championship team.

With Blood clearly approaching the end of his playing career, the Packers released him following the conclusion of the 1936 campaign, after which the Pirates named him their head coach. After spending his first two years in Pittsburgh functioning in the dual role of player-coach, Blood began the 1939 season serving the team strictly as head coach, before handing in his resignation during the early stages of the campaign following an embarrassing 32–0 loss to the Chicago Bears at Forbes Field. Although Blood ended his coaching career in Pittsburgh with an overall record of just 6-19, team owner Art Rooney later called him the most memorable character he knew during his career, stating, "Nobody would even believe some of the things he did."

After leaving Pittsburgh, McNally spent two years coaching the Kenosha Cardinals, an independent pro team that had formerly played in the

American Professional Football Association in 1939, before enlisting in the US Army Air Corps the day after the Japanese attacked Pearl Harbor. After serving in India as a cryptographer during the war, McNally attempted a comeback with the Packers in 1945, but subsequently announced his retirement after suffering an injury while returning a punt during an exhibition game. He then spent the next few years teaching and coaching several different sports at St. John's University, before returning to his hometown of New Richmond, Wisconsin, where he opened an employment agency. Inducted into the Pro Football Hall of Fame as part of its 17-member inaugural class of 1963, McNally later received the additional honor of being one of the first eight men inducted into the Packers Hall of Fame in 1970. He lived 15 more years, dying from complications of a stroke on November 28, 1985, just one day after he turned 82.

PACKERS CAREER HIGHLIGHTS

Best Season

Playing in a defensive-minded era dominated by the ground game, Blood compiled relatively modest offensive numbers over the course of his career. Nevertheless, he annually ranked among the league leaders in receiving yards and touchdown receptions during his time in Green Bay, establishing career-high marks in receptions (25) and receiving yards (404) in 1935. Still, even though the NFL did not begin to keep an official record of offensive statistics until 1932, Blood's 1931 campaign would have to be considered his finest because, based on unofficial and incomplete statistics from *The Football Encyclopedia*, he led the league with 84 points scored and 14 touchdowns, scoring 11 times on pass receptions, twice on runs, and once on an interception return.

Memorable Moments/Greatest Performances

Blood helped the Packers maintain their one-game lead over the second-place New York Giants with one game remaining in the 1929 regular season by scoring on a 29-yard pass reception from Red Dunn and a 73-yard lateral on a punt return during a 25–0 win over the Providence Steam Roller on December 1, 1929.

Blood displayed his explosiveness on October 5, 1930, when he took a short pass from Red Dunn and ran 55 yards for a 70-yard, fourth-quarter touchdown that gave the Packers a 14–7 victory over the Giants.

Nearly two months later, on November 27, 1930, Blood hauled in a pair of TD passes from Dunn during a 25–7 win over the Frankford Yellow Jackets, with his scoring plays covering 41 and 30 yards.

Blood had a huge game against the Chicago Cardinals on October 11, 1931, leading the Packers to a 26–7 victory over their overmatched opponents by scoring three second-half touchdowns, two of which came on receptions that covered 40 and 14 yards, and the other coming on a 35-yard interception return.

Blood provided most of the offensive firepower during a 15–0 win over the Frankford Yellow Jackets one week later, scoring both Packer touchdowns on a 9-yard pass reception from Roger Grove and a 19-yard scamper.

Blood once again proved to be the dominant force during a 26–0 victory over the Staten Island Stapletons on November 8, 1931, hauling in a 55-yard TD pass from Red Dunn and running for a 13-yard score.

Blood led the Packers to a 38–7 rout of the Providence Steam Roller on November 26, 1931, by scoring a career-high three touchdowns, with his scores coming on pass plays that covered 22, 45, and 20 yards.

Almost exactly one year later, on November 27, 1932, Blood put the finishing touches on a 21–3 win over Staten Island by returning an interception 45 yards for a TD in the fourth quarter.

Blood collaborated with Arnie Herber twice during a 31–7 victory over the Detroit Lions on November 10, 1935, hauling in TD passes that covered 26 and 70 yards.

Blood scored another pair of touchdowns on November 24, 1935, leading the Packers to a 34–14 win over the Pittsburgh Pirates by catching a 41-yard TD pass from Bob Monnett and returning an interception 11 yards for his second touchdown of the game.

During a seesaw battle with the Lions on October 18, 1936, Blood hooked up with Arnie Herber on a critical 46-yard touchdown pass in the fourth quarter that put the Packers ahead by a score of 17–15. After Detroit subsequently took an 18–17 lead, Tiny Engebretsen gave the Packers a 20–18 victory with a late field goal.

Blood exhibited his tremendous versatility during a 42–10 rout of the Pittsburgh Pirates on October 25, 1936, returning an interception 58 yards for a touchdown and also tossing a 7-yard TD pass to Paul Miller.

NOTABLE ACHIEVEMENTS

- Returned four interceptions for touchdowns during career.
- Surpassed 400 receiving yards once (404 in 1935).
- Surpassed 500 yards from scrimmage once (519 in 1935).
- Led NFL with 11 touchdown receptions, 14 total touchdowns, and 84 points scored in 1931.
- Finished second in NFL with 25 receptions and average of 16.2 yards per reception in 1935.
- Finished third in NFL with 14 receptions and three touchdown receptions in 1932.
- Retired with more career TD receptions (38) and interceptions (40) than any other player in NFL history.
- Four-time NFL champion (1929, 1930, 1931, and 1936).
- 1931 First-Team All-Pro.
- NFL 1930s All-Decade Team.
- Pro Football Hall of Fame All-1930s Team.
- Named to Packers All-Time Team in 1946 and 1957.
- Named to Packers All–Iron Man Era Team in 1976.
- Elected to Pro Football Hall of Fame in 1963.

35

DARREN SHARPER

A hard-hitting safety with exceptional range and a nose for the football, Darren Sharper spent 14 seasons in the NFL, establishing himself as one of the league's all-time leaders in interceptions and interception-return yards. Exhibiting a propensity for making big plays throughout his career, Sharper also ranks second in league history with 11 touchdown interceptions, with his 13 non-offensive TDs placing him fifth on the NFL's all-time list. Although Sharper compiled many of those numbers while playing for the Minnesota Vikings and New Orleans Saints his final six years in the league, he had many of his finest seasons for the Packers between 1997 and 2004, leading them in interceptions five times, with his 36 picks and 677 interception-return yards both placing him extremely high in team annals. Meanwhile, Sharper's seven defensive touchdowns tie him with Herb Adderley for the second most in franchise history, with only Charles Woodson (9) having recorded more. Sharper's exceptional all-around play helped the Packers capture four division titles and one NFC championship, earning him two trips to the Pro Bowl, two All-Pro selections, and a spot on the NFL 2000s All-Decade Team.

Born in Richmond, Virginia, on November 3, 1975, Darren Mallory Sharper attended Hermitage High School in nearby Henrico County, where, in addition to excelling as a student, he played for the varsity football and basketball teams, spending most of his time on the gridiron at the quarterback position. After graduating from Hermitage High, Sharper enrolled at the College of William and Mary, where, after transitioning to defensive back, he earned All-America honors twice and First-Team All–Yankee Conference recognition three times by recording a school record 24 career interceptions and Division I-AA record 468 career interception-return yards. An outstanding punt returner as well, Sharper set another school mark by amassing a total of 1,027 yards returning punts. Performing especially well as a senior in 1996, Sharper earned Yankee Conference Defensive Player of the Year honors by picking off 10 passes.

Darren Sharper ranks among the NFL's all-time leaders in interceptions, interception-return yards, and touchdown interceptions.
Courtesy of Tulane University via Wikipedia

Subsequently selected by the Packers in the second round of the 1997 NFL Draft, with the 60th overall pick, Sharper spent most of his rookie season playing on special teams, although he also contributed on defense, giving an early indication of his ball-hawking skills by recording two interceptions, both of which he returned for touchdowns. Even though Sharper failed to pick off a single pass after he laid claim to the starting free safety job the following year, he established himself as one of the team's most consistent defenders, doing an excellent job in pass coverage, while also finishing fourth on the club with 73 tackles (53 solo). Putting together another solid season in 1999, Sharper intercepted three passes and recorded a career-high 113 tackles, with 84 of those being of the unassisted variety.

The 2000 campaign proved to be Sharper's breakout season, as, in addition to finishing third on the team with 92 tackles, he led the league with nine interceptions, earning in the process his first trip to the Pro Bowl and the first of his two First-Team All-Pro selections. Sharper continued to perform extremely well in 2001, picking off another six passes and making 94 tackles, before earning Pro Bowl and Second-Team All-Pro honors the following year by finishing third in the league with seven interceptions, recording 68 tackles, and topping the circuit with 233 interception-return yards, which ranks as the second-highest single-season total in franchise history.

Although Sharper gradually developed a reputation during his time in Green Bay for his pass coverage skills, ability to judge the flight of the ball, and tendency to make big plays, his 6'2", 210-pound frame and willingness to challenge opposing ball-carriers also made him extremely effective against the run. In addition to leading the Packers in interceptions five times, he finished first on the team in tackles twice, recording more than 70 tackles six times and more than 90 stops on three separate occasions.

Sharper remained with the Packers for another two years, recording a total of nine interceptions and 152 tackles from 2003 to 2004, while also scoring three more touchdowns, before being released by the team prior to the start of the 2005 campaign due to salary-cap reasons. Aside from his 36 interceptions and 677 interception-return yards, Sharper left Green Bay with career totals of six sacks and 605 tackles, with the last figure placing him eighth in team annals.

Following his release by the Packers, Sharper signed with the Minnesota Vikings, with whom he spent the next four seasons, recording 18 interceptions and 359 interception-return yards during that time, while also scoring another three touchdowns. Performing particularly well in his first year with the Vikings, Sharper concluded the 2005 campaign with nine interceptions, two of which he returned for touchdowns, and a league-leading 276 interception-return yards, earning in the process Pro Bowl and Second-Team All-Pro recognition. After making his fourth Pro Bowl appearance in 2007, Sharper became an unrestricted free agent at the end of 2008. Choosing to sign with New Orleans, he spent the final two years of his career with the Saints, having one of his finest seasons for them in 2009, when he earned First-Team All-Pro honors for the second time and the last of his five Pro Bowl nominations by leading the league with nine interceptions, an NFL-record 376 interception-return yards, and three defensive touchdowns. Limited by injuries to only eight games the following year, Sharper elected to announce his retirement at season's end, concluding his career with 63 interceptions, 1,412 interception-return yards, 942 tackles, and 7½ sacks. In addition to ranking fifth in NFL history in non-offensive touchdowns and being tied for second in touchdown interceptions, Sharper currently ranks eighth in interceptions and third in interception-return yards.

Unfortunately, since leaving the game, Sharper has revealed a side of himself that no one knew existed during his playing days. Found guilty of drugging and raping two women he met at a West Hollywood nightclub in

Sharper led the Packers in interceptions five times and tackles twice.
Courtesy of MainlineAutographs.com

2013, Sharper was sentenced to 20 years behind bars and ordered to register for life as a sex offender in November 2016. The charges stemmed from an incident on October 30, 2013, when Sharper invited two women he met at the club to a party. However, on the way to the fictitious gathering, he brought the women to his hotel room, where he gave each one a drink laced with the sedative zolpidem. One of the women later said that she woke up naked hours later, only to find Sharper sexually assaulting her, while her companion told prosecutors that she awakened in time to "interrupt his actions." Officials later revealed that Sharper had raped as many as 16 women in California, Arizona, Louisiana, and Nevada in similar fashion the previous few years. He will serve the time concurrently with a sentence previously handed down in Louisiana, with prosecutors stating that, under California sentencing laws, he could earn what is called "half time credit," serving just 10 years of his sentence and being eligible for parole by the year 2024.

PACKERS CAREER HIGHLIGHTS

Best Season

Sharper performed exceptionally well for the Packers in both 1999 and 2002, concluding the first of those campaigns with three interceptions and a career-high 113 tackles, before finishing third in the NFL with seven picks, leading the league with 233 interception-return yards, scoring one touchdown, and making 68 tackles three years later. However, he had his finest all-around season as a member of the Packers in 2000, earning his first Pro Bowl nomination and consensus First-Team All-Pro honors by leading the league with a career-high nine interceptions, which he returned for a total of 109 yards, recording a sack, and amassing a total of 92 tackles (72 solo).

Memorable Moments/Greatest Performances

Sharper scored the first touchdown of his career in the second quarter of a 20–10 win over the Lions on November 2, 1997, when he intercepted a Scott Mitchell pass and returned the ball 50 yards for a TD.

Sharper again lit the scoreboard three weeks later, when he returned a fumble 34 yards for a touchdown during a convincing 45–17 victory over the Dallas Cowboys on November 23.

The ever-opportunistic Sharper scored his third touchdown of the 1997 campaign in the final week of the regular season, when he returned an interception 20 yards for a TD during a 31–21 win over the Buffalo Bills.

Sharper turned in a tremendous all-around effort against Arizona on September 24, 2000, helping to lead the Packers to a 29–3 victory over the Cardinals by intercepting Jake Plummer twice, knocking down two passes, and recording 10 tackles.

Sharper had another big game on November 6, 2000, picking off a pair of Daunte Culpepper passes and making seven tackles during a 26–20 overtime win over the Minnesota Vikings.

Sharper helped the Packers begin the 2001 campaign on a positive note by recording two interceptions during a 28–6 victory over the Detroit Lions in the regular-season opener.

Sharper contributed to a 24–10 win over the Miami Dolphins on November 4, 2002, by returning an interception 89 yards for a touchdown.

Sharper recorded another pick-six on October 17, 2004, when he returned an interception 36 yards for a TD during a 38–10 victory over the Lions.

Although the Packers lost their December 19, 2004, meeting with the Jacksonville Jaguars by a score of 28–25, Sharper once again displayed his nose for the opponent's end zone by returning a recovered fumble 15 yards for a touchdown.

Sharper scored his final touchdown as a member of the Packers in the 2004 regular-season finale, when he returned an interception 43 yards for a TD during a 31–14 win over the Bears.

NOTABLE ACHIEVEMENTS

- Scored seven defensive touchdowns (five interception returns and two fumble returns).
- Recorded at least five interceptions four times.
- Surpassed 100 interception-return yards twice, topping 200 yards once (233 in 2002).
- Recorded more than 100 tackles once (113 in 1999).
- Led NFL in: interceptions once; interception-return yards once; and TD interceptions once.
- Finished second in NFL in non-offensive touchdowns twice.
- Led Packers in interceptions five times and tackles twice.
- Ranks among Packers career leaders with: 605 total tackles (8th); 468 unassisted tackles (7th); 36 interceptions (6th); 677 interception-return yards (4th); and 7 defensive touchdowns (tied—2nd).
- Ranks among NFL's all-time leaders with: 63 interceptions (8th); 1,412 interception-return yards (3rd); 11 touchdown interceptions (tied—2nd); and 13 non-offensive touchdowns (5th).
- Four-time division champion (1997, 2002, 2003, and 2004).
- 1997 NFC champion.
- Two-time Pro Bowl selection (2000 and 2002).
- 2000 First-Team All-Pro.
- 2002 Second-Team All-Pro.
- 2000 First-Team All-NFC selection.
- NFL 2000s All-Decade Team.
- Pro Football Hall of Fame All-2000s Second Team.
- Pro Football Reference All-2000s First Team.

36

LAVERN "LAVVIE" DILWEG

Had LaVern "Lavvie" Dilweg's immediate successor in Green Bay not been the incomparable Don Hutson, he likely would have received far more recognition than he has through the years for his all-around excellence. Generally considered to be the best two-way end in pro football prior to Hutson, Dilweg starred on both offense and defense for the Packers from 1927 to 1934, earning All-Pro honors in seven of those eight seasons. A tenacious blocker, reliable receiver, and dangerous runner after the catch, Dilweg recorded the second most receptions of any player who performed from 1920 to 1934. Meanwhile, in addition to being one of the game's surest tacklers on defense, Dilweg proved to be an outstanding ball-hawk, with his 27 career interceptions representing the highest total ever compiled by a defensive end. Dilweg's brilliant play on both sides of the ball helped the Packers capture their first three NFL championships, earning him in the process spots on the Pro Football Hall of Fame All-1920s Team, the Packers 50th Anniversary Team, and Green Bay's All–Iron Man Era Team.

Born in Milwaukee, Wisconsin, on November 1, 1903, LaVern Ralph Dilweg attended local Washington High School, before enrolling at Marquette University. A three-sport star in college, Dilweg excelled as a center in basketball, a shotputter in track, and an end in football, earning All-America honors for his performance on the gridiron. After two undergraduate years at Marquette, Dilweg enrolled in that institution's law school, eventually gaining admission to the Wisconsin Bar in 1927. Prior to that, though, he began playing football professionally, spending the 1926 campaign with the NFL's Milwaukee Badgers, before signing with the Packers at season's end after the Badgers folded.

Continuing to practice law after he arrived in Green Bay, Dilweg spent his mornings on the football field and his afternoons at the law office, with his hours behind a desk having little effect on his on-field performance. After being named Second-Team All-Pro in his one year with the Badgers, Dilweg earned First-Team All-Pro honors in each of his first five seasons

LaVern "Lavvie" Dilweg proved to be the NFL's best two-way end
prior to the arrival of Don Hutson.
Courtesy of Albersheims.com

with the Packers, with his superb play during the league's infancy prompting Professional Football Researchers Association founder, Bob Carroll, to
write years later, "Give him [Dilweg] today's Super Bowl hype and they'd
chisel his face on Mt. Rushmore." Performing especially well in 1929,
Dilweg helped lead the Packers to the first of their three consecutive NFL
titles by making an unofficial total of 25 receptions, which placed him first
in the league rankings.

Rawboned, with long arms and big hands, the 6'3", 200-pound Dilweg not only did an outstanding job of hauling in any passes thrown in
his direction, but he also excelled as a blocker, the primary role of offensive
ends at that time. Yet, Dilweg proved to be even more dominant on defense,
where, in addition to being a tenacious tackler, he used his long arms and

large hands to ward off blockers, making him perhaps the toughest player in the league to run against. In expressing his admiration for Dilweg, legendary running back Red Grange stated, "I have always said that Dilweg is the greatest end who ever brought me down." Dilweg also had the flexibility to drop back into coverage and defend against the pass, with his 27 career interceptions far exceeding the total compiled by any other defensive end of his time. Equally proficient in punt coverage, Dilweg drew praise from former University of Wisconsin football coach and athletic director George Little, who suggested, "The way he goes down on punts and refuses to be taken out by blockers is beyond description."

Speaking years later of the pride he took in excelling in all phases of the game, Dilweg said, "I always enjoyed defense. Nowadays, of course, the game is full of specialists, and they're wonderful at their jobs. But, for me, if I had not been permitted to play both offense and defense, I'm sure I wouldn't have enjoyed it as much as I did." Dilweg's all-around excellence prompted Hall-of-Famers Bronko Nagurski and Cal Hubbard to name him to their all-time teams. Meanwhile, *Total Football: The Official Encyclopedia of the National Football League*, once wrote: "LaVern Dilweg, by nearly all contemporary accounts, was the best end in pro football almost from his first game in 1926 until his last in 1934."

Dilweg continued his outstanding play in 1932 and 1933, earning Second-Team All-Pro honors both years, before announcing his retirement following the conclusion of the 1934 campaign. Explaining his decision to retire while still performing at an extremely high level, Dilweg said, "I had a couple more years left, I think, but I could feel myself slowing down. Bruises that had healed in a week were taking 10 days. And they didn't want to pay me what I thought I ought to get, so I thought I would just get out of it."

Although Dilweg spent all but his final three seasons competing in the NFL's pre-statistical era, he has been unofficially credited in *The Football Encyclopedia* with 126 pass receptions for 2,043 yards and 12 touchdowns. He also returned two interceptions for touchdowns and kicked two extra points, giving him a total of 86 career points. In assessing Dilweg's nine-year NFL career, Curly Lambeau stated in 1945, "Dilweg faded out of the picture just about the time the seven-man line went out of fashion, but, without question, he was the greatest end the seven-man line type of defense ever developed."

Following his playing days, Dilweg officiated Big Ten football games and continued to practice law in Green Bay until 1943, when he was elected to Congress. After serving one term representing Wisconsin's Eighth

Dilweg's 27 career interceptions represent the highest total ever
amassed by a defensive end.
Courtesy of RMYAuctions.com

District in the US House of Representatives, Dilweg returned to his law
practice, where he remained until 1961, when President Kennedy appointed
him for a three-year term to the Foreign Claims Settlement Commission.

Subsequently reappointed twice by President Johnson, Dilweg retained his government position until January 2, 1968, when he passed away at age 64 following a lengthy illness. He died just two days after Vince Lombardi's Packers captured their third consecutive NFL title by defeating the Dallas Cowboys in the Ice Bowl, thereby replicating the feat accomplished nearly four decades earlier by the Packers of Dilweg's era.

Looking back at the life and playing career of Dilweg, legendary football historian Bob Carroll stated, "You could make the case that the stuff he did after football was a little more important in the whole scheme of things than playing end for the Green Bay Packers. Still, none of that changes the fact that, at a particular time and place in the long history of football, nobody played end better than Dilweg."

PACKERS CAREER HIGHLIGHTS

Best Season

Although Dilweg spent most of his career playing in the NFL's pre-statistical era, he has been unofficially credited in *The Football Encyclopedia* with making a league-leading 25 receptions in the Packers' first championship campaign of 1929, which would have to be considered his finest season.

Memorable Moments/Greatest Performances

Dilweg scored two defensive touchdowns during his career, with the first of those coming in the fourth quarter of a 20–0 win over the Duluth Eskimos on October 9, 1927, when he returned an interception 25 yards for the Packers' final points of the game.

Dilweg recorded another pick-six during a 27–12 victory over the Frankford Yellow Jackets on October 12, 1930, putting the Packers ahead by a score of 20–0 late in the first quarter by returning an interception 50 yards for a touchdown.

Dilweg helped the Packers overcome an early 9–0 deficit to Frankford in the 1927 regular-season finale by hauling in a 40-yard TD pass from Red Dunn during the latter stages of the first half. Green Bay went on to score 17 unanswered points, to come away with a 17–9 victory.

Dilweg gave the Packers a 12–0 win over the Chicago Cardinals on November 17, 1929, by gathering in a pair of TD passes.

Dilweg again proved to be a thorn in the side of the Cardinals in the 1930 regular-season opener, making a 50-yard touchdown reception during a 14–0 Packers win.

NOTABLE ACHIEVEMENTS

- Returned two interceptions for touchdowns during career.
- Led NFL with 25 pass receptions in 1929.
- Retired with second-most career interceptions (27) of any NFL player.
- Holds NFL record for most career interceptions by a defensive end.
- Three-time NFL champion (1929, 1930, and 1931).
- Five-time First-Team All-Pro (1927, 1928, 1929, 1930, and 1931).
- Two-time Second-Team All-Pro (1932 and 1933).
- NFL 1920s All-Decade Team.
- Pro Football Hall of Fame All-1920s Team.
- Named to Packers All-Time Team in 1946 and 1957.
- Named to Packers 50th Anniversary Team in 1969.
- Named to Packers All–Iron Man Era Team in 1976.

37

JOHN ANDERSON

An extremely consistent and reliable player, John Anderson spent his entire 12-year NFL career anchoring the Packers' defense from his left-outside linebacker position, leading the team in tackles on eight separate occasions, en route to establishing himself as the franchise's all-time leader in that category at the time of his retirement. Outstanding in pass coverage as well, Anderson recorded a total of 25 interceptions over the course of his career, tying him with Ray Nitschke for the most picks by any linebacker in franchise history. Unfortunately, the fact that Anderson spent almost all his time in Green Bay playing for mediocre Packer teams with poor defenses contributed greatly to the lack of recognition he generally received when it came to postseason honors. So, too, did the presence of more spectacular linebackers such as Lawrence Taylor, Mike Singletary, Carl Banks, and Wilber Marshall. Nevertheless, even though Anderson never earned All-Pro or Pro Bowl honors during his career, he ended up landing a spot on the Pro Football Hall of Fame All-1980s Second Team. Meanwhile, his outstanding all-around play also earned him recognition as the Packers' Most Valuable Defensive Player three straight times.

Born in Waukesha, Wisconsin, on February 14, 1956, Roger John Anderson attended Waukesha South High School, where he played both football and basketball, earning All-Conference and All-State honors on both offense and defense for his exceptional play on the gridiron. Following his graduation from Waukesha South, Anderson enrolled at the University of Michigan, where he spent the next four years playing for head coach Bo Schembechler. Emerging as a star his last two seasons under Schembechler, Anderson earned First-Team All–Big Ten Conference honors as a defensive end his junior year, before being named a First-Team All-American for his outstanding play at outside linebacker in his senior year of 1977.

Subsequently selected by the Packers in the first round of the 1978 NFL Draft, with the 26th overall pick, Anderson performed extremely well his first year in the league, earning a spot on the NFL's All-Rookie

John Anderson led the Packers in tackles eight times.
Courtesy of MearsOnlineAuctions.com

Team by recording five interceptions and 102 tackles, before breaking his arm in Week 13. Although Anderson missed more than half of the ensuing campaign after breaking his arm once again during training camp, he distinguished himself enough over the course of his first two seasons that an article appearing in a September 1980 edition of the *Milwaukee Journal* referred to him as the Packers' "best overall athlete, a complete football player who doesn't make mental mistakes," adding that he "has size and speed and strength, and possesses all the stuff superstars are made of, except for color."

Bitten by the injury bug again in 1980, Anderson appeared in only nine games, before beginning a string of five straight seasons in which he started every game for the Packers. Emerging as the Packers' leader on defense during that time, Anderson led the team in tackles each season, with his dependability and solid all-around play becoming his trademarks.

In speaking of his longtime teammate, Paul Coffman said, "John was just solid all the way around. His character, his work ethic, his play. You won't see many highlights of John Anderson making big hits, but he didn't miss many tackles because he was always in good position and so fundamentally sound. He just took you down and then went back to the huddle without a word to do it again. John was just so consistent for so long."

Looking back at the progression of his career, Anderson offered, "I remember as a rookie, I thought if I could just get to five years in the NFL, that would be awesome. It took me about five years to learn how to play the position so that I knew exactly what everyone was going to do. At that point, there weren't a lot of surprises, or a question of how they were going to block me. I would get beat, that's football, but it wasn't because I wasn't sure what the other team was going to do. That's when you have a lot of confidence."

The 6'3", 226-pound Anderson, who could be considered a prototype for the smaller, more athletic linebackers in the NFL today, truly began to come into his own after the Packers switched from a 4-3 alignment to a 3-4 defensive scheme his third year in the league. Blessed with good speed and quickness, Anderson had the ability to chase down opposing ball-carriers and cover tight ends and running backs coming out of the backfield. Although he didn't blitz that often, Anderson also did an excellent job of applying pressure to opposing quarterbacks, recording 19½ sacks over the course of his career. Displaying a nose for the football as well, Anderson not only picked off a total of 25 passes, but also recovered 15 fumbles.

Anderson's string of 77 straight starts ended in 1986, when he missed the final 12 games after suffering a broken left leg vs. Minnesota in Week 4. However, he returned to the Packers the following year to start 40 out of a possible 48 games the next three seasons, before announcing his retirement following the conclusion of the 1989 campaign. In discussing his decision to end his playing career when he did, Anderson said, "I knew my best days were in the past. I wasn't going to get any faster. I had been battling some ankle injuries and, frankly, I felt like I wasn't holding up to the way I had played earlier. I wanted to be the one who would make the call on when my career ended, and I had managed to dodge the major injury bullet over all those years. I wanted to be active after my career. It all sort of came together."

Looking back at his 12 years with the Packers, Anderson stated, "I have no regrets about my time in Green Bay, other than I wish we had been more successful on the field . . . I took a great deal of pride in the fact that I didn't come off the field. I was a third-down-guy, I was a goal-line guy, I was a first and second-down guy. And I enjoyed that because it allowed you to do a lot of things. I played nickel, I played dime, I played inside and goal-line, so I got to do a lot of different things, which was fun. And, over the course of 12 years, it allows you to not get bored."

Anderson was named the Packers' Most Valuable Defensive Player three straight times.
Courtesy of SportsMemorabilia.com

Anderson, who ended his career with a total of 1,020 tackles that remained a franchise record until A. J. Hawk surpassed it in 2014, later expressed surprise that he ranked so high in team annals, claiming, "I wasn't aware of it at the time. Statistics weren't played up. We got tackle totals after the game, and you looked at them to make sure you were contributing, but you didn't put too much into them. What I'm most proud of is that I never came off the field."

As for his selection to the Pro Football Hall of Fame's All-1980s Second Team, Anderson suggested, "It's nice to be recognized, but I think it speaks more to longevity. There was a guy in New York named Lawrence Taylor that I competed against for honors during my career, and I was far behind him, rightfully. He was the best I've ever seen. There were a number of linebackers who were perennially good players during that time, so it's something I'm proud of."

After retiring as an active player, Anderson became a sportscaster for WITI in Milwaukee, where he remained until 1998, when he accepted a position to teach middle-school Earth Science at Brookfield Academy in Brookfield, Wisconsin. Hired as linebacker coach by Carroll University in his hometown of Waukesha in 2009, Anderson continued to teach at

Brookfield Academy until 2017, when he decided to concentrate solely on his coaching duties.

CAREER HIGHLIGHTS

Best Season

An extremely consistent performer, Anderson did not have one season that stood out above all others. However, he posted his best overall numbers in 1983, when he gained recognition as Green Bay's most valuable defensive player for the first of three straight times by recording more than 100 tackles, registering 4½ quarterback sacks, and intercepting five passes, one of which he returned for the only touchdown of his career.

Memorable Moments/Greatest Performances

With Green Bay's regular kicker, Chester Marcol, sidelined by an injury, Anderson assumed placekicking duties during a 27–22 loss to the Jets on November 4, 1979, converting the only field goal attempt of his career when he connected from 39 yards out.

Anderson made all three of his interceptions in 1981 count, picking off his first pass during a 26–24 victory over the Giants on November 8, before recording interceptions in back-to-back wins over the Vikings (35–23) on November 29 and Lions (31–17) on December 6.

Anderson scored his lone career touchdown during a 55–14 rout of the Tampa Bay Buccaneers on October 2, 1983, when he returned an interception 27 yards for a TD, giving the Packers seven of the 35 points they tallied during the second quarter of the contest.

Anderson recorded two sacks in one game for the first time in his career on October 17, 1983, when he got to quarterback Joe Theismann twice during a 48–47 win over the Redskins.

Anderson again brought down the opposing quarterback behind the line of scrimmage twice on November 17, 1985, when he recorded two of the six sacks the Packers registered against New Orleans signal-caller Bobby Hebert during a 38–14 victory over the Saints.

Anderson turned in another outstanding performance two weeks later, when he helped anchor a Packer defense that allowed just five first downs and 65 yards of total offense during a 21–0 shutout of the Tampa Bay Buccaneers.

NOTABLE ACHIEVEMENTS

- Scored one defensive touchdown during career on an interception return.
- Recorded five interceptions twice.
- Recorded six sacks in 1985.
- Recorded more than 100 tackles seven times.
- Led Packers in tackles eight times.
- Ranks among Packers career leaders with: 1,020 total tackles (2nd); 783 unassisted tackles (2nd); 25 interceptions (tied—12th); and 15 fumble recoveries (tied—8th).
- 1982 Central Division champion.
- Named to 1978 NFL All-Rookie Team.
- Named Packers' Most Valuable Defensive Player three straight times (1983, 1984, and 1985).
- NFL 1980s All-Decade Team.
- Pro Football Hall of Fame All-1980s Second Team.

38

DAVE HANNER

Extremely consistent and durable, Dave "Hawg" Hanner spent 13 seasons starting at defensive tackle for the Packers, missing a total of only four games his entire career. Manning both tackle positions at different times, Hanner proved to be a rock in the middle of Green Bay's defense, excelling against the run, while also doing a good job of applying pressure to opposing quarterbacks. Persevering through the dark days of the 1950s, Hanner remained in Green Bay long enough to help the Packers win their first two NFL championships under Vince Lombardi, with his steady play earning him two Pro Bowl selections and a pair of All-Conference nominations. And following the conclusion of his playing career, Hanner continued to serve the Packers in various capacities, spending most of his adult life in the organization, before finally retiring to private life in 1996.

Born in Parkin, Arkansas, on May 22, 1930, Joel David Hanner grew up on the family farm with his four siblings, before getting his first taste of organized football while attending local Parkin High School. After graduating from high school, Hanner enrolled at the University of Arkansas, where his outstanding play on the gridiron prompted the Packers to select him in the fifth round of the 1952 NFL Draft, with the 52nd overall pick.

Earning a starting job on the Packers' defensive line immediately upon his arrival in Green Bay, Hanner performed well as a rookie, appearing in every game for the first of nine straight times. Meanwhile, Hanner's hard work and affable personality endeared him to his new teammates, with veteran running back Tony Canadeo bestowing upon him the nickname "Hawg" due to his rural upbringing and burly 6'2", 260-pound frame.

Continuing to build upon the success he experienced his first year in the league, Hanner earned Pro Bowl honors in each of the next two seasons with his outstanding play at right tackle, before eventually shifting over to the left side of the Packer defense during the second half of his career. Wherever he played, though, Hanner helped stabilize Green Bay's defensive front, with former teammate Herb Adderley recalling, "His main job was

Dave Hanner missed just four games in his 13 seasons with the Packers.
Courtesy of ClaremontShows.com

to play the draw and the screen. That was the main assignment for him. If you don't see a draw, don't see a screen, then rush the passer." Bobby Dillon, who played behind Hanner in Green Bay's defensive secondary for eight seasons, said of his longtime teammate, "He was a smart player. He never looked like he was in shape, but he was; and strong as a bull and quick." Surprisingly athletic for a man his size, Hanner defended equally well against the run and the pass, with his four career interceptions and one safety serving as a testament to his versatility.

Hanner spent more than four decades serving the Packers in one
capacity or another.
Courtesy of MearsOnlineAuctions.com

After earning First-Team All-Conference honors in both 1957 and
1959, Hanner contributed significantly to Packer teams that won three
straight conference championships and two consecutive NFL titles during
the early 1960s. Commenting on Hanner's importance to the success his
ball club experienced, Vince Lombardi noted, "He is 32 now, and it is going
to be a sad day in Green Bay when the years get him because, not only has
he been All-Pro several times, but there is nobody on this squad who is
better liked than big, easy-going, quiet Dave, with that chaw of tobacco in
his right cheek and his constant weight problem."

Hanner remained with the Packers for two more seasons after they won their second straight NFL title under Lombardi in 1962, before announcing his retirement following the conclusion of the 1964 campaign. He ended his career having played in 160 out of a possible 164 games. Packer fans later voted him onto the club's all-time "modern era team" in 1976, placing him alongside Henry Jordan at defensive tackle.

Almost immediately after Hanner retired as an active player, he joined Vince Lombardi's coaching staff, spending the next seven seasons tutoring the team's defensive linemen, before becoming the first defensive coordinator in franchise history in 1972. Relieved of his duties by the Packers in 1979, Hanner subsequently spent two years working for the rival Chicago Bears, before returning to Green Bay in 1982. After serving the Packers as a scout for the next 15 years, Hanner retired from football in 1996. He lived another 12 years, passing away at the age of 78, on September 11, 2008, two days after suffering a heart attack.

Upon learning of Hanner's passing, retired Packers president Bob Harlan said, "I don't know where else he could have gone and been as comfortable as he was. Easy-going, laid-back. He was a perfect Green Bay Packer guy."

Charley Armey, the retired GM of the St. Louis Rams who worked alongside Hanner from 1985 to 1987 on Dick Corrick's scouting staff in Green Bay, commented, "If you scoured the whole world, you couldn't find one guy to say anything bad about him."

Meanwhile, retired Packers GM Ron Wolf said of Hanner, "It was all about being what's best for the Packers. That's a rare quality in people. He lived by that code."

Former Packers scouting director and current Kansas City Chiefs general manager John Dorsey added, "That man wore the Packer 'G' with more pride than anyone I've ever met."

CAREER HIGHLIGHTS

Best Season

Hanner perhaps played his best ball for the Packers in 1959, when he earned one of his two First-Team All-Conference selections and recorded the only safety of his career.

Memorable Moments/Greatest Performances

Hanner performed extremely well during a 13–0 win over San Francisco on December 10, 1960, helping to anchor a Packer defense that allowed the 49ers to accumulate just 81 yards of total offense.

Although Hanner intercepted four passes during his career, he made his most memorable play in the opening game of the 1959 regular season, when he secured a 9–6 win over Chicago in Vince Lombardi's first game as head coach by tackling Bears quarterback Ed Brown in the end zone for a safety late in the fourth quarter.

NOTABLE ACHIEVEMENTS

- Intercepted four passes during career.
- Tied for sixth in Packers history in seasons played (13).
- Missed only four games entire career.
- Three-time Western Conference champion (1960, 1961, and 1962).
- Two-time NFL champion (1961 and 1962).
- Two-time Pro Bowl selection (1953 and 1954).
- Two-time All–Western Conference First-Team selection (1957 and 1959).
- Named to Packers All-Time Modern Era Team in 1976.

39

BOYD DOWLER

The top wide receiver on most of Vince Lombardi's championship squads of the 1960s, Boyd Dowler led the Packers in pass receptions seven times and receiving yards four times, en route to establishing himself as one of the franchise's all-time leaders in both categories. A two-time Pro Bowler and two-time All–Western Conference selection, Dowler made more than 50 receptions and amassed more than 800 receiving yards twice each, despite playing for Packer teams that predicated much of their success on their running attack. Dowler, who never missed a game in his 11 seasons with the Packers, served as an integral member of Green Bay squads that won six Western Conference championships, five NFL titles, and two Super Bowls, earning in the process spots on the Pro Football Hall of Fame All-1960s Team and the NFL's 50th Anniversary Team. Yet, ironically, it is for his inability to compete in Super Bowl I that Dowler is perhaps remembered most.

Born in Rock Springs, Wyoming, on October 18, 1937, Boyd Hamilton Dowler grew up some 250 miles east, in the city of Cheyenne, where his father, a former football coach who had played college football at Wyoming, taught high school history. After starring at quarterback for Cheyenne High School, the younger Dowler enrolled at the University of Colorado, where he spent three seasons directing the Buffaloes' offense, earning All-Conference honors as a single-wing quarterback in his senior year of 1958. Looking back at the role he assumed in the team's offense, Dowler said, "We changed to a multiple-set offense, and I called all the plays. I would line up as a 'T' quarterback, and half the time we shifted into a single wing, and I was the blocking back." An outstanding all-around athlete, Dowler established himself as a sextuple threat at Colorado, excelling as a passer, runner, receiver, safety, punter, and kick-returner, while also making the school's track team as a hurdler.

Subsequently selected by the Packers in the third round of the 1959 NFL Draft, with the 25th overall pick, Dowler switched positions shortly after he arrived in Green Bay, recalling years later, "A month after the draft,

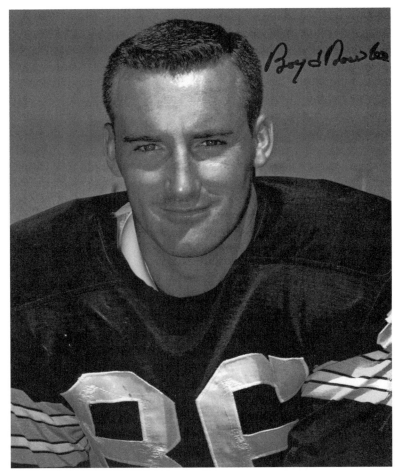

Boyd Dowler led the Packers in pass receptions seven times and
receiving yards four times.
Courtesy of PristineAuction.com

Lombardi was hired, and he brought five potential quarterbacks into a
room. Lombardi told us we were going out to pass. He turned to me and
said, 'Dowler, you're a flanker.'"

Adapting extremely well to his new position, Dowler ended up earning
NFL Rookie of the Year honors by making 32 receptions for 549 yards and
four touchdowns. He followed that up with two more solid seasons, totaling 66 receptions, 1,138 receiving yards, and five touchdowns from 1960
to 1961, before helping the Packers capture their second consecutive NFL
title in 1962 by making 49 catches for 724 yards and two touchdowns. Also

serving as Green Bay's primary punter from 1960 to 1962, Dowler averaged 43 yards per kick over the course of those three seasons.

Although the Packers failed to repeat as NFL champions in 1963, Dowler had one of his most productive seasons, ranking among the league leaders with 53 receptions and 901 receiving yards, while also making six TD grabs. He continued his outstanding play in each of the next two campaigns, making 45 catches for 623 yards and five touchdowns in 1964, before earning his first Pro Bowl selection the following year by making 44 receptions for 610 yards and four touchdowns, in helping the Packers win the first of their three straight NFL titles.

Unusually tall for a wide receiver, Dowler stood 6'5" and weighed 225 pounds, making him a difficult cover for even the league's best cornerbacks. Also blessed with excellent hands and outstanding speed, Dowler emerged as one of the NFL's top wide receivers even though the Packers rarely featured him in their offense. Subjugating his own personal statistics for the betterment of the team, Dowler discussed the attitude he and his teammates took with them to the playing field, stating:

> I don't think we ever thought of ourselves as a passing team, as a running team, as this kind of a team, or as that kind of a team. When you went out there and you played a position and ran for yards, or caught passes, or scored touchdowns, all we thought about was "what are we gonna do to contribute?" If you only caught one pass, was it meaningful? Did you make a first down? Did you score a touchdown? Did you keep a drive alive? We didn't compare stats. We didn't think "I need to get more touches . . . You need to throw me the ball more." We never felt that way. That's why the team was more important than anything we did individually.

Dowler added, "The biggest thing for me was the fact that I played every game—preseason, postseason, regular season, exhibition season—I always played. And I'm proud about that. And, in the big games—in the championship games and other big games—it always seemed that I was able to come up with a play, or two, or three, that made a difference, that led to the victory. I felt very good about that and, as a competitor, I felt that I was living up to what they expected of me."

Although Dowler started every game for the Packers for the eighth straight time in 1966, a bad shoulder, frequent double-coverage, an increased dependence on running backs in the passing game, and the emotional impact of losing his two-month-old daughter to pneumonia limited

Dowler scored the Packers' first touchdown of Super Bowl II.
Courtesy of MearsOnlineAuctions.com

him to only 29 receptions, 392 receiving yards, and no touchdowns. Dowler's woes continued in the postseason, when he aggravated his shoulder on a late hit by Dallas defensive back Mike Gaechter following a 16-yard TD reception in the NFL championship game. Subsequently forced to enter Super Bowl I at less than 100 percent, Dowler nevertheless believed that he had an excellent chance of being a huge factor in the contest, stating years later, "The Chiefs had defensive players we respected, but we knew we could attack their corners. That was the weakness. Bart [Starr] was planning to throw to me a lot."

However, Dowler slammed into Kansas City safety Johnny Robinson on the Packers' sixth offensive play, separating his already-injured shoulder, and forcing him to the sidelines for the remainder of the game. Recalling the play that knocked him out of the contest, Dowler said, "Maybe I shouldn't have [hit Robinson] because I wasn't a good blocker. I had a bad shoulder all year, and it just gave out." Dowler's injury forced little-used backup Max McGee to assume his role in the Packer offense, after which the veteran wideout, despite suffering from a hangover, went on to make seven receptions for 138 yards and two touchdowns during Green Bay's 35–10 victory.

Dowler rebounded the following year to have one of his finest seasons, making a career-high 54 catches for 836 yards and four touchdowns, earning in the process his second Pro Bowl nomination. Continuing his strong play in the postseason, Dowler totaled nine receptions for 183 yards and three touchdowns in Green Bay's three playoff contests, with his 62-yard catch-and-run giving the Packers their first touchdown of Super Bowl II. Dowler remained with the Packers for two more years, before spending one final season with the Washington Redskins. During his time in Green Bay, he caught 448 passes, amassed 6,918 receiving yards, and scored 40 touchdowns. In his one season in Washington, Dowler made 26 receptions for 352 yards and no touchdowns.

Following the conclusion of his playing career, Dowler spent nearly 15 years serving as an assistant on the coaching staffs of the Redskins (1971–1972), Philadelphia Eagles (1973–1975), Cincinnati Bengals (1976–1979), and Tampa Bay Buccaneers (1980–1984). After subsequently remaining away from the game for more than a decade, Dowler became a scout for the Atlanta Falcons in 1997. He continued to fulfill that role for the next few seasons before retiring to private life.

PACKERS CAREER HIGHLIGHTS

Best Season

Dowler performed extremely well for the Packers in 1963, making 53 receptions for a career-high 901 yards and six touchdowns. However, he had his finest season in 1967, earning one of his two Pro Bowl selections and All–Western Conference nominations by making a career-best 54 catches for 836 yards and four touchdowns.

Memorable Moments/Greatest Performances

Dowler surpassed 100 receiving yards for the first time in his career on November 15, 1959, when he made eight receptions for 147 yards during a 28–24 loss to the eventual NFL champion Baltimore Colts.

Dowler teamed up with Bart Starr for the longest play of his career during a 35–21 win over the Los Angeles Rams in the 1960 regular-season finale, collaborating with Starr on a 91-yard TD reception.

Dowler helped the Packers record a 28–10 victory over the Minnesota Vikings on October 29, 1961, by making five catches for 121 yards.

Dowler had the most productive day of his career in the final game of the 1963 regular season, making eight receptions for 188 yards and two touchdowns during a 21–17 win over the 49ers, with his scoring plays covering 53 and 50 yards.

Although the Packers lost their October 4, 1964, meeting with the Vikings by a score of 24–23, Dowler had another big afternoon, making six catches for 128 yards and two touchdowns, which covered 50 and 32 yards.

After going the entire 1966 regular season without scoring a single touchdown, Dowler hauled in a 16-yard TD pass from Bart Starr during Green Bay's 34–27 win over Dallas in the NFL championship game, finishing the contest with three catches for 49 yards.

Dowler made an even bigger impact during the Packers' 21–17 victory over Dallas in the 1967 NFL title game, making four receptions for 77 yards, and scoring Green Bay's first two touchdowns on pass plays that covered eight and 46 yards.

Dowler followed that up by scoring the first touchdown of Super Bowl II, giving the Packers a 13–0 lead over Oakland midway through the second quarter by collaborating with Bart Starr on a 62-yard catch-and-run.

NOTABLE ACHIEVEMENTS

- Surpassed 50 receptions twice.
- Amassed 901 receiving yards in 1963.
- Averaged more than 43 yards per punt twice.
- Never missed a game in 11 seasons with Packers, appearing in 150 consecutive games.
- Led Packers in receptions seven times and receiving yardage four times.

- Ranks among Packers career leaders with: 448 receptions (6th); 6,918 receiving yards (6th); 40 touchdown receptions (11th); and average of 15.44 yards per reception (6th).
- Six-time Western Conference champion (1960, 1961, 1962, 1965, 1966, and 1967).
- Five-time NFL champion (1961, 1962, 1965, 1966, and 1967).
- Two-time Super Bowl champion (I and II).
- 1959 NFL Rookie of the Year.
- Two-time Pro Bowl selection (1965 and 1967).
- Two-time All–Western Conference First-Team selection (1962 and 1967).
- NFL 1960s All-Decade Team.
- Pro Football Hall of Fame All-1960s Team.
- Pro Football Reference All-1960s First Team.
- Named to NFL's 50th Anniversary Team in 1969.

40

VERNE LEWELLEN

One of the finest all-around players of his time, Verne Lewellen spent almost his entire nine-year NFL career with the Packers, establishing himself during that time as arguably the league's most complete player. Manning numerous positions on both sides of the ball from 1924 to 1932, Lewellen excelled as a back on defense, while also starring as both a runner and a receiver on offense. Although Lewellen spent all but his final season competing during the NFL's pre-statistical era, unofficial and incomplete statistics listed in *The Football Encyclopedia* credit him with more touchdowns than any other player in the league from 1920 to 1934, with his 37 rushing TDs representing the fourth-highest total in Packers history. He is also listed as the period's second-leading scorer, sixth-leading receiver, and 12th-leading passer. But, it was as a punter that Lewellen made his greatest impact, with longtime *New York Times* columnist Arthur Daley writing in 1962, "No one who ever saw Lewellen kick could ever forget him. He was the finest punter these eyes ever saw." In addition to earning him five consecutive All-Pro selections, Lewellen's brilliant all-around play made him a key contributor to Green Bay's first three NFL championship teams.

Born in Lincoln, Nebraska, on September 29, 1901, Verne Clark Lewellen starred in baseball, basketball, football, and track while attending local Lincoln High School, before enrolling at the University of Nebraska, where he captained the football team that delivered the only two defeats Knute Rockne's "Four Horsemen" suffered in their three years together at Notre Dame. Excelling on the diamond as well as the gridiron while in college, Lewellen drew interest from the Pittsburgh Pirates, who intended to sign him to a contract until a neck injury suffered during a train wreck affected his pitching arm. Still wishing to pursue a career in pro sports, Lewellen received his big break when Jim Crowley, one of the "Four Horsemen," recommended him to his old high school coach in Green Bay, Curly Lambeau. Signed by Lambeau shortly after he graduated from Nebraska, Lewellen joined the Packers prior to the start of the 1924 campaign.

Verne Lewellen was perhaps the NFL's finest all-around player of the
1920s and early 1930s.
Courtesy of RMYAuctions.com

Taking to Green Bay immediately because, as he said years later, he
found it to be "the city with the college spirit," Lewellen started eight
games as a rookie, scoring two touchdowns while splitting his time on
offense between the halfback, fullback, tailback, and wingback positions.
He followed that up by scoring four touchdowns in 1925, en route to
earning All-Pro honors for the first of five straight times. Emerging as a
full-fledged star in 1926, Lewellen amassed 574 yards from scrimmage and
scored six touchdowns, before gaining a total of 603 yards and crossing the
opponent's goal line five times in 1927, when the Packers loaned him to the
New York Yankees for three games at the end of the year.

Blessed with superior all-around ability, the 6'1", 182-pound Lewellen
did everything well on the football field. In addition to excelling as a runner
and a receiver, he proved to be quite adept at throwing the fat football of the
day, although the Packers rarely used him as a passer. Lewellen also starred

on defense, where he served the Packers well as a sure-tackling defensive back. However, more than anything else, Lewellen excelled as a punter, gradually developing a reputation as easily the finest punter of his era.

Lewellen's unmatched ability in that particular aspect of the game gave the Packers a huge advantage over their opponents because the style of play employed at the time placed a premium on ball control and field position. With coaches often resorting to the quick-kick, and long field goal attempts not considered a viable option, punters frequently figured prominently in the outcomes of contests, with their teams asking them to deliver the ball to the opposition from practically anywhere on the field, including inside the opponent's 40-yard-line. As a result, Lewellen's uncanny knack for placing his kicks out-of-bounds deep inside enemy territory proved to be a powerful weapon for the Packers, who benefited greatly from his career punting average of 39.5 yards per kick (per *The Football Encyclopedia*, published in 1994), which is actually far more impressive than it might first appear.

Commenting on Lewellen's ability to deliver the coffin-corner kick, former Packers teammate Charlie Mathys once stated, "From 50 yards, if he aimed, he put it out of bounds on the five-yard line. He had almost dead accuracy."

Meanwhile, in describing Lewellen as a punter, George Halas said, "Who was ever better?"

Continuing his exceptional play in 1928 and 1929, Lewellen earned First-Team All-Pro honors both years, scoring a career-high nine touchdowns in the first of those campaigns, before amassing 502 yards on offense and scoring seven touchdowns for the Packers' 1929 NFL championship team. Remaining in Green Bay three more years, Lewellen helped lead the Packers to another two NFL titles, performing particularly well in 1930, when he accumulated almost 600 yards on offense and equaled his career high by scoring nine touchdowns. Choosing to announce his retirement following the conclusion of the 1932 campaign, Lewellen ended his nine-year playing career having appeared in a total of 105 games, with 102 of those coming as a member of the Packers. Although the NFL did not begin keeping an official record of offensive statistics until 1932, unofficial press counts reveal that Lewellen ran the ball 708 times for 2,410 yards and 37 touchdowns, caught 84 passes for 1,265 yards and 12 touchdowns, completed 122 of 335 passes for 2,080 yards and nine TDs, scored twice on defense, scored a total of 307 points, and punted the ball 681 times for an average of 39.5 yards per kick, with old-timers crediting him with numerous 60- and 70-yard punts.

Lewellen starred on Green Bay's first three NFL championship teams.
Courtesy of RMYAuctions.com

Following his playing days, Lewellen, who earned a degree in law at Nebraska and became district attorney for Brown County while still a member of the Packers in 1928, remained in that post briefly, before opening his own law practice when he lost his seat in 1933. After retiring from law in 1950, Lewell rejoined the Packers, with whom he spent most of the next 17 years, serving them first as a member of their executive committee (1950–1953), then, as general manager (1954–1958), and, finally, as business manager (1961–1967). Elected to the Packers Hall of Fame in 1970,

Lewellen lived another 10 years, passing away in Rockville, Maryland, at age 78, on April 16, 1980.

In discussing his former teammate, Charlie Mathys suggested, "Defensively, offensively—of the players we had in the old days, he was number one. And I'm not alone in saying that. Any of the old-timers I've talked to say the same thing. . . . He was way ahead of his time in ability. . . . If he doesn't get into the [Pro Football] Hall of Fame, it's a joke." Unfortunately, Lewellen has yet to be so honored.

PACKERS CAREER HIGHLIGHTS

Best Season

Although the NFL did not keep track of statistics until Lewellen's final year in the league, reconstruction of all but two of his games from play-by-play accounts in newspapers later revealed that he amassed close to 600 yards of total offense in four different seasons, with one of those being 1927, when he rushed for 329 yards and gained another 274 yards on 16 pass receptions, giving him a career-high total of 603 yards from scrimmage—certainly an impressive number for the day. Lewellen also scored five touchdowns in 1927, en route to earning one of his four First-Team All-Pro nominations. Nevertheless, he perhaps made his greatest overall impact in 1930, when he helped lead the Packers to their second consecutive league championship by gaining a total of 584 yards (411 on the ground and 173 through the air), scoring a career-high nine touchdowns, and averaging close to 41 yards per punt.

Memorable Moments/Greatest Performances

Lewellen gave the Packers a 7–0 win over the Milwaukee Badgers on October 17, 1926, by scoring the game's only touchdown on a 25-yard run in the fourth quarter.

Lewellen again starred against Milwaukee three weeks later, hauling in a 20-yard TD pass from Eddie Kotal and running 70 yards for another score, in leading the Packers to a 21–0 victory over the Badgers on November 7, 1926.

Although the Packers lost their November 21, 1926, meeting with the Chicago Bears by a score of 19–13, Lewellen scored the first of his two career defensive touchdowns during the contest, returning a fumble 40 yards for a TD.

Lewellen helped the Packers forge a 12–12 tie with the Bears on September 30, 1928, by recording a pair of second-half touchdowns. After making a 15-yard TD reception in the third quarter, Lewellen drew the Packers even with Chicago by scoring on a 2-yard run in the final period.

Lewellen gave the Packers their only points of a 7–7 tie with the Providence Steam Roller on December 2, 1928, by throwing a 22-yard touchdown pass to Larry Marks in the third quarter.

Lewellen again provided most of the offensive firepower during a 9–0 win over the Dayton Triangles in the 1929 regular-season opener, scoring the Packers' only touchdown of the contest on a 30-yard pass from Red Dunn in the third quarter.

Lewellen led the Packers to a 14–2 victory over the Frankford Yellow Jackets on October 13, 1929, by throwing a 46-yard TD pass to Eddie Kotal in the first quarter and scoring himself on a 2-yard run in the final period.

Lewellen followed that up one week later by running for one touchdown and scoring another on defense when he intercepted a pass in the Minneapolis end zone during a 24–0 win over the Red Jackets.

Lewellen displayed his tremendous versatility during a late-season showdown with the Giants in 1929, leading the Packers to a 20–6 win by moving from halfback to quarterback, where he replaced an injured Red Dunn. With Lewellen playing all 60 minutes, the New York sportswriters credited his punting and all-around play as being the difference in the game.

Lewellen subsequently helped the Packers clinch their first NFL title in the final game of the 1929 regular season by running for one touchdown and throwing for another during a 25–0 shutout of the Chicago Bears.

Lewellen continued his outstanding play the following year, running for two touchdowns and throwing for another during a 47–13 blowout of the Portsmouth Spartans on November 2, 1930, before leading the Packers to a 13–12 win over the Bears one week later by completing a 17-yard touchdown pass to Johnny (Blood) McNally and gathering in a 21-yard TD pass from Red Dunn.

Yet, perhaps the most memorable play of Lewellen's career took place during a 1929 contest at the Polo Grounds, when, according to George Calhoun, who covered the Packers for the *Green Bay Press-Gazette* for many years, Lewellen punted a ball from just outside the Packers' end zone that ended up going out of bounds at the New York 6 yard line. Calhoun later described the kick as the greatest he ever saw.

NOTABLE ACHIEVEMENTS

- Scored two defensive touchdowns during career (one interception return and one fumble return).
- Rushed for more than 400 yards twice.
- Surpassed 250 receiving yards twice.
- Surpassed 500 yards from scrimmage five times.
- Averaged more than 4.5 yards per carry once (4.7 in 1929).
- Scored nine touchdowns twice.
- Averaged more than 40 yards per punt four times.
- Ranks fourth in Packers history with 37 rushing touchdowns.
- Retired with second-most points scored of any player in NFL history (307).
- Three-time NFL champion (1929, 1930, and 1931).
- Four-time First-Team All-Pro (1926, 1927, 1928, and 1929).
- 1925 Second-Team All-Pro.
- Named to Packers All-Time Team in 1946.

41

FRED CARR

Spending most of his career playing in relative obscurity for losing Packer teams, Fred Carr remains one of the most overlooked and underappreciated players in franchise history. A prototype of the modern-day outside linebacker, the 6'5", 238-pound Carr combined outstanding size, speed, and athleticism to present a multitude of problems to opposing offenses. Equally capable of rushing the passer, defending against the run, or covering backs coming out of the backfield, Carr proved to be one of the finest all-around linebackers of his time, earning three trips to the Pro Bowl, one All-Pro selection, and five All-Conference nominations. Nevertheless, Carr, who led the Packers in tackles in six of his 10 seasons in Green Bay, would likely be better remembered today had he not been surrounded by inferior talent much of the time.

Born in Phoenix, Arizona, on August 19, 1946, Freddie Alton Carr attended Phoenix Union High School, where, in addition to playing football, he competed in basketball and track and field, specializing in the discus throw and the shotput. After initially enrolling at Phoenix College, Carr later transferred to the University of Texas at El Paso, where he became known as arguably the greatest all-around linebacker in school history, earning All-America honors while anchoring the Miners defense.

Subsequently selected by the Packers with the fifth overall pick of the 1968 NFL Draft, Carr drew praise from Green Bay general manager Vince Lombardi, who proclaimed him to be the best player in the country. New Packers head coach Phil Bengtson also had high hopes for the team's number one draft pick, recalling years later, "Carr had the potential to play defensive end, linebacker, tight end, or safety. Getting him was like drawing the wild card in poker."

With Ray Nitschke, Dave Robinson, and Lee Roy Caffey starting for the Packers at linebacker, the team initially tried Carr at defensive end and tight end, before moving him back to his more natural position of linebacker. He then spent his first two seasons in Green Bay playing mostly on

Fred Carr excelled at linebacker for mostly losing Packer teams during the 1970s.
Courtesy of MearsOnlineAuctions.com

special teams, while also serving as a backup to Robinson and Caffey. But, after finally breaking into the starting lineup in 1970, Carr went on to start 112 consecutive games over the course of the next eight seasons.

Quickly establishing himself as a force on the defensive side of the ball, Carr intercepted two passes and recovered three fumbles in his first year as a starter, earning in the process Pro Bowl and Second-Team All-NFC honors. Continuing his strong play in each of the next four seasons, Carr earned another trip to the Pro Bowl and Second-Team All-NFC recognition two more times, before making All-Pro for the only time in his career in 1975, when, in addition to picking off three passes and recovering two fumbles, he recorded 86 tackles.

One of the NFL's fastest linebackers, Carr once posted a time of 10.1 seconds in the 100-yard dash (in full uniform), also making him faster than most of the league's running backs, who he did an excellent job of covering one-on-one in passing situations. Carr also defended well against the run, preventing opposing backs from turning the corner on his side of the field. Carr's size, strength, and quickness made him an effective pass-rusher as well, with his unique skill set helping him to revolutionize the position of outside linebacker, as former Cowboys and Rams wide receiver Lance Rentzel noted when he said, "Fred Carr was one of the first of a different breed of linebackers that added a new dimension of speed and athleticism to the position. Not only was he a superb player in a physical sense, he had an instinctive understanding of how to play the game, and, as a result, he was always in the right place at the right time."

Because the NFL did not begin keeping an official record of sacks and tackles until after Carr retired, there is no way of knowing with any degree of certainty how many times he dropped opposing quarterbacks behind the line of scrimmage or brought down opposing ball-carriers. However, his ability to diagnose plays enabled him to record eight interceptions and 15 fumble recoveries over the course of his career, with the last figure representing the eighth-highest total in franchise history. Meanwhile, Carr's size and athleticism unquestionably would have allowed him to succeed in any era, with the only knock against him being his somewhat laid-back attitude that some felt prevented him from ever reaching his full potential. Never one to overtrain or bury his nose in his playbook, Carr sometimes drew criticism for what others perceived to be a lack of total dedication to his profession. He also smoked and drank, although those vices never seemed to affect his stamina on the playing field. Carr also proved to be an extremely durable player, never missing a game in his 10 seasons with the Packers.

After being named All-Pro the previous season, Carr earned All-Conference honors for the final time in 1976, when he unofficially recorded a team-leading 94 tackles, while also intercepting one pass, which he returned for his only career touchdown. Carr ended up spending just one

Carr's size, speed, and athleticism helped him revolutionize the position of outside linebacker.
Courtesy of MearsOnlineAuctions.com

more year with the Packers, with his time in Green Bay ending acrimoniously following a disagreement with team management. After injuring his knee, Carr told Packers trainer Dom Gentile that he considered his career to be over. However, Gentile expressed the belief that a draining of the knee, and perhaps minor surgery, would enable Carr to take the field once again. A war of words ensued, prompting the Packers to eventually cut Carr, who subsequently filed a grievance in which he claimed that the team owed him money. The two sides ultimately reached a settlement for an undisclosed amount, after which Carr never again played in the NFL. He retired having appeared in 140 consecutive games as a member of the team. In his 10 years with the Packers, they compiled an overall record of 58-77-5, finishing with a winning mark just twice and making the playoffs only once, with their lack of success throughout the period preventing Carr from receiving the recognition he so richly deserved.

CAREER HIGHLIGHTS

Best Season

Carr had an outstanding season in 1976, earning Second-Team All-NFC honors for the fifth and final time by making 94 tackles (72 solo), blocking three field goal and two extra-point attempts, and scoring the only touchdown of his career on a 10-yard interception return. However, he performed slightly better the previous year, concluding the 1975 campaign with 86 tackles (55 solo), a career-high three interceptions, and two fumble recoveries, with his excellent play earning him official Second-Team All-NFC honors from the United Press International and his lone First-Team All-Conference selection from the *Sporting News*.

Memorable Moments/Greatest Performances

Carr recorded the first of his eight career interceptions during a 30–17 win over the Philadelphia Eagles on October 25, 1970, picking off a Rick Arrington pass, which he subsequently returned 17 yards.

Carr scored the only touchdown of his career during a 32–27 victory over the New Orleans Saints on November 7, 1976, when he intercepted a Bobby Douglass pass early in the third quarter and returned the ball 10 yards for a TD that put the Packers up by a score of 23–13.

NOTABLE ACHIEVEMENTS

- Scored one defensive touchdown during career on an interception return.
- Led Packers in tackles six times.
- Tied for eighth in Packers history with 15 career fumble recoveries.
- Never missed a game in 10 seasons with Packers, appearing in 140 consecutive contests.
- 1972 Central Division champion.
- 1970 Pro Bowl Co-MVP.
- Three-time Pro Bowl selection (1970, 1972, and 1975).
- 1975 Second-Team All-Pro.
- Five-time Second-Team All-NFC selection (1970, 1972, 1974, 1975, and 1976).

42

— BILLY HOWTON —

aving spent his entire time in Green Bay playing for losing Packer teams, Billy Howton is rarely mentioned with the likes of Don Hutson, James Lofton, Sterling Sharpe, and others when conversations regarding the best wide receivers in franchise history arise. Nevertheless, Howton made a huge impact in his seven seasons with the Packers, with team historian Lee Remmel stating, "He [Howton] rates among the elite receivers in our history, without a doubt."

Howton ended his seven-year stint in Green Bay second only to the incomparable Hutson in most team receiving categories, while setting franchise marks for most touchdown receptions and receiving yards by a rookie. Also the holder of the Packers single-game records for most receiving yards and yards from scrimmage, Howton led the team in pass receptions and receiving yards six times each, en route to earning four Pro Bowl selections and three All-Pro nominations. And, after leaving Green Bay, Howton went on to establish himself as the NFL's all-time leader in pass receptions and receiving yards at the time of his retirement.

Born in Littlefield, Texas, on July 5, 1930, Billy Harris Howton attended Plainview High School, where he lettered in football, basketball, and track and field, once setting a state record that stood for several decades by recording a time of 14.3 in the 100-meter high hurdles. Continuing to star on the gridiron after enrolling at Rice University in Houston, Harris earned All-America and Southwest Conference MVP honors as a senior by making 64 catches for 1,289 yards and 12 touchdowns.

Yet, in spite of Howton's outstanding play at the collegiate level, he had to be convinced to turn pro after the Packers selected him in the second round of the 1952 NFL Draft, with the 15th overall pick, due to concerns about his size. Standing 6'2" tall and weighing only 190 pounds, Howton remained uncertain as to whether or not he had enough bulk to compete at the next level. But, after having a heart-to-heart talk with fellow Rice alum,

Billy Howton earned the nickname "The New Don Hutson" during the early stages of his career.
Courtesy of MainlineAutographs.com

Tobin Rote, a member of the Packers since 1950, Howton finally decided to make a go of it, joining the team in time for training camp.

Taking the NFL by storm, Howton earned Pro Bowl and Second-Team All-Pro honors as a rookie by making 53 receptions for a league-leading 1,231 receiving yards, while also finishing second in the circuit with 13 touchdown catches in only 12 games, which remained a rookie record until Randy Moss made 17 TD receptions in 16 games for Minnesota in 1998. Howton's fabulous performance earned him the nickname "The New Don

Hutson," with his speed, sure hands, and big-play ability rekindling memories of the greatest wide receiver in NFL history, to that point.

Plagued by injuries throughout much of the ensuing campaign, Howton experienced a significant drop-off in offensive production, making just 25 receptions for 463 yards and four touchdowns. However, he rebounded somewhat in 1954, ranking among the league leaders with 52 catches and 768 receiving yards. Howton again placed near the top of the league rankings in receptions (44) and receiving yards (697) in 1955, earning in the process the first of three straight trips to the Pro Bowl. He followed that up by finishing second in the league with 55 receptions in 1956, while also topping the circuit with 1,188 receiving yards and 12 touchdown catches, with his 1,188 yards through the air making him the first Packers receiver to top the 1,000-yard mark more than once. Howton also had a six-game scoring streak, with his superb play earning him First-Team All-Pro honors for the first time in his career.

An outstanding route-runner who excelled at distancing himself from opposing defensive backs, Howton drew praise from Hall of Fame wide receiver Raymond Berry, who said of his contemporary, "He knew what he was doing to maneuver and fake to get open. He would be effective going inside, going outside, effective going deep. He was an extremely dangerous receiver and had great technique. He wasn't just consistent over a period of years. You don't pile up the numbers he piled up."

Howton's Packer teammates also held him in extremely high esteem, with fellow wideout Max McGee stating, "He had great hands, great moves. He wasn't a tough guy. But I'll tell you, he was a hell of a receiver. Great speed. It was good having him over there. They left me alone. It took [Tobin] Rote a few games to find out I was out there, then he started throwing to me and I had like nine touchdowns as a rookie."

In discussing Howton, star Packer safety Bobby Dillon said, "He made me a better defensive back. Working against him in practice helped me a lot. He was an excellent receiver. If he had been playing for a stronger team, he would have done a lot more than he did. He had good moves and great speed. He was a high hurdler in college. Very fast. He was tough to cover. He could go over the middle or he could go deep. He was a very versatile receiver. He could change direction in a hurry, get started in a hurry, and stop in a hurry."

Dave Hanner added, "I thought he was an outstanding player. He could make things happen. He could get open, catch the ball, and run with it."

Although Howton posted far less impressive numbers in 1957, concluding the campaign with 38 receptions for 727 yards and five touchdowns,

Howton retired as the NFL's all-time leader in pass receptions and receiving yards.
Courtesy of MearsOnlineAuctions.com

he again earned Pro Bowl and First-Team All-Pro honors. He followed that up by making 36 receptions for 507 yards and two touchdowns in 1958, a season in which he became the first president of the NFL Players Association (NFLPA). While serving in that capacity, Howton played a major role in establishing a player's pension fund, which proved to be a highly contentious issue at the time.

The 1958 season also ended up being Howton's last in Green Bay. With Vince Lombardi taking over as head coach the following year, he made dealing Howton to the Cleveland Browns for halfback Lew Carpenter and defensive end Bill Quinlan one of his first moves. Those closest to the situation claimed that Lombardi made the trade because he considered Howton to be past his prime, and because the veteran wideout did not fit the coach's scheme that called for blocking ends. However, there were also whispers that Howton's involvement in the NFLPA contributed to his departure. Howton left the Packers with career totals of 303 receptions, 5,581 receiving yards, and 43 touchdowns. In addition to ranking among the Packers' all-time leaders in receiving yards and TD catches, Howton compiled an average of 18.4 yards per reception, the second-highest mark in franchise history.

After leaving Green Bay, Howton spent one season in Cleveland, making 39 receptions for 510 yards and one touchdown for the Browns, before joining the expansion Dallas Cowboys in 1960. Howton subsequently spent the next four years with the Cowboys, compiling 161 receptions for 2,368 yards and 17 touchdowns. He retired following the conclusion of the 1963 campaign with 503 receptions, 8,459 receiving yards, and 61 touchdowns, with his totals in each of the first two categories representing NFL records at the time. Yet, somewhat surprisingly, Howton's name has never been mentioned for Hall of Fame consideration.

PACKERS CAREER HIGHLIGHTS

Best Season

Howton had a big year for the Packers in 1956, earning consensus First-Team All-Pro honors by finishing second in the NFL with 55 receptions, 12 touchdowns, and an average of 21.6 yards per catch, while leading the league with 1,188 receiving yards and 12 TD receptions. Nevertheless, he made his greatest overall impact as a rookie in 1952, leading the league with a career-high 1,231 receiving yards and 1,231 yards from scrimmage, while also placing near the top of the league rankings in receptions (53), touchdown catches (13), total touchdowns scored (13), and yards per reception (23.2). Howton's 1,231 receiving yards placed him well ahead of league runner-up Bud Grant, who amassed 997 yards through the air. Meanwhile, his 13 touchdowns established an NFL record for rookies that remained the league mark for first-year players until Gale Sayers scored 22 times for the Bears in 1965. Howton's 13 TD catches also stood as an NFL rookie record until 1998, when Randy Moss eclipsed it.

Memorable Moments/Greatest Performances

Howton didn't wait long to display his explosiveness as a receiver, hooking up with quarterback Babe Parilli on an 89-yard scoring play in just the second game of his career, in helping the Packers record a 35–20 victory over the Washington Redskins on October 5, 1952. Howton finished the contest with three catches, for 128 yards and one touchdown.

Although the Packers lost their matchup with the Los Angeles Rams one week later by a score of 30–28, Howton had another big game, making five receptions for 156 yards and one touchdown, with his scoring play being a 69-yard connection with Tobin Rote late in the second quarter that gave Green Bay a 14–6 halftime lead.

Howton once again starred in defeat on Thanksgiving Day 1952, making seven catches for 123 yards and three touchdowns during a 48–24 loss to the Detroit Lions, with the longest of his scoring plays covering 54 yards.

Howton amassed 200 receiving yards for the first time in his career on December 7, 1952, when he made six receptions for 200 yards during a 45–27 loss to the Rams.

Howton followed that up with another outstanding performance in the 1952 regular-season finale, making eight receptions for 162 yards and two touchdowns during a 24–14 loss to the San Francisco 49ers. Exhibiting his game-breaking ability during the contest, Howton teamed up with Babe Parilli on a career-long 90-yard TD connection, which also proved to be the NFL's longest scoring play all season.

Howton helped the Packers defeat the Los Angeles Rams by a score of 35–17 on October 17, 1954, by making five receptions for 105 yards and one touchdown—a 28-yard hookup with Tobin Rote.

Howton had another big game the following week, making 11 catches for 147 yards during a 7–6 win over the Baltimore Colts on October 24.

Howton contributed mightily to a 30–28 victory over the Rams on October 16, 1955, making eight receptions for 158 yards and one touchdown, with his 57-yard hookup with Tobin Rote in the third quarter putting the Packers up by a score of 24–7.

Howton again torched the Los Angeles secondary on October 21, 1956, leading the Packers to a 42–17 win over the Rams by making seven receptions for a franchise-record 257 yards, with two of his catches going for touchdowns. After collaborating with Tobin Rote on a 36-yard scoring play in the first quarter, Howton connected with Jack Losch on a 63-yard TD reception in the second period.

Almost exactly one month later, on November 22, 1956, Howton helped the Packers record a dramatic 24–20 come-from-behind victory over the Lions in a contest they once trailed by a score of 20–10 midway through the fourth quarter by hooking up with Tobin Rote on a 13-yard scoring play in the game's final minutes.

Howton contributed to an even more memorable comeback on October 27, 1957, when his 75-yard TD connection with Babe Parilli late in the fourth quarter gave the Packers a 24–21 victory over the Baltimore Colts in a game they once trailed by a score of 14–0 heading into the final period.

NOTABLE ACHIEVEMENTS

- Surpassed 50 receptions three times.
- Surpassed 1,000 receiving yards twice.
- Topped 10 touchdown receptions twice.
- Averaged more than 20 yards per reception twice.
- Led NFL in: receiving yards twice; yards from scrimmage once; and touchdown receptions once.
- Finished second in NFL in: pass receptions once; touchdown receptions once; average yards per reception once; and touchdowns scored twice.
- Finished third in NFL in: pass receptions once; receiving yards once; and average yards per reception once.
- Led Packers in pass receptions and receiving yards six times each.
- Holds Packers records for most touchdown receptions (13) and receiving yards (1,231) by a rookie.
- Holds Packers single-game records for most receiving yards and most yards from scrimmage (257 vs. Los Angeles Rams on 10/21/56).
- Ranks among Packers career leaders with: 5,581 receiving yards (10th); 43 touchdown receptions (10th); and average of 18.42 yards per reception (2nd).
- Retired as NFL's all-time leader in pass receptions (503) and receiving yards (8,459).
- Four-time Pro Bowl selection (1952, 1955, 1956, and 1957).
- Two-time First-Team All-Pro (1956 and 1957).
- 1952 Second-Team All-Pro.
- Pro Football Reference All-1950s Second Team.

43

CHARLES "BUCKETS" GOLDENBERG

A versatile player who manned multiple positions on both sides of the ball during his time in Green Bay, Charles "Buckets" Goldenberg (so nicknamed for the ample size of his posterior) spent his entire 13-year NFL career with the Packers, helping them capture four Western Conference championships and three NFL titles during that time. After spending his first few seasons in Green Bay serving the Packers primarily as a blocking back on offense, Goldenberg eventually moved to guard, where he established himself as one of the league's top linemen. Goldenberg also excelled as a middle guard/linebacker on defense, with his outstanding all-around play earning him one Pro Bowl selection, one All-Pro nomination, and a spot on the NFL 1930s All-Decade Team.

Born in Odessa in the Ukraine on March 10, 1910, Charles Robert Goldenberg emigrated with his family to the United States at the age of four. After settling with his parents and siblings in Milwaukee, Wisconsin, Goldenberg went on to earn All-City honors as a halfback at West Division High School, before enrolling at the University of Wisconsin, where he starred as both a lineman and a running back.

Signed to a pro contract by Curly Lambeau following his graduation from Wisconsin in 1933, Goldenberg initially found himself being employed by the Green Bay coach as a single-wing quarterback whose primary responsibility on offense was to block for starting fullback Clarke Hinkle. Nevertheless, Goldenberg managed to gain 213 yards on the ground and lead the NFL with seven touchdowns as a rookie. Used almost exclusively as a blocker the next three seasons, Goldenberg rushed for a total of only 134 yards and scored just two touchdowns, although his ability to open up holes for Hinkle, while also delivering jarring hits on defense, helped the Packers win the 1936 NFL championship.

With veteran Mike Michalske taking note of the 5'10", 220-pound Goldenberg's exceptional blocking ability, he convinced Lambeau to convert the former Wisconsin standout into an offensive lineman in 1937.

Charles "Buckets" Goldenberg helped lead the Packers to three NFL titles.
Courtesy of RMYAuctions.com

Spending the remainder of his career serving the Packers in that capacity, Goldenberg soon emerged as one of the league's top guards on offense, developing a reputation as an outstanding lead blocker. Meanwhile, he continued to excel as a middle guard and linebacker on the defensive side of the ball, with his tenacious tackling and blitzing of opposing quarterbacks prompting many to credit him with being the originator of the draw play, because legend has it that Chicago Bears quarterback Sid Luckman grew so tired of getting sacked by Goldenberg that he finally decided to hand off the ball instead.

In discussing his fondness for playing two ways, Goldenberg said, "As for myself, I couldn't think of playing offense without playing on defense, too. I loved to block. I loved to knock down those fellows on the other side to give our ball-carriers running room. And, on defense, I liked to clobber somebody—anybody—just as long as he wore a different jersey."

Goldenberg's aggressive style of play and enthusiasm for the game helped make him one of the team's most popular players, even though he rarely touched the ball after 1935, gaining only 27 yards on just 10 carries his final 10 years in the league. After earning his lone Pro Bowl selection in 1939 and his only All-Pro nomination in 1942, Goldenberg remained with the Packers until 1945, with his badly damaged knees preventing him from joining the war effort. Announcing his retirement following the conclusion of the 1945 campaign, Goldenberg ended his career with 365 yards rushing, 111 receiving yards, eight interceptions, and 10 touchdowns, with seven of those coming on offense, two on defense, and another on special teams.

After retiring from football, Goldenberg briefly continued his offseason practice of wrestling professionally, before opening a restaurant in Milwaukee that became extremely popular with the local patrons. Remaining loyal to his former team, Goldenberg regularly attended all Packer games in Green Bay, Milwaukee, and Chicago until his health began to deteriorate in his later years. He also served on the Packers Board of Directors from 1953 until 1985. Goldenberg passed away at age 76, on April 16, 1986, with his son, Don, subsequently revealing, "He had had a major stroke in January and had been going steadily downhill since. He had been in a coma for about 10 days."

Named "Outstanding Jewish Athlete of All Time" by the Green Bay B'nai B'rith lodge in 1969 and inducted into the Packers Hall of Fame two years later, Goldenberg remains one of 10 players named to the NFL 1930s All-Decade Team that has yet to be enshrined at Canton.

CAREER HIGHLIGHTS

Best Season

Before moving to guard, Goldenberg compiled his most impressive overall numbers as a rookie in 1933, when he rushed for 213 yards and led

Goldenberg's outstanding all-around play earned him a spot on the NFL 1930s
All-Decade Team.
Courtesy of RMYAuctions.com

the NFL with seven touchdowns, scoring five times on offense, once on defense, and once on special teams.

Memorable Moments/Greatest Performances

Goldenberg helped lead the Packers to a 47–0 rout of the Pittsburgh Pirates on October 15, 1933, by returning an interception 67 yards for one touchdown and running for another score.

Goldenberg had another big game two weeks later, when, during a 35–9 mauling of the Eagles, he accomplished the rare feat of scoring touchdowns in three different ways. After scoring on a 2-yard run in the first quarter, Goldenberg scored a pair of fourth-quarter TDs, with one of those coming on a 15-yard pass reception and the other on a 34-yard return of a blocked punt.

Goldenberg continued to torment Philadelphia on November 14, 1937, when he returned an interception 27 yards for a touchdown during a lopsided 37–7 victory over the Eagles.

Goldenberg delivered a key block during the Packers' 14–7 win over the Giants in the 1944 NFL title game, leading Ted Fritsch into the end zone for the game's first score on fourth down.

NOTABLE ACHIEVEMENTS

- Scored three defensive touchdowns during career.
- Led NFL with seven touchdowns and two non-offensive touchdowns in 1933.
- Tied for sixth in Packers history in seasons played (13).
- Four-time Western Conference champion (1936, 1938, 1939, and 1944).
- Three-time NFL champion (1936, 1939, and 1944).
- 1939 Pro Bowl selection.
- 1942 Second-Team All-Pro.
- NFL 1930s All-Decade Team.
- Pro Football Hall of Fame All-1930s Team.

44

FUZZY THURSTON

Cast aside by three other NFL teams, Fred "Fuzzy" Thurston found a home in Green Bay, where he combined with Jerry Kramer to form the greatest pulling guard tandem in NFL history. A starter in eight of his nine years with the Packers, Thurston helped Vince Lombardi's squads win six Western Conference titles, five NFL championships, and two Super Bowls between 1959 and 1967, earning in the process All-Pro and All-Conference honors twice each. And, over the course of those nine seasons, the Packers led the NFL in rushing yards three times and finished second in the league on three other occasions, with Thurston's outstanding lead blocking contributing greatly to the success they experienced during that time.

Born in Altoona, Wisconsin, on December 29, 1933, Frederick Charles Thurston acquired the nickname "Fuzzy" while just a baby, when his sister assigned him that moniker because of his dark, fuzzy hair. Raised with his six siblings by his single mother after his father died of a heart attack when he was only five years old, Fuzzy eventually enrolled at Altoona High School, where he performed so well on the basketball court that he earned an athletic scholarship to Valparaiso University in northwest Indiana. Thurston subsequently spent his first two years in college competing only in basketball, before he began to exhibit more of an interest in football as a junior in 1954. Starring on the gridiron his last two years at Valparaiso, Thurston helped lead the school to an Indiana Collegiate Conference title, earning in the process All-Conference and All-America honors twice. After also being named the conference's top lineman as a senior, Thurston found himself headed to Philadelphia when the Eagles selected him in the fifth round of the 1956 NFL Draft, with the 54th overall pick.

With Thurston having previously experienced nothing but success in all his athletic endeavors, the next few years proved to be trying ones for him, as he spent three seasons accomplishing very little on the gridiron, drifting between the Eagles, the Chicago Bears, and the Baltimore Colts, while also spending time in the military. However, after serving as a backup

Fred "Fuzzy" Thurston combined with Jerry Kramer to form the greatest pulling guard tandem in NFL history.
Courtesy of MearsOnlineAuctions.com

guard on the Colts team that defeated the New York Giants in overtime in the 1958 NFL championship game, Thurston received his big break when the Packers traded linebacker Marv Matuszak for him just days before the start of training camp in 1959.

Subsequently evaluated by the Packers' coaching staff upon his arrival in Green Bay, Thurston received the following unflattering review: "Third guard type. Not good pulling guard for our type of offense. I believe we can improve this spot. Not quite NFL caliber. We can't win with Fred."

Yet, in spite of those dubious remarks, Thurston eventually made believers of Vince Lombardi and his coaching staff, laying claim to the starting left guard job his first year in Green Bay, and remaining the starter at that post for most of the next eight seasons. Proving to be the perfect complement to right guard Jerry Kramer on the other side of the Packers' offensive line, Thurston joined his cohort in helping to perfect the famed "Lombardi Power Sweep," with the head coach writing a few years later in his book *Run to Daylight*, "He's not quite as good a pulling guard as Jerry Kramer, but he's a good short-trap blocker, and he's got enough quickness, size, strength, and determination so that, when he and Jerry come out swinging around that corner together like a pair of matched Percherons, you can see that defensive man's eyeballs pop. Fuzzy's pass-protection blocking, though, is his big card, and he is as good as anyone in the league."

Thurston agreed with Lombardi's assessment, stating on numerous occasions, "There are two good reasons the Packers are world champions. Jerry Kramer is one of them, and you're looking at the other one."

In discussing his longtime line-mate, Kramer said, "Fuzz never made a mistake. We never ran into each other in the eight or nine years that we played together. He was bright and was aware about what needed to be done on a given play . . . Fuzzy also had a lot of heart. He wasn't the strongest guy in the world, but he gave it everything he had. Fuzz had a lot of energy and he also had a lot of pride. He was going to do his part in helping the team out, no matter what it took."

Kramer added, "He was a great mate. We were like a balanced team of horses. You see pictures of us today, and you can see us planting our foot at the same precise instant. There is a great picture of the sweep where Hornung plants his right foot, I plant my right foot, and Fuzzy plants his left foot. It happened almost precisely at the same instant heading up field."

Thurston, who stood 6'1" tall and weighed 247 pounds, started every game for the Packers from 1959 to 1963, helping them win three Western Conference championships and two NFL titles during that time. An All-Pro in both 1961 and 1962, Thurston made a strong impression on Dallas Cowboys' Hall of Fame defensive tackle Bob Lilly, who ranked him as one of the 10 toughest linemen he ever faced.

Thurston remained the Packers' starting left guard until Gale Gillingham finally supplanted him midway through the 1967 campaign, helping the team capture three more NFL championships during that time. Yet, even though Thurston lost his starting job to Gillingham, he remained a consummate team player, with Kramer recalling, "Fuzzy sat beside Gilly for the rest of the '67 season. He coached Gilly. They sat together in every film

Thurston helped the Packers run the "Power Sweep" to perfection.
Courtesy of MearsOnlineAuctions.com

session. Fuzzy gave him the benefit of everything he had learned about the defensive tackle that Gilly would be facing that given week. Fuzzy told Gilly what he liked to do against that tackle and told Gilly that he should think about doing the same thing. Basically, Fuzzy was Gilly's personal coach."

Choosing to announce his retirement after the Packers won their third consecutive NFL title in 1967, Thurston ended his time in Green Bay having appeared in 112 out of a possible 122 games as a member of the team. He subsequently remained in Wisconsin, where he opened a chain of restaurants named "The Left Guard" and also owned a bar not far from Lambeau Field he called "Fuzzy's." Unfortunately, Thurston spent his last several years battling Alzheimer's disease and liver cancer, before passing away two weeks shy of his 81st birthday, on December 14, 2014.

Upon learning of Thurston's passing, Pat Peppler, who served as the Packers' personnel director from 1963 to 1971, said, "I was very sad to hear about Fuzzy. He was an important part of the Packers sweep. Very mobile. A tough guy. A skilled athlete. And, with Vince, the team practiced and practiced that play until it was perfect. Every opponent knew what was coming, but they just couldn't stop it."

In discussing the special relationship that Thurston shared with the fans of Green Bay, Packers president and CEO Mark Murphy commented, "No one personified the connection between the team and the fans more than Fuzzy. His radiance attracted so many fans to him."

Speaking at a memorial service subsequently held for Thurston, former Packers linebacker Dave Robinson stated, "I thought Fuzzy was bigger than life. I thought he'd be around forever."

Referring to Thurston as "the heart and soul of that Packers team," Robinson then added, "The thing that made us a team was Fred Fuzzy Thurston. Fuzzy Thurston is going to be deeply missed. A great Wisconsinite, a great Green Bay Packer."

PACKERS CAREER HIGHLIGHTS

Best Season

Thurston had the finest season of his career in 1961, when he earned his lone First-Team All-Pro selection by helping the Packers rush for more yards than any other team in the NFL. In fact, all three major news services at that time—the Associated Press, United Press International, and Newspaper Enterprise Association—accorded Thurston First-Team honors, making him a consensus pick.

Memorable Moments/Greatest Performances

Thurston's outstanding blocking at the point of attack helped the Packers rush for 270 yards during a 20–17 win over the Giants on December 3, 1961, with Jim Taylor scoring twice and gaining a career-high 186 yards on the ground.

In addition to doing an excellent job up front during the Packers' 16–7 victory over the Giants in the 1962 NFL championship game, Thurston contributed to the Green Bay win by recovering a fumble.

NOTABLE ACHIEVEMENTS

- Six-time Western Conference champion (1960, 1961, 1962, 1965, 1966, and 1967).
- Five-time NFL champion (1961, 1962, 1965, 1966, and 1967).
- Two-time Super Bowl champion (I and II).
- 1961 First-Team All-Pro.
- 1962 Second-Team All-Pro.
- Two-time All–Western Conference First-Team selection (1961 and 1962).

45

JOHN BROCKINGTON

The first player in NFL history to rush for more than 1,000 yards in each of his first three seasons, John Brockington accomplished the feat from 1971 to 1973, gaining a total of 3,276 yards on the ground and averaging 4.3 yards per carry over the course of those three campaigns. An explosive and punishing runner, the 6'1", 225-pound Brockington earned 1971 NFL Offensive Rookie of the Year honors by rushing for 1,105 yards, before leading the Packers to their first division title in five years the following season by placing near the top of the league rankings with 1,027 yards rushing and eight rushing touchdowns. A Pro Bowl and All-NFC selection three straight times, Brockington also earned a pair of All-Pro nominations his first three years in the league. Although the powerful fullback never again reached such heights after 1973, he ended up leading the Packers in rushing five times, with his 5,024 yards gained on the ground representing the third-highest total in team annals.

Born in Brooklyn, New York, on September 7, 1948, John Stanley Brockington starred on the gridiron while attending local Thomas Jefferson High School, where he acquired the nickname "Big John." After accepting a scholarship offer from Ohio State University, Brockington spent three seasons starting in the Buckeyes' offensive backfield, helping the team compile an overall record of 27-2 during that time. Manning the left halfback position in 1968 and 1969, Brockington served primarily as a blocker for fullback Jim Otis and quarterback Rex Kern. However, he became the focal point of head coach Woody Hayes's offense after he moved to fullback in his senior year of 1970, setting a new school record by gaining 1,142 yards on the ground, while also scoring 17 rushing touchdowns.

Subsequently selected by the Packers with the ninth overall pick of the 1971 NFL Draft, Brockington took the league by storm, earning Associated Press NFL Rookie of the Year and First-Team All-Pro honors by rushing for 1,105 yards, scoring five touchdowns, and averaging 5.1 yards per carry, with both the first and last figures placing him second in the league

John Brockington rushed for more than 1,000 yards in each of his first three NFL seasons.
Courtesy of SportsMemorabilia.com

rankings. He followed that up by gaining 1,027 yards on the ground and scoring nine touchdowns for a Packers team that captured the 1972 NFC Central Division title with a mark of 10-4. Although Green Bay's record slipped to 5-7-2 the following year, Brockington earned his second All-Pro selection by rushing for a career-high 1,144 yards and scoring three touchdowns, with his exceptional play prompting the Packers' 1974 media guide to begin his bio by saying, "Rated one of the greatest running backs in pro football history after only three seasons. . . . "

Teaming up with MacArthur Lane to give the Packers one of the league's better running attacks, Brockington, in his own words, "never ran under control." Running with his shoulder pads low and his knees high, Brockington employed a style that made good use of his tremendous upper and lower body strength, becoming the very personification of the "power running back" with his powerful legs and vicious stiff arm. In discussing his high-knee action, Brockington said, "It was just natural to me. I didn't practice it. It was just the way I ran."

Preferring to run over defenders rather than run away from them, Brockington represented a throwback of sorts, intimidating defenders with his aggressive running style. More than just a power-runner, though, Brockington also possessed excellent speed, blocked well for his quarterback and running mate, and did a solid job of catching passes coming out of the backfield.

Unfortunately, the success Brockington experienced his first three years in the league proved to be short-lived. After rushing for more than 1,000 yards and averaging at least 3.7 yards per carry in each of the three previous seasons, he gained just 883 yards on the ground and averaged only 3.3 yards per carry in 1974, although he still managed to score five touchdowns and establish career-high marks in receptions (43) and receiving yards (314). But, even though Brockington scored eight touchdowns the following year, it became quite clear when he rushed for only 434 yards and averaged just three yards per carry that his days as a dominant runner had ended.

At least part of Brockington's regression could be attributed to the exorbitant number of carries he accumulated over the course of his first few seasons. His physical running style undoubtedly proved to be a huge factor as well. A straight-ahead power runner who only knew one way to attack opposing defenses, Brockington absorbed a tremendous amount of punishment his first few years in the league. Furthermore, after the Packers made changes to their coaching staff following the conclusion of the 1974 campaign, the team altered its playbook in a manner that did not take advantage of Brockington's abilities. And, with the Packers lacking a top quarterback capable of keeping opposing defenses honest, defenders crowded the line of scrimmage, making Brockington's job that much more difficult.

Brockington, though, has his own theory as to why he experienced such a dramatic decrease in offensive production, which he explained thusly: "We didn't really have anyone like him after trading Mac [the Packers dealt MacArthur Lane to Kansas City at the end of 1974]. And we changed the offense. My big play was a slant off tackle; all you did was hit it. That's how I played in college, and that's how I played in the NFL. We went to a stretch offense, where you pick your hole, and I wasn't prepared for that. I couldn't adjust. I think I sulked a little bit about that, and about Mac."

Brockington then added, "But there always comes a time when you can't do it anymore. I didn't think that was the case, but athletes are always the last to know. We think we can do it forever."

Brockington followed up his subpar 1975 performance with another poor showing in 1976, rushing for just 406 yards and two touchdowns. Convinced that the 29-year-old fullback had very little left in the tank, the Packers waived Brockington one game into the 1977 season, after which he signed with the Kansas City Chiefs as a free agent. Appearing in 10 games with the Chiefs the remainder of the year, Brockington rushed for 161 yards, accumulated another 222 yards on 19 pass receptions, and scored

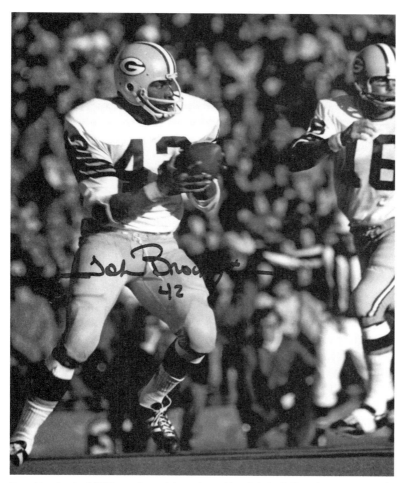

Brockington's 5,024 yards rushing place him third all-time in team annals.
Courtesy of SportsMemorabilia.com

two touchdowns, before retiring at season's end with career totals of 5,185 yards rushing, 6,482 yards from scrimmage, and 34 touchdowns, with 30 of those coming on the ground.

Following his playing days, Brockington became a financial adviser in the San Diego area, where he now lives with his wife of more than 15 years. Although the 70-year-old Brockington is currently in good health, he received a scare in 2001, when kidney problems forced him to undergo regular dialysis treatments. Saved by his wife, Diane, who donated one of her kidneys to him, Brockington has since established the John Brockington Foundation, which is dedicated to helping others affected by kidney disease. In addition to providing free screenings and educational material to those in need, the foundation provides food vouchers for people on dialysis and helps pay for kidney transplants.

PACKERS CAREER HIGHLIGHTS

Best Season

Although Brockington scored a career-high nine touchdowns in 1972 and rushed for a career-best 1,144 yards the following year, he actually had his finest all-around season for the Packers in 1971, when, en route to earning the first of his three straight Pro Bowl selections, his lone First-Team All-Pro nomination, and NFL Offensive Rookie of the Year honors, he scored five touchdowns and finished second in the league with 1,105 yards rushing and an average of 5.1 yards per carry, easily the highest mark of his career.

Memorable Moments/Greatest Performances

Brockington scored his first career touchdown in his second game as a pro, sprinting 52 yards for a score during a 34–13 win over the Denver Broncos at Milwaukee County Stadium on September 26, 1971. He finished the contest with 12 carries for 85 yards and that one touchdown.

Brockington topped the 100-yard mark for the first time in his career the following week, when he helped lead the Packers to a 20–17 victory over the Cincinnati Bengals on October 3, 1971, by gaining 120 yards on 19 carries.

Brockington helped the Packers forge a 14–14 tie with the Detroit Lions on November 1, 1971, by rushing for 111 yards on 16 carries.

Brockington followed that up with a strong outing against the Chicago Bears on November 7, helping the Packers defeat their bitter rivals by carrying the ball 30 times for 142 yards, and setting up a game-winning field goal late in the fourth quarter by toting the ball five straight times.

Although the Packers suffered a 3–0 defeat at the hands of the Minnesota Vikings one week later, Brockington acquitted himself extremely well against Minnesota's "Purple People Eaters" defense, gaining a season-high 149 yards on 23 carries.

Brockington had a huge game against San Francisco on November 5, 1972, leading the Packers to a 34–24 win over the 49ers by carrying the ball 24 times for 133 yards and scoring three touchdowns, with one of those coming on a career-long 48-yard pass reception from Scott Hunter.

Brockington helped the Packers gain a 10–10 tie with the Kansas City Chiefs on October 14, 1973, by carrying the ball 15 times for 106 yards, with one of his carries being a career-long 53-yarder.

Brockington proved to be a true workhorse during a 25–21 victory over the St. Louis Cardinals on November 11, 1973, carrying the ball 28 times for 137 yards and one touchdown.

Brockington helped the Packers record a convincing 21–0 victory over the Chicago Bears in the 1973 regular-season finale by gaining a season-high 142 yards on 22 carries.

Brockington turned in an outstanding all-around effort during a 19–7 win over the Minnesota Vikings on November 17, 1974, carrying the ball 32 times for 137 yards, and gaining another 66 yards on three pass receptions.

Brockington went over the 100-yard mark for the final time in his career on November 30, 1975, when he carried the ball 26 times for 111 yards and three touchdowns during a 28–7 win over the Bears.

NOTABLE ACHIEVEMENTS

- Rushed for more than 1,000 yards three times.
- Surpassed 1,000 yards from scrimmage four times, topping 1,200 yards three times.
- Averaged more than five yards per carry once (5.1 in 1971).
- Caught more than 40 passes once (43 in 1974).
- Amassed more than 300 receiving yards once (314 in 1974).
- Finished second in NFL in rushing yardage twice and yards per rushing attempt once.
- Led Packers in rushing five straight times.
- Ranks among Packers career leaders with 5,024 yards rushing (3rd) and 29 rushing touchdowns (tied—7th).
- First player in NFL history to rush for more than 1,000 yards in each of first three seasons.
- 1972 Central Division champion.
- 1971 NFL Offensive Rookie of the Year.
- Three-time Pro Bowl selection (1971, 1972, and 1973).
- 1971 First-Team All-Pro.
- 1973 Second-Team All-Pro.
- Three-time All-NFC First-Team selection (1971, 1972, and 1973).

46

CECIL ISBELL

Choosing to announce his retirement just five years into his NFL career, Cecil Isbell never gained admittance to the Pro Football Hall of Fame. Nevertheless, the man who ultimately replaced Arnie Herber behind center for the Packers accomplished enough during his relatively brief stay in Green Bay to earn a place in these rankings. The first NFL quarterback to pass for more than 2,000 yards and 20 touchdowns in a season, Isbell surpassed both marks in 1942, when he threw for 2,021 yards and 24 touchdowns, before calling it quits at season's end. Excelling as a runner as well as a passer, Isbell led the Packers in rushing in each of his first two seasons, finishing first in the NFL with a rushing average of 5.2 yards per carry as a rookie in 1938. And, even though Isbell shared playing time with Herber his first three years in Green Bay, he managed to earn Pro Bowl and All-Pro honors in four of his five years in the league, helping the Packers capture two Western Conference championships and one NFL title along the way. Isbell's outstanding play also earned him a spot on the Pro Football Hall of Fame All-1930s Team.

Born in Houston, Texas, on July 11, 1915, Cecil Frank Isbell attended local Sam Houston High School, before enrolling at Purdue University, where he spent three seasons starring on the gridiron. After being named the Boilermakers' most valuable player in his senior year of 1937, Isbell added to his list of accomplishments by leading the College All-Stars to a 28–16 victory over the defending NFL champion Washington Redskins at Soldier Field in Chicago, earning game MVP honors in the process.

Subsequently selected by the Packers in the first round of the 1938 NFL Draft, with the seventh overall pick, Isbell spent his rookie season alternating with Arnie Herber in the Green Bay backfield, manning both the tailback and halfback positions at different times. Yet, even though Isbell saw a limited number of snaps, he still managed to rank among the league leaders with 659 yards passing, eight touchdown passes, 445 yards rushing, and 549 yards from scrimmage, earning in the process his first trip

Cecil Isbell (right), seen here with Don Hutson, combined with the speedy receiver during the early 1940s to form the NFL's deadliest passing combination. Courtesy of MearsOnlineAuctions.com

to the Pro Bowl and the first of his three Second-Team All-Pro nominations. Continuing to platoon with Herber in each of the next two seasons as well, Isbell helped lead the Packers to the NFL title in 1939 by passing for 749 yards and six touchdowns, while also finishing first on the team with 407 yards rushing. He followed that up by throwing for 1,037 yards, tossing eight TD passes, rushing for 270 yards, and scoring four touchdowns in 1940, with his solid all-around play earning him Second-Team All-Pro honors for the second time.

Taking over as Green Bay's full-time signal-caller following the release of Herber at season's end, Isbell established himself as the league's top passer in 1941, earning his lone First-Team All-Pro nomination by leading the NFL with 15 touchdown passes and setting a new league mark by throwing for 1,479 yards. Isbell also gained 317 yards on the ground, intercepted two passes on defense, and placed near the top of the league rankings with a passer rating of 81.4 and a pass completion percentage of 56.8.

An extremely accurate passer, Isbell drew praise from Curly Lambeau, who, when asked to name the best passer he had ever seen, replied, "Isbell was the master at any range. He could throw the soft pass, bullet pass, or feathery lobs. He was the best, with Sid Luckman of the Bears a close second and Sammy Baugh of the Redskins a long third. Luckman wasn't as versatile, and Baugh couldn't compare on the long ones."

Unlike Luckman and Baugh, Isbell never had an opportunity to play quarterback in the T-formation, which Baugh later admitted added years to his career. Operating as a tailback in Green Bay's single wing, Isbell found himself being tackled on every play, whether or not the ball went to him. Isbell had the additional disadvantage of being severely limited throughout his career by a chronically bad left shoulder he dislocated several times in college. Forced to wear a chain that extended from his arm to his torso, Isbell later discussed his malady, revealing, "They decided I should have a chain on my left arm so I couldn't raise it too high. I wore the chain both at Purdue and with the Packers." He then added, "Sure it hampered me some. When I was punting, I couldn't extend my left arm all the way out, so I had to learn to drop the ball. My reach didn't have the range it would have had. The other thing was, when I was carrying the ball, I couldn't stiff-arm with my left—not effectively anyway."

Yet, in spite of his physical limitations, Isbell put together a season to remember in 1942, leading the NFL with 2,021 yards passing, 24 touchdown passes, and a passer rating of 87.0, with his totals in each of the first two categories establishing new league marks. Along the way, he continued his string of 23 consecutive games with at least one touchdown pass, which remained an NFL record until Johnny Unitas eventually eclipsed it in 1958. Teaming up with Don Hutson for 74 pass completions and 17 TD passes during the campaign, Isbell proved to be a worthy successor to Arnie Herber in getting the ball to the game's greatest receiver, with whom he developed a close personal relationship.

Nevertheless, at the very height of his career, Isbell elected to retire from the game to become an assistant coach at his alma mater, Purdue. Stating that he wanted to leave under his own terms, Isbell later explained, "I saw Lambeau go around the locker room and tell players like Arnie Herber that they were done. I vowed it would never happen to me." Announcing his retirement shortly after he celebrated his 28th birthday, Isbell ended his pro career with 5,945 yards passing, 61 touchdown passes, 52 interceptions, a completion percentage of 50.2, and a passer rating of 72.6. He also rushed for 1,522 yards and 10 touchdowns, gained another 174 yards on 15 pass receptions, amassed a total of 128 yards on special teams, and intercepted nine passes on defense.

After one year as an assistant at Purdue, Isbell became the school's head football coach—a position he maintained for the next three seasons before

In 1942, Isbell became the first player in NFL history to pass for more than 2,000 yards and throw more than 20 touchdown passes in one season. Courtesy of RMYAuctions.com

assuming the same role with the Baltimore Colts of the All-America Football Conference. While in Baltimore, Isbell helped develop the passing skills of future Hall of Fame quarterback Y. A. Tittle. After resigning his post in Baltimore, Isbell spent two years serving as backfield coach under Curly Lambeau on the coaching staff of the Chicago Cardinals, before ending his coaching career as an assistant at Louisiana State University during the mid-1950s. Isbell subsequently entered the business world, where he remained until he eventually retired to private life. Spending his final 13 years living in Calumet City, Illinois, Isbell passed away on June 23, 1985, a little over two weeks shy of his 70th birthday. Largely forgotten by recent generations of football fans, Isbell remains the only quarterback on the NFL 1930s All-Decade Team not yet inducted into the Pro Football Hall of Fame.

CAREER HIGHLIGHTS

Best Season

Playing his best ball for the Packers his final two seasons in Green Bay, Isbell finished second in the league in completion percentage (56.8) and quarterback rating (81.4) in 1941, while leading all NFL signal-callers with 117 completions, 1,479 yards passing, and 15 touchdown passes. However, he topped that performance the following year, concluding the 1942 campaign with a 54.5 completion percentage and a league-leading 146 completions, 87.0 quarterback rating, 24 touchdown passes, and 2,021 yards passing, establishing in the process new NFL records in each of the last two categories. Isbell's 24 TD passes also remained a franchise record until Lynn Dickey finally surpassed it in 1983.

Memorable Moments/Greatest Performances

Isbell put together an extremely impressive streak from 1940 to 1942, setting a new league mark by throwing at least one touchdown pass in each of the final 23 games of his career. Isbell's consecutive games streak remained an NFL record until Johnny Unitas surpassed it in 1958, en route to eventually extending it to 47.

Isbell crossed the opponent's goal line for the first time as a pro on October 23, 1938, when he ran 38 yards for a touchdown during a 20–0 win over the Pittsburgh Pirates.

Isbell displayed his versatility a few weeks later, when, during a 28–7 win over the Detroit Lions on November 13, 1938, he completed a 14-yard TD pass to Clarke Hinkle and ran 23 yards for another score.

Isbell led the Packers to a 27–20 victory over the Philadelphia Eagles in the 1940 regular-season opener by throwing a pair of TD passes and running 39 yards for another touchdown.

Isbell turned in another outstanding effort on September 29, 1940, when, during a 31–6 win over the Chicago Cardinals, he threw a 35-yard TD pass to Don Hutson and scored on runs that covered 1 and 39 yards.

Isbell completed three touchdown passes in one game for the first time on October 13, 1940, when he led the Packers to a 31–14 victory over the Cleveland Rams by hooking up with Carl Mulleneaux from 19 yards out and collaborating with Don Hutson on scoring plays that covered 19 and 47 yards.

Isbell again tossed three TD passes during a 24–7 win over the Detroit Lions on October 26, 1941, firing a 26-yard strike to Mulleneaux and connecting with Hutson from 12 and 6 yards out.

Isbell helped the Packers overcome a 17–0 halftime deficit to the Washington Redskins in the 1941 regular-season finale by throwing three second-half touchdown passes to Don Hutson that gave Green Bay a dramatic 22–17 come-from-behind victory.

Isbell set new Packer records by passing for 333 yards and five touchdowns during a 55–24 win over the Chicago Cardinals on November 1, 1942. In addition to connecting with Andy Uram from 64 and 36 yards out, Isbell collaborated with Don Hutson on scoring plays that covered 40, 73, and 65 yards.

Isbell concluded his playing career in style, throwing three touchdown passes during a 24–21 win over the Pittsburgh Steelers in the 1942 regular-season finale. After hitting Lou Brock with a 20-yard scoring strike, Isbell connected with Harry Jacunski from 49 yards out and Ray Riddick from 24 yards out.

NOTABLE ACHIEVEMENTS

- Passed for more than 1,000 yards three times, topping 2,000 yards once (2,021 in 1942).
- Threw more than 10 touchdown passes twice, topping 20 TD passes once (24 in 1942).
- Completed more than 50 percent of passes twice.
- Posted passer rating above 80.0 twice.
- Rushed for more than 400 yards twice.
- First NFL quarterback to pass for more than 2,000 yards and 20 touchdowns in a season.
- Led NFL quarterbacks in: pass completions twice; passing yardage twice; touchdown passes twice; and passer rating once.
- Finished second in NFL in: touchdown passes once; completion percentage three times; and passer rating once.
- Finished third in NFL in: touchdown passes once; passer rating once; yards from scrimmage once; and all-purpose yards once.
- Led NFL with rushing average of 5.2 yards per carry in 1938.
- Led Packers in rushing yardage twice.

- Ranks among Packers career leaders with 61 touchdown passes (7th) and passer rating of 72.6 (6th).
- Two-time Western Conference champion (1938 and 1939).
- 1939 NFL champion.
- Four-time Pro Bowl selection (1938, 1939, 1941, and 1942).
- 1941 First-Team All-Pro.
- Three-time Second-Team All-Pro (1938, 1940, and 1942).
- NFL 1930s All-Decade Team.
- Pro Football Hall of Fame All-1930s Team.

47

MAX MCGEE

A member of all five Vince Lombardi–led NFL championship teams, Max McGee spent his entire 12-year NFL career in Green Bay, leading the Packers in pass receptions four times and receiving yards five times. Displaying a knack for making big plays over the course of his career, McGee ranks extremely high in team annals in touchdown receptions and average yards per reception, averaging more than 20 yards per catch on three separate occasions. An excellent all-around athlete who also served as the Packers' primary punter his first few years in the league, McGee led the NFL in punting yards twice, averaging more than 40 yards per kick five times. Yet, with all he accomplished during his time in Green Bay, McGee will always be remembered primarily for his performance in Super Bowl I, when his brilliant play helped lead the Packers to a 35–10 victory over the Kansas City Chiefs.

Born in Saxon City, Nevada, on July 16, 1932, William Max McGee grew up in Texas, where he excelled on the gridiron while attending White Oak High School, becoming the first player in high school football history to rush for more than 3,000 yards in a season when he gained 3,048 yards on the ground as a senior in 1949. Continuing to display his athletic skills after he enrolled at Tulane University in New Orleans, McGee starred as a fullback and punter in football, while also lettering in baseball and basketball.

Selected by the Packers in the fifth round of the 1954 NFL Draft, with the 51st overall pick, McGee performed well as a rookie, making 36 receptions, amassing 614 receiving yards, and finishing fourth in the league with nine touchdown receptions, while also topping the circuit with 2,999 punting yards and ranking among the leaders with an average of 41.7 yards per punt. After missing the next two seasons while serving as a pilot in the US Air Force, McGee experienced a significant drop-off in offensive production when he returned to the Packers in 1957, making only 17 receptions for 273 yards and one touchdown. However, he regained his earlier form the following year, when he began a string of five straight seasons in which he led

In addition to starring at wide receiver, Max McGee led the NFL
in punting yardage twice.
Courtesy of LegendaryAuctions.com

the team in receiving yards. One of the few bright spots on a 1958 Packers
squad that compiled a record of just 1-10-1, McGee placed near the top of
the league rankings with 37 receptions, 655 receiving yards, seven touchdown catches, 2,625 punting yards, and an average of 42.3 yards per kick.
Continuing his solid play after Vince Lombardi assumed control of the team
in 1959, McGee made 30 receptions for 695 yards and five touchdowns,
averaged a career-high 42.4 yards per punt, and led the NFL with an average
of 23.2 yards per catch, 2,716 punting yards, and a net average of 36 yards
per punt. McGee then compiled some of the finest numbers of his career
from 1960 to 1962, averaging 46 receptions, 830 receiving yards, and five
touchdowns over the course of those three seasons, in helping the Packers
win three straight Western Conference championships and their first two

NFL titles under Lombardi. Performing particularly well in 1961, McGee earned his only trip to the Pro Bowl by making 51 receptions and placing in the league's top 10 with 883 receiving yards and seven touchdown catches.

Although the 6'3", 205-pound McGee lacked outstanding speed, he had excellent moves and a high football IQ that enabled him to gradually emerge as one of the league's better wide receivers, with Jerry Kramer recalling, "Max loved to think on his feet. He would see the corner or safety do this or that, and he would tell Bart [Starr] or Zeke [Bratkowski]. For instance, Max would go inside and make a precise move three or four times to set the guy up and then later fake that same move and go outside . . . Max just loved doing that. He thrived on mental gymnastics."

Kramer added, "Max was really a good athlete. He could play tennis. He could play golf. He could play whatever the hell you wanted to play. And he wanted to bet you on it too!"

During his time in Green Bay, McGee also developed a reputation as an exceptional big-game player who had the ability to relax in any environment and enjoy himself both on and off the field. A quipster who knew how to lighten the mood with a joke or sardonic comment, McGee became extremely popular with his teammates, particularly Paul Hornung, with whom he often partied until the wee hours of the morning. In discussing his fondness for Green Bay's nightlife, and how it affected his on-field performance, McGee stated, "When it's third-and-10, you can take the milk drinkers, and I'll take the whiskey drinkers every time."

McGee had two more productive seasons for the Packers, making 39 receptions for 749 yards and six touchdowns in 1963, before catching 31 passes, amassing 592 receiving yards, and scoring six touchdowns the following year. But, with the Packers acquiring speedy wide receiver Carroll Dale prior to the start of the 1965 campaign, the 33-year-old McGee assumed a backup role his final three seasons in Green Bay, totaling only 17 receptions, 278 receiving yards, and two touchdowns during that time.

Nevertheless, the last two years of McGee's career are the ones for which he is best remembered, because, despite being slowed by injuries and advancing age, he managed to excel when it mattered most. After catching only four passes and scoring just one touchdown during the 1966 regular season, McGee helped lead the Packers to a lopsided 35–10 victory over Kansas City in Super Bowl I by making seven receptions for 138 yards and two touchdowns. Once again displaying his ability to perform well under pressure the following year, McGee recorded a 35-yard reception in the third quarter of Super Bowl II that helped set up a touchdown during Green Bay's 33–14 win over the Oakland Raiders.

McGee's seven receptions for 138 yards and two touchdowns helped lead the Packers to a 35–10 win over the Kansas City Chiefs in Super Bowl I.
Courtesy of LegendaryAuctions.com

Choosing to announce his retirement shortly after Green Bay's victory in Super Bowl II, McGee ended his career with 345 receptions, 6,346 receiving yards, 50 touchdown catches, and an average of 18.4 yards per reception that places him third in team annals. He also carried the ball 12 times for 121 yards, scored one touchdown on a fumble recovery, and punted the ball 256 times for 10,647 yards, giving him a career average of 41.6 yards per kick.

Following his playing days, McGee entered into a restaurant partnership with former Packers' teammate Fuzzy Thurston, with whom he operated a number of steak houses all over Wisconsin. McGee also cofounded the popular Mexican restaurant chain Chi-Chi's. Remaining close to the Packers as well, McGee served as the color commentator for radio broadcasts of Packer games from 1979 to 1998, during which time his sense of humor and insightful analysis earned him Wisconsin Sportscaster of the

Year honors an unprecedented 10 times. After leaving that post, McGee founded the Max McGee National Research Center for Juvenile Diabetes at the Children's Hospital of Wisconsin, which has spent the last two decades raising money for diabetes research.

After winning his battle with colon cancer some 20 years earlier, McGee lived until October 20, 2007, when he died at the age of 75 after falling from the roof of his home in Deephaven, Minnesota, while removing leaves with a leaf blower. Upon learning of his passing, Paul Hornung told the *St. Paul Pioneer Press*, "I just lost my best friend. [McGee's wife] Denise was away from the house. She'd warned him not to get up there. He shouldn't have been up there. He knew better than that."

Hornung added, "Now he'll be the answer to one of the great trivia questions: Who scored the first touchdown in Super Bowl history? Vince knew he could count on him. . . . He was a great athlete. He could do anything with his hands."

Noting that McGee had a stubborn streak, Jerry Kramer said of his former teammate and close friend, "It's hard to admit and distinguish the fact that you're no longer what you were, and you're no longer capable of certain activities. And I think we push the limit a little bit."

CAREER HIGHLIGHTS

Best Season

McGee performed extremely well for the Packers as a rookie in 1954, making 36 receptions for 614 yards and a career-high nine touchdowns, while also leading the league in punting yards (2,999). He also had an outstanding all-around season in 1959, catching 30 passes for 695 yards, averaging a league-best 23.2 yards per reception and a career-high 42.4 yards per punt, and topping the circuit with 2,716 punting yards and a net average of 36 yards per kick. However, McGee made his greatest impact as a receiver in 1961, when he earned his lone Pro Bowl selection by scoring seven touchdowns and establishing career-high marks in receptions (51) and receiving yards (883).

Memorable Moments/Greatest Performances

McGee made the first TD reception of his career during a 23–17 loss to the 49ers on October 10, 1954, hooking up with quarterback Tobin Rote on a pass play that covered 19 yards.

McGee topped 100 receiving yards for the first time in his career during a 37–14 win over the Philadelphia Eagles on October 30, 1954, when he made three catches for 104 yards, with all three of his receptions going for touchdowns that covered 25, 49, and 30 yards.

Although the Packers lost their Thanksgiving Day 1954 meeting with the Detroit Lions by a score of 28–24, McGee collaborated with Tobin Rote on a career-long 82-yard TD reception during the contest.

McGee helped lead the Packers to a 28–10 victory over the Lions in Vince Lombardi's second game as head coach in 1959 by making a pair of fourth-quarter touchdown receptions that covered 41 and 36 yards. He finished the game with three catches for 124 yards and two TDs.

McGee helped the Packers record a resounding 41–13 win over the Chicago Bears on December 4, 1960, by making six receptions for 121 yards and one touchdown, with that being a 46-yard connection with Bart Starr in the fourth quarter.

McGee turned in an outstanding all-around effort in the 1960 regular-season finale, leading the Packers to a 35–21 win over the Rams by making four catches for 125 yards and two touchdowns, while also averaging 47.4 yards on five punts.

Although the Packers ended up losing the 1960 NFL title game to Philadelphia by a score of 17–13, McGee scored their only touchdown on a 7-yard pass from Bart Starr, after earlier keeping the drive alive on fourth down by running for 35 yards on a fake punt.

McGee had a big day against Cleveland on October 15, 1961, making five receptions for 120 yards and one touchdown during a 49–17 victory over the Browns.

McGee performed even better against Minnesota on October 14, 1962, leading the Packers to a 48–21 win over the Vikings by making a career-high 10 catches for 159 yards and two touchdowns, with his scoring plays covering 15 and 55 yards.

McGee had another huge game a few weeks later, making seven catches for a career-high 174 yards, and carrying the ball once for 36 yards during a 49–0 blowout of the Philadelphia Eagles on November 11, 1962.

McGee contributed to a 31–14 win over the Rams on December 7, 1963, by making seven catches for 105 yards and three TDs, which came on 25-, 16-, and 13-yard passes from Bart Starr.

Although well past his prime, McGee made a huge impact in the 1966 postseason, scoring what proved to be the game-winning touchdown against Dallas in the 1966 NFL championship game by hauling in a 28-yard pass from Bart Starr, before turning in the most memorable performance of his career against Kansas City in Super Bowl I. With McGee not expecting to participate in the first meeting between the NFL and AFL champions, he violated the team's curfew policy and spent the night before the Super Bowl out on the town, arriving at the stadium the following morning nursing a hangover. Upon encountering starting wideout Boyd Dowler, McGee told his teammate, "I hope you don't get hurt. I'm not in very good shape." As fate would have it, Dowler suffered a separated shoulder on the Packers' second drive of the game, causing McGee to be inserted into the contest. Shortly thereafter, the aging wide receiver recorded the first touchdown in Super Bowl history when he made a one-handed grab of a Bart Starr pass and carried the ball the rest of the way into the Kansas City end zone for a 37-yard TD. McGee ended up finishing the game with seven receptions for 138 yards and two touchdowns, earning in the process a permanent place in Packers lore.

NOTABLE ACHIEVEMENTS

- Surpassed 50 receptions once (51 in 1961).
- Surpassed 800 receiving yards twice.
- Made nine touchdown receptions as a rookie in 1954.
- Averaged more than 20 yards per reception three times.
- Averaged more than 40 yards per punt five times.
- Led NFL with average of 23.2 yards per reception in 1959.
- Led NFL in punting yardage twice.
- Led Packers in pass receptions four times and receiving yardage five times.
- Ranks among Packers career leaders with: 345 receptions (11th); 6,346 receiving yards (9th); 50 touchdown receptions (7th); and average of 18.39 yards per reception (3rd).
- Six-time Western Conference champion (1960, 1961, 1962, 1965, 1966, and 1967).
- Five-time NFL champion (1961, 1962, 1965, 1966, and 1967).
- Two-time Super Bowl champion (I and II).
- 1961 Pro Bowl selection.
- 1964 All–Western Conference First-Team selection.

48

ANTONIO FREEMAN

Adynamic playmaker who caught more than 80 passes twice and amassed more than 1,000 receiving yards three times, Antonio Freeman spent eight of his nine NFL seasons in Green Bay, establishing himself during that time as one of the Packers' all-time leaders in most pass-receiving categories. Leading the team in receptions and receiving yards four straight times, Freeman had one of the most productive seasons of any wide receiver in franchise history in 1998, when he earned Pro Bowl and consensus First-Team All-Pro honors by catching 84 passes, finishing second in the NFL with 14 touchdown receptions, and leading the league with 1,424 receiving yards. Although Freeman never again reached such heights, he proved to be an outstanding target for Brett Favre throughout his career, serving as a key contributor on Packer teams that won three division titles, two NFC championships, and one Super Bowl.

Born in Baltimore, Maryland, on May 27, 1972, Antonio Michael Freeman spent his high school years at Baltimore Polytechnic Institute, before enrolling at Virginia Tech University, where he excelled on the gridiron for three seasons at wide receiver, making 93 receptions for 1,534 yards and 16 touchdowns, while also returning 63 punts for 651 yards and one touchdown.

After being selected by the Packers in the third round of the 1995 NFL Draft, with the 90th overall pick, Freeman spent most of his rookie season returning punts and kickoffs, amassing a total of 848 yards on special teams, while making just eight catches for 106 yards and one touchdown as a backup wide receiver. Despite missing four games due to injury the following year, Freeman posted far more impressive numbers after he earned a starting job on offense, catching 56 passes, accumulating 933 receiving yards, and scoring nine touchdowns for the eventual Super Bowl champions during the regular season, before making another nine receptions for 174 yards and two touchdowns in three postseason contests.

Having established himself as quarterback Brett Favre's favorite target, Freeman subsequently began an outstanding three-year run during which he

Antonio Freeman led the Packers in receptions and receiving yards four straight times during the 1990s.
Courtesy of SportsMemorabilia.com

surpassed 70 receptions and 1,000 receiving yards each season. After ranking among the NFL leaders with 81 receptions, 1,243 receiving yards, and 12 touchdown catches in 1997, Freeman reached the apex of his career the following year, when his 84 receptions, 14 TD catches, and league-leading 1,424 receiving yards earned him Pro Bowl and All-Pro recognition for the only time. Freeman again performed extremely well in 1999, leading the Packers with 74 catches, 1,074 receiving yards, and six touchdown receptions.

Possessing good size and outstanding speed, the 6'1", 198-pound Freeman spent most of his peak seasons in Green Bay serving as the Packers' primary deep threat on offense, helping to open up the shorter passing game for running backs Dorsey Levens and William Henderson, tight end Mark Chmura, and fellow wideout Bill Schroeder. A good intermediate route-runner as well, Freeman led the Packers in receptions and receiving yards four straight times from 1996 to 1999, while also finishing first on the team in TD catches four straight times from 1997 to 2000.

Freeman led the NFL with 1,424 receiving yards in 1998.
Courtesy of MearsOnlineAuctions.com

Although Freeman had another good year for the Packers in 2000, concluding the campaign with 62 receptions, 912 receiving yards, and nine touchdown catches, the decrease in his overall production fueled speculation that the seven-year, $42 million contract he signed just prior to the start of the 1999 season caused him to become somewhat complacent. Guilty of showing up late for team meetings and complaining to reporters about his diminished role, Freeman drew criticism from some quarters for losing much of his focus, with one NFL scout noting, "He doesn't separate nearly as well, he's not as dangerous after the catch, and he doesn't seem as focused as he was at one point. I don't think he's as hungry as he was before he got the new contract, and age may have taken its toll. . . . He was an ultra-competitive player until he got the contract, and he just doesn't seem that way anymore, except for the game against Baltimore, when he really seemed focused."

Adding to the controversy surrounding Freeman was the two-year feud he began with new head coach Mike Sherman in 2000, which eventually bought him a ticket out of Green Bay. Although he posted solid numbers again in 2001, finishing the season with 52 receptions, 818 receiving yards, and six TD catches, Freeman spent most of the year bickering with Sherman about various issues, including his tardiness, which drew him a one-game suspension. Continuing to clash with Sherman during the subsequent offseason after the team's coach and general manager asked him to take a big pay cut, Freeman ended up being released by the club on June 3, 2002. He subsequently signed with the Philadelphia Eagles, for whom he made 46 catches, amassed 600 receiving yards, and scored four touchdowns in 2002. However, after mending fences with Sherman, Freeman elected to return to the Packers the following year, when, serving as a backup, he made 14 receptions for 141 yards and no touchdowns.

Commenting on his return to the Packers, Freeman said, "I never envisioned coming back. You have to take the situation as a blessing for both of us because I was available, and they were willing to welcome me back."

Meanwhile, Sherman, who blamed Freeman's earlier departure on finances, stated, "I don't hold hard feelings towards people. I'm a fairly forgiving person."

Freeman ended up spending just that one remaining season in Green Bay before announcing his retirement. He ended his playing career with 477 receptions, 7,251 receiving yards, 61 touchdown receptions, and 1,006 yards returning punts and kickoffs. While playing for the Packers, he caught 431 passes, amassed 6,651 receiving yards, and made 57 TD receptions.

Following his playing days, Freeman entered into a career in broadcasting, occasionally participating as an analyst on ESPN's *First Take* and *NFL Live*. He also works for Comcast SportsNet Washington as a commentator on *Redskins Kickoff* and *Redskins Postgame Live*, and, since 2010, he has hosted his own radio show, *The End Zone with Antonio Freeman*, which currently airs on WTSO in Madison and WOKY in Milwaukee, Wisconsin.

PACKERS CAREER HIGHLIGHTS

Best Season

Freeman had a big year for the Packers in 1997, making 81 receptions for 1,243 yards, and finishing second in the NFL with 12 TD catches. However, he performed even better the following season, earning his lone Pro

Bowl and First-Team All-Pro selections by establishing career-high marks in receptions (84), receiving yards (1,424), and touchdown catches (14), with his 1,424 yards through the air leading the league.

Memorable Moments/Greatest Performances

Freeman recorded the first touchdown reception of his career during a 34–23 win over the New Orleans Saints on December 16, 1995, hooking up with Brett Favre on an 11-yard scoring play.

Freeman gave the Packers a 20–10 second-quarter lead over the Atlanta Falcons in the 1995 NFC wild card game by returning a punt 76 yards for a touchdown. The Packers went on to win the contest by a score of 37–20.

Freeman surpassed 100 receiving yards for the first time in his career on September 29, 1996, when he made seven catches for 108 yards and two touchdowns during a 31–10 victory over the Seattle Seahawks.

Freeman followed that up with an exceptional performance against Chicago, helping the Packers record a lopsided 37–6 win over the Bears on October 6, 1976, by making seven receptions for 146 yards and two touchdowns, with his scoring plays covering 50 and 35 yards.

Freeman proved to be the Packers' top offensive threat during a 41–6 dismantling of the 12-1 Denver Broncos on December 8, 1996, finishing the afternoon with nine catches, 175 receiving yards, and three touchdowns that covered 14, 51, and 25 yards.

Freeman helped set the tone for Green Bay's 35–21 victory over New England in Super Bowl XXXI by collaborating with Brett Favre on a then–Super Bowl record 81-yard scoring play early in the second quarter that put the Packers ahead to stay. He finished the game with three catches and 105 receiving yards.

Freeman contributed to a 38–32 win over the Minnesota Vikings on September 21, 1997, by making seven receptions for 122 yards and two touchdowns, with his scoring plays—both of which came in the second quarter—covering 28 and 15 yards.

Freeman earned NFC Offensive Player of the Week honors for the first of three times for his performance during a 17–7 victory over the St. Louis Rams on November 9, 1997, when he made seven catches for 160 yards and one touchdown, which came on a 25-yard pass from Brett Favre on Green Bay's opening drive of the third quarter.

Freeman again gained recognition as NFC Offensive Player of the Week for his effort during a 31–10 win over the Carolina Panthers on December

ANTONIO FREEMAN   **347**

14, 1997, when he made 10 receptions for 166 yards and two touchdowns, hooking up with Brett Favre on scoring plays that covered 58 and 6 yards.

Freeman proved to be a huge factor in the 1997 NFC championship game, helping the Packers record a 23–10 victory over San Francisco by making four catches for 107 yards and one touchdown, which came on a 27-yard connection with Brett Favre early in the second quarter.

Although the Packers subsequently lost Super Bowl XXXII to the Denver Broncos by a score of 31–24, Freeman had another big game, amassing 126 yards on nine pass receptions, and scoring a pair of touchdowns on plays that covered 22 and 13 yards. He also gained another 104 yards on kickoff returns, giving him a total of 230 all-purpose yards that represents the third-highest figure in Super Bowl history.

Freeman helped the Packers begin the 1998 campaign on a positive note, making four catches for 110 yards and two touchdowns during a 38–19 win over the Lions in the opening game of the regular season, with his 84-yard TD reception representing the longest of his career.

Freeman proved to be the difference in a 36–22 victory over the San Francisco 49ers on November 1, 1998, making seven receptions for 193 yards and two touchdowns, with his scoring plays covering 80 yards (on the game's first play from scrimmage) and 62 yards.

Freeman provided much of the offensive firepower during a 30–22 win over the Tennessee Oilers on December 20, 1998, earning NFC Offensive Player of the Week honors for the final time by making seven catches for 186 yards and three touchdowns, which came on plays that covered 57, 68, and 32 yards.

Freeman made a dramatic 21-yard TD reception with just 1:05 left in regulation that gave the Packers a 26–23 Sunday night win over Tampa Bay on October 10, 1999. He finished the contest with seven receptions for 152 yards and two touchdowns, with his other TD coming on a 19-yard hookup with Brett Favre on the Packers' opening drive of the game.

Yet, Freeman made easily the most memorable play of his career during a 26–20 Monday night win over the Minnesota Vikings on November 6, 2000, when he ended the contest less than four minutes into overtime with an unlikely 43-yard touchdown reception. Catching what initially appeared to be an incomplete Brett Favre pass while lying on his back, Freeman rose to his feet after going untouched by his defender and ran the ball into the Minnesota end zone for the winning score. Watching the play in amazement, ABC play-by-play announcer Al Michaels famously proclaimed, "He did WHAT???" Five years later, ESPN identified the catch as the greatest play in the history of Monday Night Football.

NOTABLE ACHIEVEMENTS

- Surpassed 70 receptions three times, topping 80 catches twice.
- Surpassed 1,000 receiving yards three times, topping 1,400 yards once (1,424 in 1998).
- Surpassed 10 touchdown receptions twice.
- Led NFL with 1,424 receiving yards in 1998.
- Finished second in NFL in touchdown receptions twice.
- Led Packers in pass receptions and receiving yards four straight times (1996–1999).
- Ranks among Packers career leaders with: 431 pass receptions (8th); 6,651 receiving yards (7th); 6,668 yards from scrimmage (9th); 7,688 all-purpose yards (8th); 57 touchdown receptions (5th); and 57 total touchdowns scored (8th).
- Three-time division champion (1995, 1996, and 1997).
- Two-time NFC champion (1996 and 1997).
- Super Bowl XXXI champion.
- Three-time NFC Offensive Player of the Week.
- 1998 Pro Bowl selection.
- 1998 First-Team All-Pro.
- 1998 First-Team All-NFC selection.

49

WILLIE BUCHANON

Willie Buchanon had future superstar written all over him when he first arrived in Green Bay in 1972. A shutdown corner with good size and exceptional speed, Buchanon earned NFL Defensive Rookie of the Year honors by recording four interceptions, which he returned for a total of 62 yards. However, bad luck prevented Buchanon from ever fulfilling his enormous potential, because, over the course of the next three seasons, he broke his left leg twice, robbing him of the blinding speed he possessed when he first entered the NFL. Nevertheless, Buchanon still managed to put together an outstanding career, picking off a total of 28 passes in his 11 years in the league, seven of which he spent in Green Bay. Recording 21 of those interceptions while playing for the Packers, Buchanon earned two Pro Bowl selections and one All-Pro nomination as a member of the team, with his strong play helping the Packers capture the only division title they won between 1968 and 1981.

Born in Oceanside, California, on November 4, 1950, Willie James Buchanon attended Oceanside High School, where he starred in football and track. After subsequently earning Junior College All-America honors while playing for Mira Costa College, Buchanon transferred to San Diego State University, from which he eventually graduated. Continuing to excel on the gridiron while at San Diego State, Buchanon gained All-America recognition in his senior year of 1971, when he capped off his brilliant college career by being named the Most Valuable Player of the East-West Shrine Game.

Selected by the Packers with the seventh overall pick of the 1972 NFL Draft, Buchanon immediately earned a starting job in the Green Bay defensive backfield, combining with Ken Ellis to form one of the league's better cornerback tandems. Lining up opposite Ellis at left-cornerback, the 6-foot, 190-pound Buchanon picked off four passes, recovered three fumbles, and did an excellent job of blanketing the league's top wide receivers, prompting the Associated Press to name him the NFL Defensive Rookie of the Year

Willie Buchanon earned NFL Defensive Rookie of the Year honors
with his outstanding play at cornerback in 1972.
Courtesy of MearsOnlineAuctions.com

and the Newspaper Enterprise Association to accord him NFC Rookie of
the Year honors.

In addition to performing extremely well on the gridiron his first year
in the league, Buchanon experienced a considerable amount of growth off
the playing field, recalling years later, "I learned a lot in 1972. MacArthur
Lane pulled me aside and mentored me about the NFL. He told me about
coaches, agents, playing attitude, everything. He just told me everything
there was to know about the mental aspect of the game."

With the Packers expecting Buchanon to take another step forward in 1973, the cornerback's season ended abruptly in Week 6, when he suffered a broken leg during a 24–7 loss to the Los Angeles Rams that forced him to miss the final eight games of the campaign. Although Buchanon made a triumphant return the following year, earning his first trip to the Pro Bowl by recording four interceptions, which placed him second on the team to Ted Hendricks, his bad luck continued in 1975, when he broke the same leg during a 23–13 loss to the Denver Broncos in Week 2. Looking back at the misfortune that befell his teammate, and how it affected his career, John Brockington commented:

> He could have been one of the best-ever. He was big. He was fast. He wasn't any Deion Sanders. Willie could force on the sweep and make tackles. He wasn't soft. Deion used to say they paid him to cover. No, if you're a defensive player, you've got to tackle. You can't do the matador thing and let a guy run by you, and then jump on his back to try and make the tackle. Willie was a great, great defensive back. He did it all. Unfortunately, two (out of three) years he broke the same ankle.

Yet, even though Buchanon lacked some of the explosiveness he possessed earlier in his career when he rejoined the Packers in 1976, he remained one of the league's better cornerbacks the next few seasons. After intercepting a total of four passes from 1976 to 1977, Buchanon earned his second Pro Bowl nomination and lone All-Pro selection in 1978 by finishing second in the league with nine interceptions, four of which he recorded in one game. Nevertheless, financial considerations prompted the Packers to trade him to the San Diego Chargers for a pair of draft picks at season's end, with Buchanon later revealing, "I would have taken $150,000 from the Packers, but they told me they couldn't pay me that because I'd be the second-highest paid player on the team, behind Lynn Dickey. I wanted to stay there with my defense, but I have no regrets." In addition to intercepting 21 passes during his time in Green Bay, Buchanon amassed 234 interception-return yards, scored three touchdowns, and recovered eight fumbles.

Returning to his home state of California, Buchanon ended up spending four years with the Chargers, recording seven interceptions and seven fumble recoveries during that time. Playing his best ball for the Chargers in 1981, Buchanon picked off five passes and recovered four fumbles, making all four of those recoveries in one game, which tied an NFL record. After being reduced to part-time duty the following year, Buchanon elected to

Buchanon's four interceptions on September 24, 1978, tied a single-game franchise record.
Courtesy of SportsMemorabilia.com

announce his retirement, ending his career with 28 interceptions, 278 interception-return yards, 15 fumble recoveries, and three touchdowns.

Following his playing days, Buchanon remained in San Diego, where he taught history and geography in every school he ever attended, before going into real estate and becoming active in the community. He currently resides in his original hometown of Oceanside.

Despite his West Coast roots, Buchanon suggests that playing for the city and the fans of Green Bay represented something very special to him, stating, "It was truly the best football-playing town in America. The fans and the stadium—it was all about playing football. Green Bay really gave you an opportunity to concentrate on playing football. . . . There was nothing else to do."

PACKERS CAREER HIGHLIGHTS

Best Season

Buchanon performed brilliantly for the Packers his first year in the league, being named NFL Defensive Rookie of the Year by the Associated Press and NFC Rookie of the Year by the Newspaper Enterprise Association after recovering three fumbles and intercepting four passes, which he returned for a total of 62 yards. However, he had his finest season in 1978, when he earned First-Team All-Pro honors for the only time by leading the NFC with a career-high nine interceptions, which also placed him second in the league rankings.

Memorable Moments/Greatest Performances

Buchanon didn't wait long to assert himself as a player to be reckoned with, recording the first interception of his career in his very first game as a rookie, when he picked off a Bill Nelson pass during a 26–10 win over the Cleveland Browns in the 1972 regular-season opener.

Buchanon helped lead the Packers to a 23–7 victory over the Minnesota Vikings on December 10, 1972, by picking off a pair of Fran Tarkenton passes.

Buchanon scored the first of his three career touchdowns in the final game of the 1972 regular season, when he recovered a blocked field goal attempt by the Saints and returned the ball 57 yards for a TD that gave the Packers a second-quarter lead of 17–0 in a contest they eventually won by a score of 30–20.

Buchanon again crossed the opponent's goal line in the 1977 regular-season finale, scoring what proved to be the game-winning touchdown of a 16–14 victory over the San Francisco 49ers in the second quarter, when he picked off a Jim Plunkett pass and returned the ball 29 yards for a TD that put the Packers up by a score of 16–7.

Buchanon, though, had the most memorable day of his career on September 24, 1978, when he tied an NFL record by intercepting four passes during a 24–3 win over the San Diego Chargers. In addition to returning one of those interceptions 77 yards for a touchdown, Buchanon ended two San Diego scoring threats by picking off passes in the end zone. Meanwhile, he helped the Packers shut down San Diego's running game by also recording nine unassisted tackles.

NOTABLE ACHIEVEMENTS

- Scored three touchdowns during career (two on defense and one on special teams).
- Led NFC with nine interceptions in 1978 (finished second in NFL).
- Led Packers in interceptions twice.
- Holds Packers single-game record for most interceptions (four vs. San Diego on 9/24/78).
- 1972 Central Division champion.
- 1972 NFL Defensive Rookie of Year.
- Two-time Pro Bowl selection (1974 and 1978).
- 1978 First-Team All-Pro.
- 1978 First-Team All-NFC selection.

50

CURLY LAMBEAU

One of the most legendary figures in franchise history, Curly Lambeau spent three decades with the Packers, coaching them to 209 regular-season victories and six NFL championships. Yet, even though Lambeau built his reputation primarily on the success he experienced as a head coach, he proved to be a very solid player as well during the early stages of his career, earning a spot on the Pro Football Hall of Fame All-1920s Team with his ability to pass and run with the football. Although Lambeau competed during the NFL's pre-statistical era, he is known to be the first player in franchise history to throw a pass, throw a touchdown pass, and make a field goal, with unofficial records crediting him with 24 TD passes, eight rushing touchdowns, three touchdown receptions, and six field goals in 77 career games. Closest estimates also indicate that Lambeau was probably the first NFL player to pass for more than 1,000 yards.

Born in Green Bay, Wisconsin, on April 9, 1898, Earl Louis "Curly" Lambeau starred in multiple sports while attending Green Bay East High School, excelling in particular on the gridiron, where he spent his senior year serving as captain of the school's football team. Following his graduation in 1917, Lambeau briefly attended the University of Notre Dame, where he spent one semester playing for Knute Rockne, before returning to Green Bay. Upon his return to his hometown, Lambeau took a job as a shipping clerk at the Indian Packing Company, contributing to the local wartime meat-packing industry. However, before long, he encountered George Whitney Calhoun, an old high school friend who had since become sports editor at the *Green Bay Press-Gazette*. After a lengthy discussion, the two men decided to organize a football team, leading to the founding of the Packers on August 11, 1919.

After serving as captain and the primary signal-caller of a Packers squad that compiled a record of 10-1 in 1919 while competing against other semi-pro teams based in Wisconsin and Michigan's Upper Peninsula, Lambeau replaced Willard "Big Bill" Ryan as head coach prior to the start of

In addition to coaching the Packers to 209 regular-season victories, Curly Lambeau starred for them on the field during the 1920s.
Courtesy of RMYAuctions.com

the ensuing campaign, doing so at the tender age of 22. Following a 9-1-1 showing by his ball club in his first year at the helm, Lambeau continued to function in the dual role of player-coach in 1921, when the Packers joined the newly formed American Professional Football Association, which changed its name to the National Football League one year later.

Wielding a tremendous amount of power, Lambeau had almost complete control over the team's day-to-day operations, both on and off the playing field. In addition to managing the finances of the ball club and serving as a conduit between the other players and team ownership, Lambeau played halfback in the then-popular single-wing offensive formation, making him the team's primary runner and passer. Typically receiving the snap from center, the 5'10", 187-pound Lambeau did an excellent job of directing the Green Bay offense, which annually led the league in yards gained and ranked among the leaders in points scored. Although it is extremely difficult to gauge Lambeau's effectiveness because the NFL did not begin keeping track of offensive statistics until a few years after he retired as an active player, he performed well enough to earn Second-Team All-Pro honors three straight times from 1922 to 1924, a period during which he also coached the Packers to an overall record of 18-9-4.

After leading the Packers to their first NFL title as the team's player-coach in 1929, Lambeau elected to retire as an active player at season's end and focus exclusively on his coaching duties. He subsequently led Green Bay to five more NFL titles over the course of the next 20 seasons, experiencing his greatest success during the 1930s, when the Packers won four of those championships, compiling an overall record of 86-35-4 along the way. Blessed with an extremely innovative mind, Lambeau is credited with introducing the forward pass to the pro game, implementing pass patterns, and being the first coach to hold daily practices and fly his team to road games.

Lambeau's greatest strength, though, lay in his ability to manipulate and motivate players. Before the NFL instituted the college draft in 1936, Lambeau convinced many of the game's best young players to sign with the Packers once they turned pro. And, after they arrived in Green Bay, he helped them reach their full potential by inspiring them with his competitive fire, enthusiasm, and powers of persuasion. In discussing Lambeau's motivational skills, former Packers assistant coach Bob Snyder said, "He could really get you worked up." In addition to delivering stirring speeches to his players, Lambeau grabbed their attention by storming the sidelines, ranting and raving, stomping his feet, and kicking at the air. Before sending them into a game, he often grabbed them by the jersey and pounded them on the back for encouragement.

Yet, in spite of Lambeau's sterling reputation, many of his players did not hold him in particularly high esteem, with some of them despising him for his insincerity and others openly questioning his knowledge of the game. Said Snyder, "I don't think guys played out of respect for Curly as much as out of fear of Curly. A lot of guys didn't like Paul Brown. A lot of

Lambeau led the Packers to their first NFL title as the team's player-coach in 1929.
Courtesy of RMYAuctions.com

guys didn't like Lombardi. But they respected them. I think they were just scared of Curly."

Although not a tyrant on the field, Lambeau often incurred the wrath of players by imposing steep fines on them, threatening their jobs, and placing the blame for mistakes and defeats squarely on their shoulders. Lambeau also grew increasingly unpopular with his players due to his unwillingness to switch to the T-formation until the latter stages of his coaching career, with many of his subordinates later expressing the belief that the game had passed him by.

In the end, though, the lack of success the Packers experienced on the field following Don Hutson's retirement in 1946 and Lambeau's unpopular decision that same year to purchase the Rockwood Lodge north of Green Bay at the then-exorbitant price of $25,000 and convert it into the team's training facility ultimately proved to be his undoing. With the team struggling on the field and an internal power struggle developing between Lambeau and the members of the executive committee, the long-time coach elected to hand in his resignation following the conclusion of the 1949 campaign, ending his 31-year association with the club with an NFL regular-season coaching record of 209-104-21, making him easily the winningest coach in franchise history. Meanwhile, Lambeau's six NFL championships tie him with Chicago's George Halas for the most of any coach in the history of the league.

After leaving the Packers, Lambeau spent four more years coaching in the NFL, first with the Chicago Cardinals (1950–1951) and then with the Washington Redskins (1952–1953), experiencing very little success before being relieved of his duties in Washington. Lambeau concluded his 33-year NFL coaching career with an overall record of 229-134-22. The Pro Football Hall of Fame opened its doors to him in 1963, just two years before he suffered a heart attack that took his life at age 67. The Packers subsequently renamed their home ballpark, which had been called New City Stadium since it first opened in 1957, Lambeau Field in his honor. The team then went on to win the next three NFL titles, duplicating the feat that Lambeau's Packers accomplished from 1929 to 1931. No other team has since been able to win that many league championships in succession.

CAREER HIGHLIGHTS

Best Season

With Lambeau spending his entire career competing in the NFL's pre-statistical era, it would be extremely difficult to ascertain which season proved to be his most productive as a player. He likely played his best ball for the Packers from 1922 to 1924, earning Second-Team All-Pro honors all three years. And, despite the paucity of available statistics, it is known that Lambeau scored a career-high four touchdowns in the first of those campaigns. Nevertheless, the 1929 season would have to be considered Lambeau's most successful as a player, because, in his final year as Green Bay's player-coach, he led the Packers to a record of 12-0-1 and their first NFL championship.

Memorable Moments/Greatest Performances

Lambeau made history on October 23, 1921, when, in Green Bay's first official league game, he became the first player in franchise history to throw a pass during a 7–6 win over the Minneapolis Marines.

Lambeau starred during Green Bay's 19–0 win over the Hammond Pros in the 1923 regular-season finale, tossing a 35-yard TD pass to Stan Mills and scoring himself on a pass thrown by Charlie Mathys.

Lambeau led the Packers to a 13–0 win over the Duluth Kelleys on November 9, 1924, by throwing two touchdown passes in one game for the first time in his career.

Lambeau again tossed two TD passes and also kicked a 40-yard field goal, in leading the Packers to a 17–6 victory over the Kansas City Blues on November 27, 1924.

Lambeau paced the Packers to a 33–13 win over the Rochester Jeffersons on October 25, 1925, by throwing three touchdown passes in the fourth quarter, tossing a 15-yard strike to Dick O'Donnell, before collaborating with Myrt Basing on scoring plays that covered 45 and 60 yards.

Lambeau displayed his ability to run with the football in the 1927 regular-season opener, rushing for the Packers' only two touchdowns during a 14–0 win over the Dayton Triangles.

NOTABLE ACHIEVEMENTS

- 1929 NFL champion.
- Three-time Second-Team All-Pro (1922, 1923, and 1924).
- NFL 1920s All-Decade Team.
- Pro Football Hall of Fame All-1920s Team.
- Elected to Pro Football Hall of Fame in 1963.

SUMMARY
AND HONORABLE MENTIONS
(THE NEXT 50)

Having identified the 50 greatest players in Green Bay Packers history, the time has come to select the best of the best. Based on the rankings contained in this book, the members of the Packers' all-time offensive and defensive teams are listed below. Our offense includes a quarterback, two running backs, three wide receivers, two guards, two tackles, a center, and a tight end, who was selected from the list of honorable mentions that will soon follow. A third-down back has also been included. Meanwhile, our defense features two ends, two tackles, one middle linebacker, a pair of outside linebackers, two cornerbacks, and a pair of safeties. Special teams have been accounted for as well, with a placekicker, punter, kickoff returner, and punt returner also being included. The placekicker and kickoff returner were also selected from the list of honorable mentions.

OFFENSE		DEFENSE	
Brett Favre	QB	Randall Cobb	KR
Jim Taylor	RB	Willie Davis	LE
Paul Hornung	RB	Dave Hanner	LT
Ahman Green	3rd-Down RB	Henry Jordan	RT
Paul Coffman	TE	Reggie White	RE
Don Hutson	WR	Dave Robinson	LOLB
James Lofton	WR	Ray Nitschke	MLB
Sterling Sharpe	WR	Clay Matthews	ROLB
Cal Hubbard	LT	Herb Adderley	LCB
Mike Michalske	LG	Willie Wood	S
Jim Ringo	C	Bobby Dillon	S
Jerry Kramer	RG	Charles Woodson	RCB
Forrest Gregg	RT	Verne Lewellen	P
Mason Crosby	PK	Antonio Freeman	PR

Although I limited my earlier rankings to the top 50 players in Packers history, many other fine players have worn a Green Bay uniform over the years, some of whom narrowly missed making the final cut. Following is a list of those players deserving of an honorable mention. These are the men I deemed worthy of being slotted into positions 51 to 100 in the overall rankings. Where applicable and available, the statistics they compiled during their time in Green Bay are included, along with their most notable achievements while playing for the Packers.

51: RUSS LETLOW (OG, DT; 1936–1942, 1946)

Courtesy of RMYAuctions.com

NOTABLE ACHIEVEMENTS

- Three-time Western Conference champion (1936, 1938, and 1939).
- Two-time NFL champion (1936 and 1939).
- Two-time Pro Bowl selection (1938 and 1939).
- 1938 Second-Team All-Pro.
- NFL 1930s All-Decade Team.
- Pro Football Hall of Fame All-1930s Team.

52: LEE ROY CAFFEY (LB; 1964–1969)

Courtesy of MearsOnlineAuctions.com

NOTABLE ACHIEVEMENTS

- Scored two defensive touchdowns on interception returns.
- Intercepted nine passes.
- Three-time Western Conference champion (1965, 1966, and 1967).
- Three-time NFL champion (1965, 1966, and 1967).
- Two-time Super Bowl champion (I and II).
- 1965 Pro Bowl selection.
- 1966 First-Team All-Pro.

53: GREG JENNINGS (WR; 2006–2012)

Courtesy of Mike Morbeck

Packers Numbers

425 Receptions, 6,537 Receiving Yards, 53 Touchdown Receptions.

NOTABLE ACHIEVEMENTS

- Surpassed 75 receptions twice.
- Topped 1,000 receiving yards three times.
- Surpassed 10 touchdown receptions twice.
- Finished second in NFL with 12 touchdown receptions in 2010.
- Finished fourth in NFL in: receiving yards once; touchdown receptions once; and average yards per reception once.
- Led Packers in receptions twice and receiving yards three times.
- Made three touchdown receptions vs. Minnesota on 11/21/2010.
- Ranks among Packers career leaders in: pass receptions (9th); touchdown receptions (6th); receiving yards (8th); and average yards per reception (8th).
- 2010 NFC champion.
- Super Bowl XLV champion.
- Member of 2006 NFL All-Rookie Team.
- 2010 Week 11 NFC Offensive Player of the Week.
- Two-time Pro Bowl selection (2010 and 2011).

54: BUFORD GARFIELD "BABY" RAY
(OT, DT; 1938–1948)

Public domain

NOTABLE ACHIEVEMENTS

- Three-time Western Conference champion (1938, 1939, and 1944).
- Two-time NFL champion (1939 and 1944).
- 1939 Pro Bowl selection.
- 1941 First-Team All-Pro.
- Three-time Second-Team All-Pro (1939, 1943, and 1944).
- NFL 1940s All-Decade Team.
- Pro Football Hall of Fame All-1940s Team.

55: LARRY MCCARREN (C; 1973–1984)

Courtesy of MearsOnlineAuctions.com

NOTABLE ACHIEVEMENTS

- Started 162 consecutive games at center.
- 1982 division champion.
- Two-time Pro Bowl selection (1982 and 1983).
- Two-time First-Team All-NFC selection (1981 and 1982).
- Two-time Second-Team All-NFC selection (1983 and 1984).

56: A. J. HAWK (LB; 2006–2014)

Courtesy of Mike Morbeck

Packers Numbers

1,118 Tackles, 19 Sacks, 9 Interceptions, 121 Interception-Return Yards, 4 Forced Fumbles, 5 Fumble Recoveries.

NOTABLE ACHIEVEMENTS

- Recorded more than 100 tackles six times.
- Recorded five sacks in 2013.
- Led Packers in tackles five times.
- Holds Packers career records for most tackles (1,118) and most unassisted tackles (798).
- Missed only two games in nine seasons.
- Five-time division champion (2007, 2011, 2012, 2013, and 2014).
- 2010 NFC champion.
- Super Bowl XLV champion.
- Member of 2006 NFL All-Rookie Team.

57: CARROLL DALE (WR; 1965–1972)

Courtesy of MearsOnlineAuctions.com

Packers Numbers

275 Receptions, 5,422 Receiving Yards, 35 Touchdown Receptions.

NOTABLE ACHIEVEMENTS

- Surpassed 40 receptions three times.
- Topped 800 receiving yards four times.
- Averaged more than 20 yards per reception twice.
- Finished second in NFL with average of 23.7 yards per reception in 1966.
- Led Packers in receptions four times and receiving yards five times.
- Holds Packers career record for most yards per reception (19.72).
- Three-time Western Conference champion (1965, 1966, and 1967).
- Three-time NFL champion (1965, 1966, and 1967).
- Two-time Super Bowl champion (I and II).
- Three-time Pro Bowl selection (1968, 1969, and 1970).
- 1968 First-Team All-Conference selection.

58: DAN CURRIE (LB; 1958–1964)

Courtesy of MainlineAutographs.com

NOTABLE ACHIEVEMENTS

- Scored one defensive touchdown on interception return.
- Intercepted 11 passes during career.
- Intercepted four passes in 1960.
- Three-time Western Conference champion (1960, 1961, and 1962).
- Two-time NFL champion (1961 and 1962).
- 1960 Pro Bowl selection.
- 1962 First-Team All-Pro.
- 1963 Second-Team All-Pro.

59: EZRA JOHNSON (DE; 1977–1987)

Courtesy of MearsOnlineAuctions.com

Packers Numbers

41½ "Official" Sacks, 7 Fumble Recoveries.

NOTABLE ACHIEVEMENTS

- Recorded 20½ "unofficial" sacks in 1978.
- Finished sixth in NFL with 14½ sacks in 1983.
- Recorded four sacks vs. Minnesota on 11/11/1979.
- Led Packers in sacks four times.
- Holds Packers' single-season record for most tackles by a defensive lineman (107 in 1983).
- Ranks sixth on Packers' "official" career sack list.
- 1982 division champion.
- 1978 Packers Defensive Player of the Year.
- 1978 Pro Bowl selection.

60: MIKE DOUGLASS (LB; 1978–1985)

Courtesy of Heritage Auctions

Packers Numbers

967 Tackles, 19 Sacks, 10 Interceptions, 274 Interception-Return Yards, 16 Fumble Recoveries, 3 Touchdowns.

NOTABLE ACHIEVEMENTS

- Scored three defensive touchdowns (one interception return and two fumble returns).
- Recorded more than 100 tackles six times.
- Led Packers with nine sacks in 1984.
- Led NFL with two non-offensive touchdowns in 1983.
- Finished fifth in NFL with 126 interception-return yards in 1985.
- Ranks among Packers career leaders with: 967 tackles (5th); 766 unassisted tackles (4th); and 16 fumble recoveries (tied—5th).
- 1982 division champion.
- Two-time Packers' Defensive MVP (1980 and 1981).
- 1981 Second-Team All-NFC selection.

61: BOB JETER (DB; 1963–1970)

Courtesy of MearsOnlineAuctions.com

Packers Numbers

23 Interceptions, 333 Interception-Return Yards, 2 Touchdowns.

NOTABLE ACHIEVEMENTS

- Scored two touchdowns during career on interception returns.
- Recorded at least five interceptions in a season twice.
- Surpassed 100 interception-return yards once (142 in 1966).
- Led Packers in interceptions twice.
- Led NFL with two non-offensive touchdowns in 1966.
- Finished third in NFL with eight interceptions in 1967.
- Finished fifth in NFL with 142 interception-return yards in 1966.
- Three-time Western Conference champion (1965, 1966, and 1967).
- Three-time NFL champion (1965, 1966, and 1967).
- Two-time Super Bowl champion (I and II).
- Two-time Pro Bowl selection (1967 and 1969).
- 1967 First-Team All-Pro.

62: DORSEY LEVENS (RB; 1994–2001)

Courtesy of George A. Kitrinos

Packers Numbers

3,937 Yards Rushing, 271 Receptions, 2,079 Receiving Yards, 44 Touchdowns, 3.9 Rushing Average.

NOTABLE ACHIEVEMENTS

- Rushed for more than 1,000 yards twice, surpassing 1,400 yards once (1,435 in 1997).
- Surpassed 50 receptions twice, topping 70 receptions once (71 in 1999).
- Topped 500 receiving yards once (573 in 1999).
- Surpassed 1,600 yards from scrimmage twice.
- Scored at least 10 touchdowns three times.
- Averaged more than 4.5 yards per carry once (4.7 in 1996).
- Finished third in NFL with 1,805 yards from scrimmage in 1997.
- Finished fourth in NFL with 1,435 yards rushing in 1997.
- Finished fifth in NFL with 12 touchdowns in 1997.
- Led Packers in rushing twice.
- Ranks among Packers career leaders in rushing yards (6th) and rushing touchdowns (7th).
- Two-time NFC champion (1996 and 1997).
- Super Bowl XXXI champion.
- 1999 Week 17 NFC Offensive Player of the Week.
- 2001 Week 17 NFC Special Teams Player of the Week.
- 1997 Pro Bowl selection.
- 1997 First-Team All-NFC selection.

63: BOB SKORONSKI (OT; 1956, 1959–1968)

Courtesy of MearsOnlineAuctions.com

NOTABLE ACHIEVEMENTS

- Missed only two games in 11 seasons.
- Six-time Western Conference champion (1960, 1961, 1962, 1965, 1966, and 1967).
- Five-time NFL champion (1961, 1962, 1965, 1966, and 1967).
- Two-time Super Bowl champion (I and II).
- 1966 Pro Bowl selection.

64: PAUL COFFMAN (TE; 1978–1985)

Courtesy of MearsOnlineAuctions.com

Packers Numbers

322 Receptions, 4,223 Receiving Yards, 39 Touchdown Receptions.

NOTABLE ACHIEVEMENTS

- Surpassed 50 receptions three times.
- Topped 700 receiving yards twice, surpassing 800 yards once.
- Finished fourth in NFL with 11 touchdown receptions in 1983.
- Led Packers with 56 receptions in 1979.
- Ranks 12th in Packers history in pass receptions and touchdown receptions (tied).
- 1982 division champion.
- Three-time Pro Bowl selection (1982, 1983, and 1984).
- Two-time First-Team All-NFC selection (1983 and 1984).

65: KABEER GBAJA-BIAMILA (DE; 2000–2008)

Courtesy of Sportsmemorabilia.com

Career Numbers

74½ Sacks, 290 Tackles, 1 Interception, 72 Interception-Return Yards, 17 Forced Fumbles, 7 Fumble Recoveries, 1 Touchdown.

NOTABLE ACHIEVEMENTS

- Returned only interception of career 72 yards for touchdown.
- Recorded at least 10 sacks in a season four times, registering 13½ sacks twice.
- Finished third in NFL with 13½ sacks in 2004.
- Finished fourth in NFL with 13½ sacks in 2001.
- Led Packers in sacks five straight times (2001–2005).
- Ranks second in Packers history with 74½ career sacks.
- Four-time division champion (2002, 2003, 2004, and 2007).
- 2004 Week 17 NFC Defensive Player of the Week.
- 2003 Pro Bowl selection.

66: BILL LEE (OT, DT; 1937–1942, 1946)

Courtesy of RMYAuctions.com

NOTABLE ACHIEVEMENTS

- Two-time Western Conference champion (1938 and 1939).
- 1939 NFL champion.
- 1939 Pro Bowl selection.
- Two-time Second-Team All-Pro (1935 and 1936).
- NFL 1930s All-Decade Team.
- Pro Football Hall of Fame All-1930s Team.

67: AARON KAMPMAN (DE; 2002–2009)

Courtesy of Leivur R. Djurhuus

Packers Numbers

54 Sacks, 458 Tackles, 11 Forced Fumbles, 4 Fumble Recoveries.

NOTABLE ACHIEVEMENTS

- Recorded more than 10 sacks in a season twice.
- Recorded more than 60 tackles in a season five times, registering more than 80 tackles twice.
- Finished second in NFL with 15½ sacks in 2006.
- Led Packers in sacks three times.
- Ranks fifth in Packers history with 54 career sacks.
- Four-time division champion (2002, 2003, 2004, and 2007).
- Two-time NFC Defensive Player of the Week.
- October 2007 NFC Defensive Player of the Month.
- Two-time Pro Bowl selection (2006 and 2007).
- Two-time Second-Team All-Pro (2006 and 2007).

68: JESSE WHITTENTON (DB; 1958–1964)

Courtesy of MearsOnlineAuctions.com

Packers Numbers

20 Interceptions, 329 Interception-Return Yards, 10 Fumble Recoveries, 1 Touchdown.

NOTABLE ACHIEVEMENTS

- Scored one defensive touchdown on interception return.
- Recorded at least five interceptions in a season twice.
- Surpassed 100 interception-return yards once (101 in 1960).
- Finished second in NFL with 45 fumble return yards in 1959.
- Led Packers in interceptions twice.
- Three-time Western Conference champion (1960, 1961, and 1962).
- Two-time NFL champion (1961 and 1962).
- Two-time Pro Bowl selection (1961 and 1963).
- 1961 First-Team All-Pro.
- 1960 Second-Team All-Pro.
- 1959 First-Team All-Conference selection.

69: NICK BARNETT (LB; 2003–2010)

Courtesy of Heritage Auctions

Packers Numbers

787 Tackles, 15½ Sacks, 9 Interceptions, 175 Interception-Return Yards, 2 Forced Fumbles, 7 Fumble Recoveries, 1 Touchdown.

NOTABLE ACHIEVEMENTS

- Scored one defensive touchdown on 95-yard interception return.
- Recorded more than 100 tackles six times.
- Led NFC with 138 tackles in 2005.
- Led Packers in tackles five times.
- Holds Packers single-season record for most tackles (194 in 2005).
- Ranks sixth in Packers history with 787 total tackles and 575 unassisted tackles.
- Three-time division champion (2003, 2004, and 2007).
- 2010 NFC champion.
- Super Bowl XLV champion.
- Two-time NFC Defensive Player of the Week.
- Member of 2003 NFL All-Rookie Team.
- 2007 Second-Team All-Pro.

70: JOSH SITTON (OG; 2008–2015)

Courtesy of Kyle Engman Through Wikipedia

NOTABLE ACHIEVEMENTS

- Four-time division champion (2011, 2012, 2013, and 2014).
- 2010 NFC champion.
- Super Bowl XLV champion.
- 2010 NFL Alumni Association Offensive Lineman of the Year.
- Three-time Pro Bowl selection (2012, 2014, and 2015).
- 2014 First-Team All-Pro.
- Two-time Second-Team All-Pro (2013 and 2015).

71: TED FRITSCH (RB, LB; 1942–1950)

Courtesy of RMYAuctions.com

Career Numbers

2,200 Yards Rushing, 31 Rushing Touchdowns, 3.5 Rushing Average, 25 Receptions, 227 Receiving Yards, 1 Touchdown Reception, 10 Interceptions, 263 Interception-Return Yards, 2 TD Interceptions, 9 Fumble Recoveries, 1 Fumble-Return TD, 951 Kickoff-Return Yards, 25.7 Kickoff-Return Average, 3,671 All-Purpose Yards, 36 Field Goals Made, 98 Field Goal Attempts, 380 Points Scored.

NOTABLE ACHIEVEMENTS

- Scored three defensive touchdowns during career.
- Averaged more than 4.5 yards per carry once (4.7 in 1948).
- Intercepted six passes in 1944.
- Surpassed 100 interception-return yards once (115 in 1944).
- Led NFL with 9 rushing touchdowns, 10 total touchdowns, 100 points scored, and 9 field goals made in 1946.
- Finished second in NFL in: rushing touchdowns once; rushing average once; field goals made once; and field goal percentage once.
- Finished third in NFL in: kickoff-return yards once; interceptions once; field goals made once; and field goal percentage once.
- Ranks sixth in Packers history with 31 rushing touchdowns.
- 1944 Western Conference champion.
- 1944 NFL champion.
- 1946 First-Team All-Pro.
- 1945 Second-Team All-Pro.

72: MASON CROSBY (PK: 2007–2017)

Courtesy of Christopher Garrison

Career Numbers

277 Field Goals Made, 345 Field Goal Attempts, 80.3 Field Goal Percentage, 1,345 Points Scored.

NOTABLE ACHIEVEMENTS

- Has kicked more than 30 field goals in a season twice.
- Has posted field goal percentage in excess of 85 percent four times.
- Has scored more than 100 points 10 times, topping 140 points three times.
- Has led NFL in points scored once and extra points made twice.
- Has finished second in NFL in field goals made once.
- Has kicked five field goals in one game three times.
- Holds Packers career records for: most points scored (1,345); most field goal attempts (345); and most field goals made (277).
- Holds Packers record for longest field goal made (58 yards vs. Minnesota on 10/23/2011).
- Holds NFL record for most consecutive postseason field goal attempts successfully converted (20).
- Six-time division champion (2007, 2011, 2012, 2013, 2014, and 2016).
- 2010 NFC champion.
- Super Bowl XLV champion.
- Six-time NFC Special Teams Player of the Week.
- November 2007 NFC Special Teams Player of the Month.

73: ROGER ZATKOFF (LB; 1953–1956)

Courtesy of MearsOnlineAuctions.com

NOTABLE ACHIEVEMENTS

- Intercepted four passes and recovered six fumbles.
- Three-time Pro Bowl selection (1954, 1955, and 1956).
- 1955 First-Team All-Pro.
- 1954 Second-Team All-Pro.

74: TIM HARRIS (LB; 1986–1990)

Courtesy of George A. Kitrinos

Packers Numbers

55 Sacks, 422 Tackles, 6 Fumble Recoveries.

NOTABLE ACHIEVEMENTS

- Scored one defensive touchdown during career.
- Recorded two safeties during career.
- Recorded more than 10 sacks in a season twice.
- Registered more than 100 tackles once (110 in 1988).
- Led NFL with two safeties in 1988.
- Finished second in NFL with 19½ sacks in 1989.
- Led Packers in sacks five times and tackles once.
- Holds Packers "official" single-season record for most sacks (19½ in 1989).
- Ranks fourth in Packers history with 55 career sacks.
- Two-time NFC Defensive Player of the Week.
- 1989 Pro Bowl selection.
- 1989 First-Team All-Pro.
- 1988 Second-Team All-Pro.
- Two-time First-Team All-NFC selection (1988 and 1989).

75: RANDALL COBB (WR: 2011–2017)

Courtesy of Mike Morbeck

Career Numbers

432 Receptions, 5,141 Receiving Yards, 39 Touchdown Receptions, 352 Yards Rushing, 786 Punt-Return Yards, 9.6-Yard Punt-Return Average, 1,915 Kickoff-Return Yards, 25.9-Yard Kickoff-Return Average, 8,194 All-Purpose Yards, 43 Total Touchdowns.

NOTABLE ACHIEVEMENTS

- Has surpassed 80 receptions twice.
- Has topped 1,000 receiving yards once (1,287 in 2014).
- Has surpassed 10 touchdown receptions once (12 in 2014).
- Has surpassed 1,000 yards from scrimmage twice.
- Has surpassed 1,000 all-purpose yards three times, with mark of 2,342 yards in 2012 representing single-season franchise record.
- Has returned two punts and one kickoff for touchdowns.
- Led NFL with 2,342 all-purpose yards in 2012.
- Finished second in NFL with 27.7-yard kickoff-return average in 2011.
- Finished fourth in NFL with 12 touchdown receptions in 2014.
- Has led Packers in receptions twice and receiving yards once.
- Ranks among Packers career leaders in receptions (7th); receiving yards (13th); TD catches (tied—12th); all-purpose yards (6th); punt-return yards (6th); and kickoff-return yards (6th).
- Tied with three other players for second-longest kickoff return in NFL history (108 yards vs. New Orleans on 9/8/2011).
- Five-time division champion (2011, 2012, 2013, 2014 & 2016).
- Member of 2011 NFL All-Rookie Team.
- 2014 Pro Bowl selection.

76: NICK COLLINS (DB; 2005–2011)

Courtesy of Leivur R. Djurhuus

Career Numbers

417 Tackles, 21 Interceptions, 507 Interception-Return Yards, 6 Forced Fumbles, 4 Fumble Recoveries, 5 Touchdowns.

NOTABLE ACHIEVEMENTS

- Scored five defensive touchdowns (four interception returns and one fumble return).
- Scored touchdown on interception return in Super Bowl XLV.
- Recorded at least five interceptions in a season twice.
- Surpassed 100 interception-return yards twice.
- Led NFL with 295 interception-return yards and three non-offensive touchdowns in 2008.
- Finished second in NFL with seven interceptions in 2008.
- Ranks among Packers career leaders in interception-return yards (7th) and defensive touchdowns scored (tied—4th).
- Two-time division champion (2007 and 2011).
- 2010 NFC champion.
- Super Bowl XLV champion.
- Member of 2005 NFL All-Rookie Team.
- Three-time Pro Bowl selection (2008, 2009, and 2010).
- Three-time Second-Team All-Pro (2008, 2009, and 2010).

77: JOHN MARTINKOVIC (DE; 1951–1956)

Courtesy of MearsOnlineAuctions.com

NOTABLE ACHIEVEMENTS

- Scored two defensive touchdowns during career.
- Recovered 10 fumbles.
- Never missed a game in his six seasons in Green Bay, appearing in 72 consecutive contests for Packers.
- Three-time Pro Bowl selection (1953, 1954, and 1955).
- 1954 Second-Team All-Pro.
- 1956 First-Team All–Western Conference selection.

78: KEN BOWMAN (C; 1964–1973)

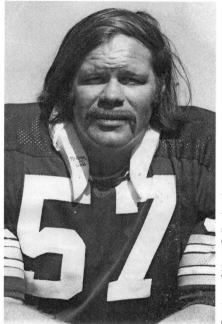

Courtesy of MearsOnlineAuctions.com

NOTABLE ACHIEVEMENTS

- Three-time Western Conference champion (1965, 1966, and 1967).
- Three-time NFL champion (1965, 1966, and 1967).
- Two-time Super Bowl champion (I and II).

79: LIONEL ALDRIDGE (DE; 1963–1971)

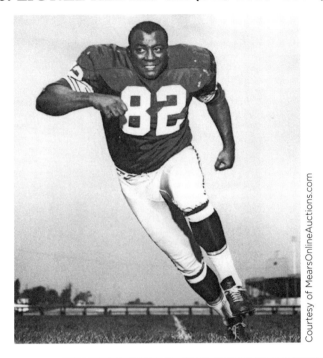

Courtesy of MearsOnlineAuctions.com

NOTABLE ACHIEVEMENTS

- Scored one defensive touchdown during career on fumble return.
- Led NFL with five fumble recoveries in 1964.
- Tied for fifth in Packers history with 16 fumble recoveries.
- Three-time Western Conference champion (1965, 1966, and 1967).
- Three-time NFL champion (1965, 1966, and 1967).
- Two-time Super Bowl champion (I and II).
- 1964 First-Team All-Conference selection.

80: CHAD CLIFTON (OT: 2000–2011)

Courtesy of Mike Morbeck

NOTABLE ACHIEVEMENTS

- Five-time division champion (2002, 2003, 2004, 2007, and 2011).
- 2010 NFC champion.
- Super Bowl XLV champion.
- Two-time Pro Bowl selection (2007 and 2010).

81: AL HARRIS (DB: 2003–2009)

Courtesy of Leivur R. Djurhuus

Packers Numbers

298 Tackles, 14 Interceptions, 233 Interception-Return Yards, 4 Sacks, 2 Touchdowns.

NOTABLE ACHIEVEMENTS

- Scored two defensive touchdowns on interception returns.
- Scored game-winning touchdown in 2003 NFC wild card game by returning interception 52 yards for TD in overtime.
- Three-time division champion (2003, 2004, and 2007).
- 2005 Week 5 NFC Defensive Player of the Week.
- Two-time Pro Bowl selection (2007 and 2008).
- 2007 Second-Team All-Pro.

82: RON KOSTELNIK (DT; 1961–1968)

Courtesy of MearsOnlineAuctions.com

NOTABLE ACHIEVEMENTS

- Five-time Western Conference champion (1961, 1962, 1965, 1966, and 1967).
- Five-time NFL champion (1961, 1962, 1965, 1966, and 1967).
- Two-time Super Bowl champion (I and II).

83: TOBIN ROTE (QB; 1950–1956)

Courtesy of RMYAuctions.com

Packers Numbers

11,535 Yards Passing, 89 Touchdown Passes, 119 Interceptions, 44.6 Completion Percentage, 54.4 Quarterback Rating, 2,205 Yards Rushing, 29 Rushing Touchdowns, 5.3 Rushing Average, 1 Touchdown Reception.

NOTABLE ACHIEVEMENTS

- Passed for more than 2,000 yards twice.
- Completed more than 50 percent of passes once (52.2 percent in 1952).
- Posted quarterback rating in excess of 80.0 once (85.6 in 1952).
- Rushed for more than 300 yards five times, topping 500 yards once (523 in 1951).
- Rushed for 11 touchdowns in 1956.
- Averaged more than five yards per carry four times.
- Led NFL quarterbacks in: pass completions twice; passing yards once; touchdown passes twice; and passer rating once.
- Finished second among NFL quarterbacks in pass completions once and passing yards once.
- Led NFL with rushing average of 6.9 yards per carry in 1951.
- Finished second in NFL with 11 rushing touchdowns in 1956.
- Led Packers in rushing three times.
- Ranks among Packers career leaders in: pass attempts (5th); pass completions (6th); passing yards (5th); and touchdown passes (5th).
- 1956 Pro Bowl selection.
- Two-time Second-Team All-Pro (1955 and 1956).

84: JOE LAWS (RB, DB; 1934–1945)

Courtesy of RMYAuctions.com

Career Numbers

1,932 Yards Rushing, 79 Receptions, 1,041 Receiving Yards, 21 Touchdowns, 3 Touchdown Passes, 4.1 Rushing Average, 339 Punt-Return Yards, 362 Kickoff-Return Yards, 18 Interceptions, 266 Interception-Return Yards, 3,942 All-Purpose Yards.

NOTABLE ACHIEVEMENTS

- Averaged more than five yards per carry twice.
- Intercepted seven passes in 1943.
- Returned one interception for a touchdown during career.
- Returned one punt for a touchdown during career.
- Intercepted three passes vs. Giants in 1944 NFL title game.
- Four-time Western Conference champion (1936, 1938, 1939, and 1944).
- Three-time NFL champion (1936, 1939, and 1944).
- 1939 Pro Bowl selection.

85: RYAN LONGWELL (PK: 1997–2005)

Courtesy of PristineAuction.com

Packers Numbers

226 Field Goals Made, 277 Field Goal Attempts, 81.6 Field Goal Percentage, 1,054 Points Scored.

NOTABLE ACHIEVEMENTS

- Kicked more than 30 field goals once (33 in 2000).
- Posted field goal percentage in excess of 85 percent four times.
- Scored more than 100 points eight times.
- Finished third in NFL in points scored once and field goals made once.
- Holds Packers career record for highest field goal percentage.
- Ranks second in Packers history in field goals made and points scored.
- Four-time division champion (1997, 2002, 2003, and 2004).
- 1997 NFC champion.
- Five-time NFC Special Teams Player of the Week.

86: MARCO RIVERA (OG; 1997–2004)

Courtesy of MearsOnlineAuctions.com

NOTABLE ACHIEVEMENTS

- Four-time division champion (1997, 2002, 2003, and 2004).
- 1997 NFC champion.
- Three-time Pro Bowl selection (2002, 2003, and 2004).
- 2003 Second-Team All-Pro.
- Two-time First-Team All-NFC selection (2003 and 2004).

87: KEN ELLIS (DB; 1970–1975)

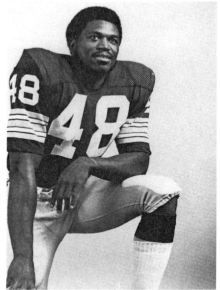

Courtesy of MearsOnlineAuctions.com

Packers Numbers

20 Interceptions, 294 Interception-Return Yards, 3 Touchdown Interceptions, 426 Punt-Return Yards, 6.8-Yard Punt-Return Average, 1 Punt-Return TD, 802 Kickoff-Return Yards, 22.3-Yard Kickoff-Return Average.

NOTABLE ACHIEVEMENTS

- Scored four defensive touchdowns.
- Returned one punt for a touchdown.
- Recorded six interceptions in 1971.
- Surpassed 100 interception-return yards once (106 in 1972).
- Led Packers in interceptions three times.
- Finished fifth in NFL with 215 punt-return yards in 1972.
- 1972 division champion.
- Two-time Pro Bowl selection (1973 and 1974).
- 1972 First-Team All-Pro.
- Two-time First-Team All-NFC selection (1972 and 1973).
- 1974 Second-Team All-NFC selection.

88: LYNN DICKEY (QB; 1976–1985)

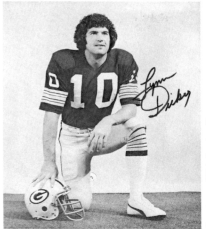

Courtesy of PristineAuction.com

Packers Numbers

21,369 Yards Passing, 133 Touchdown Passes, 151 Interceptions, 56.2 Completion Percentage, 73.8 Quarterback Rating, 9 Rushing Touchdowns.

NOTABLE ACHIEVEMENTS

- Passed for more than 3,000 yards three times, topping 4,000 yards once (4,458 in 1983).
- Threw more than 20 touchdown passes twice, tossing 32 TD passes in 1983.
- Completed more than 56 percent of passes five times.
- Posted quarterback rating in excess of 85.0 twice.
- Led NFL quarterbacks with 4,458 yards passing and 32 touchdown passes in 1983.
- Passed for 418 yards vs. Tampa Bay on 10/12/1980.
- Ranks among Packers career leaders in: pass attempts (4th); pass completions (4th); passing yards (4th); touchdown passes (4th); pass completion percentage (4th); and quarterback rating (4th).
- Holds Packers single-game record for highest completion percentage (90.48—19 of 21, vs. New Orleans on 12/13/1981).
- 1982 division champion.
- 1984 Week 11 NFC Offensive Player of the Week.
- 1983 Second-Team All-NFC selection.

89: JOHNNIE GRAY (DB; 1975–1983)

Courtesy of MearsOnlineAuctions.com

Career Numbers

22 Interceptions, 332 Interception-Return Yards, 1,001 Tackles, 771 Unassisted Tackles, 22 Fumble Recoveries, 1 Touchdown, 656 Punt-Return Yards, 7.7-Yard Punt-Return Average, 317 Kickoff-Return Yards, 15.1-Yard Kickoff-Return Average.

NOTABLE ACHIEVEMENTS

- Scored one defensive touchdown on interception return.
- Recorded five interceptions twice.
- Surpassed 100 interception-return yards once (101 in 1976).
- Recorded more than 100 tackles seven times.
- Led Packers in interceptions three times and tackles once.
- Ranks among Packers career leaders in: tackles (4th); unassisted tackles (3rd); and fumble recoveries (tied—2nd).
- 1982 division champion.
- Member of 1975 NFL All-Rookie Team.

90: IRV COMP (QB, DB; 1943–1949)

Courtesy of HeritageAuctions.com

Career Numbers

3,354 Yards Passing, 28 Touchdown Passes, 52 Interceptions, 41.0 Completion Percentage, 41.6 Quarterback Rating, 7 Rushing Touchdowns, 2 Touchdown Receptions, 34 Interceptions, 483 Interception-Return Yards, 2 TD Interceptions, 13 Fumble Recoveries.

NOTABLE ACHIEVEMENTS

- Returned two interceptions for touchdowns during career.
- Passed for more than 1,000 yards once (1,159 in 1944).
- Completed 50 percent of passes and compiled quarterback rating of 81.0 in 1943.
- Led NFL with 1,159 yards passing in 1944.
- Finished second in NFL in touchdown passes once and passer rating once.
- Finished second in NFL with 10 interceptions and 149 interception-return yards in 1943.
- Holds Packers single-season record for most interceptions (10 in 1943).
- Ranks among Packers career leaders in interceptions (7th) and interception-return yards (8th).
- 1944 Western Conference champion.
- 1944 NFL champion.

91: RON KRAMER (TE, WR; 1957, 1959–1964)

Courtesy of MearsOnlineAuctions.com

Packers Numbers

170 Receptions, 2,594 Receiving Yards, 15 Touchdown Receptions.

NOTABLE ACHIEVEMENTS

- Surpassed 500 receiving yards four times.
- Averaged more than 15 yards per reception four times.
- Made seven touchdown receptions in 1962.
- Caught two touchdown passes vs. Giants in 1961 NFL title game.
- Three-time Western Conference champion (1960, 1961, and 1962).
- Two-time NFL champion (1961 and 1962).
- 1962 Pro Bowl selection.
- 1962 First-Team All-Pro.
- 1963 Second-Team All-Pro.
- Named to NFL's 50th Anniversary Team in 1969.

92: DON CHANDLER (P, PK; 1965–1967)

Courtesy of MearsOnlineAuctions.com

Packers Numbers

48 Field Goals Made, 83 Field Goal Attempts, 57.8 Field Goal Percentage, 261 Points Scored, 41.9-Yard Punting Average.

NOTABLE ACHIEVEMENTS

- Averaged more than 40 yards per punt twice, posting average of 42.9 in 1965.
- Recorded longest punt in NFL in 1965 (90 yards).
- Finished second in NFL in field goal percentage once.
- Finished third in NFL in field goal percentage once and field goals made once.
- Finished fourth in NFL in points scored once.
- Holds Packers record for longest punt (90 yards vs. San Francisco on 10/10/1965).
- Kicked four field goals vs. Oakland in Super Bowl II.
- Three-time Western Conference champion (1965, 1966, and 1967).
- Three-time NFL champion (1965, 1966, and 1967).
- Two-time Super Bowl champion (I and II).
- 1967 Pro Bowl selection.
- NFL 1960s All-Decade Team.
- Two-time First-Team All-Conference selection (1965 and 1967).
- Pro Football Hall of Fame All-1960s Team.

93: TRAMON WILLIAMS (DB; 2007–2014)

Courtesy of Mike Morbeck

Packers Numbers

471 Tackles, 28 Interceptions, 423 Interception-Return Yards, 4½ Sacks, 5 Forced Fumbles, 8 Fumble Recoveries, 579 Punt-Return Yards, 9.7-Yard Punt-Return Average, 710 Kickoff-Return Yards, 22.2-Yard Kickoff-Return Average, 1,717 All-Purpose Yards, 2 Touchdowns.

NOTABLE ACHIEVEMENTS

- Scored one defensive touchdown on interception return.
- Scored one touchdown on 94-yard punt return.
- Intercepted three passes during 2010 postseason, returning one of those 70 yards for touchdown.
- Recorded at least five interceptions twice.
- Led Packers in interceptions twice.
- Ranks among Packers career leaders in interceptions (tied—10th) and interception-return yards (10th).
- Five-time division champion (2007, 2011, 2012, 2013, and 2014).
- 2010 NFC champion.
- Super Bowl XLV champion.
- 2007 Week 11 NFC Special Teams Player of the Week.
- 2010 Pro Bowl selection.

94: MILT GANTENBEIN (WR, DE; 1931–1940)

Public domain

Career Numbers

77 Receptions, 1,299 Receiving Yards, 8 Touchdown Receptions.

NOTABLE ACHIEVEMENTS

- Four-time Western Conference champion (1931, 1936, 1938, and 1939).
- Three-time NFL champion (1931, 1936, and 1939).
- 1939 Pro Bowl selection.
- 1936 First-Team All-Pro.
- Two-time Second-Team All-Pro (1937 and 1938).

95: JAMES JONES (WR; 2007–2013, 2015)

Courtesy of Mike Morbeck

Packers Numbers

360 Receptions, 5,195 Receiving Yards, 45 Touchdown Receptions.

NOTABLE ACHIEVEMENTS

- Surpassed 50 receptions four times.
- Topped 800 receiving yards twice.
- Surpassed 10 touchdown receptions once.
- Led NFL with 14 touchdown receptions in 2012.
- Finished second in NFL with 14 touchdowns in 2012.
- Led Packers with 890 receiving yards in 2015.
- Tied franchise record in 2012 by making two touchdown receptions in three straight games.
- Made three touchdown receptions vs. Chicago on 12/16/2012.
- Ranks among Packers career leaders in: pass receptions (10th); touchdown receptions (9th); receiving yards (12th); and average yards per reception (10th).
- Four-time division champion (2007, 2011, 2012, and 2013).
- 2010 NFC champion.
- Super Bowl XLV champion.

96: KEN RUETTGERS (OT; 1985–1996)

Courtesy of SportsMemorabilia.com

NOTABLE ACHIEVEMENTS

- Two-time division champion (1995 and 1996).
- 1996 NFC champion.
- Super Bowl XXXI champion.
- 1989 Packers' Offensive MVP.

97: DICK WILDUNG (OG, OT, DT; 1946–1951, 1953)

Public domain

NOTABLE ACHIEVEMENTS

- Recovered 11 fumbles.
- Never missed a game in seven seasons with Packers.
- 1951 Pro Bowl selection.
- Two-time Second-Team All-Pro (1947 and 1949).

98: MORGAN BURNETT (DB; 2010–2017)

Courtesy of Mike Morbeck

Career Numbers

717 Tackles, 511 Unassisted Tackles, 9 Interceptions, 52 Interception-Return Yards, 7½ Sacks, 8 Forced Fumbles, 10 Fumble Recoveries, 1 Touchdown.

NOTABLE ACHIEVEMENTS

- Has scored one defensive touchdown on a fumble return.
- Has recorded more than 100 tackles four times.
- Has led Packers in tackles three times.
- Ranks among Packers career leaders in tackles (7th) and unassisted tackles (7th).
- Five-time division champion (2011, 2012, 2013, 2014, and 2016).
- 2010 NFC champion.
- Super Bowl XLV champion.

99: FRANK WINTERS (C; 1992–2002)

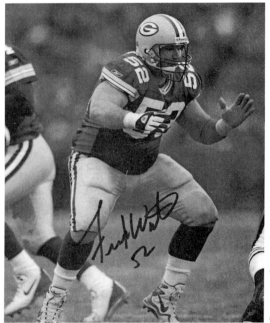

Courtesy of SportsMmorabilia.com

NOTABLE ACHIEVEMENTS

- Four-time division champion (1995, 1996, 1997, and 2002).
- Two-time NFC champion (1996 and 1997).
- Super Bowl XXXI champion.
- 1996 Pro Bowl selection.

100: BUBBA FRANKS (TE; 2000–2007)

Courtesy of Paul Cutler

Packers Numbers

256 Receptions, 2,300 Receiving Yards, 32 Touchdown Receptions.

NOTABLE ACHIEVEMENTS

- Surpassed 50 receptions once (54 in 2002).
- Finished fifth in NFL with nine touchdown receptions in 2001.
- Four-time division champion (2002, 2003, 2004, and 2007).
- 2002 NFL Alumni Tight End of the Year.
- Three-time Pro Bowl selection (2001, 2002, and 2003).

GLOSSARY
ABBREVIATIONS AND STATISTICAL TERMS

C: Center.

COMP PCT: Completion percentage. The number of successfully completed passes divided by the number of passes attempted.

DB: Defensive back.

DE: Defensive end.

DT: Defensive tackle.

FCS: Football Championship Subdivision (NCAA division once known as Division I-AA).

FS: Free safety.

INTs: Interceptions. Passes thrown by the quarterback that are caught by a member of the opposing team's defense.

KR: Kickoff returner.

LB: Linebacker.

LCB: Left cornerback.

LE: Left end.

LG: Left guard.

LOLB: Left outside linebacker.

LT: Left tackle.

MLB: Middle linebacker.

NT: Nose tackle.

OG: Offensive guard.

OT: Offensive tackle, or overtime.

P: Punter.

PAT: Point after touchdown (extra point).

PK: Placekicker.

PR: Punt returner.

QB: Quarterback.

QBR: Quarterback rating.

RB: Running back.

RCB: Right cornerback.

RE: Right end.

RECs: Receptions.

REC Yds: Receiving yards.

RG: Right guard.

ROLB: Right outside linebacker.

RT: Right tackle.

RUSH TDs: Rushing touchdowns.

RUSH Yds: Rushing yards.

S: Safety.

SS: Strong safety.

ST: Special teams.

TD PASSES: Touchdown passes.

TD RECs: Touchdown receptions.

TDS: Touchdowns.

TE: Tight end.

WR: Wide receiver.

BIBLIOGRAPHY

BOOKS

Freedman, Lew. *The Packers Experience: A Year-by-Year Chronicle of the Green Bay Packers.* Minneapolis, MN: MVP Books, 2013.

Jones, Danny. *Lost Treasures from the Golden Era of America's Game: Pro Football's Forgotten Heroes and Legends of the 50's, 60's, and 70's.* Bloomington, IN: AuthorHouse, 2011.

Maxymuk, John. *Packers by the Numbers: Jersey Numbers and the Players Who Wore Them.* Madison, WI: Prairie Oak Press, 2003.

VIDEOS

Greatest Ever: NFL Dream Team. Polygram Video, 1996.

WEBSITES

Biographies, online at Hickoksports.com (hickoksports.com/hickoksports/biograph)

Biography from Answers.com (answers.com)

Biography from Jockbio.com (jockbio.com)

CapitalNewYork.com (capitalnewyork.com)

CBSNews.com (cbsnews.com)

ESPN.com (sports.espn.go.com)

Hall of Famers, online at profootballhof.com (profootballhof.com/hof/member)

Inductees from LASportsHall.com (lasportshall.com)

LATimes.com (articles.latimes.com)

Newsday.com (newsday.com)

NYDailyNews.com (nydailynews.com/new-york)

NYTimes.com (nytimes.com)

Packers.com (packers.com)

Pro Football Talk from nbcsports.com (profootballtalk.nbcsports.com)

SpTimes.com (sptimes.com)

StarLedger.com (starledger.com)

SunSentinel.com (articles.sun-sentinel.com)

The Players, online at Profootballreference.com (pro-football-reference.com/players)

YouTube.com (youtube.com)